# First World War
## and Army of Occupation
# War Diary
## France, Belgium and Germany

59 DIVISION
Divisional Troops
Royal Army Service Corps
Divisional Train (513,514,515,516, Companies A.S.C.)
17 February 1917 - 14 August 1919

WO95/3019/4

The Naval & Military Press Ltd
www.nmarchive.com
**Published in association with The National Archives**

Published by

## The Naval & Military Press Ltd

Unit 10 Ridgewood Industrial Park,

Uckfield, East Sussex,

TN22 5QE England

Tel: +44 (0) 1825 749494

www.naval-military-press.com

www.nmarchive.com

*This diary has been reprinted in facsimile from the original. Any imperfections are inevitably reproduced and the quality may fall short of modern type and cartographic standards.*

© **Crown Copyright**
**Images reproduced by permission of The National Archives, London, England, 2015.**

# Contents

| Document type | Place/Title | Date From | Date To |
|---|---|---|---|
| Heading | WO95/3019/4 Divisional Train (513,514,515,516 Companies A.S.C) | | |
| Heading | War Diary Of Headquarters 59th Divisional Train From 17.2.17 To 28.2.17 (Volume 1) | | |
| War Diary | Fovant | 17/02/1917 | 18/02/1917 |
| War Diary | Southampton | 19/02/1917 | 23/02/1917 |
| War Diary | Havre | 24/02/1917 | 24/02/1917 |
| War Diary | Longeau | 25/02/1917 | 25/02/1917 |
| War Diary | Blangy Tronville | 26/02/1917 | 26/02/1917 |
| War Diary | Mericourt | 27/02/1917 | 28/02/1917 |
| Heading | War Diary Of O.C. Headquarters Company 59th (N.Mid.) Divisional Train. From 18-2-17 To 28-2-17 Volume 1. | | |
| War Diary | Larkhill | 18/02/1917 | 18/02/1917 |
| War Diary | S'Ampton | 19/02/1917 | 20/02/1917 |
| War Diary | Havre | 22/02/1917 | 24/02/1917 |
| War Diary | In The Field | 25/02/1917 | 27/02/1917 |
| Heading | War Diary Of O.C. No 514 Company A.S.C. From 19.2.17. To 28.2.17. (Vol. 1) | | |
| War Diary | Codford. | 19/02/1917 | 19/02/1917 |
| War Diary | Southampton. | 20/02/1917 | 21/02/1917 |
| War Diary | Havre. | 22/02/1917 | 23/02/1917 |
| War Diary | Longueau. | 24/02/1917 | 24/02/1917 |
| War Diary | Glisy. | 26/02/1917 | 26/02/1917 |
| War Diary | Morcourt | 26/02/1917 | 28/02/1917 |
| Heading | War Diary Of 515 Company Army Service Corps. From 17-2-17 To 28-2-17 | | |
| War Diary | Fovant | 17/02/1917 | 17/02/1917 |
| War Diary | Southampton | 17/02/1917 | 21/02/1917 |
| War Diary | Havre | 21/02/1917 | 22/02/1917 |
| War Diary | Point-3 Gare | 22/02/1917 | 22/02/1917 |
| War Diary | Longeau | 23/02/1917 | 23/02/1917 |
| War Diary | Salouel | 23/02/1917 | 28/02/1917 |
| War Diary | Bayonvillers | 28/02/1917 | 28/02/1917 |
| Heading | War Diary Of O.C. No 516 Company A. S. C. From 24.2.17 To 28.2.17 (Vol. 1.) | | |
| War Diary | Fovant | 24/02/1917 | 24/02/1917 |
| War Diary | Southampton. | 24/02/1917 | 24/02/1917 |
| War Diary | Havre | 26/02/1917 | 27/02/1917 |
| War Diary | Longeau | 28/02/1917 | 28/02/1917 |
| Heading | War Diary Of O.C. 59 Divisional Train From 1.3.17 To 31.3.17 Volume II | | |
| War Diary | Mericourt | 01/03/1917 | 08/03/1917 |
| War Diary | Proyart | 09/03/1917 | 30/03/1917 |
| War Diary | Pausle | 31/03/1917 | 31/03/1917 |
| War Diary | Mericourt | 01/03/1917 | 08/03/1917 |
| War Diary | Proyart | 09/03/1917 | 30/03/1917 |
| War Diary | Prusle | 31/03/1917 | 31/03/1917 |
| War Diary | In The Field | 01/03/1917 | 31/03/1917 |

| | | | |
|---|---|---|---|
| Heading | War Diary Of O.C. No. 1 Coy. 59th Division. Train From 1st To 31st March 1917 (Vol. II) | | |
| War Diary | In The Field | 01/03/1917 | 31/03/1917 |
| Heading | War Diary Of O.C. No 2 Coy. 59th Division. Train From 1st March 1917 To 31st March. 1917. Vol. II. | | |
| War Diary | Morcourt. | 01/03/1917 | 08/03/1917 |
| War Diary | Proyart. | 09/03/1917 | 09/03/1917 |
| War Diary | Estrees | 22/03/1917 | 28/03/1917 |
| War Diary | Prusles | 31/03/1917 | 31/03/1917 |
| Heading | War Diary Of O.C. No. 3 Company. 59th Divisional Train. From 1.3.17 To 31.3.17 Volume II | | |
| War Diary | Bayon-Villers | 01/03/1917 | 08/03/1917 |
| War Diary | Proyart. | 08/03/1917 | 26/03/1917 |
| War Diary | Prusle | 27/03/1917 | 31/03/1917 |
| Heading | War Diary Of O.C. 516 Coy A.S.C. 59th Divn. From 1/3/1917 To 31/3/1917 Volume II | | |
| War Diary | Glisy. | 01/03/1917 | 01/03/1917 |
| War Diary | Warfusee. | 08/03/1917 | 08/03/1917 |
| War Diary | Proyart. | 22/03/1917 | 22/03/1917 |
| War Diary | Estrees | 26/03/1917 | 26/03/1917 |
| Heading | War Diary Of Headquarters 59th Divisional Train From 1-4-17 To 30-4-17 Vol. III. | | |
| War Diary | Prusle | 10/04/1917 | 10/04/1917 |
| War Diary | Vraignes | 23/04/1917 | 30/04/1917 |
| Heading | War Diary Of O.C. 573 Coy. A.S.C. 59th Div From 1-Iv-17 To 30-Iv-17. (Vol III) | | |
| War Diary | In The Field | 01/04/1917 | 26/04/1917 |
| Heading | War Diary Of O.C. No 2 Company A.S.C. 59th Division. Volume III From 1st April 1917 To 30th April 1917. | | |
| War Diary | Prusle | 01/04/1917 | 07/04/1917 |
| War Diary | Vraignes | 10/04/1917 | 29/04/1917 |
| War Diary | War Diary Of No. 3 Company 59th Divisional Train From 1-4-17 To 30-4-17. (Volume III) | | |
| War Diary | Prusle | 01/04/1917 | 01/04/1917 |
| War Diary | Raperie | 05/04/1917 | 05/04/1917 |
| War Diary | Prusle | 10/04/1917 | 10/04/1917 |
| War Diary | Vrainges | 10/04/1917 | 30/04/1917 |
| Heading | War Diary Of O.C. North Coy A.S.C., 59th Division. From 1 April 1917 To 30th April 1917. Volume 3. | | |
| War Diary | Prusle | 10/04/1917 | 10/04/1917 |
| Heading | War Diary Of Headquarters, 59th Divl. Train From 1st May 1917 To 31st May 1917 Volume IV | | |
| War Diary | Vraignes | 01/05/1917 | 06/05/1917 |
| War Diary | S. Of Roisel | 07/05/1917 | 15/05/1917 |
| War Diary | Vraignes | 16/05/1917 | 29/05/1917 |
| War Diary | Lechelles | 30/05/1917 | 31/05/1917 |
| Heading | War Diary O.C. No 2 Coy. 59th Divl. Train Vol. IV 1st May 1917 To 31st May 1917. | | |
| War Diary | Vraignes | 01/05/1917 | 06/05/1917 |
| War Diary | Roisel | 07/05/1917 | 31/05/1917 |
| Heading | War Diary Of O.C. No. 573 Coy A.S.C. 59th Divn. From 1st To 31st May 1917. (Volume 4.) | | |
| War Diary | In The Field | 01/05/1917 | 31/05/1917 |
| Heading | War Diary O.C. 515 Coy. A.S.C. 59th Division From 1.5.17 To 31.5.17 Volume IV | | |

| | | | |
|---|---|---|---|
| War Diary | Vrainges | 01/05/1917 | 07/05/1917 |
| War Diary | Roisel | 07/05/1917 | 16/05/1917 |
| War Diary | Vrainges | 16/05/1917 | 25/05/1917 |
| War Diary | Equancourt. | 25/05/1917 | 27/05/1917 |
| War Diary | Lechelle | 27/05/1917 | 31/05/1917 |
| War Diary | Vraignes | 02/05/1917 | 06/05/1917 |
| War Diary | Roisel | 08/05/1917 | 13/05/1917 |
| War Diary | Vraignes | 17/05/1917 | 29/05/1917 |
| War Diary | Vraignes | 01/05/1917 | 01/05/1917 |
| War Diary | Roisel | 09/05/1917 | 09/05/1917 |
| War Diary | Vraignes | 21/05/1917 | 22/05/1917 |
| War Diary | Lechelle | 31/05/1917 | 31/05/1917 |
| War Diary | Vraignes | 07/05/1917 | 07/05/1917 |
| War Diary | Roisel | 16/05/1917 | 16/05/1917 |
| War Diary | Vraignes. | 30/05/1917 | 30/05/1917 |
| Heading | War Diary Of Headquarters. 59th Divisional Train From 1st June 1917 To 30th June 1917 Volume V | | |
| War Diary | Lechelles | 01/06/1917 | 30/06/1917 |
| Heading | War Diary Of O.C. 573 Coy. A.S.C. 59th Divn. From 1st To 30th June 1917. (Vol. V.) | | |
| War Diary | In The Field | 01/06/1917 | 30/06/1917 |
| Heading | War Diary Of No 2 Company, 59th Divisional Train From 1st June 1917 To 30th June 1917. Volume V | | |
| War Diary | Lechelle. P.32 cautial | 01/06/1917 | 30/06/1917 |
| Heading | War Diary Of O.C. 515 Coy. A.S.C. 59th Division From 1-6-17 To 30-6-17 (Volume V) | | |
| War Diary | Lechelle | 01/06/1917 | 30/06/1917 |
| Heading | War Diary O.C. 4 Company, A.S.C. 59th Division. From 1st June 1917 To 30th June 1917. Volume 5. | | |
| War Diary | Lechelle | 05/06/1917 | 28/06/1917 |
| War Diary | Lechelle | 01/06/1917 | 22/06/1917 |
| Heading | War Diary Of Headquarters, 59th Divisional Train From 1st July To 31st July 1917 Volume VI | | |
| War Diary | Lechelles | 01/07/1917 | 10/07/1917 |
| War Diary | Rocquigny | 11/07/1917 | 31/07/1917 |
| Heading | War Diary Of O.C. 573 Coy A.S.C. 59th Div. From 1st To 31st July 1917 Vol. VI. | | |
| War Diary | Fins | 01/07/1917 | 31/07/1917 |
| Heading | War Diary Of O.C. No 2 Coy 59th Div. Train Vol. VI 1st July 1917 To 31st July 1917. | | |
| War Diary | Lechelle P 32. Central. | 01/07/1917 | 06/07/1917 |
| War Diary | Rocquigny. O. 34. A. | 07/07/1917 | 31/07/1917 |
| Heading | War Diary Of No. 515 Coy. A.S.C. 59th Division. From 1-7-17 To 31-7-17. (Volume VI) | | |
| War Diary | Lechelle | 01/07/1917 | 10/07/1917 |
| War Diary | Rocquiny | 11/07/1917 | 31/07/1917 |
| Heading | War Diary Of O.C. 4 Company, A.S.C. 59th Division. From 1st July 1917 To 31st July 1917 Volume 6. | | |
| War Diary | Lechelle. | 01/07/1917 | 08/07/1917 |
| War Diary | Rocquigny | 09/07/1917 | 31/07/1917 |
| Heading | War Diary Of Headquarters, 59th Divisional Train From 1/8/17 To 31/8/17. (Volume VII) | | |
| War Diary | Rocquigny | 01/08/1917 | 23/08/1917 |
| War Diary | Acheux | 24/08/1917 | 31/08/1917 |
| Heading | War Diary Of 513 Coy ASC 59 Division From Aug 1st To 31st 1917. | | |

| | | | |
|---|---|---|---|
| War Diary | Field | 01/08/1917 | 31/08/1917 |
| Heading | War Diary Of O.C. No 2 Coy. 59th Div. Train. Vol VII 1st August 1917 To 31st August 1917. | | |
| War Diary | Rocquigny. | 01/08/1917 | 23/08/1917 |
| War Diary | Bouzincourt. | 24/08/1917 | 31/08/1917 |
| Heading | War Diary Of 515 Company A.S.C. 59th Division From 1-8-17 To 31-8-17 (Volume VII) | | |
| War Diary | Rocquiny | 01/08/1917 | 22/08/1917 |
| War Diary | Senlis | 22/08/1917 | 31/08/1917 |
| Heading | War Diary Of No 4 Coy. 59th Divisional Train From 1st August 1917 To 31st August 1917 Volume 7. | | |
| War Diary | Rocquigny | 01/08/1917 | 24/08/1917 |
| War Diary | Bouzincourt | 25/08/1917 | 31/08/1917 |
| War Diary | Rocquigny | 01/08/1917 | 23/08/1917 |
| War Diary | Bouzincourt | 26/08/1917 | 26/08/1917 |
| Heading | War Diary Of Headquarters 59th Divisional Train From 1st To 30th Sept 1917 Vol VIII | | |
| War Diary | Droglandt | 01/09/1917 | 23/09/1917 |
| War Diary | Brandhoek N:1 Area | 24/09/1917 | 30/09/1917 |
| Heading | War Diary Of OC 513 Company. A.S.C. 59th Division From 1st To 30th Sept 1917 Vol VIII | | |
| War Diary | Field | 01/09/1917 | 26/09/1917 |
| Heading | War Diary Of No 2 Company 59th Divisional Train From 1st To 30th Sept 1917 Vol VIII | | |
| War Diary | Hopoutre. (Poperinghe) | 01/09/1917 | 01/09/1917 |
| War Diary | Winnezeele. | 02/09/1917 | 18/09/1917 |
| War Diary | Brandhoek. | 19/09/1917 | 30/09/1917 |
| Heading | War Diary Of No. 575 Company A.S.C. 59th Division 1-9-17 30-9-17 Volume VIII | | |
| War Diary | In The Field | 31/08/1917 | 01/09/1917 |
| War Diary | Winnezelle | 01/09/1917 | 20/09/1917 |
| War Diary | Watou Area | 20/09/1917 | 23/09/1917 |
| War Diary | Vlamertinghe | 23/09/1917 | 24/09/1917 |
| War Diary | Poperinghe (Area) | 24/09/1917 | 30/09/1917 |
| Heading | War Diary Of No-4 Company 59th Divisional Train. From- 1st-Sept, 1917 To-30th Sept. 1917 Volume 8. | | |
| War Diary | Oudezeele | 01/09/1917 | 19/09/1917 |
| War Diary | Watou | 20/09/1917 | 23/09/1917 |
| War Diary | Brandhoek | 24/09/1917 | 24/09/1917 |
| War Diary | Edewaarthoek | 25/09/1917 | 30/09/1917 |
| War Diary | | 07/09/1917 | 07/09/1917 |
| Heading | War Diary Of O.C. 59th Divisional Train Vol IX From 1st October 1917 To 31st October 1917 | | |
| War Diary | Brandhoek No. 1 Area | 01/10/1917 | 02/10/1917 |
| War Diary | Steenbecque | 03/10/1917 | 05/10/1917 |
| War Diary | Rupigny | 06/10/1917 | 07/10/1917 |
| War Diary | Pressy. Les. Pernes | 10/10/1917 | 13/10/1917 |
| War Diary | Chateau de la Haie | 14/10/1917 | 30/10/1917 |
| Heading | War Diary Of 513 Company ASC. 59th Divn. From Oct 1st. 1917 To Oct. 31st 1917. Vol. VIII | | |
| War Diary | In The Field | 02/10/1917 | 28/10/1917 |
| Heading | War Diary Of O.C. No 2 Company 59th Divisional Train Vol. IX From 1st October 1917 To 31st October 1917 | | |
| War Diary | Edwaartshoek | 01/10/1917 | 01/10/1917 |
| War Diary | Isbergues. | 02/10/1917 | 06/10/1917 |

| | | | |
|---|---|---|---|
| War Diary | Lisbourg | 07/10/1917 | 10/10/1917 |
| War Diary | Hersin. | 11/10/1917 | 27/10/1917 |
| War Diary | Carency. | 28/10/1917 | 31/10/1917 |
| Heading | War Diary Of 515 Company, Army Service Corps, 59th Division From 1-10-17 To 31-10-17 (Volume IX) | | |
| War Diary | Poperinge | 01/10/1917 | 02/10/1917 |
| War Diary | Thiennes | 02/10/1917 | 06/10/1917 |
| War Diary | Berquingy | 06/10/1917 | 10/10/1917 |
| War Diary | Camblain Chatelaine | 10/10/1917 | 11/10/1917 |
| War Diary | Maisnil Les Ruitz. | 11/10/1917 | 12/10/1917 |
| War Diary | Vancouver Camp, | 12/10/1917 | 13/10/1917 |
| War Diary | Carency | 13/10/1917 | 31/10/1917 |
| Heading | War Diary Of O.C. No 4 Company 59th Divisional Train From:- 1st Oct. 1917 To 31st Oct. 1917. Volume 9. | | |
| War Diary | Edwarthoek | 01/10/1917 | 01/10/1917 |
| War Diary | St. Martin | 02/10/1917 | 02/10/1917 |
| War Diary | Aire | 04/10/1917 | 05/10/1917 |
| War Diary | Lileette | 06/10/1917 | 10/10/1917 |
| War Diary | Tangry. | 11/10/1917 | 11/10/1917 |
| War Diary | Grossart. Brittel | 12/10/1917 | 12/10/1917 |
| War Diary | Barlin. | 13/10/1917 | 13/10/1917 |
| War Diary | Gouy-Servins | 15/10/1917 | 15/10/1917 |
| War Diary | Carency | 16/10/1917 | 31/10/1917 |
| Miscellaneous | | | |
| Heading | War Diary Of Headquarter, 59th Divisional Train Vol. X. 1st November 1917 To 30 November 1917 | | |
| War Diary | Chateau-de-la-Haie | 01/11/1917 | 17/11/1917 |
| War Diary | Hermaville | 18/11/1917 | 19/11/1917 |
| War Diary | Basseux | 20/11/1917 | 21/11/1917 |
| War Diary | Achite Le Petit | 22/11/1917 | 23/11/1917 |
| War Diary | Etricourt | 24/11/1917 | 30/11/1917 |
| Heading | War Diary Of 513 Coy ASC 59 Division Vol. 10-Nov 1917 | | |
| War Diary | In The Field | 01/11/1917 | 30/11/1917 |
| Heading | War Diary Of O.C. No 2 Company, 59th Divisional Train Vol. X 1st November 1917 To 30 November 1917. | | |
| War Diary | Carency | 01/11/1917 | 18/11/1917 |
| War Diary | Simencourt | 19/11/1917 | 20/11/1917 |
| War Diary | Courcelles Le Comte | 21/11/1917 | 22/11/1917 |
| War Diary | Heudicourt | 23/11/1917 | 28/11/1917 |
| War Diary | Fins-Metz Rd. Sheet 57c | 29/11/1917 | 30/11/1917 |
| Heading | War Diary Of 515 Coy. A.S.C. 59th Division From 1-11-17 To 30-11-17. (Volume X) | | |
| War Diary | Carency | 01/11/1917 | 17/11/1917 |
| War Diary | Wanquetin | 17/11/1917 | 19/11/1917 |
| War Diary | Bailleulval | 19/11/1917 | 21/11/1917 |
| War Diary | Achiet Le Petit. | 22/11/1917 | 23/11/1917 |
| War Diary | Dessart Wood | 23/11/1917 | 26/11/1917 |
| War Diary | Fins | 26/11/1917 | 28/11/1917 |
| War Diary | Q 25. Central Sheet 57.C. | 28/11/1917 | 30/11/1917 |
| War Diary | Lechelle | 30/11/1917 | 30/11/1917 |
| Heading | War Diary Of O.C., 516 Coy. A.S.C. 59th Division From 1/11/17 To 30/11/17. Volume 10. | | |
| War Diary | Carency | 01/11/1917 | 13/11/1917 |

| | | | |
|---|---|---|---|
| War Diary | Duisans | 14/11/1917 | 19/11/1917 |
| War Diary | Hendecourt | 21/11/1917 | 21/11/1917 |
| War Diary | Gomiecourt | 23/11/1917 | 23/11/1917 |
| War Diary | Equancourt | 24/11/1917 | 29/11/1917 |
| War Diary | Metz | 30/11/1917 | 30/11/1917 |
| War Diary | Etricourt | 01/12/1917 | 01/12/1917 |
| War Diary | Vallulart Wood | 03/12/1917 | 05/12/1917 |
| War Diary | Little Wood | 08/12/1917 | 16/12/1917 |
| War Diary | Ytres | 20/12/1917 | 23/12/1917 |
| War Diary | Achiet Le Petit | 24/12/1917 | 25/12/1917 |
| War Diary | Etree Wamin | 26/12/1917 | 31/12/1917 |
| Heading | War Diary Of OC. 513 Coy. ASC 59 Divn. From 1st To 31st December 1917. (Vol. 10.) | | |
| War Diary | In The Field | 01/12/1917 | 31/12/1917 |
| Heading | War Diary Of O.C. No 2 Coy. 59th Divisional Train 1st December 1917 To 31st December 1917. Vol XI | | |
| War Diary | Lechelle | 01/12/1917 | 02/12/1917 |
| War Diary | Neuville | 03/12/1917 | 10/12/1917 |
| War Diary | Ytres | 10/12/1917 | 13/12/1917 |
| War Diary | Bertincourt | 16/12/1917 | 17/12/1917 |
| War Diary | Barastre | 20/12/1917 | 24/12/1917 |
| War Diary | Achiet Le Petit | 25/12/1917 | 25/12/1917 |
| War Diary | Etree Wamin | 26/12/1917 | 31/12/1917 |
| Heading | War Diary Of 515 Coy. A.S.C. 59th Division From 1-12-17 To 31-12-17 (Volume XI) | | |
| War Diary | Lechelle | 01/12/1917 | 03/12/1917 |
| War Diary | Havrincourt Wood | 03/12/1917 | 10/12/1917 |
| War Diary | Camp P1.d | 10/12/1917 | 16/12/1917 |
| War Diary | Bertincourt | 16/12/1917 | 22/12/1917 |
| War Diary | Rocquigny | 22/12/1917 | 24/12/1917 |
| War Diary | Achiet Le Petit | 24/12/1917 | 25/12/1917 |
| War Diary | Ambrienes | 25/12/1917 | 31/12/1917 |
| Heading | War Diary Of O.C. No. 4 Coy. 59th Divisional Train From 1/12/17 To 31/12/17 Volume II | | |
| War Diary | Lechelle | 01/12/1917 | 03/12/1917 |
| War Diary | Havrincourt Wood | 05/12/1917 | 10/12/1917 |
| War Diary | Ytres | 11/12/1917 | 16/12/1917 |
| War Diary | Bertincourt | 17/12/1917 | 21/12/1917 |
| War Diary | Rocquigny | 22/12/1917 | 22/12/1917 |
| War Diary | Beavlencourt | 24/12/1917 | 24/12/1917 |
| War Diary | Achiet-Le-Petit | 25/12/1917 | 25/12/1917 |
| War Diary | Houyin-Houyigneul | 26/12/1917 | 29/12/1917 |
| Heading | War Diary Of Headquarters 59th Divisional Train From 1-1-18 To 31-1-18 Volume I | | |
| War Diary | Etree Wamin | 01/01/1918 | 30/01/1918 |
| War Diary | War Diary Of No 1 Coy ASC 59th Division From Jany 1st To Jany 31st 1918. Vol. II | | |
| War Diary | Lucheux | 01/01/1918 | 08/01/1918 |
| War Diary | Grouches | 08/01/1918 | 31/01/1918 |
| Heading | War Diary Of No. 2 Company A.S.C. 59th Divisional Train From 1-1-18 To 31-1-18 Volume I | | |
| War Diary | Etree Wamin | 01/01/1918 | 30/01/1918 |
| Heading | War Diary Of No 3 Company A.S.C. 59th Division From 1-1-18 To 31-1-18 Volume I | | |
| War Diary | Ambrines | 01/01/1918 | 31/01/1918 |

| | | | |
|---|---|---|---|
| Heading | War Diary Of O.C. 4 Company 59th Divisional Train From 1/1/18 To 31/1/18 Volume II | | |
| War Diary | Houvin-Houvigeul | 01/01/1918 | 31/01/1918 |
| Heading | War Diary Of Headquarter, 59th Divisional Train From 1/2/18 To 28/2/18 Volume XIII | | |
| War Diary | Etree-Warmin | 01/02/1918 | 10/02/1918 |
| War Diary | Gomiecourt | 11/02/1918 | 26/02/1918 |
| War Diary | During Period | 26/02/1918 | 26/02/1918 |
| Heading | War Diary Of 513 Coy. ASC 59 Division For Month Of February 1918 Vol. No. 12 | | |
| War Diary | Field | 10/02/1918 | 20/02/1918 |
| War Diary | Grouches | 01/02/1918 | 06/02/1918 |
| War Diary | Pommier | 06/02/1918 | 07/02/1918 |
| War Diary | Courcelles Le Comte | 07/02/1918 | 10/02/1918 |
| War Diary | Gomiecourt | 10/02/1918 | 10/02/1918 |
| Heading | War Diary Of No 2 Coy. (514 Coy ASC) 59th Div. Train From 1/2/18 To 28/2/18 Volume XIII | | |
| War Diary | Etree Wamin | 04/02/1918 | 08/02/1918 |
| War Diary | Bienvillers | 08/02/1918 | 09/02/1918 |
| War Diary | Ervillers | 09/02/1918 | 10/02/1918 |
| War Diary | Gomiecourt | 10/02/1918 | 25/02/1918 |
| Heading | War Diary Of 515 Company A.S.C. 59th Division. From 1.2.18 To 28.2.18 Volume II | | |
| War Diary | Ambrines | 01/02/1918 | 08/02/1918 |
| War Diary | Monchiet | 09/02/1918 | 09/02/1918 |
| War Diary | Hendecourt | 10/02/1918 | 10/02/1918 |
| War Diary | Gunnicourt | 11/02/1918 | 12/02/1918 |
| War Diary | Gomecourt | 13/02/1918 | 25/02/1918 |
| Heading | War Diary Of O.C. 4 Company 59th Divisional Train From 1/2/18 To 28/2/18 Volume 13. | | |
| War Diary | Houvin-Houvigeul | 01/07/1918 | 08/07/1918 |
| War Diary | Gouy-En-Artois | 09/07/1918 | 09/07/1918 |
| War Diary | Mercatel | 10/07/1918 | 10/07/1918 |
| War Diary | Gomicourt | 11/07/1918 | 28/07/1918 |
| Heading | War Diary Of Headquarters, 59th (N.M) Divl. Train. 1/3/18 To 31/3/18 Vol. XIV. | | |
| War Diary | Gomicourt | 01/03/1918 | 22/03/1918 |
| War Diary | Ayette | 23/03/1918 | 23/03/1918 |
| War Diary | Bouzincourt | 24/03/1918 | 25/03/1918 |
| War Diary | Pont Noyelle | 26/03/1918 | 26/03/1918 |
| War Diary | Bonneville | 27/03/1918 | 31/03/1918 |
| Heading | War Diary Of (No-1) 513 Company A.S.C. 59th Division From 1/3/18 To 31/3/18 Volume XIV | | |
| War Diary | In The Field | 01/03/1918 | 26/03/1918 |
| Heading | War Diary Of (No-2) 514 Coy. A.S.C. 59th Division 1/3/18 To 31/3/18 Volume XIV | | |
| War Diary | Gomiecourt | 01/03/1918 | 22/03/1918 |
| War Diary | Ayette | 22/03/1918 | 22/03/1918 |
| War Diary | Bouzincourt | 23/03/1918 | 24/03/1918 |
| War Diary | Pont-Noyelles | 25/03/1918 | 26/03/1918 |
| War Diary | Bonneville | 27/03/1918 | 28/03/1918 |
| War Diary | Herlin Le Sec. | 28/03/1918 | 29/03/1918 |
| War Diary | Gauchin Legal | 29/03/1918 | 31/03/1918 |
| War Diary | Ecquedecques | 31/03/1918 | 31/03/1918 |
| Heading | War Diary Of (No-3) 515 Company A.S.C. 59th Division From 1-3-18 To 31-3-18 Volume III | | |

| | | | |
|---|---|---|---|
| War Diary | Gomiecourt | 01/03/1918 | 22/03/1918 |
| War Diary | Ayette | 22/03/1918 | 24/03/1918 |
| War Diary | Hannescamps | 24/03/1918 | 26/03/1918 |
| War Diary | Larbret | 26/03/1918 | 27/03/1918 |
| War Diary | Coullemont | 27/03/1918 | 29/03/1918 |
| War Diary | Houdain | 30/03/1918 | 31/03/1918 |
| War Diary | Lillers Area | 31/03/1918 | 31/03/1918 |
| Heading | War Diary Of O.C. No.4 Coy. 59th Divisional Train From 1/3/18 To 31/3/18 Volume 14 | | |
| War Diary | Gomiecourt | 01/03/1918 | 22/03/1918 |
| War Diary | Ayette | 23/03/1918 | 23/03/1918 |
| War Diary | Bouzincourt | 24/03/1918 | 25/03/1918 |
| War Diary | Pont-Noyelles | 26/03/1918 | 26/03/1918 |
| War Diary | Bonneville | 28/03/1918 | 28/03/1918 |
| War Diary | Herlin-Le Sec. | 29/03/1918 | 29/03/1918 |
| War Diary | Hermin | 30/03/1918 | 31/03/1918 |
| Heading | War Diary Of Headquarters, 59th Divisional Train 1/4/18 To 30/4/18 Volume XV. | | |
| War Diary | Ecquedecques | 01/04/1918 | 01/04/1918 |
| War Diary | Morbecque | 02/04/1918 | 02/04/1918 |
| War Diary | Proven | 03/04/1918 | 13/04/1918 |
| War Diary | Watou | 14/04/1918 | 21/04/1918 |
| War Diary | Bambecque | 22/04/1918 | 30/04/1918 |
| Heading | War Diary Of O.C. 513 Coy. (No-1) A.S.C. 59 Divn. From 1st To 30th April 1918. (Vol. 14) | | |
| War Diary | Field | 01/04/1918 | 30/04/1918 |
| Heading | War Diary Of No 2 Coy. 59th Divn. Train (514 Coy. A.S.C.) From 1/4/18 To 30/4/18 Volume XV | | |
| War Diary | Ecquedecques | 01/04/1918 | 01/04/1918 |
| War Diary | Morbecque | 02/04/1918 | 02/04/1918 |
| War Diary | Watou | 03/04/1918 | 10/04/1918 |
| War Diary | Vlamertinghe | 11/04/1918 | 12/04/1918 |
| War Diary | Brandhoek | 13/04/1918 | 13/04/1918 |
| War Diary | Zevecoten | 13/04/1918 | 17/04/1918 |
| War Diary | Busseboom | 17/04/1918 | 18/04/1918 |
| War Diary | Terdeghem | 19/04/1918 | 19/04/1918 |
| War Diary | Peselhoek | 20/04/1918 | 21/04/1918 |
| War Diary | Rousbrugge Camp. | 21/04/1918 | 21/04/1918 |
| War Diary | Oost Cappel | 22/04/1918 | 26/04/1918 |
| War Diary | Poperinghe (West) | 27/04/1918 | 30/04/1918 |
| Heading | War Diary Of (No-3) 515 Company A.S.C. 59th Division From 1-4-18 To 30-4-18 (Volume IV) | | |
| War Diary | Lillers Area | 01/04/1918 | 01/04/1918 |
| War Diary | Morbecque | 01/04/1918 | 02/04/1918 |
| War Diary | St-Jan-Ter Biezen | 02/04/1918 | 04/04/1918 |
| War Diary | Ypres (West) | 04/04/1918 | 12/04/1918 |
| War Diary | Bristol Camp. | 12/04/1918 | 13/04/1918 |
| War Diary | Watou Area | 13/04/1918 | 14/04/1918 |
| War Diary | Hoograf Area | 14/04/1918 | 20/04/1918 |
| War Diary | Peselhoek | 20/04/1918 | 21/04/1918 |
| War Diary | Houtkerque Area | 21/04/1918 | 26/04/1918 |
| War Diary | Schools Camp | 26/04/1918 | 27/04/1918 |
| War Diary | Farm E 30 D.4.0 | 27/04/1918 | 29/04/1918 |
| War Diary | Houtkerque Area | 29/04/1918 | 30/04/1918 |
| Heading | War Diary Of (No-4) 516 Coy. ASC. 59th Div. Train April 1918 | | |

| | | | |
|---|---|---|---|
| War Diary | Ecquedecques | 01/04/1918 | 01/04/1918 |
| War Diary | Morbecque | 02/04/1918 | 02/04/1918 |
| War Diary | St. Janster Biezen | 03/04/1918 | 07/04/1918 |
| War Diary | Steenvoorde | 08/04/1918 | 10/04/1918 |
| War Diary | Ypres | 11/04/1918 | 12/04/1918 |
| War Diary | Locre | 13/04/1918 | 13/04/1918 |
| War Diary | Westoutre | 14/04/1918 | 20/04/1918 |
| War Diary | Peselhoek | 21/04/1918 | 21/04/1918 |
| War Diary | Houterque | 22/04/1918 | 27/04/1918 |
| War Diary | St. Janster Biezen | 28/04/1918 | 29/04/1918 |
| War Diary | Hout. Kerque | 29/04/1918 | 29/04/1918 |
| Heading | War Diary Of Headquarters, 59th Divisional Train From 1/5/18 To 31/5/18 Volume XVI | | |
| War Diary | Bambecque | 01/05/1918 | 05/05/1918 |
| War Diary | St. Omer | 06/05/1918 | 09/05/1918 |
| War Diary | Hestrus. | 10/05/1918 | 31/05/1918 |
| Heading | War Diary Of O.C. 513 Coy. A.S.C. 59th Divn. From 1st To 31st May 1918 Vol. 15. | | |
| War Diary | Field | 01/05/1918 | 31/05/1918 |
| Heading | War Diary Of No 2 Coy 59th Div. Train (514 Coy. A.S.C.) From 1/5/18 To 31/5/18 Volume XVI | | |
| War Diary | St. Jan Ter Biezen. | 01/05/1918 | 06/05/1918 |
| War Diary | Kinderbelek | 07/05/1918 | 10/05/1918 |
| War Diary | Mametz | 11/05/1918 | 11/05/1918 |
| War Diary | Fiefs | 12/05/1918 | 14/05/1918 |
| War Diary | Rocourt | 15/05/1918 | 15/05/1918 |
| War Diary | Avesnes Le Comte | 16/05/1918 | 21/05/1918 |
| War Diary | Fiefs | 22/05/1918 | 23/05/1918 |
| War Diary | Therouanne | 24/05/1918 | 31/05/1918 |
| Heading | War Diary Of 515 Company A.S.C. 59th Division From 1.5.18 To 31.5.18 (Volume V) | | |
| War Diary | Houtkerque (Area) | 01/05/1918 | 06/05/1918 |
| War Diary | St Momelin (area) | 06/05/1918 | 09/05/1918 |
| War Diary | Mametz | 09/05/1918 | 10/05/1918 |
| War Diary | Sachin | 10/05/1918 | 12/05/1918 |
| War Diary | Heripre | 12/05/1918 | 31/05/1918 |
| Heading | War Diary Of O.C. No. 4 Coy A. S. C. 59th Div. Train From 1-5-18 To 31-5-18 Volume 16. | | |
| War Diary | Houtkerque | 01/05/1918 | 05/05/1918 |
| War Diary | Rubrouck | 06/05/1918 | 06/05/1918 |
| War Diary | St Omer | 07/05/1918 | 09/05/1918 |
| War Diary | Blessy | 10/05/1918 | 10/05/1918 |
| War Diary | Gricourt (Bours) | 11/05/1918 | 12/05/1918 |
| War Diary | Sachin | 13/05/1918 | 31/05/1918 |
| War Diary | In The Field | 01/06/1918 | 01/06/1918 |
| Heading | War Diary Of Headquarters, 59th Divisional Train 1st/6/18 To 30th/6/18. Volume XVII. | | |
| War Diary | Hestrus | 01/06/1918 | 17/06/1918 |
| War Diary | Greuppe | 18/06/1918 | 30/06/1918 |
| Heading | War Diary Of 513 Coy. A.S.C. 59th Division (No 1 Coy. 59th Divl. Train) From 1-6-18 To 30-6-18. Volume XVIII | | |
| War Diary | Field | 01/06/1918 | 30/06/1918 |
| Heading | War Diary Of 514 Company A.S.C. 59th Division (No 2 Coy. 59th Divl. Train) From 1.6.18 To 30.6.18. Volume XVII | | |

| | | | |
|---|---|---|---|
| War Diary | Nielles | 01/06/1918 | 17/06/1918 |
| War Diary | Beaumetz Lez Aire | 18/06/1918 | 18/06/1918 |
| War Diary | Rupigny | 18/06/1918 | 30/06/1918 |
| Heading | War Diary Of 515 Company. A.S.C. 59th Division From 1-6-18 To 30-6-18 (Volume XVII) | | |
| War Diary | Heripre | 01/06/1918 | 17/06/1918 |
| War Diary | Sachin | 17/06/1918 | 23/06/1918 |
| War Diary | Ponche | 23/06/1918 | 30/06/1918 |
| Heading | War Diary Of O.C. No 4 Coy A.S.C. 59th Div Train From 1-6-18 To 30-6-18 Volume 17 | | |
| War Diary | Sachin | 01/06/1918 | 17/06/1918 |
| War Diary | Lisbourg | 18/06/1918 | 30/06/1918 |
| Heading | War Diary Of Headquarters, 59th Divisional Train From 1st.7.18 To 31st.7.18. Volume XVIII | | |
| War Diary | Greuppe | 01/07/1918 | 11/07/1918 |
| War Diary | Crepy | 15/07/1918 | 30/07/1918 |
| Heading | War Diary Of (No-1) OC. 513 Coy ASC 59th Division From 1st To 31st July 1918. (Vol. 17.) | | |
| War Diary | Field | 01/07/1918 | 31/07/1918 |
| Heading | War Diary Of (No-2) 514 Company A.S.C.-(No 2 Coy. 59th Divl. from) 1/7/18 To 31/7/18 Volume XVIII | | |
| War Diary | Rupigny | 01/07/1918 | 09/07/1918 |
| War Diary | Herbeval | 10/07/1918 | 23/07/1918 |
| War Diary | Gouy En Artois | 24/07/1918 | 31/07/1918 |
| Heading | War Diary Of (No-3) 515 Coy. A.S.C. 59th Division From 1-7-18 To 31-7-18 Volume XVIII | | |
| War Diary | Ponche | 01/07/1918 | 10/07/1918 |
| War Diary | Teneur | 10/07/1918 | 25/07/1918 |
| War Diary | Gouy. En. Artois | 25/07/1918 | 31/07/1918 |
| Heading | War Diary Of O.C. No-4 Coy. 59th Divisional From 1-7-18 To 31-7-18 Volume 18. | | |
| War Diary | Lisbourg | 02/07/1918 | 23/07/1918 |
| War Diary | Gouy-En-Artois | 25/07/1918 | 31/07/1918 |
| Heading | War Diary Of Headquarters 59th Divisional Train 1st Aug 1918 To 31st Aug 1918 Volume XIX | | |
| War Diary | Gouy-En-Artois | 01/08/1918 | 23/08/1918 |
| War Diary | Rebreuvette | 24/08/1918 | 24/08/1918 |
| War Diary | Anvin | 25/08/1918 | 25/08/1918 |
| War Diary | La Goulee | 26/08/1918 | 27/08/1918 |
| War Diary | War Diary Of No 1 O.C. 513. ASC. 59 Division From 1st To 31st Aug 1918. Vol 18. | | |
| War Diary | Field | 01/08/1918 | 31/08/1918 |
| Heading | No 2 Company 59 Divisional Train War Diary Vol. XIX.-August. | | |
| War Diary | Gouy En Artois | 01/08/1918 | 23/08/1918 |
| War Diary | Rebreuviette | 24/08/1918 | 24/08/1918 |
| War Diary | Monchy-Cayeaux | 25/08/1918 | 25/08/1918 |
| War Diary | Bourecq | 26/08/1918 | 26/08/1918 |
| War Diary | Guarbecque | 27/08/1918 | 27/08/1918 |
| War Diary | Busnes | 28/08/1918 | 29/08/1918 |
| Heading | War Diary Of No-3 515 Company A.S.C. 59th Division From 1.8.18 To 31.8.18 (Volume VIII) | | |
| War Diary | Gouy. En Artois | 01/08/1918 | 24/08/1918 |
| War Diary | Rebreuviette | 24/08/1918 | 24/08/1918 |
| War Diary | Wail | 24/08/1918 | 24/08/1918 |
| War Diary | Anvin | 24/08/1918 | 25/08/1918 |

| War Diary | Lambres | 25/08/1918 | 26/08/1918 |
| War Diary | Busnes | 26/08/1918 | 31/08/1918 |
| Heading | War Diary Of O.C. No-4 Coy. 59th Divisional Train From 1-8-18 To 31-8-18 Volume 19. | | |
| War Diary | Gouy-En-Artois | 01/08/1918 | 23/08/1918 |
| War Diary | Rebreuvette | 24/08/1918 | 24/08/1918 |
| War Diary | Wavrans | 25/08/1918 | 25/08/1918 |
| War Diary | Mollinghem | 27/08/1918 | 27/08/1918 |
| War Diary | Guarbecque | 28/08/1918 | 31/08/1918 |
| Heading | War Diary Of Headquarters 59 Div Train From Month Of Sept 1918 (1st To 30th) Volume XX | | |
| War Diary | Busnes | 01/09/1918 | 07/09/1918 |
| War Diary | Carvin | 09/09/1918 | 16/09/1918 |
| War Diary | Paradis | 17/09/1918 | 27/09/1918 |
| Heading | War Diary Of OC. 513 Coy. A.S.C. For Month Of September 1918 (1st To 30th) Vol. No. 20 | | |
| War Diary | Field | 01/09/1918 | 27/09/1918 |
| Heading | War Diary Of 514 Coy. A.S.C. For Month Of Sept 1918 (1st To 30th) Vol XX | | |
| War Diary | Busnes | 01/09/1918 | 01/09/1918 |
| War Diary | St. Floris | 02/09/1918 | 08/09/1918 |
| War Diary | Q.S.A.-Sect. 36A. | 09/09/1918 | 30/09/1918 |
| Heading | War Diary Of 515 Company A.S.C. 59th Division From 1.9.18 To 30.9.18 Volume XX | | |
| War Diary | Busnes | 01/09/1918 | 01/09/1918 |
| War Diary | Pompadour Farm | 01/09/1918 | 06/09/1918 |
| War Diary | Merville | 09/09/1918 | 30/09/1918 |
| Heading | War Diary Of O.C. No-4 Coy. 59th Divisional Train From 1-9-18 To 30-9-18 Volume 20 | | |
| War Diary | Quarbecque | 01/09/1918 | 01/09/1918 |
| War Diary | St. Floris | 04/09/1918 | 09/09/1918 |
| War Diary | Beaupre | 10/09/1918 | 30/09/1918 |
| Heading | War Diary Of H.Q. 59th Divisional Train From 1-10-18 To 31-10-18 Volume XXI | | |
| War Diary | Paradis | 01/10/1918 | 04/10/1918 |
| War Diary | Chavulle Deville | 06/10/1918 | 17/10/1918 |
| War Diary | Bac St Maur | 18/10/1918 | 18/10/1918 |
| War Diary | St Andree | 19/10/1918 | 19/10/1918 |
| War Diary | Flers | 20/10/1918 | 24/10/1918 |
| War Diary | Hem | 21/10/1918 | 31/10/1918 |
| Heading | War Diary Of OC. 513 Coy. A.S.C. 59 Divn. From 1st To 31st October 1918 (Vol. 20.) | | |
| War Diary | Field | 01/10/1918 | 30/10/1918 |
| Heading | War Diary Of O.C. No 2 Coy. 59 (NM) Divisional Train From 1-10-18 To 31-10-18 Volume XXI | | |
| War Diary | Q.5.a/sheet 36 A. 100yds. S.W. Of Merville. | 01/10/1918 | 04/10/1918 |
| War Diary | K.24.d.3.6. Sheet 36a. | 06/10/1918 | 06/10/1918 |
| War Diary | G.27.b.6.6./sheet 36. | 13/10/1918 | 14/10/1918 |
| War Diary | Lambersart | 18/10/1918 | 18/10/1918 |
| War Diary | Lambersart St Andre | 19/10/1918 | 19/10/1918 |
| War Diary | St. Andre Hemponpont | 20/10/1918 | 20/10/1918 |
| War Diary | Hemponpont | 21/10/1918 | 31/10/1918 |
| Heading | War Diary Of 515 Company A.S.C. 59th Division From 1.10.18 To 31.10.18. (Volume XXI) | | |
| War Diary | Merville | 01/10/1918 | 04/10/1918 |
| War Diary | Estaires | 04/10/1918 | 17/10/1918 |

| | | | |
|---|---|---|---|
| War Diary | Sailly Sur. La. Lys. | 17/10/1918 | 18/10/1918 |
| War Diary | Lambersart | 18/10/1918 | 19/10/1918 |
| War Diary | St-Andre | 19/10/1918 | 20/10/1918 |
| War Diary | Flers-Berg | 20/10/1918 | 31/10/1918 |
| Heading | War Diary Of O.C. N-4 Coy. 59th Divn. Train From 1-10-18 To 31-10-18 Volume 21 | | |
| War Diary | Beaupre | 01/10/1918 | 04/10/1918 |
| War Diary | Neuf-Berquin | 06/10/1918 | 17/10/1918 |
| War Diary | Sailly-Sur-Lys | 18/10/1918 | 18/10/1918 |
| War Diary | Lambersart | 19/10/1918 | 19/10/1918 |
| War Diary | St. Andre | 20/10/1918 | 20/10/1918 |
| War Diary | Hem | 22/10/1918 | 30/10/1918 |
| Heading | War Diary 59th (N.M.) Divisional Train From 1-11-18 To 30-11-18 Vol. 22 | | |
| War Diary | Sailly-Les Lannoy | 01/11/1918 | 10/11/1918 |
| War Diary | Bailleul | 11/11/1918 | 16/11/1918 |
| War Diary | Wattignies | 17/11/1918 | 30/11/1918 |
| Heading | War Diary Of O.C. 513 Coy A.S.C. 59 Division From 1st To 30th November 1918 Vol. 21. | | |
| War Diary | Field | 01/11/1918 | 30/11/1918 |
| War Diary | Hempempont L. 29. L. 8.6/Sh. 36 | 01/11/1918 | 09/11/1918 |
| War Diary | Nechin H.14.D.7.8/Sheet 37. | 10/11/1918 | 12/11/1918 |
| War Diary | Templeuve H.33.a.9.7/Sheet 37. | 15/11/1918 | 15/11/1918 |
| War Diary | Larbrisseau Q.26.6.7.2./Sheet 36. | 16/11/1918 | 26/11/1918 |
| Heading | War Diary Of 515 Company A.S.C. 59th Division From 1/11/18 To 30/11/18 (Volume XXII) | | |
| Heading | 59th Divl. Train Herewith War Diary for The Month Of November 1918 | | |
| War Diary | Flers-Berg | 01/11/1918 | 02/11/1918 |
| War Diary | Petit Lannoy | 02/11/1918 | 10/11/1918 |
| War Diary | Carnog Farm | 10/11/1918 | 15/11/1918 |
| War Diary | Le-Marequiet | 15/11/1918 | 16/11/1918 |
| War Diary | Seclin | 16/11/1918 | 30/11/1918 |
| Heading | War Diary Of O.C. N-4 Coy. 59th Divn. Train From 1-11-18 To 30-11-18 Volume 22. | | |
| War Diary | Hem | 01/11/1918 | 10/11/1918 |
| War Diary | Nechin | 11/11/1918 | 16/11/1918 |
| War Diary | Willems | 17/11/1918 | 17/11/1918 |
| War Diary | Perit Ronchin | 19/11/1918 | 29/11/1918 |
| Heading | War Diary Of Headquarters 59th Divl Train 1-12-18 To 31-12-18 Volume XXIII | | |
| War Diary | Wattignies | 01/12/1918 | 06/12/1918 |
| War Diary | Verquin | 07/12/1918 | 29/12/1918 |
| Heading | War Diary Of OC 513 Coy ASC. 59th Divn. From Dec. 1st To 31st 1918 Vol. 22. | | |
| War Diary | Field | 01/12/1918 | 31/12/1918 |
| Heading | War Diary Of 514 Coy. R.A.S.C. 59 Division From 1-12-18 To 31-12-18 Volume XXIII | | |
| War Diary | L'Arbrisseav Q.26.C.7.2 Sheet 36. | 01/12/1918 | 05/12/1918 |
| War Diary | Fournes Barlin | 06/12/1918 | 30/12/1918 |
| Heading | War Diary Of 515 Company A.S.C. 59th Division From 1-12-18 To 31-12-18 Volume XXIII | | |
| War Diary | Seclin | 01/12/1918 | 05/12/1918 |
| War Diary | Braquemont | 05/12/1918 | 31/12/1918 |
| Miscellaneous | 515 Coy R.A.S.C. 59th Division | | |
| Miscellaneous | 515 Coy. A. S. C. 59th Division | | |

| | | | |
|---|---|---|---|
| Heading | War Diary Of O.C. 516 Coy. R. A. S. C. From 1/12/18 To 31/12/18 Volume 23. | | |
| War Diary | Petit Ronchin | 02/12/1918 | 03/12/1918 |
| War Diary | Fournes | 04/12/1918 | 04/12/1918 |
| War Diary | Ruitz | 06/12/1918 | 10/12/1918 |
| War Diary | Calonne-Ricouart | 11/12/1918 | 11/12/1918 |
| War Diary | Dunkirk | 12/12/1918 | 30/12/1918 |
| Heading | War Diary Of Headquarters. 59th Divisional Train From 1st Jan 1919 To 31st Jan 1919 Volume XXIV | | |
| War Diary | Verquin | 01/01/1919 | 31/01/1919 |
| Heading | War Diary Of O.C. 513 Coy. R.A.S.C. 59th Division From 1st To 31st Jany. 1918 (Vol. 23) | | |
| War Diary | Field | 01/01/1919 | 14/01/1919 |
| Heading | War Diary Of No 2 Coy. 59th Divl. Train From 1/1/19 To 31/1/19 Volume 24 | | |
| War Diary | Barlin | 01/01/1919 | 06/01/1919 |
| War Diary | St Venant | 07/01/1919 | 07/01/1919 |
| War Diary | Les Cinqrues | 08/01/1919 | 08/01/1919 |
| War Diary | Wallon-Cappel | 09/01/1919 | 11/01/1919 |
| War Diary | Hondeghem | 12/01/1919 | 30/01/1919 |
| Heading | War Diary Of 515 Coy. R.A.S.C. 59th Division From 1-1-19 To 31-1-19 Volume XXIV | | |
| War Diary | Braquemont | 01/01/1919 | 30/01/1919 |
| War Diary | Verquin | 30/01/1919 | 31/01/1919 |
| War Diary | Dunkirk | 02/01/1919 | 30/01/1919 |
| Heading | 59th Div. Train War Diary Vol. 25 | | |
| War Diary | Verquin | 01/02/1919 | 24/02/1919 |
| Heading | War Diary Of O.C. 513 Coy R.A.S.C. 59 Division From 1st To 28th February 1919 (Vol. 24.) | | |
| War Diary | Barlin | 01/02/1919 | 28/02/1919 |
| War Diary | Hondeghem | 01/02/1919 | 11/02/1919 |
| War Diary | Dunkirk | 12/02/1919 | 14/02/1919 |
| Heading | War Diary Of 515 Company R.A.S.C. 59th Division From 1-2-19 To 28-2-19 Volume XXV | | |
| War Diary | Verquin | 01/02/1919 | 28/02/1919 |
| Heading | War Diary Of O.C. 516 Coy. R. A. S. C. From 1-2-19 To 28-2-19 Volume 25. | | |
| War Diary | St. Polsun Mer | 01/02/1919 | 27/02/1919 |
| War Diary | War Diary 59th (N.M.) Divisional Train Vol XXVI From 1.3.19 To 31.3.19 Vol 26 | | |
| War Diary | Verquin | 01/03/1919 | 08/03/1919 |
| War Diary | Balinghem | 09/03/1919 | 11/03/1919 |
| War Diary | LeBeau Maris | 14/03/1919 | 30/03/1919 |
| War Diary | War Diary Of O.C. 513 Company RASC 59 Division From 1-3-19 To 31-3-19 Volume 25 | | |
| War Diary | Barlin | 01/03/1919 | 31/03/1919 |
| War Diary | Dunkerque | 01/03/1919 | 28/03/1919 |
| War Diary | War Diary 515 Coy R.A.S.C. Volume XXVI From 1/3/19 To 31/3/19 | | |
| War Diary | Verquin | 01/03/1919 | 07/03/1919 |
| War Diary | Aire Barracrs | 08/03/1919 | 08/03/1919 |
| War Diary | Serques | 09/03/1919 | 09/03/1919 |
| War Diary | Balinghem | 09/03/1919 | 17/03/1919 |
| War Diary | Frethun | 17/03/1919 | 31/03/1919 |
| Heading | War Diary Of O.C. 516 Coy. R. A. S. C. From 1/3/19 To 31/3/19 Volume 28. | | |

| | | | |
|---|---|---|---|
| War Diary | St. Pol Sur Mer | 02/03/1919 | 30/03/1919 |
| War Diary | Le Beaumaris | 01/04/1919 | 30/04/1919 |
| Heading | War Diary Of O.C. 513 Coy R.A.S.C. 59 Divn. From 1/4/19 To 30/4/19 Volume 26 | | |
| War Diary | Barlin | 01/04/1919 | 30/04/1919 |
| War Diary | Dunkerque | 01/04/1919 | 28/04/1919 |
| Heading | War Diary 515 Coy R.A.S.C. April 19 Volume XXVII | | |
| War Diary | Frethun | 01/04/1919 | 15/04/1919 |
| War Diary | Coquelles Vet. Hospital | 16/04/1919 | 30/04/1919 |
| Heading | War Diary Of O.C. 516 Coy. R. A. S. C. From 1/4/19 To 30/4/19 Volume 27. | | |
| War Diary | St. Pol. Sur-Mer | 03/04/1919 | 30/04/1919 |
| Heading | War Diary Of H.Qs. 59th Divisional Train From 1/5/19 To 31/5/19 Volume 28. | | |
| War Diary | Beaumaris. Near Calais | 01/05/1919 | 31/05/1919 |
| War Diary | Dunkirk | 01/05/1919 | 30/05/1919 |
| Heading | War Diary Of O.C. 513 Coy. R.A.S.C. 59th Divn. From 1/5/19 To 31/5/19 Volume 27 | | |
| War Diary | Barlin | 01/05/1919 | 31/05/1919 |
| War Diary | War Diary 515 Company. R.A.S.C. 59th Division. May 1919 Vol. XXVIII | | |
| War Diary | Coquelles Vet Hospital | 01/05/1919 | 31/05/1919 |
| Heading | War Diary Of O.C., 516 Coy. R. A. S. C. From 1/5/19 To 31/5/19 Volume 28 | | |
| War Diary | St. Pol-Sur-Mer | 01/05/1919 | 31/05/1919 |
| War Diary | Beaumaris | 01/06/1919 | 30/06/1919 |
| War Diary | Dunkirk | 01/06/1919 | 16/06/1919 |
| War Diary | Fort Nieulay Calais | 19/06/1919 | 30/06/1919 |
| Heading | War Diary No. 515 Coy. A.S.C. 59th Division. June 1919. | | |
| Heading | 59th Division Train Herewith War Diary For The Month Of June | | |
| War Diary | Coquelles | 01/06/1919 | 30/06/1919 |
| Heading | War Diary Of O.C. 516 Coy. R. A. S. C. From 1/6/19 To 30/6/19 Volume 29 | | |
| War Diary | St. Pol-Sur-Mer | 01/06/1919 | 30/06/1919 |
| Heading | War Diary Vol XXX From 1.7.19-31.7.19 H.Q. 59 Div. Train | | |
| War Diary | Beaumaris | 01/07/1919 | 01/07/1919 |
| Heading | War Diary Vol. XXX From 1.7.19-31.7.19 No. 2 Coy 59 Div. Train | | |
| War Diary | Fort Nieulay Calais | 01/07/1919 | 31/07/1919 |
| Heading | War Diary Vol XXX From 1.7.19-31-7-19 No. Coy 59 Div Train | | |
| War Diary | Coquelles | 01/07/1919 | 31/07/1919 |
| Heading | War Diary Of O.C. 516 Coy. R. A. S. C. From 1/7/19 To 31/7/19 Volume 30 | | |
| War Diary | St-Pol-Sur-Mer | 01/07/1919 | 31/07/1919 |
| War Diary | Beaumaris | 01/08/1919 | 31/08/1919 |
| War Diary | Balaes | 01/08/1919 | 01/08/1919 |
| War Diary | Dunkirk | 04/08/1919 | 15/08/1919 |
| Heading | War Diary Of O.C. 516 Coy R.A.S.C. From 1/8/19 To 31/8/19 Volume 24 | | |
| War Diary | Coquelles | 01/08/1919 | 06/08/1919 |
| War Diary | Dunkirk | 07/08/1919 | 15/08/1919 |
| War Diary | St. Pol-Sur-Mer | 02/08/1919 | 14/08/1919 |

WO95/30194

Duononal Train
(513, 514, 515, 516
Companies A, S, Y)

Confidential

War Diary
of
Headquarters 59th Divisional Train

From 14.2.14 to 28.2.14

(Volume 1)

Army Form C. 2118.

# WAR DIARY Vol I.
## INTELLIGENCE SUMMARY.
*(Erase heading not required.)*

Instructions regarding War Diaries and Intelligence Summaries are contained in F.S. Regs, Part II. and the Staff Manual respectively. Title pages will be prepared in manuscript.

| Place | Date | Hour | Summary of Events and Information | Remarks and references to Appendices |
|---|---|---|---|---|
| FOVANT | 17.2.17 | | 515 Coy A.S.C. entrained for SOUTHAMPTON and embarked on S.S. "HUNTSCRAFT" | AST |
| FOVANT | 19/2/17 | 10:30AM | Entrained Train H.Q. (6 Officers, 24 Otherranks, 6 Rifles) 7 H.D. 3-4 wheel + 12 wheel + 10 Bicycles) | AST |
| | | | 515 Coy A.S.C. entrained at LATKHILL for SOUTHAMPTON | AST |
| | | | for SOUTHAMPTON arriving there 1.30 P.M. 513 Coy A.S.C. entrained at CODFORD for SOUTHAMPTON | AST |
| SOUTHAMPTON | 19.2.17 | | Train H.Q. Detrained SOUTHAMPTON DOCKS. 514 Coy embarked on S.S. "NORTH WEST MILLER" | AST |
| " | 20.2.17 | | Train H.Q. Detrained SOUTHAMPTON DOCKS. 513 Coy embarked on S.S. "ARCHIMEDES" | SRT |
| " | 21.2.17 | 5PM | Train H.Q. embarked on S.S. "SIPTAH" 514 Coy Embarked on S.S. "SIPTAH" | SRT |
| | 22.2.17 | | Train H.Q. Detained St HELEN'S ROADS by FOG. 513 Coy disembarked HAVRE 515 Coy entrained HAVRE | SRT |
| | 23.2.17 | | Train H.Q. Entrained K SOUTHAMPTON K Take on board Rations for Troops + Horses. 514 Coy disembarked HAVRE | SRT |
| | | | 515 Coy detrained at LONGEAU + proceeded by march route to SALOUEL | SRT |
| HAVRE | 24.2.17 | | Train H.Q. disembarked at HAVRE and entrained with 513 Coy for LONGEAU. 514 Coy detrained at LONGEAU | SRT |
| | | | + proceeded to GLISY. 516 Coy entrained at FOVANT and embarked at SOUTHAMPTON | SRT |
| | | | on S.S. "KARNAK." C.O. and ADJT proceeded to LONGEAU by Motor Car. | SRT |
| LONGEAU | 25.2.17 | | Detrained Train H.Q. with 513 Coy at LONGEAU + proceeded by Route March to BLANGYTRONVILLE. | SRT |
| BLANGY TRONVILLE | 26.2.17 | | Train H.Q. proceeded with 513 Coy to MERICOURT. 514 Coy proceeded to MORCOURT. 516 Coy disembarked HAVRE | SRT |
| MERICOURT | 27.2.17 | | 516 Coy entrained HAVRE. | SRT |
| " | 28.2.17 | | 515 Coy proceeded to BAYONVILLERS. 516 Coy detrained at LONGEAU + proceeded to GLISY. | SRT |
| | | | C.O., Adjt + Interpreter proceeded from LONGEAU to MERICOURT to rejoin Train H.Q. | SRT |

J. Maylerer / Cc
Comd 51st Div. Train

CONFIDENTIAL

WAR DIARY

of

O.C. HEADQUARTER (COMPANY) 59th (N. MID.) DIVISIONAL TRAIN.

from 18-2-17 to 28-2-17

VOLUME 1.

# WAR DIARY

## INTELLIGENCE SUMMARY

Army Form C. 2118.

| Place | Date | Hour | Summary of Events and Information | Remarks and references to Appendices |
|---|---|---|---|---|
| LARKHILL | 18/2/17 | | Entrains at AMESBURY — arrives SOUTHAMPTON | |
| S'AMPTON | 19/2/17 | | Entrains horses and wagons on H.M.T. "North East Miller" | |
| " | 20/2/17 | | Entrains men on "North East Miller" | |
| HAVRE | 22/2/17 | | Arrives HAVRE — disembarks — proceeds to No. 2 Rest Camp | |
| " | 23/2/17 | | In Rest Camp — HAVRE | |
| " | 24/2/17 | | Entrains at HAVRE | |
| " | 25/2/17 | | Arrives LONGUEAU — detrains — proceeds by Route March to BLANGY TRONVILLE | |
| In the Field | 26/2/17 | | By route march from BLANGY TRONVILLE to MERICOURT | |
| " | 27/2/17 | | In billets at MERICOURT | |

Confidential

War Diary

of O.C. No 514 Company A.S.C.

from 19.2.14. to. 26.2.14.

(Vol. 1)

514 Coy. A.S.C. 59th Divn.

Vol. No. 1.

Army Form C. 2118.

# WAR DIARY
## or
## INTELLIGENCE SUMMARY

*(Erase heading not required.)*

Instructions regarding War Diaries and Intelligence Summaries are contained in F.S. Regs, Part II. and the Staff Manual respectively. Title Pages will be prepared in manuscript.

| Place | Date | Hour | Summary of Events and Information | Remarks and references to Appendices |
|---|---|---|---|---|
| CODFORD. | 19.2.17 | 9.15am | Having despatched Baggage & Supply Wagons to Minds of 176th Inf. Bde. entrained at CODFORD Station. Headquarters of Company plus Train Wagons of Machine Gun Coy., Southamencourt Staff, 4 Officers (including Lt. Off. 176 Inf Bde), 52 Other ranks, 13 Riding horses (including Ridr of Lt Off) 4.L.I. 12 H.D. 5 G.S. 1 limbered G.S. 1 Motor Car. 4 Bicycles. Two H.D. horses required to complete to Establishment. [Supply Officer, 176 Inf. Bde. with 16 Supply Detail + 1 cycle proceed onward in advance on 13.2.17]. | T.M.H. |
| SOUTHAMPTON | 20.2.17 | 12.50pm | Arrived SOUTHAMPTON and proceeded to EMBARKATION REST CAMP. | T.M.H. |
| SOUTHAMPTON | 21.2.17 | 11 a.m. | Embarked horses and vehicles on S.S ARCHIMEDES. | T.M.H. |
| SOUTHAMPTON | 21.2.17 | 2.30 pm | Embarked personnel on S.S. ARCHIMEDES. Sailed at 3.50 p.m. | T.M.H. |
| HAVRE. | 22.2.17 | 10 a.m. | Arrived off port of HAVRE. | T.M.H. |
| HAVRE. | 23.2.17 | 7 a.m. | Disembarked. | T.M.H. |
|  |  | 12.30pm | Entrained. | T.M.H. |
|  |  | 3.15pm | Left HAVRE. | T.M.H. |
| LONGUEAU | 24.2.17 | 7.30am | Arrived LONGUEAU, detrained, proceeded by March Route to GLISY at 12 noon. Lay at GLISY for nights of 24 & 25 2/17. | T.M.H. |
| GLISY | 26.2.17 | 9 a.m. | Proceeded to MORCOURT under orders of Brig. Gen. Cornwall 176th Inf. Bde. | T.M.T. |
| MORCOURT | 26.2.17 | 4 pm | Arrived MORCOURT. | T.M.H. |
| MORCOURT | 27.2.17 |  | Drew Supplies for troops in MORCOURT Area from Refilling Point of No 3 C.T.S.C. at VILLERS - BRETONNEUX. Withdrew Supply Wagons from Units. | T.M.H. |
| MORCOURT | 28.2.17 |  | Drew Supplies as above. 5th + 6th Batt'n North Staff's Regt. arrived at MORCOURT. | T.M.H. |

CAPT.
O. O. No. 514 COY.
59TH. DIVL. TRAIN.

Confidential

War Diary

of

515 Company, Army Service Corps.

From 17-2-17 to 28-2-17

Army Form C. 2118

# WAR DIARY
## or
## INTELLIGENCE SUMMARY
(Erase heading not required.)

Instructions regarding War Diaries and Intelligence Summaries are contained in F.S. Regs., Part II. and the Staff Manual respectively. Title Pages will be prepared in manuscript.

515 by A.S.C. 56th Div: from February 1917

| Place | Date | Hour | Summary of Events and Information | Remarks and references to Appendices |
|---|---|---|---|---|
| FOVANT | 19/2/17 | 10.20 p.m. | Entrained at Railhead for Southampton AG | |
| SOUTHAMPTON | 20/2/17 | 9.30 a.m. | Embarked on Troopship HUNTSCRAFT. AG | |
| | | | Remained in the SOLENT until 4.0 p.m. 20/2/17 AG | |
| | | | Sailed for HAVRE 4.0 p.m. 20/2/17 in dense fog AG | |
| | 21/2/17 | 12.15 a.m. | Stranded on Rocks about 16 Miles N.W. of HAVRE AG | |
| HAVRE | 21/2/17 | 9.30 a.m. | Landed in HAVRE Harbour (Personnel) on Torpedo Boats-22 and Taylour 1174 AG | |
| | 21/2/17 | 8.15 a.m. | Moved up to No.1 Rest Camp AG | |
| No.1 Rest Camp HAVRE | 22/2/17 | 16.30 | Left for Entraining Station HAVRE. AG | |
| Gare | 22/2/17 | 21.30 | Left for Longeau AG | |
| LONGEAU | 23/2/17 | 15.30 | Detrained and Left for Colonel AG | |

A Green Capt
o/c No 515 Coy. A.S.C.
58th Division.

Army Form C. 2118

# WAR DIARY
## INTELLIGENCE SUMMARY
*(Erase heading not required.)*

575 Coy A.S.C. 15th M.T. Coys. — February 1917

| Place | Date | Hour | Summary of Events and Information | Remarks and references to Appendices |
|---|---|---|---|---|
| SALOUEL | 23/2/17 | 8.30 a.m | In quarters | |
| SALOUEL | 28/2/17 | 6.0 a.m | Left for BAYONVILLERS | |
| BAYONVILLERS | 28/2/17 | 4.0 p.m | In quarters | |

Green Capt.
o/c No. 615 Coy. A.S.C.
58th Division

Confidential

War Diary
of O.C. N° 516 Company. A.S.C.
from 24.2.17. To. 28.2.17

Vol. 1.

# WAR DIARY
## or
## INTELLIGENCE SUMMARY.

(Erase heading not required.)

516 G. A.S.C.

Army Form C. 2118.

| Hour, Date, Place | Summary of Events and Information | Remarks and references to Appendices |
|---|---|---|
| 9.5 A.M. 24.2.17. FOVANT. | Entrained with Headquarters of Company. | nil. |
| 7.0 P.M. 24.2.17 SOUTHAMPTON | Embarked on S.S. 'KARNAK' | nil. |
| 12.30 P.M. 26.2.17 HAVRE | Disembarked at HAVRE & proceeded to rest Camp. | nil |
| 3.15 P.M. 27.2.17 HAVRE | Entrained at Point III HAVRE. | nil |
| 8.0 A.M. 28.2.17 LONGEAU | Detrained & proceeded to GLISY. | nil. |

W.R. [signature]
CAPTN.
O.C. 516 COY., A.S.C., 59th (N.M.) DIV.

59

Vol II

CONFIDENTIAL

WAR DIARY

OF

O.C. 59 DIVISIONAL TRAIN.

FROM 1.3.17 TO 31.3.17

VOLUME II

**WAR DIARY**
or
**INTELLIGENCE SUMMARY**

Army Form C. 2118.

Headquarters 59th Divisional Train.
Vol II

| Place | Date | Hour | Summary of Events and Information | Remarks and references to Appendices |
|---|---|---|---|---|
| MERICOURT | 1917 March 1 | | Railhead WIENCOURT. Refilling Points for 513, 514, 515 and 516 Coys H.T. respectively MERICOURT, VILLERS-BRETONNEUX, BAYON-VILLERS, WARFUSEE. Mechanical Transport used for drawing Supplies from Railhead to Refilling Points | J.K.B |
| | 2 | | Refilling Point for 514 Coy M.T. MORCOURT | K.B |
| | 6 | | Railhead WARFUSEE. Baggage Section of the Train used as Supply Column from Railhead to Refilling Points | K.B |
| | 8 | | 59th Divisional Train proceeded by route march to PROYART | K.B |
| PROYART | 9 | | Railhead LA FLAQUE. Commenced drawing all Baggage Section of Train from Railhead to Refilling Points and thence by Supply Section to Units Quartermaster Stores | J.K.B |
| | 22 | | Nos 514 and 516 Companies moved to ESTREES | J.K.B |
| | 23 | | Refilling Points for 176th & 178th Infy Brigade Troops ESTREES | J.K.B |
| | 26 | | Nos 515 & 516 Coys moved to PRUSLE. No 513 Coy moved to ESTREES. Headquarters PROYART | J.K.B |
| | 27 | | Refilling Points for 176 Bde Group & Div Hars & attached troops ESTREES. Refilling Points for 177th & 178th Bde Groups. PRUSLE and for the Divisional Troops & attached units PROYART | J.K.B |
| | 29 | | 514 Coy M.T. moved from ESTREES to PRUSLE. Supply Section of 42nd Divisional Train arrived FOUCOURT to assist 59th Div.nl Train with transport | J.K.B |
| | 30 | | Headquarters 59th Div.l Train moved from PROYART to PRUSLE | J.K.B |
| PRUSLE | 31 | | Railhead FAY. Refilling Points for Div.l & Attached troops PROYART and ESTREES for Headquarters Divisional PRUSLE | J.K.B |
| | 31 | | General these reports. Weather Conditions during month bad. Roads in bad state of repair, rendering use of Mechanical Transport impossible in parts. ESTREES Health of Train good. Horses suffering | J.K.B |

Major George ?
Comdg. 59th Div. Train

**Army Form C. 2118.**

# WAR DIARY
## or
## INTELLIGENCE SUMMARY.
*(Erase heading not required.)*

Headquarters 59th Divisional Train.
Vol II

| Place | Date | Hour | Summary of Events and Information | Remarks and references to Appendices |
|---|---|---|---|---|
| MERICOURT | 1917 March 1 | | Railhead WIENCOURT Refilling Points for 513, 514, 515 and 516 Coys. H.T. respectively MERICOURT, VILLERS-BRETENEUX, BAYON-VILLERS, WARFUSSEE. Mechanical Transport used for drawing Supplies from Railhead to Refilling Points. | G.R.B |
| | 2 | | Refilling Point for 514 Coy H.T. MORCOURT | G.R.B |
| | 6 | | Railhead WARFUSSEE. Baggage Section of the Train used as Supply Colm to draw from Railroad to Refilling Points | G.R.B |
| | 8 | | 59th Divisional Train proceeded by route march to PROYART | G.R.B |
| PROYART | 9 | | Railhead LA FLAQUE Commenced drawing with Baggage Section of the Train from Rail head to Refilling Points and thence by Supply Section to Units Quartermasters Stores | G.R.B |
| | 22 | | Nos 514 and 516 Companies moved to ESTREES | G.R.B |
| | 23 | | Refilling Points for 176th & 178th Infy Brigade Groups ESTREES. | G.R.B |
| | 26 | | Nos 515 & 516 Coys. moved to PRUSLE No 573 Coy. moved to ESTREES & left detachment PROYART | G.R.B |
| | 27 | | Refilling Points for 176 Bde Group & Some Nor 2 Attached troops ESTREES. Refilling Points for 177 & 178 Bde Groups PRUSLE and for other Divisional Troops & attached units PROYART. | G.R.B |
| | 28 | | 514 Coy. H.T. moved from ESTREES to PRUSLE. Supply Section of 42nd Divisional Train arrived | G.R.B |
| | | | Foucacourt to assist 59th Div'l Train with transport | G.R.B |
| | 30 | | Headquarters 59th Div'l Train moved from PROYART to PRUSLE | G.R.B |
| PRUSLE | 31 | | Railhead FAY Refilling Points for Horse & Attached troops PROYART and ESTREES | G.R.B |
| | 31 | | General Observations. Weather conditions during month bad. Roads in Captured territory abnormally bad. Rendering use of Mechanical Transport impossible east of ESTREES. Health of the Train Good. Horses suffering from OVERWORK. | G.R.B |

Major Comdg. 59th Div Train

Army Form C. 2118

# WAR DIARY
## or
## INTELLIGENCE SUMMARY
*(Erase heading not required.)*

Instructions regarding War Diaries and Intelligence Summaries are contained in F.S. Regs., Part II. and the Staff Manual respectively. Title Pages will be prepared in manuscript.

[Stamp: 1st NORTH MIDLAND VETERINARY ...]

| Place | Date | Hour | Summary of Events and Information | Remarks and references to Appendices |
|---|---|---|---|---|
| In the field | 1/3/17 | 6.30 am to 5.30 | General parade. Capt Corby going to Beaumettes for grease and tallow. | |
| | 2/3/17 | | Capt Corby gone to Beaumettes for grease and tallow. | |
| | 3/3/17 | | Inspection of sick horses at Hoppewell. | |
| | 4/3/17 | | Capt Corby went to hospital at Breuil and also to Jules Crublin. | |
| | 5/3/17 | | General parade and gas drill instruction. Trouble to have defective ambulances for aft incurred. | |
| | 6/3/17 | | Lecture on Montreal. Capt E. Corby gone to Bavincourt. | |
| | 7/3/17 | | Horses and men. | |
| | 8/3/17 | | General Routine. Gas Helmet inspection Dr Richings lecture to General Routine. Nothing except final Chiv day. | |
| | 9/3/17 | | | |
| | 10/3/17 | | Went to Bougnies and Hoppewell to inspect Chivel. | |
| | 11/3/17 | | General Routine. Capt Hutchings to Boyenville to mouth horses of no. 94 at M.S.C. Stables. 6 heads chevilles received. | |
| | 12/3/17 | | General Routine. | |
| | 13/3/17 | | General Routine. Mail from A.D.V.S. gth Division. | |
| | 14/3/17 | | Inspection - sick parade. Capt Corby visits sick horses at Hoppewell. | |
| | 15/3/17 | | General Routine. Capt Corby. Mullens horse of Division from a point 9th Division. | |

Army Form C. 2118

# WAR DIARY
## or
## INTELLIGENCE SUMMARY
*(Erase heading not required.)*

Instructions regarding War Diaries and Intelligence Summaries are contained in F. S. Regs., Part II. and the Staff Manual respectively. Title Pages will be prepared in manuscript.

| Place | Date | Hour | Summary of Events and Information | Remarks and references to Appendices |
|---|---|---|---|---|
| | | | Continued | |
| In the Field | 16/3/17 | 6.30 a.m. | General Routine. R.C.O. sent to Hervicourt - Sus-Somme to answer Horse S.I. | |
| | 17/3/17 | 5.30 p.m. | Head Quarters. | |
| | | | General Routine. Cap't Cosby goes to Hem-Quarters. | |
| | 18/3/17 | | General Routine. Collecting parties sent to Tincourt to bring in sick Horses | |
| | 19/3/17 | | General Routine. 9 G.H. Cart. 30 G.S. Cart. 93 R.D.M. to Hospital, evacuated to Bray Clearing Station | |
| | 20/3/17 | | Party sent to Bray Hospital with Horses for Evacuation | |
| | 21/3/17 | | General Routine | |
| | 22/3/17 | | Party sent to Estrees. Party sent to Bray Hospital with Horses for Evacuation | |
| | 23/3/17 | | General Routine | |
| | 24/3/17 | | General Routine. Visit paid a.p.v.d. 59th Division | |
| | 25/3/17 | | Quarters. Sus-Somme to remove Saddlery belonging to Horses | |
| | 26/3/17 | | General Routine. a.p.v.d. 59th Division inspected horses for Evacuation | |
| | 27/3/17 | | Party sent to Base Veterinary Hospital with Horses for Evacuation | |
| | 28/3/17 | | Routine. Instructions received to move to Moreuve - Chaussee | |
| | 29/3/17 | | Move to St Christ, arrangements for horses - Chaussee | |
| | 30/3/17 | | Case St Christ for move - en - Chaussee, and take-up Quarters there | |
| | 31/3/17 | | General Routine. Party sent to St Christ to collect Sick Horses left there on route. | |

Guy J Lody
Capt-ave
O/C

2 APR. 1917

WAR DIARY
—of—
O.C. No. 1 Coy, 59th Div'l Train

from 1st to 31st March 1917

(Vol. II)

# WAR DIARY
## INTELLIGENCE SUMMARY
*(Erase heading not required.)*

Army Form C. 2118

Instructions regarding War Diaries and Intelligence Summaries are contained in F.S. Regs., Part II. and the Staff Manual respectively. Title Pages will be prepared in manuscript.

| Place | Date | Hour | Summary of Events and Information | Remarks and references to Appendices |
|---|---|---|---|---|
| In the Field | 1/3/17 | | In billets at MERICOURT – Repairing Road MERICOURT – Sapphire | ADR |
| | 6/3/17 – 8/3/17 | | Caught up to R.T.P. by M.T. Supply Column | ADR |
| | 8/3/17 | | Sapphire Dawn from Railhead by Horse Transport | ADR |
| | 9/3/17 | | By road route to PROYART | ADR |
| | | | In billets at PROYART – Repairing Road from PROYART – Sapphire brought | ADR |
| | | | from LA FLAQUE Railhead to PROYART Repairing Road by H.T. | |
| | 3/5 | | Sapphire drawn from Railhead & R.T.P. by M.T. Supp Column | ADR |
| | 26/3/17 | | By Road route to PROYART to ENTREES – Detachments left at PROYART | ADR |
| | 29/3/17 | | In camp at ENTREES – Repairing roads – PROYART & ENTREES | |
| | 31/3/17 | | Sapphire drawn from new Railheads SATYRE WOOD, FAY. | |

M.Dillon Major KC
C.E. S.T.S. 50[?] Div

War Diary
of
O.C. No 2 Coy, 59th Field Train
from 1st March 1917 to 31st March 1917.

Vol. II.

# WAR DIARY or INTELLIGENCE SUMMARY

Army Form C. 2118.

No 2 COMPANY. 59th DIVL. TRAIN. Vol. II.

| Place | Date 1917 | Hour | Summary of Events and Information | Remarks and references to Appendices |
|---|---|---|---|---|
| MORCOURT | 1, Mch. | | REFILLING POINT for troops of T attached to 176 Inf. Bde. VILLERS-BRETONNEUX. Refilling Point MORCOURT. | THH |
| " | 2 " | | On commencement of move of units of 176" Inf. Bde. Group from concentration area at MORCOURT | THH |
| " | 5 " | | Carried out Supply arrangements in accordance with Appendices No 1/15. 3 hours transport being used to draw supplies from Railhead at MORCOURT. Mechanical Transport being used for | THAT |
| " | 6 " | | drawing supplies from MORCOURT (R.P.) to Units which had already reached FOUCAUCOURT area. | THAT |
| " | 8 " | | in accordance with Appendix 4, moved Headquarters of Company to PROYART, retiring No 3 Coy. of 50-Divl. TRAIN. | THAT |
| PROYART. | 9 " | | Commenced supply operations in accordance with orders contained in Appendix 4, drawing with Baggage wagons from Railhead at LA FLAQUE to Refilling Point and Thence by supply wagons to Units Quartermasters Stores in FOUCAUCOURT area. | THAT |
| ESTRÉES | 22 " | | In accordance with orders contained in Appendices 5+6 moved Headquarters of Company to ESTRÉES and (despatched) Baggage wagons to units. 5+6 Refilling Point for Units of 176" Inf Bde Group at ESTRÉES. | THAT |
| " | 23 " | | 469 Field Co. R.E. + 180" Tunnelling Co R.E. added to 176" Infantry Group for Supply purposes. | THAT |
| " | 24 " | | "A" Battm. 296 Bde R.F.A. added to 176" Inf Bde Group for Supply purposes. | THAT |
| " | 25 " | | Rations withdrawn for transport of Supplies for 3" Corps Mounted Troops from ESTRÉES to BRIE. | THAT |
| " | 26 " | | "B, C + D" Battm. + Hd. 295 Bde R.F.A. added to 176" Inf Bde Group for Supply purposes. | THAT |
| " | 27 " | | 2/5 Lond. Staff. 2/3 North. Staff. with 174" Inf. Bdes. moved to BRIE, to which point supplies carried on Train wagons. 2/1 Nat. Fld. Amb. rations on Group change for supplies and Hdqrs, A + B. Railways, 2/6 R.Lk.SR. and 470 Fld. Co. R.E. | THAT |
| " | 28 " | | 469 2nd Co. R.E. 2 Divl Salvage Dump, 2/1 Mn. Gun. Co. added to Group strength for supplies. 2/5 North Staff. to ESTRÉES to change Hdqrs. Til "A" Bde. moved to BRIE. 2/6 South Staffs & Mens-en-Chaussee, and 2/6 North Staff. to ESTRÉES so. change Hdqrs. of Company moved to point on main road 2600 yds E of BRIE. W of PROYART 1/4 R.Lk.SR and 2/5 Lond. Inf. | THAT THAT THAT |
| PROYART | 31 " | | General circumstances. Weather conditions during month had. Road conditions in consequence abnormally bad rendering use of Mechanical Transport impossible. Health of Company good. | THAT |

[Signature] Capt
O.C. No 2 Coy 59th Divl Train

Confidential

War Diary

of

O.C. No. 3 Company, 59th Divisional Train.

From 1·3·17 to 31·3·17

Volume ii

# WAR DIARY
## INTELLIGENCE SUMMARY
(Erase heading not required.)

Army Form C. 2118

| Place | Date | Hour | Summary of Events and Information | Remarks and references to Appendices |
|---|---|---|---|---|
| BAYON-VILLERS | 1/3/17 | | In quarters | March 1917 |
| BAYON-VILLERS | 8/3/17 | a.m. 9.30 | moved by road to PROYART. | |
| PROYART. | 8/3/17 | a.m. 11.15 | In quarters | |
| PROYART | 26/3/17 | p.m. 6.0 | moved by road to PRUSLE. | |
| PRUSLE | 29/3/17 | p.m. 2.15 | In quarters | |
| PRUSLE | 31/3/17 | | In quarters | |

H. Green Capt.
O.C. N.º 36 C.C.S.
55th Div. Train

Confidential
War Diary
of
H.Q. 5th Bde. R.F.C. 59th Divn
From 1/9/17 to 31/12/17

VOLUME II

Army Form C. 2118.

# WAR DIARY
## or
## INTELLIGENCE SUMMARY.
*(Erase heading not required.)*

Instructions regarding War Diaries and Intelligence Summaries are contained in F.S. Regs., Part II. and the Staff Manual respectively. Title pages will be prepared in manuscript.

| Hour, Date, Place | | Summary of Events and Information | Remarks and references to Appendices |
|---|---|---|---|
| 9 a.m. | 1.3.17 | GLISY. | Proceed by route march to WARFUSEE-ABANCOURT. | |
| 11 a.m. | 9.3.17. | WARFUSEE. | Proceed to PROYART. | |
| 8 a.m. | 22.3.17. | PROYART. | Proceed to ESTREES-DENIECOURT. | |
| 10 p.m. | 26.3.17. | ESTREES | Proceed E. of R. Somme to PRUSLE. | |

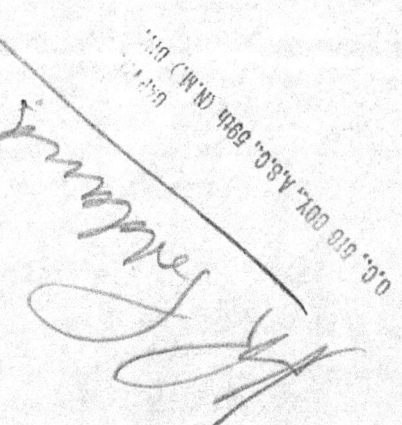

O.C. 616 Coy. A.S.C. 59th (N.M.) Div.

Vol 3

CONFIDENTIAL.

WAR DIARY

of

HEADQUARTERS 59th DIVISIONAL TRAIN

from 1-4-17 to 30-4-17

Vol. III.

# WAR DIARY

## INTELLIGENCE SUMMARY

HEADQUARTERS 59th Division Army Train VOL III

Army Form C. 2118.

(Erase heading not required.)

| Place | Date | Hour | Summary of Events and Information | Remarks and references to Appendices |
|---|---|---|---|---|
| PRUSLE | 1917 APRIL 10 | | Headquarters and Nos. 1. 2. 3. and 4 Coys 59th Divisional Train moved from PRUSLE to VRAIGNES. Refilling Points of 59th Divl Troops and 176th Infantry Brigade moved from ESTREES and PROSLE respectively and R.Ps of 177th & 178th Inf Bdes moved from THE RAPERIE on VRAIGNES – HANCOURT Rd to Divisional R.P. on VRAIGNES – BOUVINCOURT Rd where supplies for issue 11.4.17 were dumped by 59th Divl Supply Coy. | SOS SOS SOS SOS SOS |
| VRAIGNES | 23 | | After issue of Supplies, the Supply Details proceeded to new Refilling Points on the ROISEL – HANCOURT Road via the Supply CROSS in quite. Trains bivouaced for the night. Passed Reference were drawn by supply Sections from III Corps Reserve Dump ROISEL and dumped on the new Refilling Points fix next day. | SOS SOS SOS SOS |
| | 24 | | 244th Train Transport "A" "B" & "D" Batteries 210th Brigade R.F.A. arrived & attached to No 2/5 59 Division on flow units coming on the reach attacker of the Division. Refilling Points for Divl Troops, 176th Infy Bde 177th Infy Bde & 178th Infy Bde Groups all on HANCOURT – ROISEL ROAD. After issue of Supplies Train Transport again drew Reserve Rations from Corps Reserve Dump ROISEL and dumped on Refilling Points for issue following day. | SOS SOS SOS |
| | 25 | | Refilling Points as for 24th inst. After issue the Supply Details of the Train proceeded to the Refilling Points on VRAIGNES – BOUVINCOURT ROAD and received supplies from R.D.S.C. for issue 26th inst. Supply Sections returned to Coy lines VRAIGNES after delivering supplies. | SOS SOS SOS |

**Army Form C. 2118.**

# WAR DIARY
## or
## INTELLIGENCE SUMMARY.
*(Erase heading not required.)*

Instructions regarding War Diaries and Intelligence Summaries are contained in F. S. Regs., Part II. and the Staff Manual respectively. Title pages will be prepared in manuscript.

| Place | Date | Hour | Summary of Events and Information | Remarks and references to Appendices |
|---|---|---|---|---|
| VRAIGNES | 1917 APRIL 26. | | Refilling Point VRAIGNES - BOUVINCOURT ROAD. All horses of the Train inspected by D.D.V.S. 4th Army - Captain M.B.H. LAMBERT A.S.C. reported for duty to complete Establishment, and was posted to No 1 Coy 59th Divl Train as 2nd in Command. Capt A.J.A. REID posted to Headquarters 59th Divl Train as Requisitioning Officer and 2/Lt P.R.R. DIBBEN posted to No 2 Coy 59th Divl Train. Supply Wagons of 2nd Bn WELCH REGT arrived from 1st Divisional Train and were attached to No 2 Coy 59th Divisional Train for duty. | 2RF SRF 2RF 2RF |
| | 30. | | | |

War Diary
of
O.C. 513 Coy. A.S.C. 59th Div.
from 1-iv-17 to 30-iv-17

(Vol III.)

Castlewade

Army Form C. 2118.

# WAR DIARY
## or
## INTELLIGENCE SUMMARY

*(Erase heading not required.)*

Instructions regarding War Diaries and Intelligence Summaries are contained in F. S. Regs., Part II. and the Staff Manual respectively. Title Pages will be prepared in manuscript.

| Place | Date | Hour | Summary of Events and Information | Remarks and references to Appendices |
|---|---|---|---|---|
| 2/c Fus | 1/4/17 | | At ESTREES – Relying points at ESTREES & PROYART | ADS |
| | 3/17 | | Moves by road north to PRUSLE – Relying points skn at ESTREES and PROYART | ADS |
| | 9/17 | | Moves by mail route to VRAIGNES – Relying point at VRAIGNES | ADS |
| | 24/17 & 25/17 | | Relying point to Div Tempo at ROISEL | ADS |
| | 26/17 | | Relying point on VRAIGNES – BOUVINCOURT Road | ADS |
| | 26/17 | | Capt M.L.B.H. Lenton upster to h/g — 2/Lt. P.R.R. Disher posts to No. 2 Coy, 59 Div Train. | |

M Lenton Major
New Coy 59² Div Train
Capt (513 Coy)
New Coy 59 A.S.C.
(513 Coy)

Confidential

War Diary

of

O.C. No 2 Company, O.S.C. 59th Division.

Volume III

From 1st April 1917 to 30th April 1917.

# WAR DIARY or INTELLIGENCE SUMMARY

*(Erase heading not required.)*

Army Form C. 2118.

No 2 COMPANY. 59th DIVL. TRAIN. VOL III.

Instructions regarding War Diaries and Intelligence Summaries are contained in F.S. Regs, Part II. and the Staff Manual respectively. Title Pages will be prepared in manuscript.

| Place | Date | Hour | Summary of Events and Information | Remarks and references to Appendices |
|---|---|---|---|---|
| PRUSLE. | 1.4.17 | | Weather continues abnormally cold with frequent snowstorms. Condition of horses shows general deterioration consequent on exposure. 1 H.D. horse destroyed. 1 H.D. evacuated to 59 Div. Mob. Vet. Sec. (destroyed 3.4.17). Refilling point on Main Road, PRUSIG. Baggage & Supply Wagons of 5 N. Staffs to 6 South Staffs handed over 15 G.S. No 2 Coy motors (Battalions being struck off ration strength of group). | Ref. Map Sheet 62.C. 1/40,000. Nil. |
| | 2.4.17 | | | Nil. |
| | 3.4.17 | | 1st Line Transport of HQ. R.A. HQ. R.E. 467 310 Co. R.E. 59 Div. Sig. Co. R.E. No 1 & No 2 Sec. III A.T. 59 Div. Mob. Vet. Sec. 1st 2nd & 3rd Ammn. r 2nd 3rd Aids. 59 Div. collected on Moss land (with also) being on ration strength of group. 1 H.D. horse died. | Nil. Nil. Nil. |
| | 4.4.17 | | Train Transport of HQ. 178 Bde 7 B. Echelon 59th Divn collected on these lands being added to ration group for rations. | Nil. |
| | 5.4.17 | | | Nil. |
| | 6.4.17 | | 1 Draught + 3 H.D. evacuated for illness. | |
| | 7.4.17 | | 1 Draught horse left at Estates shed | Nil. |
| VRAIGNES. | 10.4.17 | | Moved Headquarters of Company to VRAIGNES. R.P. for 11th Speed at present P. 18 G central. | Nil. |
| | 11.4.17 | | On completion of delivery of supplies transferred mess wagons of 3rd B.L. Amb. to 2nd, No 4 Coy and wagons of all other But. Troops (excepting 467 310 Co. R.E. & 1st Field Amb.) to O.C. No 1 Coy on resuming rationing of units of 176th Inf. Bde. | Nil. |
| | 12.4.17 | | Limited amount of stabling and stable of walls available and utilised for horses for part time sec 23rd March. | Nil. |
| | 23.4.17 | | 3 motor Lor M/36 59th Div. Train collected from BOUCLY Drew wagons of "A"+"B" Battn. 210 13th R.F.A. and from HAMLET Drew wagons of "D" (Batt.), 210 Bde R.F.A. and there will Serving an Ration strength of Group. Supply Section of Company arrived at point K. 22. a 9. 2. Previously known as Forward Refilling Point for 176th Inf. Bde. Dump fixed for 24.4.17. | Nil. |
| | 25.4.17 | | Train Transport after delivering Supplies drew rations in bulk (for week in 24.4) from point K. 15. c. 10.3.B. | Nil. |
| | 29.4.17 | | Supply Section returned to VRAIGNES and rejoined Company headquarters upon delivery of supplies to units. | Nil. |
| | | | Units of 176th Inf. Bde. commenced to draw rations from Refilling Point by Divl. Train Transport. | |

O.C. No 2 Coy. 59th Divl. Train

Confidential

War Diary

of

No. 3 Company, 59th Divisional Train.

From 1-4-17 to 30-4-17.

(Volume iii/III)

Army Form C. 2118

# WAR DIARY
## or
## INTELLIGENCE SUMMARY
*(Erase heading not required.)*

Instructions regarding War Diaries and Intelligence Summaries are contained in F. S. Regs., Part II. and the Staff Manual respectively. Title Pages will be prepared in manuscript.

515 Coy A.S.C. 5th Div Train                April 1917

| Place | Date | Hour | Summary of Events and Information | Remarks and references to Appendices |
|---|---|---|---|---|
| PRUSLE | 1/4/17 | | In quarters | KG |
| RAPERIE | 5/4/17 | | Detachment of Supply wagons sent forward to RAPERIE (advanced dump) | KG |
| PRUSLE | 10/4/17 | 7.0 a.m. | moved by road to VRAINGES. | KG |
| VRAINGES | 10/4/17 | 9.0 a.m. | In quarters | KG |
| Do | 23/4/17 | | In quarters | KG |
| Do | 30/4/17 | | In quarters | KG |

A Green Capt —
O.C. No 3 Coy
5th Div Train

1875  Wt. W593/826  1,000,000  4/15  J.B.C. & A.  A.D.S.S./Forms/C. 2118.

Confidential

War Diary
of
Lt. Nort. Col. A.A.Q., 59th Division.
From 1st April 1917 to 30th April 1917.

Volume 3

Army Form C. 2118.

# WAR DIARY
*or*
INTELLIGENCE SUMMARY.
*(Erase heading not required.)*

Instructions regarding War Diaries and Intelligence Summaries are contained in F.S. Regs., Part II. and the Staff Manual respectively. Title pages will be prepared in manuscript.

| Hour, Date, Place | Summary of Events and Information | Remarks and references to Appendices |
|---|---|---|
| 7-0 am. 10-4-1917 PRUSSE | Proceed by route march to VRAIGNES. | M. |

M.
O.C. 516 COY. A.S.C.
CAPTN.

Vol 4

Confidential

War Diary

of

Headquarters, 59th Divl. Train

From 1st May 1917 to 31st May 1917 inclusive

Volume IV

Army Form C. 2118.

# WAR DIARY of Headquarters
## INTELLIGENCE SUMMARY. 59th Divisional Train.

(Erase heading not required.)

Instructions regarding War Diaries and Intelligence Summaries are contained in F.S. Regs., Part II. and the Staff Manual respectively. Title pages will be prepared in manuscript.

| Place | Date | Hour | Summary of Events and Information | Remarks and references to Appendices |
|---|---|---|---|---|
| | 1917 May | | | |
| VRAIGNES | 1st | | Railhead PERONNE. Refilling Points for the whole division in VRAIGNES – BOUCHOIR ROAD. C/D Batteries 241 Bde (T.F.A.) & Ref HQ & DAC taken on ration strength. 1/48 Bde R.A. | SGT |
| " | 2nd | | K n° 2 Coy for supply duties of 1/48 Bde R.A. A detachment of the Train proceeded to TINCOURT. 1/48 Bde detachment of NCOs & Men, 1 NCO 10/R/Brit & 3 complete Transport + 3 complete Transport. N° 2 Coy 1 NCO, 1 Driver & 3 complete Transport, Detachment bivouaced on South side of Road by TINCOURT. Detachment to proceed to 142 A.T. Train on 143rd Bde Artillery being relieved off ration strength of Division. | SGT SGT SGT |
| " | 3rd | | Explosion in cellar of Artillery billet occupied by N° 3 Coy men, due to Rifle gren. One D.R. injured, burnt. T/25/19 | SGT SGT |
| " | 4th | | 2 O.R. & 6 of 1st N.M. Field Ambulance to report as S.B. on Transport + 2 OR ditto | PGF SGT |
| " | 5th | | Loaders of Ad Bde & 2nd Bde wagons returned to their Units under orders of Bde H.Q. | |
| " | 6th | | Supply wagons of 6 of WELCH Regt returned to 1st Divisional Train on the Regt being relieved off ration strength of Division | SGT SGT |
| " | 7th | | Train H.Q. and 1, 2, 3 & 4 Bns and Refilling points for Div Troops (cars 178 - 173 + 176) Bde moved to location of Refilling Points. | |
| S. of ROISEL | | | ROISEL as follows: Train HQ K27.d.6, 311 coy K22.d.14, n° 2 Coy K27.c.1.8, n° 3 Coy K28.a.1.8, n° 4 Coy K28.b. Refilling Points on Road through K27.d. and K28.b. | PGF PGF SGT |
| " | 8th | | Railhead ROISEL. Supplies drawn from railhead by Train Transport. 55 wagons kept detailed for the purpose. | SGT |
| " | 9th | | Remounts drawn from LA CHAPELLETTE, 23 HD by K Train and SHD & 2 Bns for 5th div Transport Pk. | SGT |
| " | 11th | | Bombs dropped by enemy aircraft near Refilling Point but no damage done. | PGF PGF |
| " | 13th | | Train Transport of C/D Batteries 241 Bde R.F.A. & Sect. 48th DAC returned to 48th Div Train on the Units being relieved of ration strength of Division – | PGF |
| " | 14th | | D/293 A.F.A.Bde and Train Transport to arrive min.d HAMELET & come on ration strength of division. | SGT |
| " | 15th | | Drew from ROISEL Railhead for last time by Train Transport. | PGF |
| VRAIGNES | 16th | | Train HQ + N°s 1, 3 + 4 Coys + R.Ps of Bde Troops, 174, 178th Bde from road and 5th div Transport. Road respectively. N° 2 Coy + R.P. 176 Bde from road Div South of ROISEL. Railhead PERONNE. | SGT PGF |
| " | | | N° 2 Coy + R.P. 176 Bde Railhead reserve and allotted to 1/8/2 Bde D.S.S. | SGT |
| " | | | Railhead PERONNE. N° 3/67 + 177 Bde R.P. moved as before. Removed supply + Transport order carried out. N° 3/67 + 177 Bde R.P. moved off & refilling to 1/6/2 and V/6/5.3 and 137 Supply Coy. | PGF PGF SGT |
| " | 17, 24th | | 60 Remounts drawn from LA CHAPELLETTE and distributed as follows: 1 Rdn to S.O.B., 25 HD + 1 Rdn 5 H.D. | SGT PGF |
| " | | | N° 3 Coy and 1 Rdn + remainder of Remounts to 1st 2 lines Transport of Infantry | PGF SGT |
| " | 27th | | N° 3 Coy moved K P32A + 179 K.R.P.3 P32A (North 572) | SGT |
| " | 28th | | N° 1 Coy H.Q. moved K P32A (North 572) Train Transport P9/57 1 Bde R.F.A. and rem'n 159 DAC moved 203 A.R. ration strength | PGF |
| LECHELLES | " | | Train HQ + N°4 Coy + 179th Ad. R.P. move from VRAIGNES to P32A (North 572) LECHELLES | SGT SGT |
| " | 31st | | N° 2 Coy + 176 Bde R.P. move from South of ROISEL to P32A (North 572). Remainder of HQ Remounts from Field Remount Depot BRIE. 6 for Train Corps + H.Q. for 1st line Transport of Division. Div Troops R.P. withdrawn. N° 176 Remounts VRA SPR. | SGT SGT |
| | | | conditions of horses improving. | SGT |

[Signature]
Lt. Col.
Commanding 59th Divl Train

War Diary
of
O.C. No 2 Coy 59th Divl Train
Vol. IV
1st May 1917 to 31st May 1917.

Confidential

# WAR DIARY or INTELLIGENCE SUMMARY

Army Form C. 2118.

Vol. IV

No 2 Coy 59th Div. Train

Ref. Map 62.C. 1/40000

| Place | Date 1917 | Hour | Summary of Events and Information | Remarks and references to Appendices |
|---|---|---|---|---|
| VRAIGNES | 1st May | | Commenced work with following units on ration strength of Brigade Groups viz. Helqus 7th Battns 175th 2/H Bde, 175th 2 T.A.B. 174 M.Gun Co. 467 310 Co R.E. 1st FAD Ambce, 59th W. No 2 Coy 59 Div. Train, also A.C. + H B.A.C. 2/0 1st A.C. 175 B.R.F.A + 1st + 2nd D.A.C. and 13th the Welch Regt. Pt Bde Nation strength. C-"H" Batt. 241 Bde R.F.A + No 9 Sec 4th D.A.C taken in supply. Two wagons sent with detachment of Train to TINCOURT on Coal(?) work. | That |
| " | 2 " | | Detachment of 4th + 2nd Div Train rejoined 42nd Train on 43rd Div being struck off Group ration strength. | That |
| " | 5 " | | All loading of Baggage wagons reduced to 3 Infantry Battns for draft. | That |
| " | 6 " | | Resumed drawing supplies of Brigade with Train Transport now Brigade going into the line. Detachment of 1st Div. Train rejoined their Train on Bde. of which Regt. being struck off of Group ration strength. | That |
| ROISEL | 7 " | | Moved Hdqrs of Coy to K.22.b.1.5 (South of ROISEL). TINCOURT detachment returned (Coy Hdqrs) | That |
| " | 8 " | | Hqr H Batn 175 Inf Bde. Commenced drawing supplies from Villiers Front Dp. Rail Hd. Transport & continued to do so up to 16th inclusive. All ammn wagons of Coy employed during same period carrying supplies in bulk from Rail Hd. at ROISEL | That |
| " | 9 " | | Moved 6 Kennels (through No 1 Coy.) from LA CHAPELLETTE | That |
| " | 13 " | | "D" Battery, 241 Bde R.F.A moved at HANCOURT. Sections of Group Rations as from 15th and Train Transport attached | That |
| " | 15 " | | Detachment of 43rd Div Train rejoined their Train on 43rd Div Artillery being struck off Group ration strength. | That |
| " | 17 " | | 469 341 Co. R.E. & 295 Bde. R.F.A taken on group ration strength and Train Transport attached. 1st Field Amb. struck off group ration strength | That |
| " | 19 " | | Resumed drawing of Supplies for Units of 175 Inf Bde. with Train Transport. | That |
| " | 20 " | | Convoy (unarmed) with R.E. Stores to HARGICOURT QUARRIES. L.10.d.4.4 | That |
| " | 21 " | | Convoy to HARGICOURT again 19th | That |
| " | 23 " | | 295 Bde. R.F.A. + No 2 Sec 59 D.A.C taken on group ration strength | That |
| " | 26 " | | HQ 175 Inf. Bde. + 174 M.Gun. Co. moved to BOUVINCOURT, 2/8 Notts sent to Villiers Faucon Detachment to draw supplies from R.P. of 175 Inf Bde. 467 3rd D Co R.E. moved to EQUANCOURT + were struck off Group ration strength to rations on list of 178 Inf Bde. D' Batty 241 Bde R.F.A moved to CONTAYCOURT but were retained on group ration strength. | That |
| " | 28 " | | Any H.Q. wagons required hourly No 1 Coy. D' Batty 241st Bde R.F.A, 295 + 296 8.40 R.F.A + No 2 sec 59 D.A.C. struck off ration strength of Bde. Group after refilling and Train Transport sent to units prior to the wound. Horses of Baggage wagons & ammunition personnel of No1 Coy received West Coy. | That |
| " | 29 " | | 469 3rd D Co. R.E. struck off ration strength of Brigade Group after refilling to Belking on Unit moving to new area. Baggage wagons 2/8/2/6 sherwood Foresters sent to Railhead for units 175 Inf. B.Ds. in readiness for move. | That |
| " | 30 " | | 2/6 & 2/6 Sherwood Foresters struck off ration strength of Brigade Group after refilling on Battalions moving to new area. Baggage wagons sent into units 176 Inf. B.Ds. in readiness for move. | That |
| " | 31 " | | Supplies for 174 Machine Gun Co. delivered at BOUVINCOURT. Baggage of 175 + 178 Hd + Bde. HQ + 175 Battns delivered at EQUANCOURT area. Hqrs of Coy. Moved to P.32 Central (Ref. Map 57.C.) Two H.Q. Ammunition Wagons Div Train. | That |

DC No 2 Coy, 59th Div. Train

**No. 1 COMPANY**
59th DIVL. TRAIN
(No. 513 Coy. A.S.C.)

War Diary
— of —
O.C. No. 513 Coy A.S.C. 59th Div.
From 1st to 31st May, 1917.

(Volume 4.)

Confidential

# WAR DIARY

## INTELLIGENCE SUMMARY

*(Erase heading not required.)*

Army Form C. 2118

Instructions regarding War Diaries and Intelligence Summaries are contained in F.S. Regs., Part II and the Staff Manual respectively. Title Pages will be prepared in manuscript.

| Place | Date | Hour | Summary of Events and Information | Remarks and references to Appendices |
|---|---|---|---|---|
| 2ic Fiet | 1/5/17 | | In billets at VRAIGNES – R.T. to Div's troops at VRAIGNES – BOUVINCOURT Road | AB |
| | 7/5/17 | | Move by road to ROISEL – R.T. horses into Coy. | AB |
| | 8/5/17 | | Draw from Railhead by M.T. – 10 H.D. remounts received. | AB |
| | 14/5/17 | | 1 H.D. Horses returned from No. 516 Coy A.S.C. | AB |
| | 15/5/17 | | Div. H.Q. Coy Supply Bgde returned from VRAIGNES – BOUVINCOURT Road – R.T. horses into Coy. | AB |
| | 16/5/17 | | Move by road to Coys on VRAIGNES – BOUVINCOURT Road | AB |
| | 5/5/17 | | 2Lt Baskine + Buffer + Supply Bgde to No. 2 Sect D.A.C. returned to No. 514 Coy A.S.C. | AB |
| | 23/5/17 | | 1 H.D. Horse inspected by V.O. | AB |
| | 25/5/17 | | 11 H.D. Remounts received | AB |
| | 26/5/17 | | 1 H.D. Horse destroyed by V.O. | AB |
| | 29/5/17 | | R/1117 begun sent to C.R.A. + C.R.E. in reference to men to remount Supply Bgde to D.H.Q. – Sig Coy – C.R.A + C.R.E. would be used to supply to O.C 575 Coy as required supplying. D.A.C. Hors No 2 Sect materially Butter + Supply Bgde | AB |
| | 28/5/17 | | returned to D.A.C. after reporting. | AB |

# WAR DIARY
## INTELLIGENCE SUMMARY
*(Erase heading not required.)*

Army Form C. 2118

| Place | Date | Hour | Summary of Events and Information | Remarks and references to Appendices |
|---|---|---|---|---|
| | 28/9 | | Fini Post Office work to meet demand. 470 R.E. Coy supply train return from No. 516 Coy | |
| | 29/9/17 | | Coy HQ Coy moved by road FLECHELLE – Details TCy on Coy transport with 515 Coy started for DK9 – MNB – MYR MVS by supply return left behind | |
| VRAIGNES | 30/9 | | Supply trains – DHQ – Signal Coy CRA – C.R.E. – 467 + 469 R.E. Coy – C.R.E. 515/Tc. Coy transport from 515 Coy ASC | |
| | 31/9 | | CRA Bay/Tc. Bryn. details to Coy – 2 H.D. Remounts received (Lieut Simmonds HKSC) 10 H.D. Remounts from BRIE | |

Williams HKSC
Cpt 513 Coy 54th Div. T

Confidential

War Diary

No. 515 Coy. A.S.C. 59th Division

From 1·5·17 to 31·5·17

Volume IV

Army Form C. 2118

# WAR DIARY
## INTELLIGENCE SUMMARY
(Erase heading not required.)

Instructions regarding War Diaries and Intelligence Summaries are contained in F. S. Regs., Part II. and the Staff Manual respectively. Title Pages will be prepared in manuscript.

| Place | Date | Hour | Summary of Events and Information | Remarks and references to Appendices |
|---|---|---|---|---|
| VRAINGES | 1/5/17 | | 575 Coy ASC 59th Division May 1917 | |
| | | | In Billets | |
| | | | additional units on Ration strength of Bde. Group. | |
| | | | HQ's A. B. C. D Batteries 295 Bde RFA. | |
| | | | 469 Coy RE. | |
| | | | 2/2nd NMFA. | |
| D° | 9/5/17 | 11.0 a.m | Moved by road to ROISEL | |
| ROISEL | 9/5/17 | 12.30 p.m | In Camp | |
| D° | 9/5/17 | | took over 6 H.D. Accounts | |
| D° | 16/5/17 | 11.30 a.m | Moved by road to VRAINGES | |
| VRAINGES | 16/5/17 | 12.45 p.m | In Camp | |

HFGreen Capt
OC 575 Coy ASC 59 Div

1875 Wt. W593/826 1,000,000 4/15 J.B.C. & A. A.D.S.S./Forms/C. 2118.

## WAR DIARY

### INTELLIGENCE SUMMARY

*(Erase heading not required.)*

Army Form C. 2118

| Place | Date | Hour | Summary of Events and Information | Remarks and references to Appendices |
|---|---|---|---|---|
| | | | 575 by A.S.C. 59th Division May 1917 | |
| VRAINGES | 14/5/17 | | all Battery of 295 Bde RFA. Attacks off Ration Strength | 1bl |
| Do | 18/5/17 | | 2/1st NMFA came on Ration Strength | 1bl |
| Do | 21/5/17 | | 2/1st NMFA Struck off Ration Strength | 1bl |
| Do | 24/5/17 | | Received 2 Horses Reinforcements | 1bl |
| Do | 25/5/17 | a.m. P.O | Moved by Road to EQUANCOURT. | 1bl |
| EQUANCOURT | 25/5/17 | 2.30 | In Camp | 1bl |
| Do | 26/5/17 | | 59th Div. Salvage Corps came on Ration Strength | 1bl |
| | | | 177 T.M.B. struck off Ration Strength | 1bl |

Wilson Capt —
OC 575 Coy ASC 59th Div

Army Form C. 2118.

# WAR DIARY

## INTELLIGENCE SUMMARY

*(Erase heading not required.)*

515 Coy A.S.C. 59th Division    May 1917

| Place | Date | Hour | Summary of Events and Information | Remarks and references to Appendices |
|---|---|---|---|---|
| EQUANCOURT | 27/5/17 | 9.0 a.m. | Moved by road to LECHELLE. | /SEE |
| LECHELLE | 27/5/17 | 10.40 a.m. | In Camp. | /SEE |
| D° | | | 2/3rd NM.F.A. ) Came in Ration strength<br>467 Coy. R.E. ) | /SEE |
| D° | 28/5/17 | | Took over 5. M.D. and 1 Pdre Reinforcements<br>59th Div. Brigade school came in Ration strength | /SEE /SEE |
| B° | 29/5/17 | | 59th Div. HQ 15 A. Div. )<br>HQrs R.E. HQrs R.A. ) Came in Ration strength<br>D.A.D.O.S. Div Signals )<br>59th Div. Cavalry ) | /SEE |
| D° | 30/5/17 | | Detachment from 8/1 Coy 35th Div. TRAIN, under 2L R.T. Hill came attd to Coy | /SEE |

W Green Capt-
OC 515 Coy A.S.C. 59th Div.

Army Form C. 2118.

# WAR DIARY
## INTELLIGENCE SUMMARY
*(Erase heading not required.)*

Instructions regarding War Diaries and Intelligence Summaries are contained in F. S. Regs., Part II. and the Staff Manual respectively. Title Pages will be prepared in manuscript.

| Place | Date | Hour | Summary of Events and Information | Remarks and references to Appendices |
|---|---|---|---|---|
| | | | 575 Coy A.S.C. 57th Division  May 1917 | |
| LECHELLE | 30/5 | | No 1 Section 35th Div DAC  <br> 470 Coy R.E.  <br> HQrs A.B.C.D Battery, R.F.A (157th Bde) } Came on Ration strength <br> Detachment of No 1 Coy 35th Div Train. | G.C |
| " | 31/5 | | Took over 2 H.D. Remounts <br> 57th Div HQrs (13 men) } Came on Ration <br> M.M.P. <br> No 1 Coy 57th Divl Train | A.C <br> A.C |
| " | 31/5 | | In camp at LECHELLE <br> General health of the Company during the month has very good <br> Horses greatly improved in condition | V.G.S <br> V.G.S <br> V.G.S |

Arthur Capn—
OC 575 Coy ASC 57th Div.

Army Form C. 2118.

# WAR DIARY
or
## INTELLIGENCE SUMMARY.
(Erase heading not required.)

Instructions regarding War Diaries and Intelligence
Summaries are contained in F.S. Regs., Part II.
and the Staff Manual respectively. Title pages
will be prepared in manuscript.

| Hour, Date, Place | | | Summary of Events and Information | Remarks and references to Appendices |
|---|---|---|---|---|
| 6.0 a.m | 2.5.17. | VRAIGNES | 5 wagons under Lt. PIGGIN detached for duty at TINCOURT to continue material for road repairing. | M. |
| 5.0 p.m | 5.5.17 | VRAIGNES. | 2 drivers sent to 2/1st Field Ambulance to replace casualties. All drivers employed on loading & baggage wagons on returned to their units. | M. |
| 11.0 a.m. | 6.5.17 | VRAIGNES | C.Q.M.S. ROBINSON proceeds to ENGLAND on transfer to R.F.A Cadet Corps. | M. |
| 4.0 p.m | 8.5.17 | ROISEL | Water cart in returned from PERONNE with repairs completed | M. |
| 3.0 p.m | 10.5.17. | ROISEL | O.C. Train inspects camp. | |
| | 13.5.17 | ROISEL | Reveille time changed to 6.0 a.m. Cpl IRVING proceeds to ENGLAND on transfer to R.F.A Cadet Corps. A.H.D Ivan dies. | M |
| | 19.5.17 | VRAIGNES | Time for reveille changed to 8.0 a.m | M |
| 7.30 a.m | 18.5.17 | VRAIGNES. | Horses inspected by A.D.V.S. | M. |

Army Form C. 2118.

# WAR DIARY
## or
## INTELLIGENCE SUMMARY.
(Erase heading not required.)

Instructions regarding War Diaries and Intelligence Summaries are contained in F.S. Regs., Part II. and the Staff Manual respectively. Title pages will be prepared in manuscript.

| Hour, Date, Place | Summary of Events and Information | Remarks and references to Appendices |
|---|---|---|
| 11.0 a.m. 19.5.17 VRAIGNES | O.C. Train inspects camp, wagons and personnel of 2/5th Battn and 2/8th Battn Stewards Trailers and attached to No. 2 Coy at ROISEL | W |
| 20.5.17 VRAIGNES | Wagons & personnel of 296th Bde. R.F.A. (attached from No.1 Coy) are detached to No. 2 Coy at ROISEL | W |
| 10.0 a.m. 26.5.17 VRAIGNES | 3. H.D. (Renouf K) taken on strength | W |
| 2.0 p.m. 28.5.17 VRAIGNES | 2. H.T. Drivers taken on strength (reinforcements) | W |
| 2.40 p.m. 29.5.17 VRAIGNES | L/Sgt START proceeds to ENGLAND on transfer to Infantry Cadet Corps. | W |

[signature]

Army Form C. 2118.

# WAR DIARY
## INTELLIGENCE SUMMARY.
(Erase heading not required.)

| Hour, Date, Place | Summary of Events and Information | Remarks and references to Appendices |
|---|---|---|
| 1.5.17. VRAIGNES. | Units in return Strength of Brigade Group :- Hdqrs 178 Infantry Brigade, No 4 Sectn Signal Coy, 2/5 Sherwood Foresters, 2/6 Sherwood Foresters, 2/7 Sherwood Foresters, 2/8 Sherwood Foresters, 178 T.M.B, 195 Machine Gun Coy, Hdqrs 296 Bde R.F.A, A.B.C.D Batteries 296 Bde R.F.A, 470 Field Coy R.E. No 4 Coy A.S.C 59th Divisional Train. Town Major ROISEL (on return strength May 1st) Expeditionary Force Canteen Staff (on interpreter). | |
| 9.5.17 ROISEL | Town Major ROISEL struck off return strength. | W. |
| 21.5.17 VRAIGNES | Expeditionary Force Canteen Staff struck off return strength. 2/6 Sherwood Foresters 1 officer off return strength 2/8 Sherwood Foresters 1 officer off return strength | W. W. |
| 22.5.17 VRAIGNES | Hdqrs, 296 Bde R.F.A. A.B.C.D. Batteries 296 Bde R.F.A } struck off return strength W. | W. |
| 31.5.17. LECHELLE | 470 Field Coy, R.E. struck off return strength. | W. |

Army Form C. 2118.

# WAR DIARY
## or
## INTELLIGENCE SUMMARY.
*(Erase heading not required.)*

Instructions regarding War Diaries and Intelligence Summaries are contained in F. S. Regs., Part II. and the Staff Manual respectively. Title pages will be prepared in manuscript.

| Hour, Date, Place | Summary of Events and Information | Remarks and references to Appendices |
|---|---|---|
| 7.0 a.m. 7-5-1917 VRAIGNES | Proceed by route march to ROISEL. | N. |
| 8.0 a.m. 16-5-1917 ROISEL | Proceed to VRAIGNES. | N. |
| 7.0 a.m. 30-5-1917 VRAIGNES. | Proceed by route march to LECHELLE. (P 32 Central) | N. |

Vol 5

CONFIDENTIAL

WAR DIARY
of
HEADQUARTERS. 59th DIVISIONAL TRAIN
from 1st June 1917 to 30th June 1917

VOLUME IV

# WAR DIARY / INTELLIGENCE SUMMARY

**Army Form C. 2118.**

Instructions regarding War Diaries and Intelligence Summaries are contained in F.S. Regs., Part II. and the Staff Manual respectively. Title pages will be prepared in manuscript.

HEADQUARTERS. 59th DIVISIONAL TRAIN.

MAP REFERENCE Sheet 57c 1/40000

(Erase heading not required.)

| Place | Date | Hour | Summary of Events and Information | Remarks and references to Appendices |
|---|---|---|---|---|
| LECHELLES | 1917 JUNE 1st | | RAILHEAD PERONNE. Refilling Points for 176th 177th & 178th Bdes P32a. & for Divl Troops VRAIGNES. Refilling Point for Divisional Troops moved from VRAIGNES to P32a. | Sgt |
| " | 2nd | | Railhead ROCQUIGNY. Supplies drawn from Railhead by Horse Transport in relief of 59th D.S.C. | Sgt Sgt |
| " | 3rd | | Capt KEARNEY C.I.S. R.A.M.C. proceeded to Depot 15 D.M.3. 2nd Army for duty. | Sgt |
| " | 4th | | Commenced a standing detail of 2 GS wagons, complete turnout, for conveyance of RE Stores to front line and HSt. | Sgt |
| " | 5th | | L/C.G.S. SEAWARD and 15 O.R. with 12 pairs HD. Harness started haymaking work at V2 C.2.d.2. | Sgt |
| " | 8th | | Haymaking party of 1 Officer 15 O.R. 3 Riding horses and 20 HD horses proceeded R.735.d.8.1 detached | Sgt |
| " | 9th | | 4 Lorries detailed from 59th D.S.C. to assist in clearing Railhead owing to withdrawal of 16-30th. Horse King | Sgt |
| " | 11th | | During to very bad state of Roads consequent on severe Thunderstorm during night 10/11. M.T. lorries unable to work at Railhead so 15 GS wagons were sent to Railhead after delivering supplies to Units | Sgt |
| " | 12th | | 5 M.T. lorries assisted in drawing supplies from Railhead. 24 loadings of 250 Divisional Employ Company reported | Sgt |
| " | 13th | | for duty as loaders for R.A. Tram Transport. | Sgt |
| " | 14th | | 13 Other Ranks moved from Base Depot as Reinforcements. | Sgt |
| " | 17th | | 1 Officer & 24 O.R. proceeded to FINS, to prepare Refilling Points and Camps for a Divisional Train under orders of III Corps in connection with arrangement of Divisional Areas. (NCOs & Dvrs 4 HD attached to III Corps Refilling) | Sgt Sgt |
| " | 18th | | Commenced a daily standing detail of 2 GS Wagons (complete turnout) for work under 256 Tunnelling Coy RE. | Sgt |
| " | 19th | | M.T. again unable to work on the roads & Train Transport had to make second journey to Railhead commenced at 3 P.M. | Sgt |
| " | 22nd | | Haymaking party under 1 Officer proceeded to AIZECOURT LE HAUT as previous. 27 Other Ranks & 8 GS wagons, 36 HD & Riding Arranged for increased MT assistance to clear Railhead. | Sgt Sgt |
| " | 28th | | 7 O.R. evacuated from Base Depot as Reinforcements. | Sgt |
| " | 30th | | Weather conditions during the month good. General health of the personnel of the Train good. Horses improving in condition. | Sgt |

Bayleves  
Lieut Colonel  
Commanding 59 Divisional Train

WAR DIARY
—of—
O.C. 513 Coy. A.S.C. 59th Divn
1st to 30th June 1917.

(for O.C.)

# WAR DIARY / INTELLIGENCE SUMMARY

Army Form C. 2118.

Instructions regarding War Diaries and Intelligence Summaries are contained in F. S. Regs., Part II. and the Staff Manual respectively. Title Pages will be prepared in manuscript.

*(Erase heading not required.)*

| Place | Date | Hour | Summary of Events and Information | Remarks and references to Appendices |
|---|---|---|---|---|
| Le Fest Refer Sheet 57S 1:40000 | 1/9/17 | | 2nd Cmt at P.32 A (nr LECHELLE) Div: Troops R.P. on VRAIGNES — BOUVINCOURT Road about Capt Lamb's Detachment & Supply Details reports arrival of to P.32.A. | MR |
| | 2/9/17 | | Div Troop R.P. opens at P.32.A. — Dump Supplies from ROCQUIGNY Railways by H.T. — I.H.D. Horses transport. | MR |
| | 5/9/17 | | Lt Seward & 2 M.T. lorries attached to unit for duties. | MR |
| | 6/9/17 | | Water complete 6th etc horse & Divn Sec to 6 PÉRONNE walk on Rainwear — Billets. | MR |
| | 7/9/17 | | I.H.D. Horse transport. I.d. 2 Dupers on R.E. work nightly to Trench for 10 I.N.C.O. & 2 I.d. — | MR |
| | 8/9/17 | | M.W.Gs 3 officers on R.E. duty, lorry carrying. Lt Seward 2 N.C.O.s & I Pmoner to Div for 2 hr lorries Set on details duty. | MR |
| | 9/9/17 | | | MR |

# WAR DIARY
## or
## INTELLIGENCE SUMMARY

Army Form C. 2118.

*(Erase heading not required.)*

| Place | Date | Hour | Summary of Events and Information | Remarks and references to Appendices |
|---|---|---|---|---|
| | 4/7 | | 1 N.C.O. & 1 private sent on Lewis [?] course 21-6-17 for course at Corps in N.C.O. School | ADS |
| | 11/7 | | L/Sgt Morris sent on [?] Course | ADS |
| | 14/7 | | Wagon received from PERONNE | ADS |
| | 14/7 | | O.C. Dragon on leave Sunday until 20-11-17 | ADS |
| | 14/7 | | O.C. Dragon on [?] leave B. Reveley [?] duty | ADS |
| | 10/7 | | 1 N.C.O. + 2 O.R. Dragon on [?] [?] | ADS |
| | 21/7 | | Detached to 1 N.C.O. + 12 Rank & File sent to him at [?] Corps | ADS |
| | 22/7 | | 1 Mounted NCO 4 Duns + 3 [?] H[?] sent on [?] Instruction | ADS |
| | 24/7 | | Lt Philip [?] to hosp [?] Di[?] Bombing School to Corps & Instruction | ADS |
| | 27/7 | | 4 Col R [?] sent [?] Area - [?] - left no charge | ADS |
| | 11.30pm | | Detached troops [?] [?] from Capt A[?] + Lt [?] received | ADS |
| | | | Draft of 4 [?] Sent Transport Drivers, [?] [?] [?] supplies from Rhine & vicinity to [?] | |

A.D.Silverthys[?] Capt
Cmd 573 Coy A.S.C.

CONFIDENTIAL.

# War Diary

of

No 2 Company, 59th Divisional Train

From 1st June 1917 to 30th June 1917.

Volume V

Army Form C. 2118.

# WAR DIARY
# or
# INTELLIGENCE SUMMARY

(Erase heading not required.)

Vol. V

No 2 Coy. 57th Div. Train.

| Place | Date | Hour | Summary of Events and Information | Remarks and references to Appendices |
|---|---|---|---|---|
| LECHELLE P.32 Central | 1 June | | Commenced march with following units on reduced strength of Brigade Group:— Hdqrs & H Battn 176 Inf. Bde. 174 M.Gun.Co. No 2 Coy 57th Div. Train. Supplies delivered by Supply Section of Train to EQUANCOURT. | Nil |
| " | 2 June | | All available wagons (other than supply wagons) were used daily for transport of supplies in bulk from Railhead at ROISIGNY to Supplying points at P.32 central, in lieu of Divl Supply Col. | Nil |
| " | 3 " | | No 467 Indl Co. R.E. taken on reduced strength of Brigade Group, instructions issued prohibiting unloading of company horses at public troughs and for details of establ— cars, officers, drivers and orders issued. | Nil |
| " | 4 " | | transport for horsemanship of R.S. Materiel. 15 Pack Bdy of A.T. R.A. 18. 6. 8. 9. ... Divl Train annexed to furnish same. | Nil |
| " | 5 " | | 176 Bde T.M.B. taken on reduced strength of Brigade Group on return from school. | Nil |
| " | 7 " | | 178 Infl Bde. subsided 178 Inf. Bde. in Bth—Sub sector but owing to rodent strain on night of 9/10. " rendering roads impassable interchange | Nil |
| " | 11 " | | of accommodation sites was postponed. | Nil |
| " | 12 " | | Interchange of accommodation sites between 176 & 178 Inf. Bdes effected. Supplies were being brought forward to destination of supplies in use. | Nil |
| " | 14 " | | 2 Pairs details to cavalry Remounts to Rivalo on 14 June. Dull from 14 to 20th inclusive. | R. |
| " | 18 " | | Capt? M Bengtery...proceeded to ENGLAND on one months Special Leave. 2 Lieut O.M. Diff taken over command of No2Coy 57th Divl Train Company...during 18 December.      during the absence of Cap? M Bengtery. | R. |
| " | 22 " | | Quartermasters stores of No 467 moved to FINS. Bangay moved by Supply wagon & Ambulance to Advanced Ridst 6 C.R.E. | R. |
| " | 24 " | | 2 Pair horses wagon, 2 limber wagon, 1 Sudge, & horsesforhorse attached to Hqrs returned  from Train under ASO.S.M. 4 filled wagon Rtd to C.A.E. | R. |
| " | 30 " | | Work started at new Camp at FINS. History of Horsemanshp stations etc. | R. |
|  |  |  | 78 Wagon weak during month on loan of Road, E.H.O, Columns from Railhead to Supplying Point. Reconstructed rdwy 540 — 15 do 92 workng Essex sqns working conduits to Bde and Bn Hdqrs Reconstructed rdwy p 255 — head do. Very large number of men all the time in the Arpilette. Weather & road unfit for movement & remained ... | R. |
|  |  |  | Weather conditions— Very bot weather prevalent conditions 1st to 20 Leh, mgs a slaim cooler and more dryset ... | R. |
|  |  |  | ..... ..... ...... outside ..... FINS. | R. |

30 June 1917

O.C. No 2 Coy 57th Divl Train

Confidential

War Diary

of

O.C. 515 Coy. A.S.C. 59th Division

From 1-6-17 to 30-6-17

(Volume V)

Army Form C. 2118.

# WAR DIARY
## INTELLIGENCE SUMMARY.
(Erase heading not required.)

Instructions regarding War Diaries and Intelligence Summaries are contained in F. S. Regs., Part II. and the Staff Manual respectively. Title pages will be prepared in manuscript.

575 Coy A.S.C. 59th Divl. Train      June 1917

| Hour, Date, Place | | Summary of Events and Information | Remarks and references to Appendices |
|---|---|---|---|
| LECHELLE | 1/6/17 | In Camp | H.G. |
| " | 2/6/17 | Took over 2 H.D. Hencoops | H.G. |
| " | 3/6/17 1.40 p.m | Took over 1 Rake, Cement | H.G. |
| " | " | Baggage wagons commenced daily journey to ROCQUIGNY Rail Head as supply Column in place of 59 D.S.C. | H.G. |
| " | 5/6/17 2.30 p.m | Gas alarm this was took off at 12 midnight all ranks wore non-off ration strength | H.G. H.G. |
| " | " 3.0 p.m | Camp inspected by the A.D.M.S. | H.G. |
| " | " | 1 H.D. Horse Rug | H.G. |
| " | 8/6/17 | 8 H.D. Horses sold. 6 n.c.o's and men detached for Hay Cutting | H.G. |
| " | " 1.45 p.m | Gas alarm, Taken off at 2 a.m | H.G. H.G. |
| " | 10/6/17 4.0 p.m | Camp inspected by the G.O.C. 59 Div | H.G. |

Forms/C. 2118/10.

Horsen Capt
OC 575 Coy A.S.C.
59th Divl. Train

# WAR DIARY
## INTELLIGENCE SUMMARY

*(Erase heading not required.)*

Army Form C. 2118.

| Hour, Date, Place | Summary of Events and Information | Remarks and references to Appendices |
|---|---|---|
| LECHELLE 12/17 6.30 a.m. | 575 Coy A.S.C. S9th Divn | June 1917 |
| " 13/6/17 | Inspection of horses by A.D.V.S. | |
| " 22/6/17 | Received 1 W.O. Class I and 8 O.R. Reinforcements | |
| | 177th Bde being in reserve 1st line Transport supplied | |
| " 24/6/17 | 12 H.D. Horses and 8 O.R. detached for the Cattery | |
| | Lieut H. Wood left for Veterinary Course (10 days) Driver Shuttlewood sent to 59th D.E. Stationary School for 7 day course | |
| " 3.30 a.m. | Inspection of D.O. of S+T. IV Army of Camp | |
| " 25/6/17 6.0 a.m. | Inspection of Horses by A.D.V.S. | |
| " 28/6/17 | Received one Driver, Reinforcement | |
| " 30/6/17 | In Camp at LECHELLE - General health of the Coy during the month was very good and losses still below normal in condition | |

Confidential

War Diary

of

O.C, H Company, A.S.C., 59th Division

From:- 1st June 1917 To:- 30th June 1917.

Volume 5.

WAR DIARY
or
INTELLIGENCE SUMMARY.
(Erase heading not required.)

Army Form C. 2118.

| Hour, Date, Place | Summary of Events and Information | Remarks and references to Appendices |
|---|---|---|
| 5.6.17 "LECHELLE" | 2 drivers & horses detached for Haymaking under Lt. Seamouf. A.S.C. | Nil. |
| 2.30pm 6.6.17 " | A.D.M.S. Sgt Anson inspects camp. | Nil. |
| 9.6.17 " | Company Sgt Major admitted 34 C.C.S. & struck off strength | Nil. |
| 2.45 pm 10.6.17 " | G.O.C. 59th Division inspects camp. | Nil. |
| 6.45pm 12.6.17 " | A.D.V.S. 59th Division inspects horses & Coy. | Nil. |
| 13.6.17 " | 1 Cpl & 1 Driver taken on strength. | Nil. |
| 14.6.17 " | 4 Drivers & 4 H.D are detached for road making duties at P.18. D.S.2. | Nil. |
| 15.6.17 " | a/c.Q.M.S. WOODFORDE attached from Train Hdqrs & assumes duties of C.S.M. | Nil. |
| 16.6.17 " | 2 Cpls proceed for 1 week course of instruction in Anti-Gas Defence | Nil. |
| 21.6.17 " | Baggage wagons proceed to mills to move to new area. | Nil. |

Army Form C. 2118.

# WAR DIARY
## or
## INTELLIGENCE SUMMARY.
(Erase heading not required.)

Instructions regarding War Diaries and Intelligence Summaries are contained in F. S. Regs., Part II. and the Staff Manual respectively. Title pages will be prepared in manuscript.

| Hour, Date, Place | Summary of Events and Information | Remarks and references to Appendices |
|---|---|---|
| 22.6.17. LECHELLE | 7 pm H.D. proceed to "AIZECOURT" on detachment for Horse watering duties under Lt. Piggin. | hd. |
| 23.6.17 " | Q.S.C. 1 Driver struck off strength. | hd. |
| 4.0 pm 23.6.17 " | D.D.S.T. 4th Army inspects cars/s. | hd. |
| 25.6.17 " | 1 c/pl proceeds for one weeks course of instruction in Bombing. | hd. |
| 6.0 pm 25.6.17 " | A.D.V.S. 59th Division inspects all horses of Cy. | hd. |
| 28.6.17 " | 1 c/pl proceeds for one weeks course of instruction in Anti-Gas defence. | hd. |
| | 2 Drivers taken on strength. | hd. |

W. Schmidt cart
O.C. No 4 Cy. 59th Divisional Train

# WAR DIARY
## INTELLIGENCE SUMMARY.
(Erase heading not required.)

Army Form C. 2118.

| Hour, Date, Place | Summary of Events and Information | Remarks and references to Appendices |
|---|---|---|
| 1.6.17. LECHELLE | Units on petn strength 7 M.G. 2 of Bayonets Coy/s :— H.Qrs 178th Inf. Brigade — No 4 Sec Signals R.E. — 2/5 Sherwood Forester — 2/6 Sherwood Forester — 2/7 Sherwood Forester — 2/8 Sherwood Forester — 178 Trench Mortar Batter — 178 Machine Gun Co — 470 Field Co. R.E. — No 4 Co. A.S.C. 59 Divnl Train — | |
| 3.6.17 " | 2/3 Field Ambulance R.A.M.C taken on Ration Strength | H. H. |
| 22.6.17 " | 178 Trench M.G. Battery struck of Ration Strength H. | |

M. C. [signature]
O.C. No 4 Co. 59 Divnl Train

CONFIDENTIAL.

WAR DIARY
OF
HEADQUARTERS, 59th DIVISIONAL TRAIN
from 1st July to 31st July 1917

Volume VI

# WAR DIARY

## INTELLIGENCE SUMMARY.

(Erase heading not required.)

Army Form C. 2118.

HEADQUARTERS 59th DIVISIONAL TRAIN

MAP REFERENCE O27a Sheet 57 C 1:40000

VOLUME VI

| Place | Date | Hour | Summary of Events and Information | Remarks and references to Appendices |
|---|---|---|---|---|
| LECHELLES | July 1917 1st | | Railhead ROCQUIGNY. Refilling Points P32a. for all formations. Coy & Train Headquarter Camp in rear of Refilling points. | Ref. |
| | 2nd | | | Ref. |
| | 3rd | | CAPT R.J. GREEN D.C. No.3 Coy proceeded on 14 days Special Leave. New recruits from BRIE. Lieut G. SEAWARD admitted No 21 Casualty Clearing Station having had the thumb of Right hand cut off by cutting machine. | Ref. |
| " | 6th | | Second Ring fingers of right hand cut off by cutting machine. Detachment of 35th Divisional Train left No 38 Coy k returned own Unit on 35th Div billeting passing under command of A.S.C.R.A. 35th Div. | Ref. |
| " | 7th | | Lieut. H. WARDILL 1102 Coy 59th Div Train proceeded to Headquarters Royal Flying Corps on transfer. | Ref. |
| " | 8th | | No 2 Coy moved to O34a. after refilling + Refilling point 15 O27 a S.6 for 176 & 177 Infy Bde Groups | Ref. |
| " | 9th | | 1 C.S.M. & 1 Wheeler Corpl reported from Base at new hand. | Ref. |
| " | | | after refilling No 4 Coy moved to O34a & 178 Inf Bde Refilling Point 15 O27a. | Ref. |
| ROCQUIGNY | 10th | | after refilling No 3 Coy moved to O34a and 177th Refilling Point H O27b. Capt Peach proceeded on leave | Ref. |
| | 11th | | after refilling Train Headquarters and No 1 Coy moved to O34a and Div Troops Refilling Point to O27 10.10 165 | Ref. |
| " | 12th | | Under orders of IV Corps Detailed in Sector to join IV Corps B.O.C. for duty | Ref. |
| " | 15th | | 2nd Lieut W.B. HARRISON reported for duty in relief of 2nd Lieut H WARDILL A.S.C.RC N°1 Coy | Ref. |
| " | 16th | | 7 O.Rs reported from Base as reinforcements | Ref. |
| " | 17th | | Capt R.I GREEN returned from leave | Ref. |
| " | 18th | | Capt BUTLER R.A.M.C. reported for duty as M.O. Capt T.M. HAZLERIGG returned from leave + Lieut LIDDIARD proceeded on leave | Ref. |
| " | 20th | | 19 Remounts received from LA CHAPPELETTE Railhead | Ref. |
| " | 24th | | Lieut J.G. Fairfax - Ross reported for duty Posted K No18 Coy in relief of Lieut G. Seaward who have evacuated to England 9.7.17 | Ref. |
| " | 26th | | Establishment of Ride Horse reduced by 3 per Coy ie 1 SRMs & 2 Drivers & 12 Pack Horses Capt Peach + Lieut T.K. BROWN returned from leave. All Infantry kits allow Supplies by 1st Line Transport by 1st June to enable Train Transport to hand for RE connects from HUTS & other Building material | Ref. |
| | | | Major Williams and Capt P.J.G. Smith proceeded on leave. | Ref. |
| " | 29th | | | Ref. |
| " | to 31st | | Supplies drawn from Railhead by Train Transport. General Health of the Train good. Ref. condition of horses improved. Weather conditions fair with heavy thunder storms. | Ref. |

R.G. Cecil
Lieut Colonel
Commanding 59th Divisional Train

War Diary
— of —
A.S.C. 59th Divn
513 Coy 1st to 31st July 1917

Vol. VI.

O.C.

Copy No 2

# WAR DIARY
## INTELLIGENCE SUMMARY
*(Erase heading not required.)*

Army Form C. 2118

| Place | Date | Hour | Summary of Events and Information | Remarks and references to Appendices |
|---|---|---|---|---|
| Fins | 1/7 | | 2 Coys at P.32.A. (near LECHELLE) — Div<sup>l</sup> Troops R.P. Same place — Supplies horse from ROCQUIGNY Railhead | ADS |
| | 3/7 | | Lt. G.S. SEAWARD admitted to Hospital | ADS |
| | 4/7 | | 1 H.D. Horse evacuated — 1 Remount (H.D.) received | ADS |
| | 7/7 | | 2/Lt. H. WARDILL proceeds to join R.F.C. — 1 H.D. Horse from Base | ADS |
| | 8/7 | | 15th Coy<sup>l</sup> reports for duty from Base | ADS |
| | 10/7 | | Capt. A.N. PEACH proceeds on leave to England — also Sgt PERROTT | ADS |
| | | | Sgt GODFREY, A.T.R.S. P.32.A. to O.24.A. (near ROCQUIGNY) went from Company | ADS |
| | 11/7 | | Div<sup>l</sup> Troops R.P. opens at O.27.a. — Supplies still come from ROCQUIGNY Railhead | ADS |
| | 12/7 | | 2 men sent to 35 Army School of Cookery for course of Instruction | ADS |
| | 13/7 | | 2/Lt. W.B. HARRISON reports for Duty | ADS |
| | 15/7 | | 1 Sec. Coy<sup>l</sup> + 2 Divs reports to Coy | ADS |

Army Form C. 2118

# WAR DIARY
## or
## INTELLIGENCE SUMMARY
(Erase heading not required.)

Instructions regarding War Diaries and Intelligence Summaries are contained in F.S. Regs., Part II. and the Staff Manual respectively. Title Pages will be prepared in manuscript.

| Place | Date | Hour | Summary of Events and Information | Remarks and references to Appendices |
|---|---|---|---|---|
| | 17/7/17 | | Capt. CUTLER R.A.M.C. joins for duty | MB |
| | 20/7/17 | | Six H.D. Recruits received | MB |
| | 24/7/17 | | Lt. J.G. FAIRFAX R.O.N. reports for duty | MB |
| | | | 1 H.D. Horse evacuated | |
| | 26/7/17 | | Capt. A.N. PEACH returns from leave | MB |
| | 29/7/17 | | Major A.T. WILLIAMS and S.S.M. HATFIELD proceed on leave to England — Capt. B.H. LAMBERT take over as Company Transport. | MB |
| | 18/7 to 31/7/17 | | General Transport Duties, including drawing supplies from R.P. & lorries, R.P. to trains, & delivering of supplies from R.P. to lorries. | MSmith Major ASC O.C. |
| | 30/7/17 | | | |
| | 31/7/17 | | | |

NO. 1 COMPANY
59th DIVL. TRAIN
(No. 513 Coy. A.S.C.)

F. Hawkins Capt.
O.C. 513 Coy A.S.C.

CONFIDENTIAL.

# WAR DIARY
## OF
## O.C. No 2 Coy, 59th Divl Train
### Vol VI

1st July 1917 to 31st July 1917.

Army Form C. 2118.

# WAR DIARY
## or
## INTELLIGENCE SUMMARY
*(Erase heading not required.)*

VOL VI.

No 2 Coy 59TH DIVL TRAIN

Instructions regarding War Diaries and Intelligence Summaries are contained in F. S. Regs., Part II. and the Staff Manual respectively. Title Pages will be prepared in manuscript.

| Place | Date 1917 | Hour | Summary of Events and Information | Remarks and references to Appendices |
|---|---|---|---|---|
| LECHELLE P32 CENTRAL | 1st July | — | Commenced move with following units on Roban strength: H.Q. & Billets, 115 & Lanky Co Engrs, 174 MGC, 467 Coy RE. No2 Coy 59th Divl Train. Brigade HQ moved to Equancourt by 3rd Bde. We are after delivering Rations QM stores remained at Fins. | REFCE MAP 57B |
| " | 2nd " | — | First lot of Daylight commenced running billets from Lechelle out to Aizecourt. Supply & Gun drawing Rations supplied ........ Billets of .... | R |
| " | 6th " | — | 12 men of German Sheltos at Fins Camp completed | R |
| ROCQUIGNY O 34 A | 7th " | — | Brigade cinema. HQ & Billets 1/4 Infantry Engrs, 174 MGC, 467 Coys RE. Engrs & O.IO.C. Brigade Bayge moved by Bde HQ to new Camp by Supply & Train from Headquarters of Capt Whyte of O 34 A. | R |
| " | 10th " | — | 2 loads of water delivered to R.S.O. at Rocquigny boxcart from Lechelle | R |
| " | 7th " | — | Horses Hyacutting on ....... State grazes. | R |
| " | 18th " | — | 5 " " " | R |
| " | 19th " | — | " " " " | R MGT |
| " | 20th to 31st " | — | Routine continued by No 2 Coy 59th Divl Train. 2/hat P.R.R. EBBEN attached to 59th D.T.S.C. from course of Instruction in duties of roads & Transport Train: CAPT M. HAZLETON ...... Summary of Transport During July:- Wagons used in line of ..... Cavalry prov Rations & Supplies & Repairing Point 351. Sahmas mileage 963. Horses hypogin held in Iltres of Supply 40. mileage 209. Horses material for emberking 105. mileage 480. Drawing materials ........ during month 2549 (exclusive of trans supplied) on experience. | MGT Trust |
| | | | Total mileage of Vehicles during month 2549 (exclusive of trains supplied) on experience. B ........ of ..... & Grod ..... report. | Trust |

WMHyland Cpt.
M. No2 Coy, 59th Divl Train.

Confidential

War Diary

of

No. 515 Coy. A.S.C. 59th Division.

from 1-7-17 to 31-7-17.

(Volume VI)

Army Form C. 2118.

# WAR DIARY
## or
## INTELLIGENCE SUMMARY.
*(Erase heading not required.)*

Instructions regarding War Diaries and Intelligence Summaries are contained in F.S. Regs., Part II. and the Staff Manual respectively. Title pages will be prepared in manuscript.

575 Coy A.S.C. 59 Div.                                                                July 1917

| Hour, Date, Place | Summary of Events and Information | Remarks and references to Appendices |
|---|---|---|
| LECHELLE 1/7 | Capt Brown OC C.L. on leave (r) to Lechelle Special leave | a/fr |
|  | Wed D. Blakely sent to Nurse | a/fr |
|  | Baggage wagon sent for Brigade horse (77 F.A.) | a/fr |
| " 2/7 | Pte Locke (attached from 7th Londons for Instruction) returns to Units | a/fr |
|  | Maj. Stanfount returns from Musketry Course | a/fr |
|  | Maj. Foulsham return on course of Furnature | a/fr |
|  | 2nd line transport Commenced delivery of supplies | a/fr |
|  | Supply Column Commenced to Company | a/fr |
|  | O/C Proudly went to 7 F.A. Hospital | a/fr |
|  | Gas alarm from 10.30pm to 11.45pm | a/fr |
|  | Sgt Loosly sent to Hospital | a/fr |
| " 3/7 | Commenced with new Coy on Rations | a/fr |
| " 4/7 | Gas Alarm 1.45 to 2 am | a/fr |
|  | 1.H.D. (305) Lonsdale was hurt by Car | a/fr |
|  | Horse Lines completed | a/fr |
|  | Dr Riley sent to Hospital | a/fr |
| " 5/7 |  |  |

A. F. Green Capt.
OC 575 Coy A.S.C. 59 Div.

Army Form C. 2118.

# WAR DIARY
## or
## INTELLIGENCE SUMMARY.
(*Erase heading not required.*)

Instructions regarding War Diaries and Intelligence Summaries are contained in F.S. Regs., Part II. and the Staff Manual respectively. Title pages will be prepared in manuscript.

575 Coy ASC MT Bn 54th Div  July 1917

| Hour, Date, Place | Summary of Events and Information | Remarks and references to Appendices |
|---|---|---|
| LECHELLE 6/7 | 10 Laundries returned from CCS as 72 NZ Yeomans | ajh |
| " 7/7 | 35th Div Train Details reis before | ajh |
| " 6.30pm | 7th wound returned from body convoy | ajh |
| | proceed | ajh |
| | D. Couriers reported from Hospital | ajh |
| " 8/7 | D Relay working. | ajh |
| " 9/7 | Refilling 7am | ajh |
| " 10/7 17 12nn | 177th Inf Regt + Company here to Rocigny | ajh |
| ROCIGNY 11/7 | In camp. Horses in good condition the weather | ajh |
| " 12/7 10am | D. horses wed LF oversunde hospital | ajh |
| " | [?] Inspects of horses by ADVS Sgt Bm | ajh |

A J Green Capt
OC 575 Coy ASC 54th Div

Army Form C. 2118.

# WAR DIARY
## or
## INTELLIGENCE SUMMARY.
*(Erase heading not required.)*

Instructions regarding War Diaries and Intelligence Summaries are contained in F.S. Regs., Part II. and the Staff Manual respectively. Title pages will be prepared in manuscript.

575 Coy A.S.C. 59 Div.     July 1917

| Hour, Date, Place | Summary of Events and Information | Remarks and references to Appendices |
|---|---|---|
| COEQUINCY 15/7/17 | Received three drivers (Reinforcements) | AG |
| " 16/7/17 | Sergt Leahy discharged from hospital | AG |
| " 18/7/17 | Captain R.J. GREEN returned from special leave and again assumed command of Company | AG |
| " 20/7/17 | Lieut A.J. LIDDIARD leave for 14 days special leave | AG |
| " 23/7/17 | Four H.D. Horses (Remounts) received | AG |
| " 26/7/17 | Inspection of Horses by A.D.V.S. 59th Divn | AG |
| " 29/7/17 | 1st line transport of 177th–13th draw their own supplies from R.P. | AG |
|  | Captain F.G. SMITH. leave for 14 days special leave | AG |

R.J. Green Capt.
O.C. 575 Coy A.S.C. 59th Div

# WAR DIARY
## ~~INTELLIGENCE~~ SUMMARY.
*(Erase heading not required.)*

Army Form C. 2118.

Instructions regarding War Diaries and Intelligence Summaries are contained in F. S. Regs., Part II. and the Staff Manual respectively. Title pages will be prepared in manuscript.

515 Coy A.S.C. 59 Divn    Summary for July 1917

| Hour, Date, Place | Summary of Events and Information | Remarks and references to Appendices |
|---|---|---|
| ROCQUINCY 29/7/17 | LIEUT J.K. BROWN, took over duties as Supply Officer 177th Bde, during absence on leave of CAPTAIN F.C. SMITH. | |
| " 31/7/17 | In Camp at ROCQUINCY. Units on Ration strength during the month were 177th Inf Bde, 469 Coy R.E., 177th M.G.C., 2/2nd Field Amb., 515 Coy A.S.C. General health of the Company during the month was good. Horses in good condition. | |

A.J. Brown Capt.
OC 515 Coy 59th Divn

Confidential

War Diary

of

O.C. 4 Company, A.S.C. 59th Division.

From 1st July 1917 To 31st July 1917.

Volume 6.

Army Form C. 2118.

# WAR DIARY
## or
## INTELLIGENCE SUMMARY.
(Erase heading not required.)

Instructions regarding War Diaries and Intelligence Summaries are contained in F.S. Regs., Part II. and the Staff Manual respectively. Title pages will be prepared in manuscript.

| Hour, Date, Place | Summary of Events and Information | Remarks and references to Appendices |
|---|---|---|
| 1.7.17 LECHELLE. | Unit a return strength of 178 Infantry Brigade Troops:— Hqrs 178 Inf. Bgde — No 4 Section Signal — 2/5. 2/6. 2/7. 2/8 Batts Sherwood Foresters — 178 Trench Mortar Battery — 178 Machine Gun Coy — No 70 Field Coy R.E — 2/3 Field Ambulance R.A.M.C — No 4 Coy. A.S.C. Sgt. Arrived Train | K.I. |
| 2.7.17 LECHELLE | 1 O.R. admitted to Hospital.— Gas alarm sounded 10.30 pm. | M |
| 3.7.17 LECHELLE. | Abrams parties 17, 176th 177th & 178th Infantry Brigades taken to Coy return strength.— | |
| 4.7.17 LECHELLE | 22 Reserves received & taken as return strength. 21 Reservists dispatched to various units in Division N.C.O returns to Coy from Gas Course | K.I. |
| 5.7.17 LECHELLE | Advance party of a returnees sent to ROCQUIGNY to select new camp.— | W.I. K.I. |
| 6.7.17 LECHELLE | One ride horse taken on strength from Signal Coy R.E — 1 O.R. admitted to hospital. | K.I. |

(73989) W4141—463. 400,000. 9/14. H.&J.Ltd. Forms/C. 2118/10.

Army Form C. 2118.

# WAR DIARY
## or
## INTELLIGENCE SUMMARY.
(Erase heading not required.)

Instructions regarding War Diaries and Intelligence Summaries are contained in F. S. Regs., Part II. and the Staff Manual respectively. Title pages will be prepared in manuscript.

| Hour, Date, Place | Summary of Events and Information | Remarks and references to Appendices |
|---|---|---|
| 7.7.17 LECHELLE | 1 O.R admitted to Hospital | M. |
| 8.7.17 LECHELLE | Baggage wagons sent to units to move — 1 O.R. discharged from Hospital. | M. |
| 9.7.17 ROCQUIGNY | Coy move to ROCQUIGNY close to rail head — supply dump in the village — Baggage wagons return from units — 2 O.R discharged from Hospital. | M. |
| 10.7.17 ROCQUIGNY | 1 O.R. admitted to Hospital — 2 O R discharged from Hospital. | M |
| 11.7.17 ROCQUIGNY | A.D.V.S inspects horses. | M |
| 12.7.17 ROCQUIGNY. | 1 O.R admitted to Hospital. | M. |
| 13.7.17 ROCQUIGNY. | 1 O R admitted to Hospital — 1 O.R. discharged from Hospital | M. |
| | 1 O.R admitted to Hospital — 1 O.R discharged from Hospital | M. |
| | 2/3 field Ambulance supply wan attached to Coy. | |
| 16.7.17 ROCQUIGNY | 1 O R admitted to Hospital — AMIENS leave for 6 starts. | M. |
| 17.7.17 ROCQUIGNY | 1 O.R. admitted to Hospital | M. |
| 19.7.17. ROCQUIGNY. | 1 O R discharged from Hospital — Divisional transport Competition held, Coy won 2 prizes. | M. |

Army Form C. 2118.

# WAR DIARY
## or
## INTELLIGENCE SUMMARY.
*(Erase heading not required.)*

Instructions regarding War Diaries and Intelligence Summaries are contained in F.S. Regs., Part II. and the Staff Manual respectively. Title pages will be prepared in manuscript.

| Hour, Date, Place | | Summary of Events and Information | Remarks and references to Appendices |
|---|---|---|---|
| 20.7.17 | ROCQUIGNY. | 1 Pioneer driver transferred from No 1 Coy. | M |
| 22.7.17 | ROCQUIGNY | 2. O.R transferred to No 2 Coy. — 1 O.R discharged from Hospital | M |
| 23.7.17. | ROCQUIGNY. | 3 O.R. discharged from Hospital | M |
| 24.7.17. | ROCQUIGNY. | 1 O.R. discharged from Hospital | M |
| 25.7.17 | ROCQUIGNY. | 1. O.R discharged from Hospital — 1 O.R admitted to Hospital | M |
| 26.7.17. | ROCQUIGNY | 1st line transport having returned from DUMP until further orders. | M |
| 27.7.17 | ROCQUIGNY. | Coy. sends wagons to BAPAUME for R.E. services which will continue until further orders. — 1 O.R admitted to Hospital — Ammunition from DADOS. Inspection all rifles. Violent thunderstorm in the morning. | M |
| 29.7.17 | ROCQUIGNY. | | M |
| 31.7.17 | ROCQUIGNY. | S.S.M BENNETT transferred to No 3 Coy — Violent rain storm in evening which lasted all night | M |

J.R. Paterson CAPT.
O.C., 516 C.Cy., A.S.C., 55th (W.M.) Div.

(73989) W4141—463. 400,000. 9/14. H.&J.Ltd. Forms/C. 2118/10.

Vol 7

Confidential

War Diary

of

Headquarters 59th Divisional Train

From 1/8/17 to 31/8/17.

(Volume VII)

# WAR DIARY

**Army Form C. 2118.**

Instructions regarding War Diaries and Intelligence Summaries are contained in F. S. Regs., Part II. and the Staff Manual respectively. Title pages will be prepared in manuscript.

## INTELLIGENCE SUMMARY. 59th DIVISIONAL TRAIN   Vol. VII

HEADQUARTERS

(Erase heading not required.)   MAP REFERENCES. SHEET 57c 1/40000
SHEET ALBERT (COMBINED) 1/100000

| Place | Date | Hour | Summary of Events and Information | Remarks and references to Appendices |
|---|---|---|---|---|
| ROCQUIGNY | 1917 Aug. 1 | | RAILHEAD ROCQUIGNY. Refilling Points as follows Divisional Troops Group O.27.a.10.10. 176th Infy Bde Group O.27.a.2.6. 177th Infy Bde Group O.27.h. 178th Infy Bde Group O.27.a. Train Headquarters and all 4 Coys encamped at O.34.a. Lieut H. Wood No 3 Coy proceeded to England on attachment to No 2 Infantry School BEDFORD. All Supplies drawn from Railhead by Train Transport. | SOT |
| " | 4 | | 2/Lt W. TODD reported for duty on relief of 2/Lt H. WOOD | SOT |
| " | 5 | | 2/Lt C.W. BLINDELL proceeded on 14 days Special Leave under A.C.I. 2527. | SOT |
| " | 7 | | Lieut A.J. LIDDIARD returned from leave | SOT |
| " | 9 | | Major A.T. WILLIAMS returned from leave. | SOT |
| " | 10 | | 2/Lt A. JACOBSOHN reported from Base for duty & posted to No 2 Coy. 14 O.Rs reinforcements arrived from Base to replace men inadequately fit to attend away for M.T. Transport detached for duty with Lines Regns on Huyματkινγ Scheme returned to Nos 1, 2 and 3 Coys. | SOT |
| " | 15 | | MAJOR A.T. WILLIAMS handed over Command of No 1 Coy to CAPT M.L.B.H. LAMBERT and proceeded to Headquarters 58th Divisional Train for duty. Capt H.J.A. REID, Requisitioning Officer proceeded to Central Purchase Board with 1 Clerk 1 Batman and 1 Motor Car and Orderly for permanent duty. Capt J.S. SMITH returned from leave. Lieut PIGGIN returned with transport of No 4 Coy from Huyματkινγ day | SOT |
| " | 19 | | Lieut E.J.H. Gaines proceeded on leave. | SOT |
| " | 20 | | 2/Lt C.W. BLINDELL returned from leave. | SOT |
| " | 21 | | Refilling for 177th Bde Group at 5 P.M. | SOT |
| " | 22 | | No 3 Coy moved to SENLIS W. of ALBERT. Divisional Troops and 176 Bde Groups had 2nd refill at 6 pm. for consumption 24th. 2/Lieut W.S.A. BROWN 5th Bn. North Staffs Regt attached to Train Headquarters as Divisional Claims Officer. | SOT |
| " | 23 | | Train Headquarters No 1 Coy moved to ACHEUX and No 2 Coy to BOUZINCOURT. 178th Bde Group had 2nd refill at 6 pm for consumption 25th. Refilling Point for 177th Bde Group opened at New R.P. Line N.g | SOT |
| ACHEUX | 24 | | Railhead ALBERT. Supplies drawn by 59 D.S.Column. New Refilling Points opened for Divisional Troops Group at R.P. S.E. of ACHEUX immediately N. of S.T.A. and for 176 Bde Group at R.P. 100 yards W. of BOUZINCOURT on main Road 8 M. N. of Camp E of BOUZINCOURT. 5 H.Q. removals received. | SOT |
| " | 25 | | New Refilling Point opened for 178th Bde Group at R.P. 50 yards W. of BOUZINCOURT on Main Road at 8 A.M. | SOT |
| " | 28 | | Advance Parties of 1 Officer + 1 N.C.O. per Coy proceeded to New Area at WINNEZEELE (SHEET HAZEBROUCK S.I.) | SOT |
| " | 29 | | Orders received for Entrainment of the Division on 30 Inst. +31 Inst. | SOT |
| " | 31 | | Baggage Wagons & 2 Units sent to train preparatory to moving. Orders received postponing move of Division for 24 hours. ie. till 31st - 1st Train Headquarters and Nos 1, 2, 3, + 4 Coys entrained for J.10. Ref. Sheet 27. 1/40000 | SOT |

[signature] Lieut Colonel
Commanding 59th Divisional Train

Confidential.    Vol. VI.

WAR DIARY.
—o—
513 Coy ASC 59 Division
from Aug. 1st to 31st 1917.

Army Form C. 2118

Vol. VI

**WAR DIARY**
or
**INTELLIGENCE SUMMARY**

(Erase heading not required.)

Instructions regarding War Diaries and Intelligence Summaries are contained in F. S. Regs., Part II. and the Staff Manual respectively. Title Pages will be prepared in manuscript.

| Place | Date | Hour | Summary of Events and Information | Remarks and references to Appendices |
|---|---|---|---|---|
| Field | August 1917 | | | |
| | 1st | | War Diary and detachment return from Haymaking | |
| | 10th | | Major A.T. WILLIAMS returns from leave and resumed command | |
| | 13th | | Major A.T. WILLIAMS transferred to 58 Divisional Train | |
| | | | Capt B.H. LAMBERT assumes command of 575 Coy A.S.C. | |
| | | | 2nd Lieut F.N. DIGBY is transferred from 514 Coy A.S.C. | |
| | | | Capt H.J.A. REID and other ranks did M.T. motor car course of duty with Central Purchase Board | |
| | | | Capt M.H. DAWES A.S.C. proceeds on indefinite leave to ENGLAND | |
| | 16th | | Horse No 331 transferred to 3/8 North Midland Regt Northerly remount | |
| | 21st | | Baggage & Supply waggons horses used to hot with 2/1 L.N. Lancs 2nd Line | |
| | 22nd | | R.F.A. Brigades prior to move | |
| | 23rd | | Move from TORQUAY to KATIGNY | |
| | 14th | | Mule remounts received from ABBEVILLE | |
| | 15th | | Move from ACHEUX to QUESNOY | |

1875   Wt. W593/826   1,000,000   4/15   J.B.C. & A.   A.D.S.S./Forms/C. 2118.

CONFIDENTIAL.

WAR DIARY

OF

O.C. No 2 Coy. 59th Div. Train.

VOL VII.

1st August 1917 to 31st August 1917.

# WAR DIARY
## or
## INTELLIGENCE SUMMARY

*(Erase heading not required.)*

Army Form C. 2118.

Vol. VII

N° 2 Coy. 59 Div. Train.

Instructions regarding War Diaries and Intelligence Summaries are contained in F. S. Regs., Part II. and the Staff Manual respectively. Title Pages will be prepared in manuscript.

| Place | Date | Hour | Summary of Events and Information | Remarks and references to Appendices |
|---|---|---|---|---|
| ROCQUIGNY. | 1.8.17 | — | Commenced march with HQ and 4 Sectn 176 Inf. Bde. 176 L.T.M.B. 174 M.G.Co. Rd. Hq. 57 c. 40,000. on rations strength of Brigade Group. Company echelons at 0.28.c.3.a. 467 314 Co. R.E. N°2 Coy. 59 Div Train Unit drawing supplies with 1st Line Transport from R.P. Rocquigny. Units at 0.10.c. | |
| | 6.8.17 | — | Railhead as R.P. and for movement of R.E. & other stores mainly from BAPAUME to LE MESNIL areas. Train wagons drawing supplies in bulk from Rocquigny. Supplies delivered to Units by Train wagons. | 711111. |
| | 10.8.17 | — | ditto — | 711111. |
| | 22.8.17 | — | Baggage wagons sent to all units for loading and to move with Brigade transport. Supply wagons loaded. | 111111. 111111. |
| | 23.8.17 | — | 1st 3rd Ant. 59th Advance in rather stronger of Brigade Group. In accordance with orders of HQ. 59 Div. Train Company Headquarters with Supply Section left Rocquigny at 5 a.m. and proceeded via BAPAUME to camp 1 kilometre S.E. of BOUZINCOURT on main road to ALBERT. Supplies of 176 Inf. Bde. HQ. 5th & 6th South. Staff. Regt. T 4/67 313 Co. R.E. 176 L.T.M.B. 1st 3rd Ant. 59 Div and 174 M. Gun Co. delivered at Bouzincourt, those of 5th & 6th North. Staff Regt. 4/67 313 Co. R.E. delivered at FORCEVILLE. | 711111. |
| BOUZINCOURT. | 24.8.17 | — | Supplies drawn by Train Wagons from R.P. at BOUZINCOURT. | 711111. |
| | 25.8.17 | — | ditto — | 1111111. |
| | 26.8.17 | — | ditto — | 71111. |
| | 27.8.17 | — | ditto — | 11111. |
| | 28.8.17 | — | Advance party proceeded to next area | 11111. |
| | 29.8.17 | — | Baggage wagons despatched to units. Supply wagons refilled at BOUZINCOURT at 8 a.m and 4 p.m. and proceeded to units after last refilling. Orders received at 11 pm post-poning move for 24 hours. | 11111. |
| | 30.8.17 | — | Supply wagons refilled at BOUZINCOURT at 6.30 a.m. and delivered with units. (1st Fd Amb, 59 Div. 467 313 Co. R.E. T N°2 Coy 59 Div Train now rations for 2/3.9.17) | 11111. |
| | 31.8.17 | 7.11 pm | Entrained Headquarters & Coy at BOUZINCOURT AVELUY. | 11111. |
| | | 6 a.m. | at R.P. BOUZINCOURT at 6 a.m. | |

M. Mapledoff Capt.
OC N°2 Coy. 59 Div. Train.

Confidential

War Diary
of
515 Company A.S.C. 59th Division

From 1-8-17 to 31-8-17

(Volume VII)

Army Form C. 2118.

# WAR DIARY
## or
## INTELLIGENCE SUMMARY.
(Erase heading not required.)

575 Coy A.S.C. 59th Div Summary of Events and Information  August 1917

| Hour, Date, Place | Summary of Events and Information | Remarks and references to Appendices |
|---|---|---|
| ROCQUINY. 1/8/17 | In Camp | — |
| " | 2/Lieut H. WOOD. Proceeded to England on attachment to Infantry | — |
| " | 5. O.R's and 7. H.D. Horses returned to Coy from Haymaking | — |
| 2/8/17 | Camp inspected by G.O.C. 59th Div | — |
| 4/8/17 | 2/Lieut W. TODD. posted to the Coy | — |
| 7/8/17 G.O. | Inspection of Transport by the A.D.T.S.T. III Army | — |
| " | Lieut. A.J. LIDDIARD returned from special leave | — |
| " | Received 4 Drivers Reinforcements | — |
| 10/8/17 | 7. O.R. 1 N.C.O. 12 H.D. Horses 2 S.S. Wagons returned to Coy from Haymaking | — |

A. Green Capt. O.C. 575 Coy A.S.C. 59th Div

Army Form C. 2118.

# WAR DIARY
## or
## INTELLIGENCE SUMMARY.
*(Erase heading not required.)*

Instructions regarding War Diaries and Intelligence Summaries are contained in F.S. Regs., Part II. and the Staff Manual respectively. Title pages will be prepared in manuscript.

375 Cy A.S.C. 5y NMD  Summary of Events and Information  August 1917

| Hour, Date, Place | Summary of Events and Information | Remarks and references to Appendices |
|---|---|---|
| ROCQUIGNY 12/8/17 | One Driver evacuated to CCS and struck off strength | KL |
| " 13/8/17 5.30 a.m | Horses inspected by the DADVS | KL |
| " 15/8/17 | One Private (Supply) transferred to 373 Cy A.S.C. | KL |
| " " | Captain F.G. SMITH reported back from Leave | KL |
| " 17/8/17 | Farr Corpl and 1 Driver evacuated to CCS | KL |
| " 22/8/17 6.0 a.m | Coy H.Q. (Smith Supply Section of Bde Group moved by road to SENLIS | KL |
| SENLIS 22/8/17 4.0 p.m | In quarters (Matamato) | KL |
| " 28/8/17 | Hbq Coy R.E. } Came on ration strength of Bde Group 1/3rd NMFA } | KL |

Webrey Capt OC 375 Cy A.S.C. 5y Divn

Army Form C. 2118.

# WAR DIARY
## ~~or~~
## INTELLIGENCE SUMMARY.
*(Erase heading not required.)*

Instructions regarding War Diaries and Intelligence Summaries are contained in F.S. Regs., Part II. and the Staff Manual respectively. Title pages will be prepared in manuscript.

| Hour, Date, Place | 515 Gy A.S.C. 5<sup>th</sup> Summary of Events and Information August 1917 | Remarks and references to Appendices |
|---|---|---|
| SENLIS. 26/8/17 | One Sergeant evacuated to C.C.S. | AG |
| " 28/8/17 | One Officer and 2 O.R. proceeded to the WIENNEZEELE area in advance party. | AG |
| " 30/8/17 2.0 pm | Supply and Baggage Waggons sent to units of 17<sup>th</sup> Bde Group, for move to WIENNEZEELE. One Wheeler Serg<sup>t</sup> reported (Reinforcement) | AG |
| " 31/8/17 8.30 am | Coy H.Q. moved by road to ALBERT Station to entrain for the WIENNEZEELE area. General health of the Company during the month was fairly good. Horses in good condition. | AG |

A Green Capt=o.c. 515<sup>th</sup> A.S.C. Sy Coln

Confidential

War Diary

of

No. H Coy. 59th Divisional Train

From 1st August 1917 to 31st August 1917

Volume 1.

# WAR DIARY
## or
## INTELLIGENCE SUMMARY.
*(Erase heading not required.)*

Army Form C. 2118.

Instructions regarding War Diaries and Intelligence Summaries are contained in F.S. Regs., Part II. and the Staff Manual respectively. Title pages will be prepared in manuscript.

| Hour, Date, Place | Summary of Events and Information | Remarks and references to Appendices |
|---|---|---|
| 1.8.17. ROSQUIGNY | 1. Sadler (Pte Booth) transferred to A.S.C. (anthrits A.S.C. recruits) & taken on strength. | H.J. |
| 2.8.17 " | Lt. Jimison & haymaking party return to Coy. — C.S.M. admitted to Hospital | H.J. |
| 3.8.17 " | 1.O.R. admitted to Hospital — 1.O.R. discharged from Hospital — | H.J. |
| 4.8.17 " | C.S.M. discharged from Hospital | H.J. |
| 5.8.17 " | 1.O.R. evacuated to C.C.S. & struck off strength — Work on new standings commenced | H.J. |
| 6.8.17 " | " 2.8.17 in completed to Coy. | H.J. |
| 7.8.17 " | 1.O.R. discharged from Hospital — | H.J. |
| 8.8.17 " | 1.O.R. proceeds (ENGLAND) on leave (Pte Barker). | |
| 9.8.17 " | 2.O.R. evacuated to C.C.S. & struck off strength — 1.O.R. admitted to Hospital | H.J. |
| 11.8.17 " | 1.O.R. reverts to rest station for 14 days — | H.J. |
| 12.8.17 " | Sgt Hutchinson tried by F.G.C.M. for Drunkenness & acquitted. — | H.J. |
| | 1.O.R. at base for dental treatment struck off strength. — Farrier Gunner Marshall struck off strength as a deserter 22.6.17 never heard from | H.J. |
| 13.8.17 " | Field Ambulance to which he has been attached. — | H.J. |
| | D.A.D.V.S. inspects all horses — 1.O.R. admitted to Hospital — | H.J. |
| 15.8.17 " | Lt Piggin & haymaking party return to Coy. — 1.O.R. admitted to hospital | H.J. |
| 16.8.17 " | 1.O.R. (A. Broadhurst) proceeds ENGLAND on 3 months special leave | H.J. |
| 17.8.17 " | 1.O.R. evacuated to C.C.S. & struck off strength | H.J. |
| | 2.O.R. admitted to hospital — | H.J. |
| 19.8.17 " | 3.O.R. proceed to rest station for 14 days — 2.O.R. admitted to hospital — 1.O.R. evacuated to C.C.S. & to struck off strength. | H.J. |

Army Form C. 2118.

# WAR DIARY
## or
## INTELLIGENCE SUMMARY.
(Erase heading not required.)

Instructions regarding War Diaries and Intelligence Summaries are contained in F.S. Regs., Part II and the Staff Manual respectively. Title pages will be prepared in manuscript.

2

| Hour, Date, Place | | Summary of Events and Information | Remarks and references to Appendices |
|---|---|---|---|
| 20.8.17 | ROCQUIGNY. | S.O. 118 Inf Brigade proceeds to ENGLAND on leave — 1 O.R. admitted to hospital. | M. |
| 21.8.17 | " | 3 O.R. admitted to hospital — 3 O.R. reported to duty & taken on strength — | M. |
| 22.8.17 | " | 1 O.R. discharged from hospital | M. |
| 23.8.17 | " | Baggage wagons sent to unit — rations drawn 4.0 pm for consumption 25.8.17 — | M. |
| 24.8.17 | " | 1 officer 1 O.R. proceed to new camp. | |
| 25.8.17 | BOUZINCOURT | Coy moves to BOUZINCOURT by route march BAPAUME - ALBERT — Coy quartered in Nissen huts — wagons return from units — | M. |
| 26.8.17 | " | Refilling at 10.0 am — 4 O.R. evacuated to C.C.S. strength 97 & strength — | M. |
| 27.8.17 | " | 1 O.R. reports for duty & is taken on strength | M. |
| 28.8.17 | " | 3 Supply clerks medically examined & 2 found category A for infantry. | M. |
| 29.8.17 | " | Supply & baggage wagons report to units — rations drawn 8.0 am & 4.0 pm for consumption 30.8.x 31.8. — Now half feed 24 hours — wagons return to Coy. | M. |
| 30.8.17 | " | Refilling at 6.0 am — 2 O.R. discharged from hospital — Baggage & Supply wagons report to units. | M. |
| 31.8.17 | " | Refilling 6.0 am — Coy leave camp 9.45 pm to entrain at BOUCOURT — en route to WINNEZEELE | M. |

(73989) W4141—463. 400,000. 9/14. H.&J.Ltd. Forms/C. 2118/10.

Army Form C. 2118.

# WAR DIARY
## or
## INTELLIGENCE SUMMARY.

*(Erase heading not required.)*

Instructions regarding War Diaries and Intelligence Summaries are contained in F.S. Regs., Part II. and the Staff Manual respectively. Title pages will be prepared in manuscript.

3

| Hour, Date, Place | Summary of Events and Information | Remarks and references to Appendices |
|---|---|---|
| 18.17 ROCQUIGNY | Units on return strength of 178 Infantry Brigade Group :— | |
| | H.Qrs 178 Inf. Brigade — No 4 Sec. 59 Sgnl Coy — 2/5 Sherwood Foresters — 2/6 Sherwood Foresters — 2/7 Sherwood Foresters — 2/8 Sherwood Foresters — 470 Field Co. RE — No 4 Coy 59 Div Train — 178 T.M. Battery — | |
| 23.8.17 | 178 M.G. Coy. — 2/3 N.M.W. Field Ambulance. 2/3 N.M. Field Ambulance struck off return strength — 200 Machine Guns — 2/1 Mobile Veterinary Section — 2/2 N.M.W. Field Ambulance taken on return strength or Ramp. | h.l. |
| | | h.l |
| | | h.l |
| 26.8.17 BOUZINCOURT | 200 Machine Guns Coy Established struck off return strength of Brigade Group. | |

M. Earhart Cmpl.
O.C. No 4 Coy. A.S.C. 59 D.W Train.

Vol 8

Confidential

War Diary

of

Headquarters 59th Divisional Train

from 1st to 30th Sept 1917

Vol VIII

# WAR DIARY
## INTELLIGENCE SUMMARY

Army Form C. 2118.

HEADQUARTERS 59th DIVISIONAL TRAIN VOL. VIII

MAP REFERENCES SHEETS 27 & 28 40cc & HAZEBROUCK 5-?

| Place | Date 1917 September | Hour | Summary of Events and Information | Remarks and references to Appendices |
|---|---|---|---|---|
| DROGLANDT | 1 | | Detrained at GODEVERSVELDT at 12 Noon and marched to WINNIZEELE AREA where the Train went into billets as follows:- TRAIN H.Q. and Nº1 Coy DROGLANDT. Nº2 Coy WINNIZEELE. Nº3 Coy. J.O.8.6. Nº4 Coy. J.8.a.6. Refilling Points established as follows:- DIVISIONAL TROOPS GROUP and 177th INFY. BDE GROUP at J.10 d.3.5 and 176th & 178th BDE GROUPS at J.10.d.b.4. Supplies drawn from WIPPENHOEK RAILHEAD by Lorries at 5 A.M. | SNT SNT SNT SNT SNT SNT |
| " | 2 | | RAILHEAD WIPPENHOEK 5AM by M.T. Refilling at above R.P.s 8am | SNT |
| " | 3 | | Received medical certificate from Lieut E.J.H.EAMES, S.O. 178th BDE GROUP stating that he is unfit to travel and no further extension of leave had been applied for to WAR OFFICE. The 4 G.S. Wagons held on strength by Nº1 Coy for Train Transport of "PIONEER BATT" handed over to R.T.O. POPERINGHE for return to Base Ordnance Depot and 8 single G.S horses for same landed on E.D.A.D.O.S. 59th DIVISION. | SNT SNT SNT |
| " | 4 | | RAILHEAD changed to ARNEKE 10.30am. M.T.- CAPT H.W.DAWES A.V.C. Vet Officer to rejoin us from leave | SNT |
| " | 5 | | Commenced drawing from RAILHEAD ARNEKE by Horse Transport, 35 G.S Wagons being sent. Total distance of return trip 20 miles. Finished not | PST PST |
| " | 6 | | RAILHEAD Convoy returned to 24 G.S Wagons moving to 7 lorries being allotted from 59th D.S.C. | SNT |
| " | 7 | | 20 G.S Wagons detailed for Railhead Convoy. 10 days extension of leave granted to Lieut EAMES by WAR OFFICE | PST |
| " | 8 | | 21 G.S Wagons detailed for Railhead Convoy. After refilling Nº1 Coy and Co. Brit. Field moth. & supply details moved to G.J.15 t.8.2 Pkut 28. to relieve 59th T.R.A & D.A.C. Train Transport of other Divisional Troops handed over to OC Nº2 Coy + the MILIT. Kinetograph & 176-178 feeding through. | PST PST RT |
| " | 9 | | Proceedings of B.R.M. in the case of Whiler W.B. HARRISON A.P.C. promulgated and sentence " to be dismissed from His Majesty's Service" duly carried out. Prisoner being handed over to A.P.M. | PST PST |
| " | 10 | | Lieut E.J.H. EAMES reported for duty on return from sick leave | SNT |
| " | 12 | | Lieut Colonel T. HAZLERIGG, Commanding 59th Div. Train proceeded on leave to England. Major V.D.R. CONLAN assumed command in his absence. One of the "spare" G.S wagons of Nº1 Coy. handed over to 5th Bn. Depot Battalion at MERKEGHEM detached on permanent duty with the 59th Div Depot Battalion at MERKEGHEM | PST PST PST |
| " | 13 | | Capt R.W. HARTLEY S.O. 176th Infantry Brigade proceeded on leave to ENGLAND & Lieut J.H. BROWN took over his duties. | PST |
| " | 14 | | The remaining "spare" vehicles of Nº1 Coy. 1 e. 2 G.S. + 2 limber G.S Wagons handed over to 59th Div. Salvage Coy | PST |
| " | 19 | | for duty near YPRES.- Nº2 Coy + Supply Officer resuppl details 176th Infantry. Bde moved to G.11 a. Pkut 19 with Refilling Point at 5:30 P.M. Divisional Troops details other than R.A + D.A.C. transferred to 178th Bde Group. Second Refilling Point 177+178 Bd. at 5:35 P.M. | SNT PST PST |
| " | 20 | | Railhead ARNEKE for 177+178 Bde Groups by M.T. and EDEWAARTHOEK for 176th Bde and 59 T.R.A groups - Nº2. Coy and S.O 177 Bde moved to WATOU Nº1 Area and Nº4 Coy + S.O 178 Bde moved to WATOU Nº2 Area. | PST PST RT |

T2134. Wt. W708—776. 500000. 4/15. Sir J. C. & S.

# WAR DIARY or INTELLIGENCE SUMMARY

Army Form C. 2118.

Head Quarters 59th Divisional Train VIII
Map references Sheet 27 & 28 & HAZEBROUCK 5A

| Place | Date 1917 | Hour | Summary of Events and Information | Remarks and references to Appendices |
|---|---|---|---|---|
| DROGLANDT | Sept 20 | | Lieut P.R.R. DIBBEN proceeded to ENGLAND on 21 days Special Leave | |
| " | 21 | | Nº 4142605 Dr. JOHNSTONE, H. of Nº 1 Coy. wounded whilst attached to 31st Salvage Coy and his two horses destroyed | |
| " | 22 | | Lieut Colonel T.H. AZZLERIGG returned from leave at reassumed command of the Train | |
| " | 23 | | Nº 3 Coy moved to YPRES Nº 1 AREA and Nº 4 Coy moved to G15 a 64 Sht 28. 17th Bde R.P. moved to G15 a 64 | |
| " | 24 | | 178th Bde R.P. moved to G15 a 4.7 Sht 28. Railhead for all units changed to EDEWAARTHOEK. Supplies drawn for 176th Fd Field Group and 59th T.T. Group by H.T. and for 177th & 178th Adv. Groups by M.T. Train H.Q. moved to G4.65.3. BRANDHOEK Nº 1 AREA and Nº 2, 3 & 4 Coys moved from above localities into same camp. A Convoy of 14 G.S. wagons under Lieut M.C. JOHNSTON | |
| BRANDHOEK Nº 1 AREA | 25 | | convoyed 2093 wagons under Capt T.M. HAZLERIGG went with S.A.A. from MAIN GRENADE DUMP to the line at SPREE FARM. Train transport of Nº 1, 64, 108, 2d2 of 178 Bde R.F.A. reported to Nº 1 Coy for attachment and their units convoy on Railway Siding at the Division. Nº 1 Coy moved into Train camp at G4.65.3. IDS R.P. moved to G4.65.3. 10 G.S. wagons under 2/Lieut WESTWICK supplied with S.A.A. at SPREE FARM and returned at 4.10 A.M. 26th. 1 G.S. wagon & M.C.O. went up to WESTVAR supplies for advanced SOUP KITCHENS. 8 G.S. wagons under Lieut J.G.F. ROSS went up to the line with water. | |
| " | 26 | | 13th Infantry Bde arrived in Divisional area on attachment to the Division. Attachment of 10 G.S wagons supplied therefrom arrived from 5th Army Auxiliary H.T. Coy & French Transport in 13 Infy. Bde. Attached to Nº 1&2 for accommodation & rations. These 10 G.S. wagons were issued out at 10.30 P.M. 6.90 to V.LAMERTINGHE to pick up rear details & Munitions and the ration brought by rail by 13th Infy Bde. 2/Lieut BROWNE in charge of wagons met near an Munitions but shortly returned. | |
| " | 27 | | Supplies drawn from Railhead by M.T. with some lorries to assist with Forage. Feeding strength of the Division above Rank & Details 9762 animals - 1 G.S. wagon carried forward detailed from Nº 1 Coy Headquarters for duty with the Divisional Burial Officer. | |
| " | 28 | | 13th Infy Bde left Divisional area. Detachment of 5 Army Aux H.T. Coy sent under S.S.M. HEILIG R.A.F. Nº 26 def to refill supplies and march with the Bde and provide for the night and thereafter to return to same camp. | |
| " | 29 | | 9 G.S. wagons under Lieut JOHNSTON sent to the line with Grenadier Company rationed to 3.30 A.M. 1 G.S. wagon sent to ST JEAN with supplies for SOUP KITCHENS. Orders received reducing Establishment of Nº 1 Coy by 1 H.T. Capt & 1 Ride Horse. 1 N.C.O. & 5 Drivers taken on the Strength of 5 Army Aux H.T. Coy. | |
| " | 30 | | returned to their own H.Q. S.S.Q. 15th. outfit & equipment for ambt G.S. Solution up to strength R.A. Headquarters by Con. 59th Coy, 1 N.C.O. Wounded. Nº 2 Coy, 1 N.C.O. wounded - 1 Ride Horse wounded. Nº 3 Coy KILLED 2 O.R. WOUNDED, 2 O.R. (1 including 1 slightly wounded) & 1 Rd.H. Horses wounded. Following casualties caused by enemy aircraft. General Health of all ranks very good. Weather conditions very good. Horses obtain the ration & have got much more welfare and are in the main in good condition. | |

P. Hazlerigg
Lieut Colonel
Commanding 59th Divisional Train

Confidential

War Diary

of

513 Company A.S.C. 59th Division

from 1st to 30th Sept 1917

Vol VIII

# WAR DIARY
## or
## INTELLIGENCE SUMMARY
*(Erase heading not required.)*

Army Form C. 2118

| Place | Date | Hour | Summary of Events and Information | Remarks and references to Appendices |
|---|---|---|---|---|
| Field | September 1917 | | | |
| | 1st. | | Move from ACHEUX to DROGLANDT completed. Refilling point Sheet 27. T.0.d.2.5. Company in fields, also Rating Horses. 1D. Horses in open. | |
| | 3rd. | | 4 Wagons returned to Entrance. | |
| | 4th. | | Capt S.H.W. DAVIES returns from leave. 4 double sets of harness returned to DADS | |
| | 8th. | | Moved by Route March from DROGLANDT to Sheet 28. B.16.a.2.b. and attached to 42nd Division. 1 Ride Horse transferred to No.2 Coy 59 Divil. Train. | |
| | 9th. | | 2/Lt M.B. Harrison struck off the strength. | |
| | 11th. | | 1 Ride Horse sent to V.O (Yr. Horse c.g.) | |
| | 12th. | | Lieut. Cve T. Hayling proceeded to U.K. on leave. | |
| | 18th. | | 1 Ride Horse and 3 H.D. transferred to No.3 Coy 59 Div. Train. | |
| | | | 1 H.D. transferred to 2/5. S. Staffs. | |
| | | | 1 H.D. transferred to 2/6. S. Staffs. | |
| | 19th. | | Company attached to 9th Division. | |
| | 22nd. | | Lieut. Cve T. Hayling returns from leave. 2 draught horses killed and three wounded by bomb from enemy aircraft. Company moves to units attachments from Cct Bgde | |
| | | | March from Sheet 28. B.16.a.2.6. to B.16. D.8.4. | |
| | | | and 108/Bgde at a rate attached to its Company. | |
| | 23rd. | | 2/Lieut M. Jenkinson Browne posted to the Company. | |
| | 25th. | | March from B.16.b.8.4. to B.4.6.2. Sheet 28. V. Refilling Point at G.4.7.6.2. | |
| | 26. | | 232 Bgde R.F.A. attachment is broken. | |

*R.A. Accushush* Capt.

Confidential

War Diary

No 2 Company Sqth Divisional Train

from 1st to 30th Sept 1917

Vol VIII

# WAR DIARY
## INTELLIGENCE SUMMARY
*(Erase heading not required.)*

Army Form C. 2118.

Vol. VIII

Instructions regarding War Diaries and Intelligence Summaries are contained in F. S. Regs., Part II. and the Staff Manual respectively. Title Pages will be prepared in manuscript.

| Place | Date | Hour | Summary of Events and Information | Remarks and references to Appendices |
|---|---|---|---|---|
| HOPOUTRE. (POPERINGHE) | 1917 Sept. 1 | | Detained Headquarters of Company and proceeded via ABEELE and STEENVOORDE to WINNEZEELE. H'qrs & W Bn. of the 176 Inf. Bde. drew supplies at R.P. WINNEZEELE during morning. Delivered supplies to Brigade Dumps in Divn. wagons. | Nil. |
| WINNEZEELE. | 2 | | diff. | Nil. |
| | 3 | | 467 Bde.Co. R.E. drew at 7.30 p.m. rations for consumption 5th and moved entrenching train on 6th. | Nil. |
| | 4 | | Supplies delivered to Brigade Dumps by Divn. wagons | Nil. |
| | 5 | | 10 wagons and carts of Train convey of 35 wagons, in lieu of D. Supply/Col. to draw supplies from ARNEKE mills to Railhead in WINNEZEELE area. 10th Line transport drew supplies from Railhead store. | Nil. |
| | 6 | | Refilling point in WINNEZEELE area. 7 wagons sent to Railhead convoy. | Nil. |
| | 7 | | Do. No.1 Coy. 59 Div. Train moved to forward area from this day transport for Div. troops running in WINNEZEELE area. | Nil. |
| | 8 | | | Nil. |
| | 9 | | 7 wagons used in lieu of D.S.C. daily consumption up to & including 17 Sept. Div. troops running in WINNEZEELE area commenced. | Nil. |
| | 12 | | Drew supplies from R.T.O. 176 Inf. Bde. with 59th Bde Depot Batt. at MERCKEGHEM. | Nil. |
| | 14 | | 4 wagons of No.1 Coy. despatched to VLAMERTINGHE area for duty with 59 Divl. Salvage Coy. Supplies for consumption 20th inst. drawn at 5.30 p.m. Batchment of No.1 Coy. | Nil. |
| | 15 | | Bagage wagons sent to O.C. No. 3 Coy. handed over to O.C. No. 3 Coy. | Nil. |
| BRANDHOEK. | 19 | | Headquarters of Coy. with Bagage & Supply Sections, and 18th Line Transport of Brigades Group (less Divl.G. RE. & Divl Amn.) moved via STEENVOORDS and POPERINGHE to BRANDHOEK No.1 area under command of 59 Bde., Supply train, under command of D.T. No.2 Coy. to Company. | Nil. |
| | 20 | | Refilling Point at G. b. d. 1. 4. Supplies drawn by motor transport. Railhead EDWARRTSHOEK. | Nil. |
| | 24 | | Supplies drawn in bulk by Divn. wagons. Rd Coy. H'qrs. & Sect. 2.B. & D. S. S. Train wagons supplied by Local Government employed on transport services to WISTTN | Nil. |
| | 30 | | Month ended. Condition of Horses good. Health of men good. | Nil. |

[signature] Capt.
O.C. 2 Coy. 59 Div. Train

Confidential

War Diary

of

No. 575 Company A.S.C. 37th Division

1-9-17    30-9-17

Volume VIII

Army Form C. 2118.

# WAR DIARY
## INTELLIGENCE SUMMARY.
*(Erase heading not required.)*

575 Coy A.S.C. 59 Div  September 1917

| Hour, Date, Place | Summary of Events and Information | Remarks and references to Appendices |
|---|---|---|
| 31/8/17 } Midnight 1/9/17 | En route by rail to WINNEZEELE Area. | KE |
| WINNEZEELE 1/9 ar. 10.30 | In quarters | KE |
| " 5/9 | Began again acted as pantry Supply Column from ARNEKE Railhead | KE |
| " " | One Ride Horse transferred to 75th Civic Regt | KE |
| " " | 2/3rd Field Amb. struck off ration strength of Bde. | KE |
| " " | One other casualty | KE |
| " 6/9/17 | 469th Coy R.E. struck off ration strength of Bde | KE |
| " 8/9/17 | 2 Ride Horses transferred to Camp Comdt 4th 59th Div | KE |

Kelson Capt
O.C. 575 Coy A.S.C.
59th Divn

Army Form C. 2118.

# WAR DIARY
## INTELLIGENCE SUMMARY.
*(Erase heading not required.)*

Instructions regarding War Diaries and Intelligence Summaries are contained in F. S. Regs., Part II. and the Staff Manual respectively. Title pages will be prepared in manuscript.

| Hour, Date, Place | Summary of Events and Information September 1917 | Remarks and references to Appendices |
|---|---|---|
| WINNEZELLE 11/9/17 | 515 Coy A.S.C. S₉ S.D. One Driver Reinforcement received | |
| " 12/9/17 | One Driver Evacuated | |
| " 15/9/17 | A.C.O. from Supply detail, 191 Coy transferred to Coy | |
| " 18/9/17 | One Sergeant Reinforcement received | |
| " 19/9/17 h. 4.0 | Detachment of No 1 Coy taken over from No 2 Coy | |
| " 19/9/17 h. 10.0 | Station of No 1 Coy handed over to No 4 Coy | |
| " 5.30 | All Baggage begun sent to North of Bac Saint Maur | |
| " 19/9/17 20/9/17 | The following Units came in Ration strength (for 2 days) D.H.Q. M.M.P. Traffic Control. O.R.K. 10th Signal M.V.S. C.R.E. DO. 9th Canadian. 200 M.G.C. T.H.Q. 2/1st Field Amb. | |

Forms/C. 2118/10.

Army Form C. 2118.

# WAR DIARY
## INTELLIGENCE SUMMARY.
*(Erase heading not required.)*

Instructions regarding War Diaries and Intelligence Summaries are contained in F.S. Regs., Part II. and the Staff Manual respectively. Title pages will be prepared in manuscript.

| Hour, Date, Place | Summary of Events and Information | Remarks and references to Appendices |
|---|---|---|
| | 575 Co A.S.C 59 Div September 1917 | |
| WINNEZEELE 20/9 5:40 a.m. | Coy H.Q.rs with supply wagons move by road to WATOU area. | A.P.S |
| WATOU area. 20/9 11:30 a.m. | In camp at L.9 sheet 27 | A.P.S |
| " 23/9 1:30 p.m. | Coy H.Q.rs moved by road to VLAMERTINGHE | A.P.S |
| VLAMERTINGHE 23/9 | In Camp | A.P.S |
| " 24/9 3:30 p.m. | Coy H.Q.rs with supply wagons move by road to POPERINGHE area. | A.P.S |
| POPERINGHE 24/9 4:30 (area) | In Camp at G.4. sheet 28 | A.P.S |
| " 25/9 | Train wagons commence supply Col duties from EDWARDSHOEK railhead | A.P.S |

A.P.Green Capt. O.C. 575 Co. A.S.C. 17

(9 29 6) W 3332—1107 100,000 10/13 H W V Forms/C. 2118/10.

Army Form C. 2118.

# WAR DIARY
## INTELLIGENCE SUMMARY.
*(Erase heading not required.)*

Instructions regarding War Diaries and Intelligence Summaries are contained in F. S. Regs., Part II. and the Staff Manual respectively. Title pages will be prepared in manuscript.

| Hour, Date, Place | Summary of Events and Information 515 Coy A.S.C. 59 Divn September 1917 | Remarks and references to Appendices |
|---|---|---|
| POPERINGHE 25/9/17. Wks. G.4. Sheet 28. | 10. G.S. Wagons detailed for night work up to SPREE FARM. 2/Lieut W. TODD i/c. | |
| " 29/17. 2.0 a.m | 2 Drivers killed 1 Driver and 1 Horse wounded by bombs from enemy aircraft. 1 Ride Horse wounded in Camp | } |
| " 30/9/17 | General health of the Company during the month was good, good all Horses in good condition | } |

A. Green Capt.
O.C. 515 Coy A.S.C.
59 Divn

Confidential

War Diary

of

No. 14 Company 59th Divisional Train

From:- 1st Septr. 1917   To:- 30th Septr. 1917

Volume 8.

Army Form C. 2118.

# WAR DIARY
## or
## INTELLIGENCE SUMMARY.
(Erase heading not required.)

Instructions regarding War Diaries and Intelligence Summaries are contained in F.S. Regs., Part II and the Staff Manual respectively. Title pages will be prepared in manuscript.

| Hour, Date, Place | Summary of Events and Information | Remarks and references to Appendices |
|---|---|---|
| 1.9.17 OUDEZEELE | Entrained at BAUCOURT 3.0 a.m. — Detrained at GODEWAERSVELDE at 3.30 p.m. — proceeded to camp at OUDEZEELE — | M. |
| 2.9.17 " | Refitting at 9.30 a.m. at Brigade Dump at WINNEZEELE. | M. |
| 4.9.17 " | Supply checks meanwhile examined. | M. |
| 5.9.17 " | 3 O.R. return from III Army Rest Camp — 1 O.R. discharged from Hospital — 1 Rds horse transferred to 2/8 Sherwood Foresters — Return drawn by 'bus transport | M. |
| 6.9.17 " | Baggage wagons forward to ARNEKE to railhead Scoury — Supplies Dump moved to OUDEZEELE — | M. |
| 8.9.17 " | 10 Spare men of Coy medically examined — | M. |
| 10.9.17 " | Rdrs & Drvrs Saddlers attd. Hrsmn from Coy & returned to Ordnance | M. |
| 13.9.17 " | Supply details & Staff Sergt reports to duty & taken on strength — | M. |
| 16.9.17 " | 1 O.R. discharged from Hospital — | M. |
| 19.9.17 " | Reveillez at 2.0 a.m. moved 8 a.m. — Baggage wagons report to work — | M. |
| 20.9.17 WATOU | Supply wagons return to Coy in readiness for move to-morrow — Coy forward by route march to WATOU area, deliver supplies to troops there & return to Coy together with Baggage wagons | M. |
| 21.9.17 " | Reveillez at 8.0 a.m. from Suppl Dump L & D 8.2 (Sheet 27) | M. |
| 23.9.17 " | Baggage wagons report to work — Coy move with Supplies wagons to BRANDHOEK — | M. |

# WAR DIARY or INTELLIGENCE SUMMARY.

*(Erase heading not required.)*

Army Form C. 2118.

| Hour, Date, Place | Summary of Events and Information | Remarks and references to Appendices |
|---|---|---|
| 24.9.17 BRANDHOEK | Coy moves to EDEWAARTHOEK — 12 wagons under Lt. JOHNSTON took S.A.A. to packhorse Coys in the line near BRIDGE HOUSE — | W |
| 25.9.17 EDEWAARTHOEK | Baggage wagons return to Coy — Supply dump situated at G.6.d.1.3 (sheet 28) — 6 wagons under Lt JOHNSTON took S.A.A. to WIELTJE FARM — | W. |
| 26.9.17 " | 15 wagons go to _____ Packhorses to enemy — 1 O.R. admitted to hospital — | W |
| 27.9.17 " | 15 wagons Packhorses covered — area shelled by enemy aeroplanes — | W. |
| 28.9.17 " | 15 wagons Packhorses covered — Our guns shelled at night — | W |
| 29.9.17 " | 6 wagons Packhorses to enemy — Own shelled again — 5 wagons under Lt JOHNSTON took S.A.A. to VON RUCK FARM — | W. |
| 30.9.17 " | Pte Edmunds on Supply details proceeds to ENGLAND to join officers cadet corps in stead of joining K — area shelled again — Baggage unsuccessful to work — 2/6 Sherwd Foresters wagons attached to my 2nd Brigade — | W |

Signed [illegible] Lt. Col. Commanding 53rd Div Train

Army Form C. 2118.

# WAR DIARY
## or
## INTELLIGENCE SUMMARY.
(Erase heading not required.)

Instructions regarding War Diaries and Intelligence Summaries are contained in F. S. Regs., Part II and the Staff Manual respectively. Title pages will be prepared in manuscript.

| Hour, Date, Place | Summary of Events and Information | Remarks and references to Appendices |
|---|---|---|
| Units patrolled by 178 Infantry Brigade during Month of September 1917 with dates :— | Hdqrs 178 Infantry Brigade from 1st Sept. To 30 Sept. | |
| | No 4 Section 59 Div Signals " " | |
| | 2/5 Sherwood Foresters " " | |
| | 2/6 Sherwood Foresters " " | |
| | 2/7 Sherwood Foresters " " | |
| | 2/8 Sherwood Foresters " " | |
| | 178 Trench Mortar Battery " " | |
| | 178 Machine Gun Coy " " | |
| | 430 Field Coy R.E. " " | |
| | No 4 Coy 59 Div Train A.S.C. " " | |
| | 21/M Mobile Veterinary Section A.V.C. " 8th and 22nd to 30th = | |
| | 2/2 Field Ambulance R.A.M.C " 1st " 6 30 = | |
| | 1 Hdqrs 59th Division " 22 " 30th | |
| | " Stff M.M.? " | |
| | " Stff Traffic " | |
| | " R.E. & Workshop " | |
| | 59 Signal Coy R.E " | |
| | D.A.D.O.S. " | |
| | 59 Laundry " | |
| | 200 Machine Gun Coy " | |
| | 2/1 Field Ambulance R.A.M.C. " | |
| | Stanley Ammunition Dump for 28 Sept only | |

M. Oakley Capt
O.C. HQ 178 Inf Brig

Confidential

11
959

War Diary
of
O.C. 59th Divisional Train

Vol IX

From 1st October 1917 to 31st October 1917

**WAR DIARY** HEADQUARTERS 59th DIVISIONAL TRAIN

**INTELLIGENCE SUMMARY.**

Army Form C. 2118.

(Erase heading not required.)

Reference Maps. HAZEBROUCK S.A.
Vol. IX. LENS II. Sheets 28 & 36 B.

| Place | Date 1917 | Hour | Summary of Events and Information | Remarks and references to Appendices |
|---|---|---|---|---|
| BRANDHOEK No 1 AREA G.4.5-3 Sheet 28 | Oct 1 | | RAILHEAD EDEWAARTHOEK. No 2 Coy at Refilling Point for 176th Bde Group moved KEISBERGUES. No 4 Coy and Refilling Point 178th Bde Group moved ST MARTIN both up HAZEBROUCK. No 2 T.H Corps New Zealand Train took over the camps of the outgoing Coy's. CRE and Forward Divisional H.Q. at WATOU. Rear Divisional H.Q. moved K. STEENBECQUE. | SGT BPF BPF PPT SGT |
| " | 2 | | RAILHEAD EDEWAARTHOEK by M.T. Train H.Q. and No 3 Coy moved to STEENBECQUE and THIENNES respectively. No 1 Coy and Supply Details remained to take over 59th Divn Cattery Train H.Q. and drew rations from Pack Train by New Zealand Division. | GET PAT BPF PAT |
| STEENBECQUE | 3 | | No 3 Coy New Zealand Divisional Train took over camps vacated by 59th Div Train. Railhead changed to LILLERS. Refilling Points for 176th Bde Group BOESEGHEM Group ISBERGUES. 177th Sup Bde Group THIENNES. 178th Bde Group BOESEGHEM | SGT BPF |
| " | 4 + 5 | | No 1 Coy moved with 59th R.A. to XIV Corps area at ST. SIXTE. The Coy sent refilling Point per attached in farm S. of EYKHOEK. No 4 Coy moved to LILLETTE Railhead LILLERS. Train H.Q moved from STEENBECQUE. No 3 Coy moved from THIENNES to BERGUIGNY with Refilling point at LAIRES. Capt GODDARD OC No 4 Coy proceeded on leave to ENGLAND | SGT BPF SGT PAT |
| RUPIGNY | 6 | | No 2 Coy moved to LISBOURG Railhead LILLERS. | SGT |
| PRESSY-LES-PERNES | 7 / 10 | | From new area under Brigade Orders being supplied for the night-- No 2 refilling at TANGRY. No 3 refilling DPT and some Units DWK Targos where did not move until 14th refilling Points 176 Bde Group HERSIN - 177 and 178 Sup Bde Group SACHIN. No 3 Coy CAMBLAIN - CHATELAIN. No 4 Coy TANGRY. Co Establishment of Train H.Q. remained at RUPIGNY to feed Divisional H.Q. and some Units. | SGT PAT PPF BGT BGT PPT BGC |
| " | 11 | | No 3 Coy moved to MAISNIL-LES-RUITZ. No 4 Coy moved K BRITTE L. Refilling Points 176th Bde Group GAVION - 177th Bde Group ESTREE CAUCHIE. 178th Bde Group SACHIN. | WAT GRC ART |
| " | 12 | | Refilling Points for 3 Inf Bde Groups at PETIT SERVINS | BRE |
| " | 13 | | RAILHEAD HOUDAIN. Train H.Q moved from PRESSY LES PERNES. took on strength about 8 N.W.A. 9000 men and 3000 horses to Refilling Points by Light Railway commenced | PPF PAT |
| CHATEAU DE LA HAIE. | 14 | | Railhead BARLIN and Horses to Refilling Points by Light Railway commenced delivering supplies to 1st 2nd and 3rd Canadian Infantry Training Depots. The following Train serving complete turnout, detached for duty. 2 G.S. Wagon to DISTRICT COMMANDANT CALONNE-RICOUART. 1950 Inch R. and 1 Limb G.S Wagon to 8th Enemy Coy. | NPT RTS MPT |
| " | 15 | | A daily standing detail of 12 G.S Wagons for work on Roads commenced. Supplies drawn from Refilling Points by Divn Transport. | SGT |
| " | 16 | | No 3 + 4 Coys moved into camps at CARENCY, and Refilling Points for 177th + 178th Inf Bde at CARENCY. Refilling Points 176 Inf Bde moved to SAINS-BOUVIGNY. Siding on Light Railway. | BPT SGT PAT BPT |

# WAR DIARY or INTELLIGENCE SUMMARY.

*(Erase heading not required.)*

Army Form C. 2118.

VOL IX Part 2.

| Place | Date 1917 | Hour | Summary of Events and Information | Remarks and references to Appendices |
|---|---|---|---|---|
| CHATEAU de la HAIE | Oct 17 | | Supplies loaded at Railhead BARLIN on Light Railway did not arrive at 17 2nd Inf Bde Refilling Point but lie 3.30 A.M. on 17th inst. for issue on the same day. | SAF |
| | 18 | | No. 1 Coy which had been detached from the Divisional with the 59th Division arriving in the Divisional Area and went into camp at CARENCY. Refilling Point for Divisional Troops guard at Light Railway Siding CARENCY. 1 Limber & 3 wagons attached for duty with A.P.M. Y Corps at COUPIGNY. CAPT. H.R. GODDARD returned from leave and resumed Command of No 4 Coy. | SAF SAF SAF SAF |
| | 22 | | Lieut. F. PIGGIN No 4 Coy Proceeded on 10 days leave to ENGLAND. | SAF |
| | 23 | | 1st Canadian Div Artillery drew from 59th Division's Pack to loose twine. | SAF |
| | 24 | | 5 Canadian Div Artillery Canadian Div Reinforcement Camps and Nos 1, 2, & 3 Canadian Training Depots rationing for last time. 1 NCO & 7 O.R.s having completed tour now attached for duty with 4 Reserve Park Section under 9 Corps T.S. Col. | SAF SAF SAF |
| | 25 | | No. 1 Coy moved to new Camp W. of ABLAIN ST NAZAIRE at X 3 c central Sht 36 B. | SAF |
| | 26 | | Refilling Point for Divisional Troops group changed to X 3 c central Sht 36 B for issue 27th for 1st time. | SAF |
| | 28 | | No 2 Coy moved from HERSIN to CARENCY. 176th Refilling Point changed to N.E. of Sibing GREENE. | SAF |
| | 30 | | Ammunition & drinking waters to the Queckmaster's Store guards of the Inf. Brigades in the Lefts Section of the Divisional Grant. | SAF SAF |

*[signature]* Majors Lieut Col.
COMMANDING
59TH DIVISIONAL TRAIN

Confidential.

WAR DIARY
of
53 Company R.E.
54th Divn.
From Oct 1st 1917 to Oct 31st 1917.

Vol. VIII

Army Form C. 2118.

# WAR DIARY
## or
## INTELLIGENCE SUMMARY.
(Erase heading not required.)

Instructions regarding War Diaries and Intelligence Summaries are contained in F.S. Regs., Part II. and the Staff Manual respectively. Title pages will be prepared in manuscript.

| Place | Date | Hour | Summary of Events and Information | Remarks and references to Appendices |
|---|---|---|---|---|
| In the field | 2/10/17 | | Detachment of 104, 109, and 232 Bytes Coys struck off to bring up to Company | |
| | 5/10/17 | | Moved by Marchorts to Myk Rafa F.M.O. Bonfire Sheet 27. | |
| | 9/10/17 | | Unloading from Railhead at Elverdinghe and delivering to Refilling Point at F.M.Q. Central Sheet 27. | |
| | 10/10/17 | | 1 Sgt and 1 Rifle Horse struck off establishment for 76th Aza Byle | |
| | 11/10/17 | | 1 Gur and 1 Rifle Horse struck off strength on repting to 76th Aza Byle. | |
| | 12/10/17 | | 1 Ryt Horse un-earmarked. | |
| | 15/10/17 | | Moved by Mech Conts to EECKE. Company wheels unearmarked. | |
| | 16/10/17 | | Moved by Mech Conts to MORBECQUE, Near HAZEBROUCK Company wheels, horses on lines. | |
| | 17/10/17 | | Moved by Mech d'onts to GONNEHEM Company wheels known on stall. 1 RD Horse Evacuated. | |
| | 18/10/17 | | Moved by Mech Conts to CARENCY. Company in Camp horses in Stables. Refilling Point at CARENCY — Supplies obtained at Decauville Rly at Dump. | |
| | 20/10/17 | | Moved by Mech Conts to CARENCY (Change of Camps) Company in Camp. Horses in lines and in stables. 1. RD Horse Received. | |
| | 23/10/17 | | 1 MD Horse Evacuated. | |
| | 25/10/17 | | Moved by Mech Conts to ABLAIN ST NAZAIRE. Company in camp. Horses in Shelters which as no yet completed. Refilling Point in Camp. Supplies obtained by Decauville Rly at Dump. | |
| | 28/10/17 | | 243189 Sgt Ist Gardner reports to Command at Canadian Corps Gas School for Gas Course. | |

T.R. Hackett Capt
O.C. 313 Coy. 59th Div Train

CONFIDENTIAL

# WAR DIARY

of

O.C. No 2 Company 59th Divisional Train

## Vol. IX

From 1st October 1917 to 31st October 1917

Army Form C. 2118.

# WAR DIARY
## INTELLIGENCE SUMMARY
(Erase heading not required.)

Vol. IX

No 2 Coy. 59th Divl. Train.

| Place | Date | Hour | Summary of Events and Information | Remarks and references to Appendices |
|---|---|---|---|---|
| EDWARTSHOEK. | 1917 1st Octr | | Baggage wagons having been despatched to all units and supply wagons of 6th Batt. South Staff Regt & 174th M. Gun Coy having been detached to No 8 Coy. 59 Divl Train, HdQrs. of Company and Supply Section marched to ISBERGUES via POPERINGHE, HAZEBROUCK and STEENVOORDE and delivered supplies at ISBERGUES and GUARBEQUE on arrival in new area. Distance 29 miles. | Pnnt. |
| ISBERGUES. | 2 " | | Drew supplies from Railhead Point at THIENNES and delivered to units. 174th M. Gun Coy. & 6th South Staff Regt arrived in area and were with 3rd Inf. Bde. | Pnnt. |
| " | 3 " | | 59th Divl Train on Ration strength of Coy. HdQrs. | Pnnt. |
| " | 6 " | | Refilling Point moved from THIENNES to Market Square, ISBERGUES. Baggage delivered by Train Transport | Pnnt. |
| " | 7 " | | #67 3rd Co. R.E. rations on ration strength of Boiry (?) Coy. Supplies despatched to all units in readiness for move. Baggage wagons despatched to all units in BERGUENEUSE Area. | mnt. |
| LISBOURG | 8 " | | Refilled for consumption 9th at 5.30 p.m. Co. HdQrs. and supply section proceeded by mareche route to LISBOURG. Supplies delivered to all units of Group in BERGUENEUSE Area. | Pnnt. |
| " | 9 " | | Baggage wagons recalled from units. | Pnnt. |
| " | 10 " | | Baggage wagons despatched to units. Refilled for consumption 11th at 5.30 p.m. Co. HdQrs. and supply section proceeded by mareche route to HERSIN. Delivered supplies to units in new area. | Pnnt. |
| HERSIN. | 11 " | | #67 3rd Co. R.S. & 2/2 M.M. Field Amb. struck off B.A. ration strength after 11th | Pnnt. |
| " | 13 " | | Baggage wagons returned with units. Supplies delivered to all Units by Train Transport. | Pnnt. Pnnt. |
| " | 15 " | | 171 Field Refilling Point moved with time to PETIT SERVINS for dates 14th inst. | Pnnt. |
| " | 16 " | | All Transport wagons generally from units on completion of move of Brigade to BOUVIGNY BOYEFFLES. | Pnnt. Pnnt. |
| " | 17 " | | 176-7 & 8 R.F.A. Brigades joined Division from units in charge of Brigade E. BOUVIGNY BOYEFFLES. Supplies drawn by 1st Line Transport to units one extra commencing 16th June. | Pnnt. |
| " | 24 " | | Two H.R. remounts received. | Pnnt. |
| " | 26 " | | Mixed Coy. 15 was union at GANSN. - N. and of HERSIN. | Pnnt. |
| " | 27 " | | Advance party moved to HERSIN. | Pnnt. |
| " | 28 " | | Baggage wagons of units made up for any move with units drawn from BOUVIGNY area to CARENCY. | Pnnt. |
| CARENCY. | | | Mixed HdQrs. of Coy to CARENCY. Supply Section drew supplies from Saint-BOUVIGNY Refilling point to Coys Store at BOUVIGNY and took from there to CARENCY baggage of units. Baggage wagons of units returned supplies from units drawn to carry rations load on 29th. BOUVIGNY was to drew at CARENCY and returned to BOUVIGNY Area in order to carry further load on 29th. | Pnnt. |
| " | 29 " | | Supplies drawn by Train Transport from Railhead Point at CARENCY and issued to Units stores. Baggage wagons returned from BOUVIGNY area to CARENCY and left 4 Brigades from the line to CARENCY area. Two wagons on command. | Pnnt. Pnnt. |
| " | 30. | | Stores of 176-7-8 R.F.A. 59th Divl. Amn & Corps Reinforcement Camp. 1st Line Transport drew supplies. | Pnnt. Pnnt. |
| " | 31 | | Two wagons attended (?) to (?) Loads of (?) wagons employed in transferring ammunition & at 470th Bde G. R.S. | Pnnt. |

M. Hagler Capt.
O.C. No 2 Coy. 59 Divl. Train.

Confidential

War Diary
of
515 Company Army Service Corps. 59th Division

From 1-10-17 to 31-10-17

(Volume IX)

# WAR DIARY
## INTELLIGENCE SUMMARY

515 Coy A.S.C. 59th Divn. October 1917

| Place | Date | Hour | Summary of Events and Information | Remarks and references to Appendices |
|---|---|---|---|---|
| POPERINGE Area B 4 sheet 28. | 1/10/17 | | In Camp | |
| " | " | 5.0 a.m. | 430 Coy R.E. <br> 431 " " <br> 432 " " <br> 10th Btk Div R. J. } Came on Ration strength to 1st + 2nd Setts | |
| " | 2/10/17 | 3.30 | Company HQs with Supply section of Bde Group moved to THIENNES | |
| THIENNES " | " | | In Billets | |
| " | " | | H.Q. & 59th Div Train <br> 2/1st — M.V.S. <br> 2/6th Sinth Staff <br> 2/6th Ches. Fd Amb <br> 2/1st — N.M. F.A. } Came on Ration strength for 2nd = 3rd & 4th Octr | |
| " | " | | A. Green Capt — <br> OC 515 Coy A.S.C. 59th Divn. | |

Army Form C. 2118.

# WAR DIARY
## or
## INTELLIGENCE SUMMARY

*(Erase heading not required.)*

Instructions regarding War Diaries and Intelligence Summaries are contained in F.S. Regs., Part II. and the Staff Manual respectively. Title Pages will be prepared in manuscript.

515 Coy. A.S.C. 5th A.H.D.          October 1917

| Place | Date | Hour | Summary of Events and Information | Remarks and references to Appendices |
|---|---|---|---|---|
| THIENNES | 6/10/17 | 8.0 a.m. | Company H.Q. with Supply section of 3rd Bde. Group moved to BERQUINGY | 66 |
| BERQUINGY | " | 3.0 p.m. | In Billets | 166 |
| " | 7/10/17 | | 7/1st N.M.F.H. came in Ration Strength | A66 |
| " | 8/10/17 | | 1 driver Reinforcement received | 66 |
| " | 10/10/17 | 10.0 a.m. | Company H.Q. moved by road to CAMBLAIN CHATELAINE | 66 |
| CAMBLAIN CHATELAINE | " | 4.0 p.m. | In Billets | 166 |
| " | 11/10/17 | 11.0 a.m. | Coy. H.Q. with Supply section of Bde. Group, moved by road to MARNILL LES RUITZ | 166 |
| MARNILL LES RUITZ | 11/10/17 | 3.0 p.m. | In Billets | 166 |

Arthur Capt
OC 515 Coy A.S.C 5th A.H.D.

Army Form C. 2118.

# WAR DIARY
## INTELLIGENCE SUMMARY
*(Erase heading not required.)*

Instructions regarding War Diaries and Intelligence Summaries are contained in F. S. Regs., Part II. and the Staff Manual respectively. Title Pages will be prepared in manuscript.

| Place | Date | Hour | Summary of Events and Information | Remarks and references to Appendices |
|---|---|---|---|---|
| | | | 515 Co. A.S.C. 59th Div'n  5 October 1917 | |
| MAISNIL LES RUITZ | 12/10/17 | a.m. 10.0 | Coy H.Q. & pack supply section of Ech. Group moved by road to VANCOUVER CAMP. | G.E. |
| VANCOUVER CAMP. | 12/10/17 | p.m. 3.0 | In Camp | G.E. |
| " | 13/10/17 | a.m. 9.0 | Coy H.Q. & moved by road to CARENCY. X 21a. sheet 36 B | G.E. |
| CARENCY | " | p.m. 4.30 | In Camp and quarters | G.E. |
| " | 15/10/17 | | 1 Driver with G.S. Wagon & Pair sent on Det'mt to CALONNE RICOURT | G.E. |
| " | " | | 2 Drivers Reinforcements received | G.E. |
| " | " | | 1st Canadian Inf'y Bde School  }<br>2nd  "    "    "    "    "    } Came on ration strength<br>3rd  "    "    "    "    "    } | G.E. |

A. Green Capt
OC 515 Coy A.S.C. 59th Div'n

Army Form C. 2118.

# WAR DIARY
## INTELLIGENCE SUMMARY
*(Erase heading not required.)*

Instructions regarding War Diaries and Intelligence Summaries are contained in F. S. Regs., Part II. and the Staff Manual respectively. Title Pages will be prepared in manuscript.

| Place | Date | Hour | Summary of Events and Information | Remarks and references to Appendices |
|---|---|---|---|---|
| CARENCY | 16/10/17 | | 515 Coy A.S.C. 59th Divn. October 1917 | |
| | | | 3 Lorries with G.S. Wagons + Pairs sent on Detmt CHATEAU DE LA HAIE | A/1 |
| " | " | | Offr & Bretr's 2.I. } 2nd Battn Coy, 79th Bde RFA | A/2 |
| | | | 66 Gr Kilren Coy H Q 5/177 F.A. — come in |
| | | | 127 " 303rd Batt R.F.A. Position |
| | | | T.A. 35th Trench Batty 463rd " Strength |
| " | 17/10/17 | | One Corpl. issuer Transferred to 514 Coy ASC 59th Divn | A/4 |
| " | 18/10/17 | | 7 Gr Batt. Lincolns returned to Bde. Group | A/5 |
| " | 19/10/17 | | 2 Lorries Transferred to 2/2nd W.M.F.A. | A/6 |
| " | 22/10/17 | | 3 Lorries and 1 Lorry Reinforcement received | A/2 |

K.B. Green Capt.
O.C. 515 Coy A.S.C. 59th Divn

2449 Wt. W14957/M90 750,000 1/16 J.B.C. & A. Forms/C.2118/12.

Army Form C. 2118.

# WAR DIARY
## INTELLIGENCE SUMMARY
*(Erase heading not required.)*

515 Coy A.S.C. 59th Bde 3hs — O.C. 515 Coy 10/17

| Place | Date | Hour | Summary of Events and Information | Remarks and references to Appendices |
|---|---|---|---|---|
| CARENCY | 24/12/17 | | P. O. R⁵ with 7. G. S. Wagons + Pair extra Setts to 5ᵗ Bgn Inf. R.E. | Col |
| " | 27/12/17 | | 1 Farr Corpl received as supernumery | Rez |
| " | 28/10/17 | | 1 officer with 50 O.R⁵ Amm Sub. Park taken on ration strength | Col |
| " | 29/12/17 | | 1 Driver Reinforcement - Received | Rez |
| " | 31/12/17 | | 2/1 N.M.F.A. 200ᵗʰ M.Q.C. struck off ration strength | Rez |
| " | " | | 2/2 N.M.F.A. Came on ration strength | Rez |
| CARENCY | 31/12/17 | | In quarters. General health of the company during the month was fairly good, all horses in good condition | Rez |

(Green Capt)
O.C. 515 Coy A.S.C. 59ᵗʰ Bde TMs

Confidential
War Diary
of
106, M.G. Company 5q.th Divisional Train
From 1st Oct. 1917 To 31st Oct. 1917.

Volume 9.

Army Form C. 2118.

# WAR DIARY
## or
## INTELLIGENCE SUMMARY

(Erase heading not required.)

Instructions regarding War Diaries and Intelligence Summaries are contained in F.S. Regs., Part II. and the Staff Manual respectively. Title Pages will be prepared in manuscript.

| Place | Date | Hour | Summary of Events and Information | Remarks and references to Appendices |
|---|---|---|---|---|
| EDWARTHOEK | 1.10.17 | 5.0 AM | Coy move by Route March to ST MARTIN. — Supply Dump at BOESEGHEM. | L.W. |
| ST. MARTIN | 2.10.17 | 2.0 PM | Coy move ½ mile to AIRE | W. |
| AIRE | 4.10.17 | | Baggage wagons sent to units | W. |
| " | 5.10.17 | 9.0 am | Coy move to LILLETTE — Supply Dump at LAIRS. | W. |
| LILLETTE | 6.10.17 | | 1 O.R. admitted to Hospital. | W. |
| | 7.10.17 | | Supply Dump move to GLEM. | W. |
| | 8.10.17 | | S.S.M Young reported for duty & taken on Strength — | W. |
| | 9.10.17 | | Baggage wagons sent to units. | W. |
| | 10.10.17 | | Coy move to TANGRY. (Route March) | W. |
| TANGRY. | 11.10.17 | 9.0 am | Coy move to GROSSART-BRITTEL (hit) | W. |
| GROSSART-BRITTEL | 12.10.17 | 9.30 am | Coy move to BARLIN. (hito) | W. |
| BARLIN. | 13.10.17 | 9.0 am | Coy move to GOUY-SERVINS. (hito) | W. |
| GOUY-SERVINS | 15.10.17 | 10.0 am | Coy move to CARENCY. (hito). | W. |
| CARENCY | 16.10.17 | | Baggage wagons return from units. | W. |
| | 19.10.17 | | 1 O.R. discharged from Hospital. | W. |
| | 20.10.17 | | 1 Farrier Shoer taken on Strength. | W. |
| | 21.10.17 | | 1 O.R. struck off Strength on transfer to Kampa & Details. | W. |
| | 22.10.17 | | 1 F/Cpl reports for duty & is taken on Strength. — 1 O.R. admitted to Hospital. | W. |
| | 23.10.17 | | 1 O.R. discharged from Hospital. | W. |
| | 26.10.17 | | 1 O.R. returned to duty with Supply Details & taken on Strength. | W. |

2449 Wt. W14957/M90 750,000 1/16 J.B.C. & A. Forms/C.2118/12.

Army Form C. 2118.

# WAR DIARY
## or
## INTELLIGENCE SUMMARY
*(Erase heading not required.)*

| Place | Date | Hour | Summary of Events and Information | Remarks and references to Appendices |
|---|---|---|---|---|
| CARENCY | 28.10.17 | | 1 O.R. evacuated from Hospital & struck off strength. | N. |
| | 29.10.17 | | 1 O.R. admitted to Hospital. — C.S.M. Proceeds to COUPIGNY for a R.A.S. Course. | N. |
| | 31.10.17 | | Scout Platoon rejoined to Company. | N. |

W. Gilbert Capt.
O.C. No 4 Coy 39 Div A W Train.

# WAR DIARY
## or
## INTELLIGENCE SUMMARY

Army Form C. 2118.

| Place | Date | Hour | Summary of Events and Information | Remarks and references to Appendices |
|---|---|---|---|---|
| | | | The following units have been attached to the Supply Officer 178 Infantry Brigade from the month of October:— | |
| | | | Headquarters 178 Inf Brigade 1.10.17 to 31.10.17 | |
| | | | No 4 Section 59 Div Signals 1.10.17 to 31.10.17 | |
| | | | 2/5 Sherwood Foresters 1.10.17 to 31.10.17 | |
| | | | 2/6 Sherwood Foresters 1.10.17 ONLY and 4.10.17 to 31.10.17 | |
| | | | 2/7 Sherwood Foresters 1.10.17 to 31.10.17 | |
| | | | 2/8 Sherwood Foresters 1.10.17 to 31.10.17 | |
| | | | 178 Trench Mortar Battery 1.10.17 to 31.10.17 | |
| | | | 178 Machine Gun Coy 1.10.17 to 31.10.17 | |
| | | | 470 Field Coy R.E. 1.10.17 ONLY and 5.10.17 to 31.10.17 | |
| | | | No 4 Coy A.S.C. 59 Div Train 1.10.17 to 31.10.17 | |
| | | | 2/1 Field Ambulance RAMC 1.10.17 ONLY | |
| | | | 467 Field Coy R.E. 1.10.17 ONLY and 5.10.17 to 30.10.17 | |
| | | | 2/2 Field Ambulance R.A.M.C. 11.10.17 to 17.10.17 | |
| | | | Headquarters 59 Division 1.10.17 to 20.10.17 | |
| | | | " M.M.P. " 1.10.17 to 20.10.17 | |
| | | | " Traffic " 1.10.17 to 20.10.17 | |
| | | | 59 Signal Coy 1.10.17 to 20.10.17 | |

Army Form C. 2118.

# WAR DIARY
## or
## INTELLIGENCE SUMMARY

*(Erase heading not required.)*

Instructions regarding War Diaries and Intelligence Summaries are contained in F. S. Regs., Part II. and the Staff Manual respectively. Title Pages will be prepared in manuscript.

| Place | Date | Hour | Summary of Events and Information | Remarks and references to Appendices |
|---|---|---|---|---|
| D.A.D.O.S. | 1.10.17 | | to 20.10.17 | |
| 59 Laundry | 1.10.17 | | to 20.10.17 | |
| 59 Salvage Coy | 8.10.17 | | to 20.10.17 | |
| 2/4 Lincolns | 11.10.17 | | to 16.10.17 | |
| Lt Col. H.A.A. Dump | 18.10.17 | | to 31.10.17 | |
| 86 Labour Coy | 25.10.17 | | to 31.10.17 | |
| 331 Road Construction Coy | 25.10.17 | | to 31.10.17 | |
| E. Ant-Aircraft Battery | 25.10.17 | | to 31.10.17 | |
| 59 Hqrs R.E. 4th M/C Coy | 1.10.17 | | to 20.10.17 | |
| 21 Mobile Veterinary Section | 1.10.17 | | ONLY and 4.10.17 to 20.10.17 | |
| 216 Sanit. Section | 1.10.17 | | ONLY | |
| 200 N.G.C. | 1.10.17 | | ONLY and 4.10.17 to 20.10.17 | |
| H.Q. 59 Divn. | 1.10.17 | | to 20.10.17 | |
| H.Q. 59 R.A. | 1.10.17 | | to 20.10.17 | |
| 2/3 Field Ambulance | 2.10.17 | | to 31.10.17 | |

O.C. No. 9 Coy 59 A.W.

Confidential.

Vol 10

# War Diary

of

Headquarters, 59th Divisional Train

Vol. X.

1st November 1917 to 30th November 1917

# WAR DIARY or INTELLIGENCE SUMMARY

Army Form C. 2118.

Vol. X

Headquarters 39th Divisional Train
Ref: Photos LENS 11 Sheet 57c Reel 57c

| Place | Date 1917 | Hour | Summary of Events and Information | Remarks and references to Appendices |
|---|---|---|---|---|
| CHATEAU-de-la-HAIE | Nov 1 | | Reached BARLIN Refilling Points for 176, 177 and 178 Bde. Troops. LIGHT Ry. SIDING CARENCY. | K.B |
| " | 3 | | R.P. for Div Troops X.3.C. | K.B |
| | | | R.H. and R.P's same as 1st inst. Air/c No 4 Coy. horses found shoe oil/rat-a-arsenic/R.S. | K.B |
| | 8 | | Light worn on VIMY RIDGE | K.B |
| | | | R.H. and R.P's no change R.H (Mules) 700 steel plates for (Mule Rail show ing) issued to No 2 Coy. | K.B |
| | 11 | | 39th Divisional Rail Hd for 3 mounts to rest | K.B |
| | 14 | | R.H. & R.P's same as 11th inst. No 4 Coy. moved to No. 3 Camp. DUISANS officer's billetting at CARENCY | K.B |
| | | | R.P. for Div Troops 176 & 177 Bde. Troops. BARLIN R.H. for 178 Bde. Troops AGNEZ-lez-DUISANS | K.B |
| | 17 | | R.H. for 178 Bde. C-o-y moved to M.12.A.9.C. Sheet 57c. Capt SA THORNBERY admitted to Corps. | K.B |
| | | | Rest Station. Lt. J.N. BROWN continued this duty of actg. Adjt. | K.B |
| | | | R.H. for 39th Divisional Artillery BARLIN ( ed by S.S.O. 1st Canadian Division R.H for 176 Bde. 6r Trally | K.B |
| | | | attached to 177 Bde. Troops for feeding. BAIN, HEADQUARTERS moved to HERMAVILLE No. 3 Coy. work 178 Bde | K.B |
| HERMAVILLE | 18 | | moved to CARENCY to WANQUITIN | K.B |
| | | | R.H. 176 Bde. BARLIN R.H. 177 & 178 Bdes. AGNEZ-lez-DUISANS R.P. 176 Bde. CARENCY 177 Bde. NOYELETTE | K.B |
| | 19 | | 178 Bde. same as 15th inst. French interpreter permanently attached to Trans H.Q. | K.B |
| | | | R.H. no change R.P's 176 & 177 Bde no change. 178 Bde. R.P. on DUISANS-AGNES Road | K.B |
| | | | T.H.Q. moved from HERMAVILLE to BASSEUX. No 2 Coy moved from CARENCY to SIMENCOURT | K.B |
| | | | No. 3 Coy moved from WANQUITIN to BAILLEUAL. All moves were carried out by hand. | K.B |
| BASSEUX | 20 | | R.H. " BOISLEUX " R.P's 176 Bde. SIMENCOURT 177 on BASSEUX-BAILLEUAL road 178 on BLAIREVILLE-HENDECOURT | K.B |
| | | | " DUISANS to HENDECOURT | K.B |
| | 21 | | Second Line 20 from parcel all towns in the Division | K.B |
| | | | R.H. & R.P's no change. T.H.Q. moved from BASSEUX to ACHIET-le-PETIT | K.B |
| | | | No 2 Coy " " SIMENCOURT to COURCELLES-le-COMPT | all moved |
| | | | No 3 Coy " " WANQUITIN to ACHIET-le-PETIT | carried out |
| | | | No 4 Coy " " HENDECOURT to GOMIECOURT | by Lt Inf } |
| ACHIET-le-Petit | 22 | | R.H. ACHIET-le-GRAND R.P's 176 Bde. A.21.B. 178 Bde. A.28.6. 177 Bde. R.H.B. Sheet 57c. | K.B |
| | 23 | | R.H. & R.P's same as 22nd inst. 177.Q. moved from ACHIET-le-PETIT to ESTRICOURT } Train Corps arrived | K.B |
| | | | No 2 Coy " " COURCELLES " HEUDECOURT } by road. Infantry | K.B |
| | | | No 3 Coy " " ACHIET-le-PETIT " DESART WOOD } moved by Rail. | K.B |
| | | | No 4 Coy " " GOMIECOURT " EQUANCOURT | K.B |
| ETRICOURT | 24 | | R.H. FINS R.P's for the three Bde. Groups V.12.C.5.2 Sheet 57c. Supplies drawn from R.H. same | K.B |
| | | | by supply section of the Train limits drawn from R.P. by Bde. Transport on Baggage Wagons | K.B |
| | 25 | | R.H. same as 24th Suffolks covered from R.H. & R.P. by Light Railway R.P's moved | K.B |
| | | | from V.12.C.5.2 as follows 176 to N.14.B.56 177 Bde to W.I.d.2.8 178 Bde | K.B |
| | | | Supplies of 178 Bde unloaded from Ly. Ry. at P.25.a. Re from here by Train Wagons 6 EQUANCOURT | K.B |

# WAR DIARY
## or
## INTELLIGENCE SUMMARY.

Army Form C. 2118.

Vol X Sheet 2

Headquarters 59th Divisional Train

| Place | Date 1917 | Hour | Summary of Events and Information | Remarks and references to Appendices |
|---|---|---|---|---|
| ETRICOURT | Nov 27 | | R.H. and R.Ps. Iexchange Supply wagons of Nos. 2 & 3 Coys had to be hurriedly called in from Convoy with R.E. material as 176 & 177 Bdes were moving. Wagons accompanied Units on march * returned to Coy Lines for the night | App 3 |
| | 28 | | R.H. & R.Ps. In Change Nos. 2 & 3 Coys moved to Q.25. Central Ref. Sheet 57.C LT. J.H. BROWN appointed Adjutant 59th Divisional Train from 18/11/17 vice Capt. S.R. THORNSBERY. | App 3 |
| | 29 | | R.H. In change of R.Ps. to 176 and 177 Bdes, Q.25.C. No.1 78 Bde E9 advanced | App 3 |
| | 30 | | R.H. to Change to Nos. 2,3 & 4 Coys. 59th Divisional Train ordered to move to LECHELLES at | App 3 |
| | | 12.30 p.m. | Nos. 2 & 3 Coys to A.25.C.5.6 " 4 " to A.25.C.6.3 | App 3 |

Haylor+Kent Col
COMMANDING 59TH DIVISIONAL TRAIN

Confidential

War Diary
of
513 Coy ASC
59 Division.

Vol. 10 — Nov 1917.

G.

Army Form C. 2118.

# WAR DIARY
## INTELLIGENCE SUMMARY.
*(Erase heading not required.)*

Instructions regarding War Diaries and Intelligence Summaries are contained in F. S. Regs., Part II and the Staff Manual respectively. Title pages will be prepared in manuscript.

| Place | Date | Hour | Summary of Events and Information | Remarks and references to Appendices |
|---|---|---|---|---|
| In the Field. | 1/11/17 to 2/11/17 | — | Company in Camp at ABLAIN. ST. NAZAIRE. Refilling Point in Camp. Supplies received by Deckauville Rly to Camp. Drawn in Skeltons. | |
| | 5/11/17 | — | 2 Rides (dismounted) received from "D" Batty 295 Bgde Ata. | |
| | 13/11/17 | — | 1 Ride Force Force. No 150. | |
| | 15/11/17 | — | Cpt. & Adj. S. R. Townsbery admitted to Give les Station and transferred to I.C.C.S. | |
| | 16/11/17 | — | I.O.D. received from D.H.Q. Capt. & Adj. S. Townsbery evacuated to 22 C.C.S. | |
| | 29/11/17 | — | Company moved by Narrow route from ABLAIN. ST. NAZAIRE to ESTREES' COUCHIE. Men in Shackletts. Lorries. Open Skeltons. Supplies drawn from BARLIN Railhead by Motor Lorry. | |
| | 30/11/17 | — | Company moved by March Route from ESTREES' COUCHIE to ARRAS ("A" AREA). Men in Barracks. Horses in open on lines. Supplies drawn from BARLIN RAILHEAD by Motor Lorry. Move not yet completed. | |

R. A. Buckley Capt.
Commdg 575 Coy A.S.C. 59 Division.

CONFIDENTIAL.

# WAR DIARY
## of
O.C. No 2 Company, 59th Divisional Train

### Vol. X

1st November 1917 - 16 - 30 November 1917.

Army Form C. 2118.

# WAR DIARY
## INTELLIGENCE SUMMARY
*(Erase heading not required.)*

Vol. X

No 2 Coy. 59 Div. TRAIN.

Instructions regarding War Diaries and Intelligence Summaries are contained in F.S. Regs., Part II. and the Staff Manual respectively. Title Pages will be prepared in manuscript.

| Place | Date | Hour | Summary of Events and Information | Remarks and references to Appendices |
|---|---|---|---|---|
| CARENCY. | 1917 1st Nov | — | Commenced work with normal Brigade Group. Unit drew supplies by 1st Line TRANSPORT. Train wagons employed on Road making and general services within Div. Area. Attachments with 122 Labour Coy, ARM.Y Corps, 59 Div Wing I Corps Reinforcement Camp. #69 + #70 Field Co R.E. + 2/3 N.M. Field Amb. Rations ex Brigade Group, 2/1 N.M. Brit Amb. Transferred to 177th Inf. Bde. Group. | TWR. |
| " | 14th " | | Baggage wagons dispatched to all units. | TWR. |
| " | 18th " | | Supplies drawn by Train Transport. Moved Bdy. Hdqs. - Supply Section from CARENCY to SIMENCOURT under orders | TWR. |
| SIMENCOURT. | 19th " | | of 176th Inf. Bde. | TWR. |
| " | 20th " | | #69 + #70 Brit Co. R.E. proceeded to join 177th +178th Inf. Bdes respectively. Refilling point SIMENCOURT to 20th 21st Second mob ration vans accompanied Brigade Groups. 2/1 N.M. Brit Amb marched by night from SIMENCOURT via RAMPART, ADINGER and AYETTE to | TWR. |
| COURCELLES 21/22. | | | Marlin orders of 176th Inf. Bde. | TWR. |
| HEUDICOURT | 23rd | | COURCELLES LE COMTE and encamped. Refilling point at S.E. end of COURCELLES. Under orders of Hdqrs. 59 Div. Train moved from COURCELLES LE COMPTE via BAPAUME, LE TRANSLOY and LECHELLE to HEUDICOURT. and delivered supplies on arrival. | TWR. |
| " | 24th " | | Refilling Point and Railhead at FINS. | TWR. |
| " | 26th " | | Supplies drawn from R.P. FINS with Baggage wagons. Moved R.P. from FINS to near HEUDICOURT (W.14.6. - Sheet 57c). #67 Brit Co. R.E. transferred to 177th Bde. Group. | TWR. |
| " | 26th " | | 10 despatch on R.E. Convoy FINS to HEUDICOURT. 2/6 - 2/7 Glenwood Battalion attd. to Bde. Group march 28th Nov | TWR. |
| " | 27th " | | 6 wagons on R.S. Convoy HEUDICOURT to TYKE DUMP + CRUZEAUCOURT, 4 wagons on R.E. Convoy Fins to HEUDICOURT. 2/6 Glen (Notts) running to RIBECOURT area. Dispatch'd wagons at 2.15 p.m. return to Rail III wagons + dispatch same to unit as crop supplies on Brigade. Supply Convoy Coy. Hdqrs. atrd by and collected same at night at HEUDICOURT | TWR. |
| " | 28th " | 1 p.m. | Refilled at 8 a.m. Dispatch'd wagons of 6 + 7 Sherwoods as note of 59 Div Train. #67 Brit Co. R.E. returned to Brigade Group. joining orders till 1 p.m. It was a limits on Road from FINS to METZ (Q.25.c. - sheet 57c). Supply Convoy proceeded via VILLERS. Moved Coy Hdqrs. | TWR. |
| FINS - METZ Rd. Sheet 57c. | 29 | 11 a.m. | PLUICH with divided supplies at RIBECOURT and FLESQUIERES. Refilled and delivered supplies in RIBECOURT and FLESQUIERES. Camp shelled from 7.30 a.m. to 5.12 noon. Refill order was old unstill supply wagons under bed. Received orders to move to LECHELLE 4 p.m. (P.25.c.8.8. - sheet 57c) and delivered supplies | TWR. |
| " | 30 | | Coy. Hdqrs. + Supply Section to LECHELLE area. Moved at 1.30 a.m. via YTRES - HERMIES - HATRICOURT - HERMIES and arrived LECHELLE Group 5 p.m. Supply wagons of #67 Brit Co R.E. and 119/176 Inf. Tk Bn. Getd. by. Despatched Supply Convoy of full Brigade Group at 3 a.m. on morning of 1st Dec. Supply wagons will 6 horses for an hour. Rates were under fire at RIBECOURT and FLESQUIERES and after driving to reserve some rations taken, but took S.W. of FLESQUIERES. One male horse got on wound, Robins mules lost + found lost. | TWR. |

M. Hagland Capt
OC N°2 Coy. 59 Div Train.

Confidential

War Diary
of
515 Coy. A.S.C. 59th Division
from 1-11-17 to 30-11-17.
(Volume X)

Army Form C. 2118.

# WAR DIARY
## INTELLIGENCE SUMMARY
(Erase heading not required.)

| Place | Date | Hour | Summary of Events and Information | Remarks and references to Appendices |
|---|---|---|---|---|
| MATIGNY | 1/11/17 | | 375th Coy A.S.C 59th Divn November 1917 | |
| " | | | In quarters | |
| " | | | 2/Lieut. N. Todd reported to 514 Coy | |
| " | | | 2/Lieut. A. Jackstedter reported to 516 Coy (vice 2/Lieut W. Todd) | |
| " | | | H.Q.'s 179th & 7th Am Col 179th Bde ⎫ Taken on ration strength 1st to 9th | |
| " | | | 303 Batt. R.F.A. 463rd Batt. R.F.A. ⎬ | |
| " | | | 100 Fat. Coy taken on ration strength 1st to 5th | |
| " | | | Batt'n T.A. French No. 2 Ballon Coy, 469th F.E. taken on Rat-strength 1st to 673 | |
| " | | | 59th Divl. Grenade Dump taken on 3rd to 15th | |
| " | 3/11/17 | | 2 Drivers Reinforcements received | |
| " | 5/11/17 | | 1 Driver transferred to 516 Coy | |
| " | " | | 1 Driver evacuated | |

A Green Capt.
OC 375 Coy 59th Divn

**Army Form C. 2118.**

# WAR DIARY
## or
## INTELLIGENCE SUMMARY

*(Erase heading not required.)*

Instructions regarding War Diaries and Intelligence Summaries are contained in F. S. Regs., Part II. and the Staff Manual respectively. Title Pages will be prepared in manuscript.

515 Coy A.S.C. 59th Divn.  Summary of Events and Information  November 1917

| Place | Date | Hour | Summary of Events and Information | Remarks and references to Appendices |
|---|---|---|---|---|
| CARENCY | 6/11/17 | | 1 Driver transferred to 516 Coy | A/9 |
| " | 8/11/17 | | Detachment on duty with I Corps Troops Supply Col. Returns Coy | B/9 |
| " | 10/11/17 | | 1 Cyclist Pair Corps transferred to 17th Divl Train | C/9 |
| " | 13/11/17 | | 1 Driver Reinforcement received | D/9 |
| " | 14/11/17 | | 200 A.S.C. taken in Ration strength | E/9 |
| " | " | | 2/1st NMFA HQrs 59th Divn M.M.P. G.R.E. 59th Divl. Repair DADOS Divl Laundry THQs | Again in Ration Strength 14th to 25th inst. |
| " | 17/11/17 | 11.30 a.m. | Coy HQrs moved by road to WANQUETIN | F/9 |
| " | " | 4:0 p.m. | " Billets | G/9 |
| WANQUETIN | 17/11/17 | | Mot. Vet. Sect. Troops taken into Ration Strength 12th to 21st | H/9 |
| " | 18/11/17 | | | I/9 |

Kilbee. Capt.
O.C. 515 Coy A.S.C. 59th Divn.

# WAR DIARY / INTELLIGENCE SUMMARY

Army Form C. 2118.

**515 Coy A.S.C. 59th Divn** November 1917

| Place | Date | Hour | Summary of Events and Information | Remarks and references to Appendices |
|---|---|---|---|---|
| WANQUETIN | 19/11/17 | 5.30 a.m. | Coy H.Q.rs move by road to BAILLEULVAL | RG |
| BAILLEULVAL | " | 8.0 p.m. | In Billets | RG |
| " | 21/11/17 | 11.30 a.m. | 464th Coy R.E. taken on Car strength 21st to 30th | RG |
| " | 21/11/17 | | Coy H.Q.rs with Supplies Bde Group moved by road ACHIET LE PETIT. | RG |
| ACHIET LE PETIT | 22/11/17 | 6.30 a.m. | In Camp | RG |
| " | 23/11/17 | 9.30 p.m. | Coy H.Q.rs with Supplies Bde Group moved by road to DESSART WOOD (W.1.a about 5.9°) | RG |
| DESSART WOOD | 23/11/17 | 9.0 p.m. | In Camp | RG |
| " | 25/11/17 | | X Batt. 59th T.M.B. taken on ration strength 25th to 29th | RG |
| " | 26/11/17 | | 467 Coy R.E. 470th Coy R.E. taken on Ration strength 26th to 29th | RG |
| " | 26/11/17 | 9.30 a.m. | Coy H.Q.rs moved by road to FINS. | RG |

Reden Capt.
OC 515 Coy A.S.C. 59th Divn

# WAR DIARY
## INTELLIGENCE SUMMARY

575 Coy A.S.C. 59th Divn — November 1917

| Place | Date | Hour | Summary of Events and Information | Remarks and references to Appendices |
|---|---|---|---|---|
| FINS | 26/11 | 11.0 | In Billets | |
| " | 28/11 | 11.0 | Coy H.Q. to meet supplies. Pole Group moved to Ronl to Q.2.S. Central 57.c. | |
| Q.2.S. Central Sheet 57.c. | 29/11 | n | In Camp | |
| " | 30/11 | 4.0 | The Camp and lines heavily shelled by enemy artillery from 7.0 to 2.0 | |
| " | 30/11 | 7.15 | Coy H.Q. to meet supplies. Pole Group moved by road to LECHELLE | |
| " | 30/11 | 2.0 | | |
| LECHELLE | 30/11 | 6.0 | In Camp | |

General result of the company during the month was very heavy losses
But horses are losing condition

Ebreu Capt
O.C. 575 Coy A.S.C. 59th Divn

Confidential

War Diary

of

O.C., 516 Coy. A.S.C. 59th Division

From :— 1/11/17    To :— 30/11/17

Volume 10.

# WAR DIARY or INTELLIGENCE SUMMARY

Army Form C. 2118.

*(Erase heading not required.)*

Instructions regarding War Diaries and Intelligence Summaries are contained in F. S. Regs., Part II. and the Staff Manual respectively. Title Pages will be prepared in manuscript.

| Place | Date | Hour | Summary of Events and Information | Remarks and references to Appendices |
|---|---|---|---|---|
| CARENCY | 1.11.17 | | C.R.E inspects camp — A.D.M.S inspects camp — | N/ |
| | 2.11.17 | | Baggage wagons went for R.E. night work on VIMY RIDGE — | N/ |
| | 3.11.17 | | 1.O.R admitted to Hospital. | N/ |
| | 5.11.17 | | 2 drivers report to Duty and are taken ON Strength — 7 O.R. inoculated. | N/ |
| | 6.11.17 | | C.R.E inspects camp — 1 O.R taken ON Strength — 1 O.R admitted to Hospital — | N/ |
| | 9.11.17 | | Draw of horses striking to Company — | N/ |
| | 12.11.17 | | 1.O.R admitted to Hospital — 1 O.R reports for duty + is taken ON Strength — | N/ |
| | 13.11.17 | | Baggage wagons went to Vimy — | N/ |
| DUISANS | 14.11.17 | 1.30 PM | Company moves to DUISANS — Supply dump AGNEZ-LES-DUISANS — | N/ |
| | 15.11.17 | | Baggage wagons report from Vimy | N/ |
| | 17.11.17 | | 1.O.R. discharged from Hospital | N/ |
| | 19.11.17 | 2 a.m | Baggage wagons went to Vimy — 1 O.R. evacuated to C.C.S sick off Strength — | N/ |
| HENDECOURT | 21.11.17 | 4.0 P.M | Coy moves to HENDECOURT — | N/ |
| | | | Coy moves to GOMIECOURT — | N/ |
| GOMIECOURT | 23.11.17 | 10.0 AM | Coy moves to EQUANCOURT — Supply dump at FINS — | N/ |
| EQUANCOURT | 24.11.17 | | Supply wagons went to Railhead — 1 Cpl transferred to Stables — Baggage wagons return | N/ |
| | 25.11.17 | | 1 W.O.II admitted to hospital + taken off Strength — 1 O.R taken ON Strength from 2.C.S | N/ |
| | 26.11.17 | | Stable Dumps moves to EQUANCOURT — | N/ |
| | 29.11.17 | | Baggage wagons are sent to Vimy — 1.O.R admitted to Hospital — | N/ |
| | | | Supply Dump moves to METZ — | N/ |
| METZ | 30.11.17 | 9.0 AM | Coy moves to METZ — Camber are shelled — Coy moves to LECHELLE | N/ |
| | | | NEUVILLE-BOURJONVAL – HAVRINCOURT road — Supply Dump to | M/ |

A. Rutherford Capt.
O.C 48 Coy 5th Div. Train A.S.C

**Army Form C. 2118.**

**WAR DIARY** or **INTELLIGENCE SUMMARY**
*(Erase heading not required.)*

Instructions regarding War Diaries and Intelligence Summaries are contained in F. S. Regs., Part II. and the Staff Manual respectively. Title Pages will be prepared in manuscript.

| Place | Date | Hour | Summary of Events and Information | Remarks and references to Appendices |
|---|---|---|---|---|
| November 1917 | | | Unit composition showing 178 & 178 Infantry Brigade Groups:— | |
| | | | | FROM | TO |
| | | | Headquarters 178 2nd Brigade | 1.11.17 | 30.11.17 |
| | | | New Books Sig Signal Coy | 1.11.17 | 30.11.17 |
| | | | 2/5 Sherwood Foresters | " | " |
| | | | 2/6 Sherwood Foresters | " | 29.11.17 arrival 29.11.17 To 30.11.17 |
| | | | 2/7 Sherwood Foresters | " | 29.11.17 ... 29.11.17 . 30.11.17 |
| | | | 2/8 Sherwood Foresters | " | 29.11.17 ... 29.11.17 . 30.11.17 |
| | | | 178 T.M.B. | " | 30.11.17 |
| | | | 175 M.G.C. | 1.11.17 | 30.11.17 |
| | | | 470 Coy R.E. | " | 30.11.17 |
| | | | S.C. Coy A.S.C. | " | 13.11.17 ... 22.11.17 & 30.11.17 |
| | | | 2/3 2/1st Ambulance R.A.M.C. | " | 30.11.17 |
| | | | S.C.H.A. Dinkyville Dump | 1.11.17 | 13.11.17 |
| | | | 86 Labour Coy | 1.11.17 | 13.11.17 |
| | | | 331 Road Construction Coy | 1.11.17 | 13.11.17 |
| | | | E.A.A Battery | 1.11.17 | 13.11.17 |
| | | | 59 Schemes Coy | 3.11.17 | 13.11.17 |
| | | | 50 Labour Coy | 14.11.17 | 13.11.17 |
| | | | 2/1 D.A. R.A.M.C. | 21.11.17 | 30.11.17 |
| | | | 200 M.G.C. | 21.11.17 | 25.11.17 |
| | | | S.A.O Section D.A.C. | 26.11.17 | 30.11.17 |
| | | | Headquarters 59 Division | 26.11.17 | 30.11.17 |
| | | | 59 M.M.P. | 26.11.17 | 30.11.17 – 30.11.17 |
| | | | 59 Traffic | | |

(CONTINUED)

Army Form C. 2118.

# WAR DIARY
## or
## INTELLIGENCE SUMMARY

*(Erase heading not required.)*

| Place | Date | Hour | Summary of Events and Information | Remarks and references to Appendices |
|---|---|---|---|---|
| | | | CONTINUED:- | |
| | | | SR Signal Cox R.E.    From 26.11.17 To 30.11.17 | |
| | | | HQ 5g Div R.E.                26.11.17      30.11.17 | |
| | | | 21 Mobile Vet-Sectn.           26.11.17      30.11.17 | |
| | | | DADOS 5g Division              26.11.17      30.11.17 | |
| | | | HQ 5g Div Train A.S.C.         26.11.17      30.11.17 | |
| | | | X Batten T.M.B.                30.11.17 | |

Instructions regarding War Diaries and Intelligence Summaries are contained in F. S. Regs., Part II. and the Staff Manual respectively. Title Pages will be prepared in manuscript.

**Army Form C. 2118.**

# WAR DIARY
## or
## INTELLIGENCE SUMMARY.
*(Erase heading not required.)*

**WAR DIARY** of **Headquarters 59th Divisional Train**

**Vol. XI**

Instructions regarding War Diaries and Intelligence Summaries are contained in F.S. Regs., Part II. and the Staff Manual respectively. Title pages will be prepared in manuscript.

| Place | Date | Hour | Summary of Events and Information | Remarks and references to Appendices |
|---|---|---|---|---|
| ETRICOURT | 1 Dec | | Railhead FREMICOURT. Refilling Points 176, 177, 178 Bdes at P.17.a. | App B |
| VALLULART WOOD | 3rd " | | Train Headquarters moved to VALLULART WOOD | App B |
| " | " | | R.H. and R.P's same as 2nd. Nos. 2 & 4 Coys moved from LACHELLES to P.17.d. No. 3 Coy from LACHELLES to P.18.c | App B |
| LITTLE WOOD | 5th " | | Train Headquarters moved to LITTLE WOOD | App B |
| " | 8th " | | R.P's & R.H. no change. Supplies were drawn from T.R.H.'s. Kirver by 1st line transport. Owing to no supplies being brought up to R.H. No. 24. Outpost train Transport organised by D.H.O. brought supplies from R.H. to N. 24. Outpost trains | App B |
| " | 10 " | | Nos. 1 T.H.Q. Remained. Cores drawn for the Train | 2 App B |
| " | 12 " | | Nos. 2, 3rd & 4 Coys moved to P.27.a. | App B |
| " | 13 " | | No. 1 Coy moved into Bivouac Area at NEUVILLE | App B |
| " | 15 " | | Refilling Points moved to P.21. 29.B.A.F.A. Bde lorries on feeding through 2 Divisions | App B |
| " | 16 " | | Iron Rations to FLESQUIERES & tomorrow moved to P. 26. 6. 3. 9. | App B |
| " | | | 1000 Iron Rations. Train Headquarters moved to P.10.a.3.13. | App B |
| " | | | R.H. & R.P.'s no change | P.7.6.6.8 MAR 3/6/Net 576 |
| " | | | Nos. 1 Coy 2, 3 & 4 Coys | App B |
| YTRES | 20 " | | All rifles & small arms moved to R.P.6 on YTRES-BEATINCOURT road. No 2 Coy | App B |
| " | | | T.H. FREMICOURT Refill Points R.P.6 Incorps. to Q.10.a. Q.6 6 Morl. & 6 South. Stoffs transport moved under orders of O.C. | App B |
| " | 21 " | | No. 2 Coy moved to ROCQUIGNY | App B |
| " | 22 " | | R.H. FREMICOURT. R.P's 176 Bde on BARASTRE-HAPLINCOURT road 178 Bde ROCQUIGNY | App B |
| " | 23 " | | No 3 Coy moved to ROCQUIGNY. No 4 Coy moved to BEAULENCOURT | App B |
| ACHIET LE PETIT | 24 " | | Train Headquarters moved to ACHIET L PETIT | App B |
| " | 25 " | | Railhead ROCQUIGNY as transport of Division moved to ACHIET L PETIT | App B |
| " | | | Railhead ROCQUIGNY R.P's H.34.c.6.4. for 176 Bde + Outposts | App B |
| " | | | All transport moved over " H. 1. c. 2.1 " 177 " + Outposts | App B |
| " | | | orders of O.C. Train & two area " H. 14.a.2.2 " 178 | App B |
| " | | | No. 2 Coy " " " to " | App B |
| " | | | " 3 " " " " 6 AMBRINES | App B |
| " | | | " 4 " " " " HOUVIN | App B |
| ETREE WAMIN | 26 " | | Railhead FREVENT R.P's H.36.c.6.6. on Light Railway at ETREE | App B |
| " | 31 " | | Railhead FREVENT. R.P's Same as 26. 5th Divl Artillery joined Divison | App B |

W. Brown
CAPT. & ADJT.
59th DIVISIONAL TRAIN

_Confidential_

# WAR DIARY

- of -

O.C. 513 Coy ASC 59 Div.

from 1st to 31st December 1917.

( Vol. 10.)

Army Form C. 2118.

# WAR DIARY
## or
## INTELLIGENCE SUMMARY
*(Erase heading not required.)*

Instructions regarding War Diaries and Intelligence Summaries are contained in F.S. Regs., Part II. and the Staff Manual respectively. Title Pages will be prepared in manuscript.

| Place | Date | Hour | Summary of Events and Information | Remarks and references to Appendices |
|---|---|---|---|---|
| In the Field. | 1/12/17 | | Company moved by March Route from ARRAS to COURCELLES. Supplies drawn by Div Supply Col. from ACHIET-LE-GRAND. | |
| | 2/12/17 | | Company moved by March route to HAPLINCOURT. New quarters in Nissen huts & screen in Shelters. ACHIET-LE-GRAND. | |
| | 4/12/17 | | 2/Lieut R.R. DIBBEN A.S.C. to be temporary Lieut. as from 1st July 1917. (Authority pub GR.No 4/12/17) | |
| | 6/12/17 | | Lieut. (T. Capt.) S.R. Jambery ASC. was transferred to England "Sick" 22/11/17 and struck off the formation accordingly. (Vide List No. 970 6-12-17) Lieut G. Brown is appointed adjt. of 59 Div from VICE Capt. S.R. Jambery from 16/11/17. (Authority Div. G. A56 1389 22-11-7) | |
| | 9/12/17 | | 2/Lieut J.R. Brown ASC is appointed Actg. Captain with pay and allowances as Lieut. whilst employed as Adjt. 59 Div from (Auth G/HQ List 165 of 1917) Company moved by Route March from HAPLINCOURT to NEUVILLE. Quarters in Nissen huts. Nissen Huts. Supplies drawn by Div Sup Col. from FREMICOURT. | |
| | 12/12/17 | | | |
| | 16/12/17 | | Company moved by Route March from NEUVILLE to RYAUX COURT. New quarters in huts and ruined buildings. Leave in Shelters. Supplies drawn by Div. Supply Col. from FREMI COURT. | |

2449  Wt. W14957/M90 750,000 1/16 J.B.C. & A. Forms/C.2118/12.

Army Form C. 2118.

# WAR DIARY
or
## INTELLIGENCE SUMMARY
(Erase heading not required.)

Instructions regarding War Diaries and Intelligence Summaries are contained in F. S. Regs., Part II. and the Staff Manual respectively. Title Pages will be prepared in manuscript.

| Place | Date | Hour | Summary of Events and Information | Remarks and references to Appendices |
|---|---|---|---|---|
| In Field | 19/11/17 | | Capt. J.C. Jaupes R.S.O. granted leave to U.K. from 19/11/17 to 2/12/18 inclusive. | |
| | 20/11/17 | | No. 4440 Pte J. Blain A.S.C. reported for duty with the formation from A.S.C. Base Depot. Same was ordered to proceed to No. 1 Cav. Sig. Dvl. Drm as Requisitioning Officer. | |
| | 29/11/17 | | Company moved by March Route from RUYAULCOURT to COURCELLES. Quartered in huts / canvas Stables on lines. Supplies drawn from FREMICOURT by Div Supply Coe. | |
| | 30/11/17 | | Company moved by March Route from COURCELLES to FOSSEUX. Quartered in huts / Canvas Shelters. Supplies drawn from M. BOISLEUX by Div Supply Coe. | |
| | 31/11/17 | | Company moved by March Route from FOSSEUX to LUCHEUX. Quartered in Billets and Barns. Horses on Lines. Supplies drawn from FREVANT by Div Supply Coe. and Refilling point at MILLY. | |

R. Crowley Capt.
O.C. 1 Cav S? S? B.E.F. France.

CONFIDENTIAL

WAR DIARY
— OF —
O.C. No 2 Coy. 59th Divisional Train

1st December 1917 to 31st December 1917.

VOL XI

Army Form C. 2118.

# WAR DIARY
## INTELLIGENCE SUMMARY
*(Erase heading not required.)*

Vol. XI

No 2 Coy. 59 Div. Train.

Instructions regarding War Diaries and Intelligence Summaries are contained in F.S. Regs., Part II. and the Staff Manual respectively. Title Pages will be prepared in manuscript.

| Place | Date | Hour | Summary of Events and Information | Remarks and references to Appendices |
|---|---|---|---|---|
| LECHELLE | 1917 1st Dec. | 5 p.m. | Reference Map Sheet 57C. Refilled at P.17.d.3.0 and delivered supplies to 4 Battery, 174 M. Gun Coy and 176 Bde. H.Q., 467 Field Coy R.E. and 2/3 N.M. Field Amb. in the Village of FLESQUIERES under considerable shell fire. Refilled from R.16.d., wagons of 467 Field Coy. R.E. which had been abandoned dropped under fire during previous night. Bound wagons of 176 Bde H.Q. (Supply) had become dismounted and shell fire. Both teams of Baggage wagon of H.Q. 176 Bde. H.Q. killed by shell fire at FLESQUIERES. Personals 176 horse & received one wounded by | Trans. |
| " | 2nd " | | Refilled at P.17.d.3.0 and delivered as on 1st. at R.16.d. dismounted and returned same camp shell fire. | Trans. |
| NEUVILLE | 3rd " | | Moved H.Qrs. of Coy to P.17.A.8.8. Delivered supplies as on 1st. | |
| " | 4th to 10th | | Supplies drawn from Refilling Point by Train Transport. | |
| " | 10th " | 9 a.m. | Came here at P.17.A.8.2. Horsed & ambushed to searches for my expedition of some hostile aircraft. Received 1 K.R. 2 H.D. reinforcements. | Trans. |
| YTRES | " | 2 p.m. | Moved H.Qrs. of Coy. under orders of H.Qrs 59 Div. train to GENERATING STATION, YTRES at P.27.a.5.9. Evacuated 1 H.D. horse. | Trans. |
| " | 11th " | | 1st time Transport of 6th North Staffs & 6th South Staffs remaining behind after baths moved to RUE attached to No 2 Coy, 59 Div. Train. Detachment of Transport drawing supplies with ration Transport. | Trans. |
| " | " | | Refilled Baggage Wagons from 6th North Staff & 6th South Staff. Moved Rations Transport to Railway CAMP WEST, LECHELLE. | Trans. |
| " | 12th " | | After Refilling moved Refilling Point to P.27.a.5.9. | |
| " | 13th " | 9 a.m. | Refilled at P.27.a.5.9 moving train wagons & delivering to 2/5 South & 2/5 North Staff & 174 M. Gun Coy at NEUVILLE. | Trans. |
| " | " | | 2/3 N.M. Fld. Amb at RUYAULCOURT & 467 Field Co. R.E. at METZ. And round transport trucks by 2/5 North & 2/5 South. | |
| BERTINCOURT | 16th " | 11 a.m. | Moved H.Qrs. of Coy to BERTINCOURT after refilling at P.27.a.59. | Trans. |
| " | 17th to 19th | | Staff. As usual Trains. Refilled in BERTINCOURT - YTRES area. | Trans. |
| BARASTRE | 20th " | | Moved H.Qrs. of Coy. and Details of 2/5 North & 2/5 South Staff to BARASTRE (D.10.a.1.2.) 467 Bd. Co. R.E. & 2/3 N.M. Fld. Amb. transferred as the Rear group for Supplies. Train wagons drew supplies as usual from FREMICOURT Railhead. | Trans. Trans. |
| " | 21st " | | Refilled at O.10.a.1.2. 15 1st Line Transport. | Trans. |
| " | 23rd " | | Refilled at O.10.a.2.2. 15 1st Line Transport Awaits during day for communication 24th 25th Dec. Train wagons drew supplies in bulk from | Trans. |
| " | 24th " | 7 a.m. | FREMICOURT Railhead and 467 Field Co R.E and 2/3 N.M. Field Amb. rations now issued through the Brigade Group Proceeded by march route in command of 67th horse Transport of 176 1st Bde Group via BARCOURT and BARAUNE & ACHIET LE PETIT and embarked for night | Trans. |
| ACHIET LE PETIT | 25th " | 7 a.m. 8.15 a.m. | Supply Section of Coy proceeded to ETREE WAMIN and drew supplies from Refilling point and delivered to Units of Brigade Group in BIENVILLERS, POMMIER, SAULTY, GRAND ROULLECOURT, and LIENCOURT as Brigade Area. Proceeded by march route in command of the Transport of 176 Brigade Group via BIENVILLERS, POMMIER - SAULTY - GRAND ROULLECOURT - LIENCOURT as Brigade Area. Route economical a transport of many difficulty. | Trans. |
| ETREE WAMIN | 26th to 31st | | Supplies drawn from R.P. McNAULT, at Refilling Point ETREE WAMIN shelter. Stable and Farrmrate work of horses. Condition of horses reasonably good, but large percentage of personnel suspected of mange in Dr. | Trans. |
| | | | T.W. Butler Duff Capt. OC. No2 Coy, 59 Div. Train. | |

2449 Wt. W14957/M90 759,000 1/16 J.B.C. & A. Forms/C.2118/12.

Confidential

War Diary
of
515 Coy. A.S.C. 59th Division

from 1-12-17 to 31-12-17

(Volume XI)

# WAR DIARY or INTELLIGENCE SUMMARY

Army Form C. 2118.

(Erase heading not required.)

515th Coy A.S.C. 59th Divn. — Summary of Events and Information — December 1917

| Place | Date | Hour | Summary of Events and Information | Remarks and references to Appendices |
|---|---|---|---|---|
| LECHELLE | 1/12/17 | | In Camp | |
| " | | | 1. H.D. Horse evacuated to M.V.S. | |
| " | 3/12/17 | 8.0 a.m. | Coy H.Q.s moved by road to HAVRINCOURT WOOD. P.I.R.U.4. 3 sheet 57c | |
| HAVRINCOURT WOOD | 3/12/17 | 3.0 p.m. | In Camp | |
| " | 4/12/17 | | 1 Driver wounded. 2 H.D. Horses killed. 2 H.D. Wounded + evacuated | |
| " | | | 2/1st Field Amb. came in ration strength | |
| " | 6/12/17 | | 1/Field Amb Jack Ross proceed to South Africa on 6 months leave | |
| " | | | 1 H.D. Horse wounded and evacuated | |
| " | 8/12/17 | | 1. R.D. and 3 H.D. 10 mounts received | |

Ashin Capt
O.C. 515 Coy A.S.C. 59 Divn

**Army Form C. 2118.**

# WAR DIARY
## or
## INTELLIGENCE SUMMARY
*(Erase heading not required.)*

Instructions regarding War Diaries and Intelligence Summaries are contained in F. S. Regs., Part II. and the Staff Manual respectively. Title Pages will be prepared in manuscript.

515 Coy A.S.C. 59th Divn.  December 1917.

| Place | Date | Hour | Summary of Events and Information | Remarks and references to Appendices |
|---|---|---|---|---|
| HAVRINCOURT WOOD | 10/12/17 | | 1 H.D. Horse evacuated to M.V.S. | AGE |
| " | 10/12/17 | | Coy H.Q. moved by road to Camp P.21.d. sheet 57C | AGE |
| CAMP P.21.d. | " | | In Camp | AGE |
| " | " | | 2/Lieut. F.G. TURTON reported and posted to the Coy | AGE |
| " | 11/12/17 | | 1 Pack Mule horse came on ration strength | AGE |
| " | 12/12/17 | | 1 Driver evacuated to CCS | AGE |
| " | 13/12/17 | | 1 " " " " " | AGE |
| " | 16/12/17 | | Iron Ration Comm Y/o Lieut A.J. Richard proceeded up to 1st Line Trenches | AGE |
| " | | | Coy H.Q. with Supply Wagons & Pole Group move by road to BERTINCOURT | AGE |
| BERTINCOURT | " | | In quarters | AGE |

A. Green Capt.
O.C. 515 Coy A.S.C. 59th Divn.

Army Form C. 2118.

# WAR DIARY
## INTELLIGENCE SUMMARY
*(Erase heading not required.)*

Instructions regarding War Diaries and Intelligence Summaries are contained in F. S. Regs., Part II. and the Staff Manual respectively. Title Pages will be prepared in manuscript.

Summary of Events and Information December 1917

515 Coy A.S.C. 59th Div.

| Place | Date | Hour | Summary of Events and Information | Remarks and references to Appendices |
|---|---|---|---|---|
| BERTINCOURT | 20/12/17 | | 1 Driver evacuated to C.C.S. | |
| " | 22/12 | 11.30 | Coy H.Q. with supply section of Bde Group moved from BERTINCOURT to ROCQUIGNY. | |
| ROCQUIGNY | 22/12 | 1.45 | In Camp | |
| " | " | | 469 Coy R.E. 2/3rd F.A. } came on ration strength | |
| " | " | | 467 Coy R.E. 1/3rd F.A. } | |
| " | 23/12 | | 200 M.G.C. came on ration strength | |
| " | 24/12 | 8.0 am | Coy H.Q. came by road to ACHIET LE PETIT. | |
| " | " | | A Command of all Transport of Bde Group on own wheels to Bivouac area. | |
| ACHIET LE PETIT | 24/12 | 4.0 pm | In Camp | |
| " | " | | H.Q. 59th Div. Salvage Coy. C.R.E. } ration strength from | |
| " | " | | Traffic Control. T.M.O.'s. C.M.A. } 24/12/17 to 25/12/17 |
| " | " | | 59 Div Laundry. M.M.P. M.V.S. | |
| " | " | | 59 Divl. Signals R.E. DADOS. | |

A. Brew Capt.
O.C. 515 Coy A.S.C. 59th Div.

Army Form C. 2118.

# WAR DIARY
## INTELLIGENCE SUMMARY
*(Erase heading not required.)*

Instructions regarding War Diaries and Intelligence Summaries are contained in F.S. Regs., Part II. and the Staff Manual respectively. Title Pages will be prepared in manuscript.

515 Cy. A.S.E. 59th Divn.                    December 1917

| Place | Date | Hour | Summary of Events and Information | Remarks and references to Appendices |
|---|---|---|---|---|
| ACHIET LE PETIT. | 25/12/17 | 8.30 a.m. | Coy. H.Qtrs. move by road to AMBRIENES. | |
| AMBRIENES | 25/12/17 | 10.0 a.m. | In Billets and quarters | |
| " | 27/12/17 | 8.0 a.m. | S.P.P. Annex took to ETRÉE WAMIN owing to severe weather and state of roads | |
| " | 31/12/17 | | In Billets and quarters. 4.H.Q. Reports received. General health of the Company during the month fairly good. Horses showing signs of falling off in condition owing to the severe strain of the move and continuous work | |

K Green Capt —
O.C. 515 Cy. A.S.E. 59 Divn

Confidential

War Diary
of

O.C., No. 4 Coy. 89th Divisional Train

From:- 1/12/17   To:- 31/12/17

Volume 11.

Army Form C. 2118.

# WAR DIARY
## or
## INTELLIGENCE SUMMARY

(Erase heading not required.)

Instructions regarding War Diaries and Intelligence Summaries are contained in F. S. Regs., Part II. and the Staff Manual respectively. Title Pages will be prepared in manuscript.

| Place | Date | Hour | Summary of Events and Information | Remarks and references to Appendices |
|---|---|---|---|---|
| LECHELLE | Dec 1st | | Supply wagons went 3 hours after refilling until information is received from Divn. Head Quarters as to the move of Q.M. Stores | M.C.T |
| LECHELLE | Dec 3rd | 2 P.M. | Coy moves by route march to edge of HAVRINCOURT WOOD – Accommodated in Tents. – Horses in open. – Supply Dump on NEVILLE – HAVRINCOURT WOOD road | M.C.T |
| HAVRINCOURT WOOD | Dec 5th | | Capt. H.R. GODDARD O.C. Coy admitted to Hospital – One Wheeler Driver taken ON strength – Lieut. F. PIGGEN A.S.C. assumes command of Coy. | M.C.T |
| " | Dec 6th | | One horse and one O.R. wounded by shell fire while out on Duty. Both evacuated well struck off strength. – Camp bombed by hostile aircraft 9. A.M. / No casualties. | M.C.T |
| " | Dec 7th | | One O.R. struck off strength. – | M.C.T |
| " | Dec 8th | | Clean underclothing issued to the Coy. | M.C.T |
| " | Dec 9th | | One O.R. (Dvr JOHNSON) severely wounded and two horses killed. – One O.R. (DRG.H.H.D.S) slightly wounded. | M.C.T |
| " | Dec 10 | | Coy proceeds by route march at 2 P.M. to YTRES – Horses in lines in Brickyard and men in Tents. – Camp is skilled as Coy is leaving. – One O.R. taken on strength. – Dvr. JOHNSON dies in 21st C.C.S. and is buried at Y 2 a 8.4 Sheet 57. C. – Two H.R. horses received from O.C. No 3 Coy. | M.C.T |
| YTRES | Dec 11th | | Hostile aircraft over camp at 7 A.M. – Two bombs dropped 50 yds from Wagon Park – No Casualties. – Supply Dump on YTRES – NEUVILLE ROAD – Bulk standings for horses started | M.C.T |

Army Form C. 2118.

# WAR DIARY
or
# INTELLIGENCE SUMMARY

(Erase heading not required.)

Instructions regarding War Diaries and Intelligence Summaries are contained in F. S. Regs., Part II. and the Staff Manual respectively. Title Pages will be prepared in manuscript.

| Place | Date | Hour | Summary of Events and Information | Remarks and references to Appendices |
|---|---|---|---|---|
| YTRES | Dec 12 | | BRICK standings for horses continued. — 9m Stores of Brigade Group now back to HAVRINCOURT WOOD | N.I. |
| " | Dec 13 | | One large sectional hut drawn and erection started | |
| " | Dec 14 | | One Supply Detail. evacuated to 2/1 C.C.S. and struck off strength | |
| " | Dec 15 | | Advance party of No 4 Coy 19th Div Train arrive to take over camp | |
| " | Dec 16 | | Coy move to BERTINCOURT by route march — Severe snow storm in afternoon. Supply Dump situated on BERTINCOURT - YTRES Road | |
| BERTINCOURT | Dec 17 | | Artificers shops are erected. — One O.R. evacuated and struck off strength. Severe frost — horses in stables and ruined buildings — men in huts. | |
| " | Dec 20 | | Advance party sent to ROCQUIGNY to take over from No4 Coy 17 Div Train | |
| " | Dec 21 | | Coy proceed by route march to ROCQUIGNY. — Wagon of 2/2 nm Field Ambulance 470 R.E. and 200 M.G.C. handed over to O.C. No 3 Coy 57th Div Train also one sick horse too ill to travel. Coy in Reinforcement Camp ROCQUIGNY — Advance party sent to BEAULENCOURT — Horses in stables — Men in huts. Coy 17th Div. Train. — Supply Dump at ROCQUIGNY - BARASTE Road | |
| ROCQUIGNY | Dec 22 | | Coy moves by Route march to BEAULENCOURT and is accommodated in same camp as 470 Field. Coy R.E. — Horses in stables — Men in huts. Supply Dump at LE TRANSLOY Sugar Factory. | |

2449 Wt. W14957/M90 750,000 1/16 J.B.C. & A. Forms/C.2118/12.

Army Form C. 2118.

# WAR DIARY
## or
## INTELLIGENCE SUMMARY

*(Erase heading not required.)*

Instructions regarding War Diaries and Intelligence Summaries are contained in F. S. Regs., Part II. and the Staff Manual respectively. Title Pages will be prepared in manuscript.

| Place | Date | Hour | Summary of Events and Information | Remarks and references to Appendices |
|---|---|---|---|---|
| BEAULENCOURT | Dec 24 | 7.30 AM | Coy move by route march to ACHIET-LE-PETIT and accommodated in tents for the night. Snow storm in evening. Wagons of 470 Field Coy R.E. and 2½ F.A. return to Coy horses in the open. | |
| ACHIET-LE-PETIT | Dec 25 | 6.30 AM | Coy proceed by route march to HOUYIN-HOUYIGNEUL. Rifling in over after arrival. Supply Dump opposite Coy H.Q. in village. Severe frost. Road very slippery and much snow. Coy in barns — horses in sheds and stables | |
| HOUYIN-HOUYIGNEUL | Dec 26 | | Being to severe frost supply dump moved to ESTRÉE-WAMIN station. Six horses required to bring each supply wagon from Dump to village owing to state of road. | |
| " | Dec 27 | | More stabling obtained — Baggage huts which have been with units over a month return to Coy. Arrangements made for leave parties from units for all supply wagons. | |
| " | Dec 25 | | Xmas dinners and Concert given to men of Coy in evening. | |

M Charleton Johnston Lt.
516 Coy ASC.

Army Form C. 2118.

# WAR DIARY
## *or*
## INTELLIGENCE SUMMARY

*(Erase heading not required.)*

| Place | Date | Hour | Summary of Events and Information | Remarks and references to Appendices |
|---|---|---|---|---|
| | | | The following units were rationed by Supply Officer 178 Infy Brigade on the dates of issue inclusive during the month of December 1917 | |
| | | | H.Q. 178 Infy. Brigade. 1.12.17 — 31.12.17. | |
| | | | No 4 Section 59 Div. Signals " " | |
| | | | 2/5 Sherwood Foresters " " | |
| | | | 2/6 " " " | |
| | | | 2/7 " " " | |
| | | | 2/8 " " " | |
| | | | 178 Trench Mortar Battery " " | |
| | | | 175 M.G.C. " " | |
| | | | No 4 Coy 59" Div Train " " | |
| | | | 2/2 Field Ambulance. 1.12.17 — 21.12.17. 24.12.17 — 31.12.17 | |
| | | | 470 Field Coy R.E 1.12.17 — 21.12.17 24.12.17 — 31.12.17 | |
| | | | 200 M.G.C. 1.12.17 — 18.12.17. | |
| | | | H.Q. 59th Division. 1.12.17 — 18.12.17. | |
| | | | H.Q. 59" Division Traffic " " | |
| | | | H.Q. " " Police " " | |
| | | | 59" Div Signals " " | |

# WAR DIARY
## or
## INTELLIGENCE SUMMARY

*(Erase heading not required.)*

Army Form C. 2118.

| Place | Date | Hour | Summary of Events and Information | Remarks and references to Appendices |
|---|---|---|---|---|
| | | | 2/1 Mobile Vet. Section. 1-12-17 — 18-12-17 | |
| | | | H.Q. R.E. 59" Division " | |
| | | | R.E. Workshops, 59" Div " | |
| | | | D.A.D.O.S. 59" Div. 1-12-17 — 4-12-17, 9-12-17 — 18-12-17 | |
| | | | Laundry 59" Div 1-12-17 — 18-12-17 | |
| | | | S.A.A. 59" D.A.C. " | |
| | | | X Batty T.M.B. R.A. " | |
| | | | Guards Div. Amb. Party. 1-12-17 — 10-12-17. | |
| | | | 36" Div. Burial Party " | |
| | | | 51" Div " " | |
| | | | Y & Z. Batty T.M.B. R.A. 9-12-17 — 18-12-17 | |
| | | | 59" Div Salvage Coy. 10-12-17 — 18-12-17 | |
| | | | 59" Div Amm R. Point. 13-12-17 — 18-12-17 | |
| | | | Y. Corps O.O. & P. Cable Section. 14-12-17 — 18-12-17 | |

M. Chastain / Johnston Lt.
516 Coy A.S.C.

Confidential

War-Diary of
Headquarters 54th Division 6 Force
from 1-1-16 to 31-1-16

Volume I

Army Form C. 2118.

# WAR DIARY
## or
## INTELLIGENCE SUMMARY.
(Erase heading not required.)

VOL. XII

Headquarters 59th Divisional Train

Instructions regarding War Diaries and Intelligence Summaries are contained in F. S. Regs., Part II. and the Staff Manual respectively. Title pages will be prepared in manuscript.

| Place | Date | Hour | Summary of Events and Information | Remarks and references to Appendices |
|---|---|---|---|---|
| ETREE WAMIN | July | | Train Headquarters and No 2 Coy billeted at ETREE WAMIN No 1 Coy & Grooms No 3 Coy of Amazines No 4 Coy at HOUVIN all in Billets. Horses in G48. Received ready to move at 4.8 hours notice. Railhead FREVENT. Refilling point for 59th Division MP44 APs No 176,177 +178 at DREUIL ETREE WAMIN Station Supplies drawn from RH LUCHEUX 1 Serjeant and from RH & ETREE WAMIN 1. | |
| | | | 1 Halalary. All h. fft reads to Unit. AM tore by Tank transport from APs | |
| | 12.1.18 | | OC 59th Div Train proceeded to England on 14 days leave. Major VD Courth DSO took | |
| | | | command of 59th Div Train | |
| | 19.1.15 | | Supply Section of Train Inspected by Divisional Commander at IRP | |
| | 22.1.18 | | Two Drivers & HD Horses + 28 Waggons of the complete Train (4 on 4) being left by Waggon C/75st Inft Inft Reft were handed over to Remount Army Clearing Kennel G. Paris and were shown on the Strength of No 2 Coy all correspondence with restrictions from 59 Tr Hdq | |
| | 27.1.18 | | J. Col T. HAZZELRIGG DSO returned from leave & assumed command of 59th Div Train | |
| | 28.1.18 | | 467+468 Field Coys RE required a second limber at 4 hp supply waggon each handed journed will not take new area on 29 inst | |
| | 30.1.18 | | The Two firm carts lent to Army Clearing Depot HOMIET 6. GRAND ont of 22nd inst returned to No 2 Coy, 59th Divl Train | |

MAP Ref 8th Aust LENS 11

[Signatures]

Confidential

WAR DIARY
OF
No 1 Coy ASC
59th DIVISION
from Jany 1st to Jany 31st 1918.

VOL. II

Army Form C. 2118.

# WAR DIARY
## INTELLIGENCE SUMMARY.
(Erase heading not required.)

513 Coy A.S.C. 59th D.V.   Summary of Events and Information  January 1918.

| Place | Date | Hour | Summary of Events and Information | Remarks and references to Appendices |
|---|---|---|---|---|
| LUCHEUX | 1/18 | | In Billets and quarters. 1 Riding horse "Redmond" received. | |
| " | 3/18 | | Lieut. F.J. Roots reported back for duty on return from leave | |
| " | 5/18 | | Captain A.J. GREEN took over Command. Vice Captain. M.L.B.H. LAMBERT (sick) | |
| " | " | | 1. H.D. Horse evacuated to M.V.S. | |
| " | 8/18 | 10. | Coy H.Q/s moved by road to GROUCHES | |
| GROUCHES | " | 11.0 | In Billets and quarters | |
| " | " | | Captain A.N. PERCH. Proceeded on 30 days special leave to England | |
| " | " | | Lieut. P.R.R. DIBBEN. assumed the duties of S.O. during the absence on leave of Captain A.N. Perch | |
| " | 13/18 | | Three Precautionary orders came into force. Bulk supplies were drawn from the F.S.D. at DOULLENS to S.R.P. by Horse Transport. The 59th DAC working | |

A.Green Capt. O.C. 513 Coy A.S.C. 59 th D.V.

Army Form C. 2118.

# WAR DIARY
## INTELLIGENCE SUMMARY.
*(Erase heading not required.)*

Instructions regarding War Diaries and Intelligence Summaries are contained in F. S. Regs., Part II. and the Staff Manual respectively. Title pages will be prepared in manuscript.

| Place | Date | Hour | Summary of Events and Information | Remarks and references to Appendices |
|---|---|---|---|---|
| | | | 513 Coy A.S.C. 59th Div | January 1918 |
| CROUCHES | 20/18 | | 12 H.D. Remounts received | |
| " | 22nd | | 1 H.D. Remount sent to 802 Coy 59th Div. train | |
| " | 22nd | | Three precaution order removed 59th D.S.C. being supplies to S.R.P. | |
| " | 31/18 | | 1 H.D. Horse attached to C.F.A. died (between 1st & 31st/1/18) | |
| | | | The general health of the Company during the month was fairly good, all horses in good condition and improving | |

K. F. Greer
Capt
O.C 513 Coy A.S.C.
59th Div —

Confidential

No 2
54th Company A.S.C. 5gq 7th Divisional Train
War Diary of
From 1-7-16 to 31-1-18.

Volume I

Army Form C. 2118.

# WAR DIARY
## or
## INTELLIGENCE SUMMARY
*(Erase heading not required.)*

Vol. XII

N° 2 Coy. 59 Div. Train.

Instructions regarding War Diaries and Intelligence Summaries are contained in F. S. Regs., Part II. and the Staff Manual respectively. Title Pages will be prepared in manuscript.

| Place | Date | Hour | Summary of Events and Information | Remarks and references to Appendices |
|---|---|---|---|---|
| ETREE WAMIN | 1.1.18 | | Coy. billeted at ETREE WAMIN. Refilling Point at Railway Station. Supplies of Brigade Groups being drawn by Train Transport. | Trpt. |
| " | 7.1.18 | | Division in G.H.Q. reserve. No casualties. No move at 48 hours notice. Captain T.M. HAZLERIGG handed over command of Company to 2/Lieut W. TODD on proceeding to United Kingdom on leave. | Trpt. 1/4 |
| " | 1/1/18 | | 3 Reinforcement - Corporals from base. One Driver on Leave Co. | 1/4 |
| | 4/1/18 | | One N.C.O. mar received from 469 F. Coy. R.E. | 1/4 |
| | 7/1/18 | | Pte N.D. Coy Fyfe he 118 Battery from Militis Home former Casualties. | 1/4 |
| | 8/1/18 | | One reinforcement from base arrived (duty detail) | 1/4 |
| | 9/1/18 | | " " " " 3" N.M. F.A. (transfers below) | 1/4 |
| | 10/1/18 | | Ten drivers transferred to 2/9 3" N.M. F.A. (left detail) | 1/4 |
| | 17/1/18 | | One reinforcement from base received | 1/4 |
| | 19/1/18 | | Company Supply section (See Bn group police regn. of 2/3 N.M.F.A. and 46 F"(Coy. R.E.) transferred for line by Major Gen. Romer G.O.C. 59 Div. or S.R.T. on the morning of 19th. An excellent report being furnished by the Deputy Assist. of 2/S L.N.L. Reg. | 1/4 |
| | 22/1/18 | | One driver 24 H.D. 26 S. HAYDON (See example below) transferred to the COMMANDANT ARMY CLEARING DEPOT AGNEZ-LE-GRAND, and new transferred men (new strength of Coy. (Authority T.H.Q. Q=(31/157/4). | 1/4 |
| | 24.1.18 25.1.18 | | Copr. T.A. HARDY? 2/Lieut W. TODD attached temporarily to N° 3 Coy. 59 Div. Train from 24.1.18. N°7 3rd (B) Coy. R.E. billets & assembly huts at 4 p.m. and Supply were transferred forwards with HdQ.T.S. area. | Trpt Trpt |
| | 30.1.18 | | 2/5 Smith Staff Regt refilled at 6.15 a.m. on splitting up of the Battalion. Transports dispatched to Army Clearing Depot on 22.1.18 returned to company. | Trpt. |

T.W. Todd 2/Lt
O.C. N° 2 Coy. 59 Div. Train

Confidential

War Diary
of
No 3 Company. A.S.C. 59th Division

From 1-1-18 to 31-1-18

Volume I

Army Form C. 2118.

# WAR DIARY
## or
## INTELLIGENCE SUMMARY

(Erase heading not required.)

Instructions regarding War Diaries and Intelligence Summaries are contained in F. S. Regs., Part II. and the Staff Manual respectively. Title Pages will be prepared in manuscript.

515 Coy A.S.C. 59th Div.  January 1918

| Place | Date | Hour | Summary of Events and Information | Remarks and references to Appendices |
|---|---|---|---|---|
| AMBRINES | 1/18 | | In Billets and quarters | |
| AMBRINES | 1/7/8 | | Three reinforcement arrived (2 Drs 1 Ath) | a.y.k. |
| | 4/7/8 | | Capt/R. Johnson posted to command of 515 Co. 59th Div. Train | a.y.k. |
| | 4/7/8 | | 2/Cpl Payne & 1 Rider have transferred to 515 Co 59th Div Train | a.y.k. |
| | 11/7/8 | | W.O. J. Lockhart assumed command of 515 Co. 59th Div. Train | a.y.k. |
| | 11/7/8 | | Taken in ration strength from 1/1/18. 469 RE 3/4 h. Per Cent. 200 M.G.C. | a.y.k. |
| | 10/7/8 | | 2 Riders 1 H D evacuated | a.y.k. |
| | 14/7/8 | | 1 Rider from M.V.S. (7.M.M) 1 Rider from 515 Co ASC | a.y.k. |
| | 14/7/8 | | 2/Cpl hehale transferred from 515 Co ASC A3 C | a.y.k. |
| | 17/7/8 | | (2) Divis. reinforcement H/Cpl hehale is transferred to 515 Co. 2/Cpl Bristow | a.y.k. |
| | | | transferred from 515 Co ASC to 515 Co ASC | |
| | 19/7/8 | | Supply Section inspected by D.O.C. Division at ETRA-WAMIN. | a.y.k. |
| | 20/7/8 | | 2 HD reinanly arrived | a.y.k. |
| | 21/7/8 | | 1 Driver previously relieved to 7/4 h. Per Cent. | a.y.k. |
| | 21/7/8 | | 1 Dr. to Hospital | a.y.k. |

2449  Wt. W14957/M90  750,000  1/16  J.B.C. & A.  Forms/C.2118/12.

Army Form C. 2118.

# WAR DIARY
or
# INTELLIGENCE SUMMARY

(Erase heading not required.)

Instructions regarding War Diaries and Intelligence Summaries are contained in F. S. Regs., Part II. and the Staff Manual respectively. Title Pages will be prepared in manuscript.

| Place | Date | Hour | Summary of Events and Information | Remarks and references to Appendices |
|---|---|---|---|---|
| AMBRINES | 21st | 10.45 a.m | Inspection of lines by ADVS 59th Divn. | a/k |
| | 23rd | | Sgt Scooby posted to 7th h. Fd Amb in a/s S&U. | a/k |
| | | | L/Cpl Challinor promoted to a/s S&U. It wants permitting appt | a/k |
| | 26th | | Ptes Lowe arrived. 1 Dr to Hospital | a/k |
| | 28/1/18 | | Lieut A.J. Liddiard proceeded on 14 days leave. | 2444 |
| | | | 2/Lieut W. Good Assumes command | |
| | 29/1/18 | | 469 Yester R.E. Shock offinale Strength | way |
| | 29/1/18 | | S. Killed and 9 oranks at AMBRINES. | way |

Wm Good 2/Lt.
for O.C. 515 Coy A.S.C.
59th Divn

Confidential

War Diary

of

O.C., H Company 59th Divisional Train.

From:- 1/7/18          To:- 31/7/18

Volume 11.

Army Form C. 2118.

# WAR DIARY
## or
## INTELLIGENCE SUMMARY
*(Erase heading not required.)*

Instructions regarding War Diaries and Intelligence Summaries are contained in F. S. Regs., Part II. and the Staff Manual respectively. Title Pages will be prepared in manuscript.

| Place | Date | Hour | Summary of Events and Information | Remarks and references to Appendices |
|---|---|---|---|---|
| HOUVIN-HOUVIGEUL | Jan 1st 1918 | | Leave allotment received. 7 vacancies for the Coy. – One O.R. proceeds on leave. | |
| | Jan 2 | | O.C. Train inspects camp. – Severe frost. – | |
| | Jan 4 | | O.C. Train and C.O. Coy inspect 1st line transport – Regul buses for Supply Wagons obtained from units of Brigade | |
| | Jan 12 | | 2. O.R. admitted to hospital. | |
| | Jan 13 | | 1 O.R. admitted to hospital having been thrown off horse by horses bolting. – Church parade 6 P.M. | |
| | Jan 14 | | 1 O.R. admitted to hospital – Transport of 2/1 N.M. Field Ambulance inspected by O.C. | |
| | Jan 15 | | Heavy rain | |
| | Jan 17 | | 1 O.R. proceeds on leave to England – 1 O.R. evacuated and struck off strength | |
| | Jan 18 | | 1 O.R. proceeds on leave to England – 5 O.Rs taken on strength 30Rs posted to 2/1 N.M. Field Ambulance – 1 O.R. evacuated and struck off strength | |
| | Jan 19 | | 2 O.R. proceed on leave to England – G.O.C. inspects Supply Section at refilling point | |
| | | | Dvr. MOONEY returns from leave 3 days late – Church parade 6.0 P.M. | |
| | Jan 20 | | Wagons sent to TINQUES for R.E. material. | |
| | Jan 21 | | Dvr. STOCKTON transferred to Supply Details | |
| | Jan 24 | | 4 O.R. proceed on one days leave to AMIENS. – Church parade 11.45 A.M. | |
| | Jan 27 | | 2 O.R. proceed on leave to England. | |
| | Jan 28 | | F.G.C.M. on Dvr. MOONEY | |
| | Jan 31 | | 2 O.R. proceed on leave to England – Sentence of F.G.C.M. on Dvr. Mooney promulgated. | |

Army Form C. 2118.

# WAR DIARY
## or
## INTELLIGENCE SUMMARY

(Erase heading not required.)

| Place | Date | Hour | Summary of Events and Information | Remarks and references to Appendices |
|---|---|---|---|---|
| HOUVIN-HOUVIGNEUL | Jan 1 -31 | | The undermentioned units have been until enril by the Supply Coln during the month of Jan. 1918 | |
| | | | O/Pon 178 Inf Brigade | 1.1.18 — 31.1.18 |
| | | | Headquarters 178 Inf Brig | 1.1.18 — 31.1.18 |
| | | | No 4 Section Div Sig Coy | 1.1.18 — 31.1.18 |
| | | | 2/5 Sherwood Foresters | 1.1.18 — 31.1.18 |
| | | | 2/6 " | 1.1.18 — 31.1.18 |
| | | | 2/7 " | 1.1.18 — 31.1.18 |
| | | | 2/8 " | 1.1.18 — 31.1.18 |
| | | | 178 Light T.M.B | 1.1.16 — 31.1.18 |
| | | | 175 M.G.C. | 1.1.16 — 31.1.18 |
| | | | No 4 Coy 59th Div Train | 1.1.18 — 31.1.18 |
| | | | 470. Field Coy R.E. | 1.1.18 — 31.1.18 |
| | | | 2/2 N.M Field Ambulance | 1.1.18 — 31.1.18 |

M Churton Lieut Col
A.O.C. 516 Coy ASC
59th Div Train

WM/13

Confidential

War Diary

of

Headquarters, 59th Divisional Train

From 1/2/18 to 28/2/18

Volume XIII.

# WAR DIARY or INTELLIGENCE SUMMARY.

(Erase heading not required.)

Army Form C. 2118.

VOL. XIII

Head Quarters. 59th Div. TRAIN

| Place | Date | Hour | Summary of Events and Information | Remarks and references to Appendices |
|---|---|---|---|---|
| ETREE-WARMIN | 1.2.18 | | HEADQUARTERS and No 2. COY. at ETREE-WARMIN in billets. No 1 COY at GROUCHES No 3 COY at AMBRINES No 4 at HOUVIN-HOUVIGNEL all in billets. 59th Div ARTILLERY in BILLETS Division in VI CORPS in GHQ Reserve. Railhead FREVANT SRD 59 Div Artillery at MILLY. SRD's for 176. 177 178 Inf Brigades at ETREE WARMIN STATION. Supplies of DIV ARTILLERY drawn from Railhead by lorry and for the Inf Brigades by light railway to ETREE-WARMIN. | MCJ |
| " " | 2.2.18 | | O.C. TRAIN inspects 1st line transport of 177 Inf Brig. | MCJ |
| " " | 4.2.18 | | Instructs for 295- Bde. R.F.A. passed from S.O. 176 Inf Brig. to S.O. DIV TROOPS. | MCJ |
| " " | 6.2.18 | | RP for RFA less DAC on POMMIER - BIENVILLERS until DAC draws from detail issue store at FREVANT. No 1 COY moved under orders of TRAIN HQ en route for GOMIECOURT. 4 ORs joined Train | MCJ |
| " " | 7.2.18 | | 176 and 178 Inf Brig. upfilled twice. 1st of to 1st line transport hand. 2nd on to SUPPLY WAGONS | MCJ |
| " " | 8.2.18 | | Railhead closed by lorry R.P. for 177 Inf move at ETREE-WARMIN and three times to DIV TROOP units. in the area owing to early move of 177 Brig on 9.2.18. No 2 and No 4 Coys moved under orders of 176 and 178 Inf Brigs en route for GOMIECOURT | MCJ |
| " " | 9.2.18 | | Railhead BEAUMETZ (by lorry). 176. R.P at POMMIER 178 at GOUY-EN-ARTOIS No 3 Coy moved with 177 Brig en route for GOMIECOURT. | MCJ |
| " " | 10.2.18 | | Railhead BEAUMETZ. T.H.Q moved from ETREE-WARMIN to GOMIECOURT 176 RP at ERVILLERS. 177 GOUY-EN-ARTOIS 178. MERCATEL No 1. 2. 4. COY arrive at GOMIECOURT | MCJ |

Army Form C. 2118.

# WAR DIARY
## or
## INTELLIGENCE SUMMARY.
(Erase heading not required.)

Instructions regarding War Diaries and Intelligence Summaries are contained in F. S. Regs., Part II. and the Staff Manual respectively. Title pages will be prepared in manuscript.

| Place | Date | Hour | Summary of Events and Information | Remarks and references to Appendices |
|---|---|---|---|---|
| GOMIECOURT | 11.2.18 | | Railhead ACHIET-LE-GRAND by light railway and lorry. SB's. RFA GOMIECOURT 176 and DT. | |
| | | | Units ERVILLERS 177 and H.M.M.V.S. BLAIRVILLE 178. GOMIECOURT No. 3. Coy arrived at GOMIECOURT | |
| | | | MAJOR M.L.B.H. LAMBERT reported for duty on return from SICK LEAVE and assumed command of No 1 Coy vice CAPT. R.J. GREEN | |
| | | | who assumed command of No. 3 Coy vice LT A.J. LIDDIARD. LT G.J. FAIRFAX-ROSS transferred from No 1 Coy to No 3 Coy and 2/Lt FG | M.J/ |
| | | | TURTON from No 3 to No 1 Coy. | |
| | 12.2.18 | | RP's. RFA GOMIECOURT. 176 DIAMOND SIDING. (Ref Map 57c. B 20. b 7.2.) 177. ERVILLERS, 178. DIAMOND SIDING. M.J. | |
| | 13.2.18 | | 177. R.P. moves to DIAMOND SIDING. Supplies for Inf. Brigs delivered by light railway. MAJOR V.D.R CONRAN D.S.O. S.SO | |
| | | | 59" DIV and CAPT J.K.BROWN ADJT. 59" DIV TRAIN proceeded on 14 days leave to ENGLAND. CAPT A.M. FRASER assumed duties | |
| | | | of S.S.O. LT M.C. JOHNSTON those of ADJT. LT A.J. LIDDIARD returned from leave. | M.J. |
| | 14.2.18 | | 4 HD horses received for the TRAIN. | M.J. |
| | 15.2.18 | | Railhead for RFA closed by H.T from ACHIET-LE-GRAND to GOMIECOURT. INF. BRIGADES by light railway. | M.J. |
| | 16.2.18 | | CAPT R.J. GREEN and 2/LT W. TODD proceeded on 14 days leave to ENGLAND. LT A.J. LIDDIARD assumed command of No 3 Coy. | M.J. |
| | 20.2.18 | | 2/LT C.W. BLINDELL proceeded on 14 days leave to ENGLAND | M.J. |
| | 22.2.18 | | Three haystacks handed over by S.S.O to the FRENCH AUTHORITIES | M.J. |
| | 25.2.18 | | All Baggage wagons sent to units under orders from D.H.Q. & to stay with Units till further Orders. | M.J. |
| | 26.2.18 | | Railhead by lorry. All available TRAIN transport went to LOG EAST wood to draw wood for DIV FUEL DUMP | M.J. |
| DURING PERIOD | Heath of man condition | | GOOD. WEATHER/CONDITIONS GOOD in time of year. | |
| | | | HORSES GOOD although much extra work caused by above. Wt. W708-776. 500000. 4/15. Sir J. C. & S. T2134. | |

Hayloft
LIEUT COL
COMMANDING 59" DIV TRAIN
1/3/18

Confidential

WAR DIARY
OF
513 Coy ASC 51 Division
"
month of February 1918

VOL. Nº 12.

Army Form C. 2118

# WAR DIARY
## —OF—
## INTELLIGENCE SUMMARY
*(Erase heading not required.)*

Instructions regarding War Diaries and Intelligence Summaries are contained in F.S. Regs., Part II. and the Staff Manual respectively. Title Pages will be prepared in manuscript.

| Place | Date | Hour | Summary of Events and Information | Remarks and references to Appendices |
|---|---|---|---|---|
| Field | 10/2/18 | — | 513 Coy ASC. 59 Division. S.R.P. at GOMIECOURT. Supplies received from ACHIET le GRAND by Div. Supply Column | |
| Do. | 11/2/18 | — | Major B.R. Lambert wounded (or reported) for duty from hospital. | |
| Do. | 12/2/18 | — | Major B.H. Lambert assumed command of 513 Coy ASC 59 Division vice Capt R.J. GREEN sick to J.C. Fairfax Ross, ASC, posted to 515 Coy ASC. Lieut J.C. Fairfax Ross, A.S.C, posted to 515 Coy ASC, from 513 Coy ASC. 59 Division. 2/Lieut J.G. TURTON, ASC, posted to 513 Coy ASC from No 515 Coy ASC 59 Division. | |
| Do. | 13/2/18 | — | Capt J.K. Brown ASC Adjutant 59 Div. Train on 0-see dept on 14 days leave to England. Major Y.D.R. CONLAN. DSO. (S.S.O. 59 Division) proceeded on 14 days leave to England. Capt A.N. PEACH. S.O. 59 Div Troops assumed the duties of SSO 59 Division during the absence on leave of Major Y.D.R. CONLAN. DSO. | |
| Do. | 14/2/18 | — | 1. H.O. mount received. | |
| Do. | 16/2/18 | — | Supplies drawn by lorry transport of 59 Div. Train from ACHIET le GRAND to S.R.P at GOMIECOURT. | |
| Do. | 19/2/18 | — | 1.L.D. Vickers by V.O. result of enemy bombs. 1 H.D returned to M.V.S. while detached with CRA. | |
| Do. | 20/2/18 | — | 1 H.D destroyed while in M.V.S. (346) | |

R.H. Lambert Major.
Commdg. 513 Coy ASC 59 Division

Army Form C. 2118.

# WAR DIARY

## INTELLIGENCE SUMMARY.

(Erase heading not required.)

513 Coy A.S.C. 59th Divn. February 1918

| Place | Date | Hour | Summary of Events and Information | Remarks and references to Appendices |
|---|---|---|---|---|
| GROUCHES | 1/2/18 | | In Billets and quarters | AG |
| " | 3/18 | | 1. H.O. Horse drawn in to 59th M.V.S. | AG |
| " | 4/18 | | 1. H.O. known - received | AG |
| " | 6/18 | 9.30 a.m. | Coy H.Q.ers moved by road to POMMIER. | AG |
| POMMIER | 6/18 | 3.30 p.m. | In Billets and quarters | AG |
| " | 7/18 | 9.30 a.m. | Coy H.Q.ers moved by road to COURCELLES LE COMTE. | AG |
| COURCELLES LE COMTE | 7/18 | 3.15 p.m. | In huts and quarters at - No 3. Camp | AG |
| " | 10/2/18 | 10.0 a.m. | Coy H.Q.ers moved by road to GOMIECOURT. | AG |
| GOMIECOURT | 10/2/18 | 11.15 a.m. | In Camp (CARLTON HILL) Handed over to Major 13.H. Company at - 9 am 14/2/18 | AG Green Capt |

1577 Wt. W10791/1773 500,000 1/15 D. D. & L. A.D.S.S./Forms/C. 2118.

Confidential

War Diary

of

No 2 Coy (5th Coy ASC) 59th Divl Train

From 1/2/18 to 28/2/18

Volume XIII

Army Form C. 2118.

# WAR DIARY or INTELLIGENCE SUMMARY

*(Erase heading not required.)*

Vol. XIII

No 2 Coy. 59th DIVISIONAL TRAIN.

| Place | Date | Hour | Summary of Events and Information | Remarks and references to Appendices |
|---|---|---|---|---|
| ETREE WAMIN. | 4.2.18. | | Received from 2/1. Mdt. Vet. Sec. one H.D. Remount. | Nil. |
| " | 7.2.18 | | Handed over to 177 M. Gun Coy & 2/3 N.M. Fld. Amb. respectively, two draught mules. | Nil. |
| | | 8.30am | Despatched No 2/6 North Staff Regt. Baggage wagons to move stores from REBREUVIETTE to GRAND RULLECOURT and to march with Unit on 8th & 9th. | |
| | | 9 a.m. | Brigade Group supplied to 1st Line Transport for communication & wef. | |
| | | 2 p.m. | Brigade Group supplied to Train Transport for consumption 9th inst. and supply/forage returned to Coy. Hdqrs. under/less 2/6 North Staff. | |
| | | 2.15pm | Despatched Baggage wagons to HQ. 176th Infantry Bde. 2/6 North Staff and 2/6 North Staff. | |
| BIENVILLERS. | 8.2.18. | 7.AM. | Under orders of HQ 176 Inf Bde. Coy. Hdqrs. and Supply Section marched from ETREE WAMIN via LIENCOURT – GRAND RULLECOURT – SOMBRIN – SAULTY and POMMIER to BIENVILLERS. Delivered supplies at POMMIER – BERLES-AU-BOIS and BIENVILLERS. | Nil. |
| " | 9.2.18 | 7.30AM | Refilled at BIENVILLERS. | |
| | | 9.30AM | Delivered supplies to 2/3 N.M. Fld. Amb. at BERLES AU BOIS. Under orders of HQ. 176 Inf Bde. Coy. Hdqrs. and Supply Section marched to ERVILLERS via BUCQUOY and COURCELLES and delivered supplies at HAMELINCOURT, ERVILLERS and MORY. | Nil. |
| ERVILLERS. | 10.2.18 | 9.AM. | Refilled at ERVILLERS. Delivered supplies on 9th. Under orders of HQ. 176 Inf. Bde. Company Hdqrs & quantities moved to GOMIECOURT. Refilled at ERVILLERS and delivered at MORY & HAMELINCOURT. | Nil. |
| GOMIECOURT. | | 10.30AM | | |
| | 12.2.18 | | Refilling point moved to IZMAGNY SIDING, MORY. Delivered supplies by Train Wagons to 2/3 N.M. Fld Amb. HAMELINCOURT, HQ 176 BDE & 74 Afd. Gun Coy at MORY. | Nil. |
| | 13.2.18. | | Baggage wagons withdrawn from Units. 1 Driver/1 Cpl. Reinforcements received. | Nil. |
| | 14.2.18. | | 1 H.H. remount received - Shoeing smith extra establishment. | Nil. |
| | 15.2.18. | | Extra supplies for Div. Troops in bulk from Richard ACHIET LE GRAND for first time with train wagons. | Nil. |
| | 16.2.18. | | Supply wagons of 467 Siege Coy. R.E. 5/3rd Div. Sig. Coy. R.E. & C.R.E. 59th Div. attached from No.1 Coy. 59 Div. Train. | Nil. |
| | 17.2.18. | | Two supply rides received from 2/5th N.M. Fld Amb. | Nil. |
| | 22.2.18. | | 1 Completed transport G.S. wagons attached for duty with 9th Entrenching Battn. BASSEUX. | Nil. |
| | | | Three Drivers received as Reinforcements from Base Depot. | |
| | 23.2.18. | | Six wagons employed on moving R.S. Dump at ECOUST ST MEIN and ammunition dumped to MORY DUMP. | Nil. |
| | 25.2.18. | | Despatched Baggage wagons to Units in accordance with orders of HQ. 59th Div. Train. | Nil. |

Work of personnel during month, conditions of horses good, mules & transport wagons generally favourable.

WM Hegley Capt.
OC. No 2 Coy. 59 Div. Train.

"Confidential"

War Diary

of

515 Company. A.S.C. 59th Division.

from 1-2-18 to 28-2-18.

Volume ii

Army Form C. 2118.

# WAR DIARY
## or
## INTELLIGENCE SUMMARY

(Erase heading not required.)

515 Coy A.S.C. 59th Divn.  Summary of Events and Information  February 1918.

| Place | Date | Hour | Summary of Events and Information | Remarks and references to Appendices |
|---|---|---|---|---|
| AMBRINES | 1/2/18 | | In billets and quarters at AMBRINES | 1/44 |
| | 2/2/18 | | C.S.M. reported back from leave | 1/44 |
| | 3/2/18 | | T/4/216600 Dr Beeffer proceeded on special leave 4/2/18 to 15/2/18 | 1/44 |
| | 5/2/18 | | Cpl Richardson back from leave | 1/44 |
| | 6/2/18 | | H.D. returned from M.V.S orders it has been tested for fir. | 1/44 |
| | 7/2/18 | | Despatched 200 M.G. wagon to H.Q. Coy | 1/44 |
| | | | Dr Chilson sent to Hospital | |
| | | | Dr Sheen and Yellop attached to this Company tremor is completed | |
| | | | have been and instructors to have their men one to H.Q. Coy on arrival in numbers | |
| | 8/2/18 | | Supplies drawn by 1st Bns. at 8 A.M. Dr M. Vaughan Bren 21-12-0 over | 1/44 |
| | | | Baggage wagon return to unit | |
| | | | Two baggage wagons of 2/5 Leicesters report to 177 T.M.B. personnel | |
| | | | Cpl Shaw admitted to Hospital | |
| MONCHIET | 9/2/18 | | Company moved to MONCHIET route AVENES - LES - COMTE GOUVEN. ARTOIS | 1/44 |
| | | | Pte Greenlees admitted to Hospital | |
| HENDECOURT | 10/2/18 | | Company moved to HENDECOURT route BASSEUX. BLAIRVILLE | |
| | | | A.M. 10 ------ 2 P.M. | |

Army Form C. 2118.

# WAR DIARY
or
## INTELLIGENCE SUMMARY
(Erase heading not required.)

Instructions regarding War Diaries and Intelligence Summaries are contained in F.S. Regs., Part II. and the Staff Manual respectively. Title Pages will be prepared in manuscript.

| Place | Date | Hour | Summary of Events and Information February 1918 | Remarks and references to Appendices |
|---|---|---|---|---|
| HENDECOURT | 10/2/18 | | 515 Coy a S.C. 59th Divn. Spent night at HENDECOURT | |
| GONNICOURT | 11/2/18 | | Company moved with cars at GONNICOURT Route DOUCHY-LES-AYETTE COURCELLES LES. CONTÉ GONNICOURT. All supplies delivered and wagon back on Coy lines 5.0 P.M. Pte Suttion reported back from hospital Lucion Theon and Fallor dispatches to No 1 Coy. | W.L.Y. |
| | 12/2/18 | | Capt Green assumes command of Company vice 2/Lieut. W. Lord 2/Lt 2. Lentin transferred to 513 Co. A.S.C. 2/Lt J.B. Harpur Res transferred from 513 C. A.S.C. to Pritchard to 513 C. Dr Paris from 513 C. | ayl |
| | 13/2/18 | | Farrier Sgt reinforcement arrival, proter to 7 > 2 h. Lee Amb | |
| | 14/2/18 | | 2/L.F. Lockhart from leave. 7/20 Lorer proceeded to BAPAUME for Reinnurts 1HD Reinmts arrival | ayl |
| | 15/2/18 | | 2/Lieut W. Lord returned to S14 C.M.C. 2/L h.h. Lee and 2/Lieut. N.M.V.S. 49 C. R.E. taken in relief strength of Brigade Group. | ayl |
| | 16/2/18 | | Capt N.R.J. Green proceeded on 14 days leave W. Yorkshire assumed command. | ayl |

Army Form C. 2118.

# WAR DIARY
## or
## INTELLIGENCE SUMMARY

(Erase heading not required.)

Instructions regarding War Diaries and Intelligence Summaries are contained in F. S. Regs., Part II. and the Staff Manual respectively. Title Pages will be prepared in manuscript.

| Place | Date | Hour | Summary of Events and Information | Remarks and references to Appendices |
|---|---|---|---|---|
| GOMMECOURT | 17/2/18 | | 516 Co A.S.C. Sgt T.M. R.A. attached. | ajh |
| | 18/2/18 | | 469 Co R.E. 15th K Fusiliers, 27 Labour Co Area Commandant attached for rations | ajh |
| | 19/2/18 | | K.M. V.S. Supply wagon attached | ajh |
| | 21/2/18 | | 3 Driver Reinforcements received. 2 Lancashire returned from C.C.S. 15. 7; 2 K.M. Fusiliers | ajh |
| | 22/2/18 | | Sgt Harvey + 1 Br. evacuated | ajh |
| | 24/2/18 | | Dr Curry transferred to 516 Co A.S.C. Sgt Crockett arrived from 516 Co. Dr Shuttleworth arrived from C.C.S. Cpl Inman reported from hospital. | ajh |
| | 25/2/18 | | 7Cpl Lawson (Supply) transferred from 516 Co A.S.C. Baggage wagon sent to Route transport lines for attendance. | ajh |

Lt A/Reilphin?
OC 51st Co A.S.C.

28/2/18

Confidential

"War Diary"
of
O.C. 1st Company 69th Division dec...

From - 1/2/18 to - 28/2/18.

Volume 13.

Army Form C. 2118.

# WAR DIARY
## or
## INTELLIGENCE SUMMARY

*(Erase heading not required.)*

Instructions regarding War Diaries and Intelligence Summaries are contained in F. S. Regs., Part II. and the Staff Manual respectively. Title Pages will be prepared in manuscript.

| Place | Date 1916 | Hour | Summary of Events and Information | Remarks and references to Appendices |
|---|---|---|---|---|
| Houvin-Houvigneul | July 2nd | | 1 – O.R. reports for duty & is taken on the strength & posted to the Supply Details | |
| | " 3rd | | 1 – O.R. discharged from Hospital. – 6 – O.R. inoculated. | |
| | " 4th | | 1 – O.R. admitted to Hospital – 5 – O.R. inoculated. | |
| | " 7th | | 2 – O.R. proceed on leave – 5 – O.R. inoculated. | |
| | " 8th | | 2 two report for duty & are taken on the strength | |
| Gouy-en-Artois | " 9th | | By motor by route March to Gouy-en-Artois. | |
| Mercatel | " 10th | | By motor by route March to Mercatel | |
| Gomiecourt | " 11th | | By motor by route March to Gomiecourt — Dump is situated at Diamond Siding near Mory | |
| | " 12th | | 1 – O.R. discharged from Hospital. Lieut. M.C. Johnston detached for duty at Train Headquarters. | |
| | " 13th | | O.C. Train inspects Camp. | |
| | " 14th | | 1 – O.R. (Loader) admitted to Hospital. | |
| | " 15th | | 1 – O.R. reports for duty & is taken on the strength. | |
| | " 16th | | 1 – O.R. evacuated & struck off strength. | |
| | " 17th | | 2/Lieut. W.J.J. Brown attached to this company from No 1 Coy 59th Divisional Train. | |
| | " 18th | | 1 – O.R. (Loader) admitted to Hospital. | |
| | " 19th | | 2 loaders report for duty | |
| | " 20th | | 1 loader reports for duty | |
| | " 21st | | 1 – O.R. admitted to Hospital — 3 drivers report for duty & are taken on strength. | |
| | " 22nd | | 2 – O.R. posted to 2/1st N.M. Fd. Ambce for duty. – 2 – O.R. inoculated | |
| | " 24th | | 2 – O.R. transferred to No 3 Coy 59th Divnl. Train. – 1 – O.R. transferred to this Company from No 3 Coy 59th Divnl. Train. – 6 – O.R. inoculated. | |
| | " 25th | | 2/Lieut. J. Denton posted to this Coy. for duty. | |
| | " 25th | | 1 – O.R. admitted to Hospital. | |

Army Form C. 2118.

# WAR DIARY
## or
## INTELLIGENCE SUMMARY

*(Erase heading not required.)*

Instructions regarding War Diaries and Intelligence Summaries are contained in F. S. Regs., Part II. and the Staff Manual respectively. Title Pages will be prepared in manuscript.

| Place | Date | Hour | Summary of Events and Information | Remarks and references to Appendices |
|---|---|---|---|---|
| | | | The following units were relieved by Artillery Officer 178th Infantry Brigade on the dates of their inclusive during the month of February 1916. | |
| | | | H.Q. 78th Infantry Brigade  1-2-18 — 28-2-18 | |
| | | | 2/5th Bn. Hampshire Regt.  " " | |
| | | | 2/6th   "   " | |
| | | | 2/7th   "   " | |
| | | | 178th Trench Mortar Battery   " | |
| | | | 176th Bde. M.G.C.   " | |
| | | | 134 Bde. Sig. Sub. Section   " | |
| | | | 2/2nd Field Ambulance   " | |
| | | | 470 Fld. Coy. R.E.   " | |
| | | | H. Section Sig. 2 Div. Aig.  1-2-18 — 14-2-18. | |
| | | | 2/8th Bn. Advanced Formation  1-2-18 — 25-2-18. | |
| | | | 290 M.G. Coy.  5-2-18 — 28-2-18. | |
| | | | 6/7 Royal North Fusiliers  22-2-18 — 25-2-18. | |
| | | | 10th Trenching Battalion  23-2-18 — 28-2-18. | |
| | | | Y.M.C.A. St Leger  14-2-16 — 28-2-18. | |

Hand Wyllie Lieut
C.C. of Inf. 59th Denal. Div.

2449 Wt. W14957/M90 750,000 1/16 J.B.C. & A. Forms/C.2118/12.

Confidential.

Vol 14

# War Diary.

## OF

### Headquarters, 5Ok (N.M) Div'l Train.

1/3/18 to 31/3/18

Vol. XIV.

# WAR DIARY
## or
## INTELLIGENCE SUMMARY.
(Erase heading not required.)

Army Form C. 2118.

Vol XIV

Headquarters 59th Divisional Train

| Place | Date | Hour | Summary of Events and Information | Remarks and references to Appendices |
|---|---|---|---|---|
| GOMIECOURT | 1/3/18 | | Railhead ACHIET-LE-GRAND Refilling Points Div. Troops GOMIECOURT. | |
| | 9/3/18 | | 176, 177, 178 Inf. Bdes. at Diamond Siding MORY. Railhead & R.P's. Same as 1st Ind. drew from R.H. & R.P by M.T. to load wagons on to BOISLEUX-AU-MONT for b.ats. D.A.C. informed of being unable to furnish supply personnel to D.T.B. now to Railhead as to lorries will be used in future. 2 I.C. Coys. Sent for authority to take the use of two lorries. Consideration R.H. by home transport — | |
| " | 15/3/18 | | Railhead & R.P's. No Change. Agricultural Officer visited camp & I was arranged to plough up all Vegetables & the 4 acres in addition to the 2 acres already cleared by No. 4 Coy. | |
| " | 16/3/18 | | R.H. & R.P's. No Change. Convoy Issued Corn & One arrived at R.H. all wagons had to do a second journey to clean supplies. | |
| " | 18/3/18 | | Ten-eight lorries help collect removals for Division from ABLAINZEVILLE. | |
| " | 21/3/18 | | Railhead Refilling Points & GOMIECOURT Village shelled on commencement of German attack. Refilled at Diamond Siding. Supplies to Divn. lion 23rd Boxes & Drawn Siding Withdrawn by Douaville to LOG EAST WOOD. | |
| | 22/3/18 | | Railhead MIRAUMONT Refilling Point for 176, 177, 178 Bdes. LOG EAST WOOD. GOMIECOURT. R.P. for Div. Troops | |

# WAR DIARY
## or
## INTELLIGENCE SUMMARY.
*(Erase heading not required.)*

Army Form C. 2118.

Vol XIV.

Headquarters 59th Divisional Train

| Place | Date | Hour | Summary of Events and Information | Remarks and references to Appendices |
|---|---|---|---|---|
| GOMIECOURT | 22/3/18 | | 59th Divisional Train moved to AYETTE. On AYETTE—BOUQUOY road 2pp. | 87 |
| AYETTE | 23/3/18 | | Railhead BOUQUOY. R.Ps for the whole Division LoGEAST WOOD. Train Headquarters Nos. 2 & 4 Coys moved to BOUZINCOURT Nos 1 & 3 Coys came under orders of 40th Div.l Train | p.3 p.3 p.3 |
| BOUZINCOURT | 24/3/18 | | Railhead ALBERT RPs 176 & 178 Belos BOUZINCOURT | p.3 |
| | 25/3/18 | | Railhead CORBIE T.H.Q. Nos. 2 & 4 Coys Moved to PONT NOYELLE. Refilled PONT NOYELLE at about 10 p.m. | p.3 p.3 |
| PONT NOYELLE | 26/3/18 | | Railhead BELLEGLISE T.H.Q. & Nos. 2 & 4 Coys. moved to BONNEVILLE Refilled at BONNEVILLE | p.3 |
| BONNEVILLE | 27/3/18 | | Railhead CANAPLES | p.3 |
| | 28/3/18 | | do T.H.Q. Nos 2 & 4 Coys moved to an area just S. of ST. POL. | p.3 |
| | 29/3/18 | | Railhead CHOCQUES R.Ps on CAUCOURT — VILLERS CHATEL road | p.3 |
| | 30/3/18 | | do RPs at GAUCHIN LEGAL No 3 Coy with 177 Bde formed | p.3 |
| | | | The Division now billeted at HOUDAIN | p.3 |
| | 31/3/18 | | Railhead TINCQUES RPs 176,178 & l CAUCHIN LEGAL 177 Rd at HOUDIN | p.3 |
| | | | Train moved to ECQUEDECQUES | p.3 |

T2134. Wt. W708—776. 500000. 4/15. Sir J. C. & S.

Confidential
—

War Diary
of

(N°1) 513 Company A.S.C. 59th Division

From 1/3/18 to 31/3/18

Volume XIV

Army Form C. 2118.

# WAR DIARY
## or
## INTELLIGENCE SUMMARY
(Erase heading not required.)

Instructions regarding War Diaries and Intelligence Summaries are contained in F. S. Regs., Part II. and the Staff Manual respectively. Title Pages will be prepared in manuscript.

| Place | Date | Hour | Summary of Events and Information March 1918. | Remarks and references to Appendices |
|---|---|---|---|---|
| In the Field | | | 513 Coy A.V.C. 50. Division | |
| | 1/3/18 | | Notification received from 8/1st MMRS that MD horse 234 was evacuated to Base 26/2/18 1/Sergeant G Driver J/18 HD and 1 Rider of 26th Brigade AFA attached. | |
| | 3/3/18 | | 1 HD received from 514 Coy AVC. | |
| | 8/3/18 | | 1 Ride Horse found straying returned to 511 Coy AVC | |
| | 11/3/18 | | 1 MD horse found straying returned to 3/1 NM MVS | |
| | 10/3/18 | | 1 MD horse No 534 evacuated to 8/1st MVRS for evacuation No 534 | |
| | 21/3/18 | | Company moved by march route from GOMMEÇOURT to AYETTE. Supplies drawn from Achiet le Grand to Div. Supply Column. Refilling point at Rossignol Wood | |
| | 22/3/18 | | " " | |
| | 23/3/18 | | Company moved by march route from AYETTE to HANNESCAMP. Supplies drawn from ADINFER by 10th Div.l Supply column. Refilling point at HANNESCAMP. | |
| | 24/3/18 | | Refilling point at HANNESCAMP. 2 Riders & 2 Horses at HD horses (Remounts) handed over to Major Gibbon RFA | |
| | 25/3/18 | | Company moved by march route from HANNESCAMP to HENU. Awakened in billets & horses on lines. Supplies drawn by 62nd Div. Supply Column. Refilling point at HENU. | |
| | 26/3/18 | | 3 HD horses joined straying & taken on strength. | |

H. Parnell Major
Comdg 513 Coy AVC
50th Division

Confidential

War Diary

of

514 Coy. R.S.C. 59th Division

1/3/18 to 31/3/18

Volume XIV

(N° 2)

Army Form C. 2118.

# WAR DIARY
# INTELLIGENCE SUMMARY

(Erase heading not required.)

VOL. XIV

No 2 Coy. 59th Div!: TRAIN.

Ref. Maps. LENS. II. and AMIENS. 17/.

Instructions regarding War Diaries and Intelligence Summaries are contained in F.S. Regs., Part II. and the Staff Manual respectively. Title Pages will be prepared in manuscript.

| Place | Date | Hour | Summary of Events and Information | Remarks and references to Appendices |
|---|---|---|---|---|
| GOMIECOURT | 1.3.18 | | Commenced month with Coy. stationed S.W. of GOMIECOURT, Refilling Point at DIAMOND SIDING, MORY, Units on Barjack Group Ration Strength being HQ. 176 Inf. Bde. 2/6 South Staffs, 2/5th and 2/6 North Staffs, 176 I.T.M.B. N° 2 Coy. 59 Div. Train, 467 Fld. Co. R.E. 2/3 N.M. Fld. Amb. C.R.E. 59 Div., 59 Div. Signals, Hd Qrs 59 Div. M.M.P. 59 Div. III. A. II. 05. Laundry Officer & Salvage Coy 59 Div. 250 Div. Employmt Coy, and 174 Machine Gun Coy. Railhead ACHIET LE GRAND. | TMWT. |
| " | 8.3.18 | | Turnover of Supply wagons of 174 M. Gun Coy. Attached to N°4 Coy. 59 Div. Train on Coy. being absorbed into Machine Gun Bde. and going on hollow strength of 176 Inf. Bde. Group. | TMWT. |
| " | 21.3.18 | | On commencement of German attack Railhead, Refilling Point & Gomiecourt village shelled. Refilled at Diamond Siding. Supplies for consumption 23rd taken to Diamond Siding but withdrawn to Barastville with Supply Details to Log East Wood on road ACHIET DIECOURT to ABLAINZEVILLE. | TMWT. |
| " | 22.3.18 | 8 A.M. | Refilled at Log East Wood and delivered to Units Stores which had reached BUCQUOY, AYETTE & DOUVY LES AYETTE arena and Supply wagons collected at rendez-vous at ABLAINZEVILLE. | TMWT. |
| AYETTE | | 1 P.M. | Coy. HQrs moved via COURCELLES LE COMTE & ABLAINZEVILLE to lines on BUCQUOY - AYETTE Road and bivouacked for night of 22/23 March. | TMWT. |
| | | 8 A.M. | Supply Convoy refilled at Log East Wood and returned to AYETTE and at 10 A.M. moved with Coy. Hdqrs. via BUCQUOY - PUISIEUX au MONT - HEDAUVILLE to BOUZINCOURT. and delivered Supplies to Units in BOUZINCOURT Area. | TMWT. |
| BOUZINCOURT | 23.3.18 | | HEDAUVILLE - HEDAUVILLE to BOUZINCOURT - MILLENCOURT Road - 2/1 N.M. Fld. Amb., 4/59 Fld. Co. R.E. and 2/1 Mob. Vet. Sec. being added to Field Ration Group. Supply wagons proceeded to and remained with Units in anticipation of entrainment at 6 P.M. arrangement to be prepared to move ahead by Rail 3 A.M. during which supply cattle wagons and refilled again at 7 P.M. and assembled. Supply Section on Coy. Lines. Having received orders to be prepared to move ahead by Rail 3 A.M. | TMWT. |
| BOUZINCOURT | 24.3.18 | 8 A.M. | Refilled on BOUZINCOURT - MILLENCOURT Road | TMWT. |
| PONT NOYELLES | 25.3.18 | 3 A.M. | HQ. 59 Div. Train moved Coy. Hdqrs. and Supply Sec. via SENLIS - HENENCOURT - BAISEUX and FRANVILLERS. As units of Group at CONTAY, BEAUCOURT, main ALBERT - AMIENS Road) and billed by. At 11.30 A.M. delivered supplies to Units of Group at CONTAY, BEAUCOURT, BEHENCOURT & PONT NOYELLES. and collected Supply Convoy at PONT NOYELLES. | TMWT. |
| PONT-NOYELLES | 26.3.18 | 5 A.M. 6 A.M. | Refilled on PONT NOYELLES - BEHENCOURT Road. Moved Coy. Hdqrs. and Supply Sec. via ST GRATIENS - MOLLIENS AU BOIS - VILLERS BOCAGE - FLESELLES - HAVERNAS - CANAPLES and MONTRELET to BONNEVILLE and delivered supplies to Units of Group at FIENVILLERS, MONTRELET, BONNEVILLE and CANDAS. | TMWT. TMWT. |
| BONNEVILLE | 27.3.18 | 12 noon 5 P.M. | Refilled at BONNEVILLE to stand by under Lorry. Relieved in above order of readiness supply. Replenished Supply Convoy. | TMWT. TMWT. |
| BONNEVILLE HERLIN LE SEC | 28.3.18. | 6.30 A.M. | Refilled at BONNEVILLE and despatched wagons to relieve in above order to await Lorry with Units Refilled Coy. Hdqs. via FIENVILLERS - HEM - DOVILLERS - FREVENT to HERLIN LE SEC (2 mile S. of ST POL) and collected empty supply wagons and returned empty wagons until collected. | TMWT. TMWT. |
| | 29.3.18 | 10.15 A.M. | Moved Coy. Hdqs. and Supply Sec. via ST POL - ROELLECOURT - MARQUAY - MONCHY BRETON to FREVILLERS and Units arrived Coy. at delivering Rations at CAUCOURT VILLERS CHATEL and CAMBLIGNEUL. Moved Coy. Hdqs. via HERNIN to GAUCHIN LEGAL after delivering Rations at CAUCOURT, VILLERS CHATEL and CAMBLIGNEUL. | TMWT. TMWT. |
| GAUCHIN LEGAL | 30.3.18 | 11 A.M. | Refilled at GAUCHIN LEGAL and delivered to Units. | TMWT. |
| GAUCHIN LEGAL | 31.3.18. | 7 A.M. | Refilled supply Section and despatched loaded wagons to Units for Groups between Rail Heads for use of troops with 11th Corps Transport | TMWT. |
| ECQUEDECQUES | | 10.30 A.M. | Left GAUCHIN LEGAL and proceeded via HOUDAIN, BRUAY, LILLERS to ECQUEDECQUES arriving 6 P.M. Halted spare month during which Good weather prevailed and excellent conditions of horses and Good rides to continuing numerous moves & exposure. | TMWT. |

T.W. Haslegrove Capt.
OC N°2 Coy. 59th Div! Train.

Confidential

War Diary

of

515 Company A.S.C. 59th Division

(No 3) From 1-3-18 to 31/3/18

Volume III

Army Form C. 2118.

# WAR DIARY
## or
## INTELLIGENCE SUMMARY

(Erase heading not required.)

| Place | Date | Hour | Summary of Events and Information | Remarks and references to Appendices |
|---|---|---|---|---|
| COMIECOURT | 1/3/18 | | 515 Co A.S.C. 59th Division. March 1918. | appx. |
| | 3/3/18 | | In Camp. | appx. |
| | | | 1 Driver reinforcement J.W. Wallace. Surplus H.D. transferred to 515 Co A.S.C. | |
| | 4/3/18 | | 2 P.R.R. Dibben reported OSS.O. for duty. Capt. R.J. Green returned from leave. | appx. |
| | 5/3/18 | | CAPTAIN. R.J. GREEN assumed command of company. | appx. |
| | | | CAPTAIN. F.J.G. SMITH proceeded on 14 days leave to England — | |
| | | | 469 Field Co R.E. 5th T.M. (Heavy) Came in later strength | appx. |
| | | | 2/1st NMA Front 2/1st Return Coy from 1/3/18 to 24/2/18 | |
| | | | 1/1st M.V.S. Area Comd (Inf'try) | |
| | 7/3/18 | | 4 Septic Q.S. Wagons with complete equipment transferred to 6/7 P.R.S.F. | appx. |
| | 8/3/18 | | 17 M.G.C. Supply hypo detached to 516 Coy. | appx. |
| | 15/3/18 | | LIEUT. J.G. FAIRFAX ROSS. proceeded on 10 days special leave ——— | appx. |
| | 20/3/18 | | 1 L.D. Horse (surplus) transferred to 9th Entrenching Batt'n. | appx. |

R.J. Green Capt

Army Form C. 2118.

# WAR DIARY
or
## INTELLIGENCE SUMMARY

(Erase heading not required.)

515 Coy A.S.C. 5g[?] [?] Summary of Events and Information March 1918

| Place | Date | Hour | Summary of Events and Information | Remarks and references to Appendices |
|---|---|---|---|---|
| GOMIECOURT | 21/3 | a.m 4.45 | Vicinity of camp shelled by hostile artillery | A.F. |
| " | " | 6.0 | Supplies and Personnel of 177 Bde moved back to L.O.2. EAST WOOD from DIAMOND SIDING NIORY. | A.F. |
| " | 22/3 | 1.45 | Coy H.Q⁵ moved by road to AYETTE. | A.F. |
| AYETTE | " | 4.30 | In Camp | A.F. |
| " | 23/3 | | CAPTAIN F.J.C. SMITH returns from leave | A.F. |
| " | " | | LIEUT P.R.R. DIGBEN reports back to T.H.Q | A.F. |
| " | " | | collected to 40⁵ Div⁵ with 177 Bde | A.F. |
| " | 24/3 | a.m 6.0 | Coy H.Q⁵ with Supplies moved by road to HANNESCAMPS | A.F. |
| HANNESCAMPS | " | 9.0 | In Camp | A.F. |
| " | " | | 2.L.D and 4.H.Q (Amount taken on strength pending distribution) | A.F. |

A. Green Capt OC 515 Coy A.S.C.

2449 Wt. W14957/M90 750,000 1/16 J.B.C. & A. Forms/C.2118/12.

# WAR DIARY or INTELLIGENCE SUMMARY

Army Form C. 2118.

*(Erase heading not required.)*

Instructions regarding War Diaries and Intelligence Summaries are contained in F. S. Regs., Part II. and the Staff Manual respectively. Title Pages will be prepared in manuscript.

515 Coy A.S.C. 51st Divn.   March 1918

| Place | Date | Hour | Summary of Events and Information | Remarks and references to Appendices |
|---|---|---|---|---|
| HENNESCAMPS | 24/3 | | 6/7 R.S.F. taken on ration strength | |
| " | 25/3 | 5.0 | Supplies drawn but could not be delivered to Q.M. Stores. These were afterwards delivered during the night - 25/26th | |
| " | | | 3 G.S. Supply wagons failed to return | |
| " | | | 2 L.D Horses lost & 5, 7 & 1st Lincolns to make their way on foot. Vicinity of the Camp shelled by hostile artillery | |
| " | 26/3 | 8.0 am | moved by road to the vicinity of POMMIER | |
| " | | 12.30 | moved on to LARBRET | |
| LARBRET | " | | In Camp | |
| " | | 2.0 | Supplies for 1/7 Rde delivered during the night | |
| " | 27/3 | 5.0 am | Coy H.Q.'s moved by road to HARBACQ was diverted en route to COURLEMONT | |

 L.J. Stern Capt. O.C. 515 Coy A.S.C.

Army Form C. 2118.

# WAR DIARY
## or
## INTELLIGENCE SUMMARY
(Erase heading not required.)

315th Coy A.S.C. 59th Divn — March 1918

| Place | Date | Hour | Summary of Events and Information | Remarks and references to Appendices |
|---|---|---|---|---|
| COILLEMONT | 27/3 | 12.30 p.m. | In Camp | KG |
| " | 28/3 | 8.0 a.m. | Supplies drawn from D.S.C (40th) at Sus St LEDGER | KG |
| " | 29/3 | 8.0 a.m. | Supplies drawn by Horse transport (2 days) from STULTY Railhead | KG |
| " | | | Transferred from 40th Divn and staff of VI Corps | KG |
| " | | 8.30 a.m. | Moved by train (all night march) to HOUDAIN | KG |
| HOUDAIN | 30/3 | 8.0 a.m. | In Billets and quarters | KG |
| " | | | 3 Supply C.S. Wagons previously left now brought on to lines | KG |
| " | | | 13. O.R's with 10 Horses of 573 Coy brought on to my lines | KG |
| " | 31/3 | 10.0 a.m. | Moved by road to the LILLERS area | KG |
| LILLERS AREA | | 6.0 p.m. | In Camp and Billets. General health of the Coy during the month has been good. Men & horses all now rested. | KG |

A.P. Green Captain
O/C 315 Coy A.S.C. 59 Divn

Confidential

War Diary

O.C., 1st Pdt Coy K (SD) 59th Divisional Train.

From:- 1/3/16   To:- 31/3/16

Volume 14.

Army Form C. 2118.

No. 516 Coy A.S.C.
59 Div Train

# WAR DIARY or INTELLIGENCE SUMMARY

*(Erase heading not required.)*

Instructions regarding War Diaries and Intelligence Summaries are contained in F.S. Regs., Part II. and the Staff Manual respectively. Title Pages will be prepared in manuscript.

| Place | Date | Hour | Summary of Events and Information | Remarks and references to Appendices |
|---|---|---|---|---|
| GOMIECOURT | 1.3.18 | — | COY. at GOMIECOURT in good hutted camp. Horses in Stables. — SRP. at DIAMOND SIDING between ERVILLERS and MORY. Supplies for Brigade Group delivered at SRP by light railway and drawn by 1st line transport. COY transport assists in drawing supplies from ACHIET-LE-GRAND RAILHEAD for Div ARTILLERY. | M.I. |
|  | 2.3.18 | | One OR (DVR BRAYCOTT) reports for duty and taken on strength | M.I. |
|  | 4.3.18 | | TWO OR (DVR WARING and WILLIAMS) report for duty and posted to 2/1 N.M.F.A. | M.I. |
|  | 5.3.18 | | 1 OR (DVR DAVIES) evacuated and struck off strength — LIEUT F. PIGGIN a/o.c. No.4 Coy 59 Div Train proceeds on 14 days leave to ENGLAND. — LIEUT MC JOHNSTON assumes command. | M.I. |
|  | 9.3.18 | | 2 GS wagons (complete turnouts with DVR FOX and MISSOM) attached for duty with 177 and 178 Inf Brig HQ. | M.I. |
|  | 11.3.18 | | ONE OR (SERGT TIMMINS) proceeds on 14 days leave to ENGLAND | M.I. |
|  | 12.3.18 | | CAPT H R GODDARD returns from SICK LEAVE and assumes command of Coy. | M.I. |
|  | 16.3.18 | | ONE M.C.O (A/CPL C. F. L'ANSON) reverts to permanent rank at his own request | M.I. |
|  | 17.3.18 | | ONE OR (DVR GUTHRIE) reports for duty and taken on strength. 2 OR proceed on leave. | M.I. |
|  | 18.3.18 | | TWO OR's proceed to ABBEVILLE for remounts — 1 OR proceeds on leave. | M.I. |
|  | 21.3.18 | | Very heavy bombardment — COY. withdrew from more — SRP shifted to 106 EAST WOOD in afternoon. — 1 OR proceeds on leave. | M.I. |
| AYETTE | 22.3.18 | | Refilling 7AM at 106 EAST. WOOD. — COY moves to AYETTE | M.I. |
|  | 23.3.18 | | Refilling 7AM at 106 EAST WOOD. — COY proceeds by route march to BOUZINCOURT. SRP at X roads in village. | M.I. |
| BOUZINCOURT | 24.3.18 | | Supplies delivered by COY and forage remain with units — Refilling again at 6PM and wagons return to COY. — COY ready to move at 10PM — Great activity of hostile aircraft | M.I. |

Army Form C. 2118.

No. 516 Coy ASC
59th Div Train

# WAR DIARY or INTELLIGENCE SUMMARY

*(Erase heading not required.)*

Instructions regarding War Diaries and Intelligence Summaries are contained in F.S. Regs., Part II. and the Staff Manual respectively. Title Pages will be prepared in manuscript.

| Place | Date | Hour | Summary of Events and Information | Remarks and references to Appendices |
|---|---|---|---|---|
| BOUZINCOURT | 25.3.18 | 3AM | Coy move by nite march to PONT – NOYELLES arriving at 9 AM – Horses in lines – men in barns. – SRP in village. | M.7 |
| PONT-NOYELLES | 26.3.18 | | Coy move by nite march to BONNEVILLE – Coy arrives at 4 PM – SRP by Church in village. – Refilling at 6 PM wagons remain with units. | M.7 |
| BONNEVILLE | 28.3.18 | | Coy move by nite march at 6.30 AM. – Supply wagons move with units – Billeting party proceed by train to HERMIN, and also a party to arrange B/H for the night at HERMIN – LIE – SEC – Coy arrive at HERMIN at 4 PM. | M.7 |
| HERMIN-LIE-SEC | 29.3.18 | | Coy move by nite march to HERMIN – SRP in HERMIN | M.7 |
| HERMIN | 30.3.18 | | Refilling at 11 AM – Baggage wagons return to Coy – SRP on CAUCOURT – VILLERS–CHATIER ROAD. GAUCHIN – LIEGAL | M.7 |
| HERMIN | 31.3.18 | — | Baggage wagons report to units – Supply wagons move with units – Coy moves by nite march to ECQUEDECQUES. Sept. Timmins returns from leave. One wagon (Pte Sharky) returns from hospital. – Party of 132 under Lt Johnston left at HERMIN to be posted by rail the following day. The following units were fed by 516 Coy Inf. Bn. during the month of March 1918. | M.7 |

HQ 178. Inf. Brig. 1.3.18 – 31.3.18
2/5 Sherwood Fds. — — —
2/6 — — —
Y — — —
4 Coy Div Train — — —
470 Field Coy RE — — —
6/7 R.S.F. — — —

178 Light T.M.B. 1.3.18 – 23.3.18
175 M.G.C. 1.3.18 – 8.3.18
300 M.G.C. 1.3.18 – 7.5.18
103 Entrenching Bn.H. 1.3.18 – 2.3.18
59. M.G. Bn.H. 8.5.18 – 31.3.18

10 Chateau Johnston Lt
for O.C. 516 Coy ASC
59th Div Train

Vol 15

Confidential

War Diary

of

Headquarters, 59th Divisional Train

1/4/18 to 30/4/18

Volume XV.

# WAR DIARY
## or
## INTELLIGENCE SUMMARY.   Vol XV.

(Erase heading not required.)

Headquarters 59th Divisional Train

Army Form C. 2118.

| Place | Date June | Hour | Summary of Events and Information | Remarks and references to Appendices |
|---|---|---|---|---|
| ECQUEDECQUES | 1 | | Railhead TINEQUES. R.P's. on BOURECQ – HAMROED loop from BOURECQ | A3 |
| MORBECQUE | 2 | | T.H.Q. Nos 2, 3 & 4 Coys moved to MORBECQUE | A7 |
| | 3 | | Railhead GRUBBEM R.P's in ignore at MORBECQUE. T.H.Q. 1 Coy moved to WATOU | A8 |
| PROVEN | 4 | | do — R.P's 176 Bde in ignore at WATOU 177 & 178 Bdes at VLAMERTINGE. No. 3 Coy moved to VLAMERTINGE | A5 |
| | 5 | | do — R.P's same as 3rd inst. No 3 Coy moved to VLAMERTINGE | A5 |
| | 6 | | Railhead to Chaney E. R.P's 176 + 178 Bdes to Chaney E. R.P 177 Bde VLAMERTINGE | A3 |
| | | | R.H. & R.P's in Chaney E Town over Surplus Transport of the 33rd Division. | |
| | 7 | | No 4 Coy. Moved to abt 3000 yds W. of STEENVOORDE | A3 |
| | | | R.H. & R.P's in Chaney E Surplus Transport handed over to Capt PRESTON | |
| | | | O/C Surplus Transport VIII Corps at HAMHOEK | A5 |
| | 10 | | R.H. for 176 & 178 Bde Comps GRUBBEM. R.H. 177 Bde VLAMERTINGE. No 2 Coy moved | A3 |
| | | | to VLAMERTINGE at that H.16.a. Sheet 28. | |
| | 11 | | R.H. for Division GRUBBEM. R.P's all in H.16.a. T.H.Q. moved to H.16.a | A7 |
| | 12 | | R.H. GRUBBEM Refilling was carried out on evening of the 11th | |
| | | | No 4 Coy moved to DRANOUTRE. Nos 2 & 3 Coys to G.6.d. T.H.Q to G.7c. | A7 |
| | 13 | | R.H. in Chaney E. R.P's new Coys. T.H.Q. moved to WATOU No 4 to G.6. G.32.d.7.3. Sheet 38 | A3 |
| | | | moved to WESTOUTRE No 3 to WATOU No 4.6. G.32. d.7.3 Sheet 38 | |

**Army Form C. 2118.**

# WAR DIARY
## or
## INTELLIGENCE SUMMARY.
*(Erase heading not required.)*

Headquarters 59th Divisional ___ VOL XL

Instructions regarding War Diaries and Intelligence Summaries are contained in F. S. Regs., Part II. and the Staff Manual respectively. Title pages will be prepared in manuscript.

| Place | Date April | Hour | Summary of Events and Information | Remarks and references to Appendices |
|---|---|---|---|---|
| WATOU | 14th | | R.H. & R.P⁰ in Charge. No 2 Coy moved to C.30.C.9.4. No 3 Coy moved to G.26.C.4.4. | Ag3 |
| | 15 | | T.H.Q. moved to G.26.C.4.4. | Ag3 |
| | 16 | | R.H. in Charge. R.P⁰ in Bellacers. T.H.Q. moved to G.32.a.7.3. 2nd Lt. F.M. WHITFIELD joined from 9th Div. Train | Ag3 |
| | 17 | | No 2 Coy moved to G.15.C.2.6. Their camp was heavily shelled. Casualties 6 men wounded 20 horses killed wounded and wagon destroyed. Two wagons lost the lift in camp when Coy moved. There were got away later by Capt. T.M. HAZLERIGG & his drivers under heavy shellfire. R.H. in Charge. R.P⁰ in Coy Lines. No 2 Coy moved to A.21.b. | Ag3 Ag3 |
| | 18 | | ST MEENVOORDE. 3 men of No 3 Coy wounded | Ag3 |
| | 19 | | T.H.Q. & No 2 Coy moved to A.21.b.2.9. | Ag3 |
| | 20 | | No 3 & 4 Coys moved to A.21.b.2.9. Sheet 28 | Ag3 |
| | 21 | | R.H. ARNEKE R.P⁰ at A.21.b. —— T.H.Q. moved to BAMBECQUE No 2 Coy. moved to ROUSBRUGGE Rackled No 3 Coy. moved to D.12.a.1.2 Sheet 27 - No 2 Coy bombed No 4. —— E.20.b.2.6. Casualties 1 man & 3 horses wounded | Ag3 Ag6 Ag3 Eg6 |

# WAR DIARY
## or
## INTELLIGENCE SUMMARY.
(Erase heading not required.)

Army Form C. 2118.

Headquarters 59th Div. l Train

VOL XV

| Place | Date April | Hour | Summary of Events and Information | Remarks and references to Appendices |
|---|---|---|---|---|
| BAMBECQUE | 22 | | R.H. ARNEKE R.P's E7.L.6.4 Sheet 27. No 2 Coy moved to a farm 3 mile N. N.W. of OOST CAPPEL No1 & No2 Coy moved to E.20.c.0.9 R.H. YPRES Madame 2. L. J. BLOIN proceeded to YPRES for duty | 1,2,3 |
| | 23 | | 2. LT. A.M. BANNISTER joined the Train for duty from the Base | 4,5 |
| | 26 | | R.H. ESQUELBECQ R.P's Madame Ordering me to prepare to move Corps in half an hour at 5pm. Reflected to use Nos 2 & 3 Coys moved to H. JANTERBIEZEN area | 6,7,8 |
| | 27 | | R.H. PROVEN R.P's 176 & 178 & 177 at ST. JANTERBIEZEN near Church No 4 Coy moved to JANTERBIEZEN | 9,10 |
| | 29 | | R.H. ROUSBRUGGE R.P's in Bde areas, No 3 Coy moved to E.I.D.R.P.1. Sh.127 No 4 Coy moved to HOUTKERQUE | 11,12 |
| | 30 | | R.H. ROUSBRUGGE R.P's 176 Bd Church JANTERBIEZEN 177 & 178 Bde Group at E.7.L.6.4 (Sheet 27) | 13 |

M. Brown Capt
for Lt Col Commanding
59TH DIVISIONAL TRAIN

Confidential

# WAR DIARY
## —of—
### O.C. 513 (No.1) Coy A.S.C. 59 Div⁓
from 1st to 30th April 1918.

(Vol. 14).

Army Form C. 2118.

# WAR DIARY
## or
## INTELLIGENCE SUMMARY

(Erase heading not required.)

Instructions regarding War Diaries and Intelligence Summaries are contained in F. S. Regs., Part II. and the Staff Manual respectively. Title Pages will be prepared in manuscript.

| Place | Date | Hour | Summary of Events and Information | Remarks and references to Appendices |
|---|---|---|---|---|
| Field. | 11/4/18. | — | 513 Coy A.S.C. 59th Division. | |
| | | | Company quartered in Billets & Barns at HENU. Stores in chew Shelters. Supplies drawn from SAULTY by M.T. Refilling Point at HENU. | |
| | 12/4/18. | — | 2/Lt. J. Blair No1 Coy 59th Divisional Train posted to No2 Coy 59th Divisional Train. | |
| | | | 2/Lt. F. Benton A.S.C. taken on the strength of the company. | |
| | 13/4/18 | — | 1. A.D. No435 evacuated by 4th Dvl. Division. | |
| | 16/4/18 | — | 1. A.D. Horse No396 destroyed by V.O. | |
| | 17/4/18 | — | 2.A.S. cases No 510 – 511 transferred to No2 Coy 59 Divl. Train. | |
| | 17/4/18 | — | 1 Rider from No522 admitted to 2/3 F.M.N.S. | |
| | 30/4/18 | — | Company quartered in Billets & Barns at HENU. Stores in cha. Shelter. Supplies drawn from SAULTY by M.T. Refilling Point at HENU. | |

[signature] Major

Commdg No513 Coy A.S.C.
59th Division.

Confidential

War Diary
of
No 2 Coy 59th Dvl Train
(514 Coy. A.S.C.)

From 1/4/18 to 30/4/18

Volume XV

Army Form C. 2118.

# WAR DIARY
## or
## INTELLIGENCE SUMMARY
(Erase heading not required.)

VOL. XV

No. 2 Coy. 59th Div. TRAIN.

| Place | Date | Hour | Summary of Events and Information | Remarks and references to Appendices |
|---|---|---|---|---|
| ECQUEDECQUES | 1.4.18 | | Ref Maps LENS 11. HAZEBROUCK 5A. Sheets 27 & 28 BELGIUM. Moved Coy. HQrs. & transport of 1/4 & 59 Div. Train via HAM-en-ARTOIS, MOLINGHEM-AIRE-HAM-en-ARTOIS, MOLINGHEM-AIRE-STEENBECQUE to MORBECQUE. Refilled Supply. See for HQ 176 Bde. 2/6 SOUTH STAFFS REGT. 2/5 & 2/6 NORTH STAFFS REGT. 2/1 and 2/3 N.M. FD. AMB. 467 and 468 Field Corp R.E. 2/1 N.M. M.G.S. 1ST SEC. C.R.E. 59 Div. N.M.P. 59 Div. Sqs. at BOURECQ at 1 p.m. and moved Same via HAM- MOLINGHEM-AIRE- STEENBECQUE to MORBECQUE and delivered Rations & collected wagons to units on the march. Park North of MORBECQUE. | Nil. |
| MORBECQUE. | 2.4.18. | | Received Reserve Supply Convoy at MORBECQUE at 5:30 a.m. & loaded own Supply wagons to units  S.S.E. of WATOU (L 13. a.b.3. Sheet 27 N.W.) MORBECQUE. Moved Coy. HQrs. via HAZEBROUCK - STEENVOORDE - TROCQLAN'DT to WATOU 2 miles S.E. of WATOU (L 13. a.b.3. Sheet 27 N.W.) and collected empty wagons. | Nil. Nil. |
| WATOU. | 3.4.18. | 10 a.m. | Refilled Group Supply convoys at WATOU & delivered to units | Nil. |
| " | 4.4.18. | 10 a.m. | Refilled Group Supply Convoy (less HQ 176 Bde + 3 Bn Nos which was drawn by Infm. transport) at WATOU and delivered to units 467 & 468 Bde Co. R.E. 2/1 and 2/3 N.M. 311. Amb. supply wagons travelled over bad roads which broke up on 5.4.18 travelled roads. Convoy 6 wagons to GRUBBEM Railhead for supplies & Coal | Nil. Nil. |
| " | 5.4.18 | 10 a.m. | Convoy 6 wagons to GRUBBEM Railhead for supplies & Coal. Refilled Bde. Group (less HQ Bde + 3 Bn Nos) at WATOU. | Nil. Nil. |
| " | 6.4.18 | | Received some empty wagons & a 1 N.M. N.E. Wsg. 59 Bn. Regd. T.C.R.E. 15 St. MorOng. 59 Div. Cran & refill with 177 Bde. Group on 7.4.18. 176 Bde. drawing for Inn transport of Reisen Infantry Brit. w/o Manchester 2/6/N.M. South Staffs Regt.) Handed over 59 Div. Corps 3 9 Supply wagons to HQ horses of Ammunition transport by Train wagons. | Nil. Nil. |
| " | 7.4.18 | | | Nil. |
| " | 9.4.18 | | Drew for Bde. Group Supplies in bulk from GRUBBEM Railhead to BRANDHOEK Area. Delivered rations to Shores Pt. of Refilled WATOU & despatched supply conveys forward with wk to BRANDHOEK Area for delivery. | Nil. |
| " | 10.4.18 | 8 a.m. | Moved HQrs/Coy. 15 lorries at H.16.a.8.4. (CARGINE CAMP W.YPRES AREA) (mile S.S. of VLAMERTINGHE) reestablished Supply Pt. after delivery. YPRES. Companies conveniently shelled from 10 p.m. till 5 a.m. between communication. | Nil. |
| VLAMERTINGHE | 11.4.18 | | Refilled. at 8 a.m. & delivered supplies in BRANDHOEK YPRES Areas. Refilled again 2 p.m. and resumed tracks Supply. See on lines linings Camp was shelled during night leaving light test morning of Bristol. | Nil. Nil. |
| " | 12.4.18 | 8 a.m. | Delivered supplies at BRANDHOEK & E.YPRES areas. Refilled at H.15.a. 8.4 and moved Helicopter over and supply section & | Nil. |
| BRANDHOEK | 13.4.18 | | BRISTOL CAMP BRANDHOEK. "D" Coy Train 4 par the below to change of Brigade Camp. Reposited (with Supply wagons to travel with Unit). Moved Coy. HQrs. via BUSSEBOOM and RENINGHELST TO NEWCASTLE CAMP on ZEVECOTEN- LA CLYTTE Road (9.35 a.5.2 - Shut 28), transport on CANPHIN LINES (M.6.a.B.9). | Nil. |
| ZEVECOTEN. | 14.4.18 | 8 a.m. | Refilled at Hd Square RENINGHELST. Returned to Groups at LUERS. Camp was considerably shelled in afternoon, but damage & we were slight, hit. 1/8 Bde. R.E. & 2/1 N.M. 311. Amb. broken on reduced strength of Brigade group. | Nil. |
| " | " | 6 p.m. | Refilled again at M. 6 a.2.9. & kept wagons under load on lines. | Nil. |

M.HAgilbuff Cpt.
o.c. 2 Coy. 59 Div. Train.

PAGE I.

2449 Wt. W14957/Mg0 759,000 1/16 J.B.C. & A. Forms/C.2118/12.

# WAR DIARY

## INTELLIGENCE SUMMARY

Army Form C. 2118.

Vol. XV — Page III.

No 2 Coy. 59th Div. TRAIN.

| Place | Date | Hour | Summary of Events and Information | Remarks and references to Appendices |
|---|---|---|---|---|
| ZEVECOTEN. | 15.4.18 | 11 a.m. | Delivered supplies to units at LOCRE and refilled again in evening at M.6.a.2.9. Vaarlijn lines again shelled during evening & night. | Suff. |
| " | 16.4.18 | | Delivered supplies to units of Group on LOCRE – ZEVECOTEN Road. Lines shelled during afternoon. Applied for authority to move. At 10 p.m. received authority to move subject to warrant T/Bngdr. which was received late. During | Suff. |
| " | 17.4.18 | | Irregular advance party at 8.30 a.m. At BUSSEBOOM Area. Camp and lines commenced to be heavily shelled at 8.45 a.m. During preparations for departure of supply convoy, stables & wagon lines were hit by shells. Three men o/Coy were wounded, one Spr o/Coy S.D.A. Train. of 2 SAC Replacement Coy. R. of 2/5 North Staff. Supplies & horses mildly by shell fire on trail through 19.8. warhorse scratched. During forward march had received a Lieut J. Blair attached Mr. Burg with agreement 1 damaged vehicle and 3 others which could not be moved of 5 others which could be moved with the Bussebom and Zevegoten 5 owing to wounded & dead horses. At this time I was again wounded. Came under heavy fire from Ostendum onwards decided to abandon attempt till morning at 5 p.m. journeyed as resolute as from wounded Bussebom, same under fairly heavy fire from Ostendum onwards c/Prefilled at G.15.c.3.5. Bussebom area. (Fighting one unit in turn with one supplied) and proceeded with journey back, to proper car, Hd which was handmade of cartridges all wagons empty. M. & Hdqrs o/Coy unit Supply Section & Final passage program as could be found via ASSELE in STEENVOORDE as TERDEGHEM which was again by O.S.M. Camp under their keep during afternoon. Moved Hdqrs o/Coy ava — mine heavy damaged wagons to 32nd Corps Vety C.C.S. at IMPERINHEM. Hay being severely wounded. Evacuated two mules & three heavy damaged horses. | Suff. |
| BUSSEBOOM. | 18.4.18 | 4 p.m. | | Suff. |
| " | | | | Suff. |
| TERDEGHEM. | 19.4.18 | 7 a.m. 1 p.m. | Refilled at TERDEGHEM. Moved Hdqrs o/Coy. and Supply Sec. of Fld Group via STEENVOORDE – WATOU – POPERINGHE at PESELHOEK. | Suff. |
| PESELHOEK. | 20.4.18 | 11 a.m. 3.30 pm | Refilled at PESELHOEK and delivered supplies. Refilled again at PESELHOEK. | Suff. |
| PESELHOEK | 21.4.18 | 7.30 a.m. | Moved 1st Supply Section via CANADA CORNER, INTERNATIONAL CORNER, PROVEN, HARINGHES to ROUSBRUGGE CAMP and delivered supplies at OOST CAPPEL – ROUSBRUGGE CAMP – BLUNK and HOUTKERKE. Camp bombed by hostile aircraft at 10.15 p.m when one man was wounded, 1318 Pte Perry K.Nt.D. What side and most Bomanl herein wounded. | Suff. |
| ROUSBRUGGE CAMP | | | | Suff. |
| OOST CAPPEL | 22.4.18 | 9 a.m. 1 p.m. | Refilled at HOUTKERKE and delivered supplies. — 2/Lieut J. Blair transferred to Base. 2/Lt A.M. Barnister reported for duty. Moved Coy. Hdqrs. 15 farms 3/4 mile N.N.W. of Oost Cappel. | Suff. |
| " | 23.4.18 | 9 a.m. | Refilled at HOUTKERKE and delivered supplies. Received an extra pack No 3 Coy 59 Div Train. sight A.F.D harness for duty pending arrival of remounts. | Suff. Suff. Suff. |
| " | 24.4.18 | 9 a.m. | Refilled at HOUTKERKE – delivered supplies. | Suff. |
| " | 25.4.18 26.4.18 | 9 a.m. 9 a.m. | Refilled at HOUTKERKE and delivered supplies. Delivered supplies at L.19.a.4.1 (about 2) and refilled at St Jan ter Biezen. Moved Coy. Hdqrs & Supply Sec. via MOERKEVAL – PROVEN as L.4.1.2.S. (about 27) evening midnight & arrived St Jan ter Biezen. 2/Lt A.M. Fld Cmdr. Announced to 177 Bde attd. | Suff. Suff. |
| POPERINGHE (WEST) | 27.4.18 | | Refilled at St Jan tea Biezen – delivered supplies as/Bde. Commd. 469, 1470 2nd O.G. R2. B.C/D.S. R.F.D. S.a.a. Sig, S.a.a. Sig. 59th D.A.C. Truncated 177 Bde, 2nd OG. Group, 59/5 Div. Train, 2/Div. M. Mch. W. Sec, 21 AD. D. S & Laundry officer 59th Div. Returned to strength. C.R.E. 59 Div., 59 D.L. Sigs, 1st R.E. Pt 36, 2nd and 3rd Pl. St Jan ter Biezen. | Suff. Suff. |
| " | 28.4.18 29.4.18 | | | Suff. |
| " | 30.4.18 | | Delivered supplies & refills at 3 p.m. at St Jan ter Biezen. | Suff. |

T.M.MacBrugh Capt
O.C. No 2 Coy. 59 Div. Train.

Confidential

War Diary

of.

(No 3) 515 Company A.S.C. 59th Division

from 1-4-18 to 30-4-18.

(Volume IV)

Army Form C. 2118.

# WAR DIARY
## or
## INTELLIGENCE SUMMARY.

(Erase heading not required.)

Instructions regarding War Diaries and Intelligence Summaries are contained in F. S. Regs., Part II. and the Staff Manual respectively. Title pages will be prepared in manuscript.

515 Co. A.S.C. 39th Divn. April 1918.

| Place | Date | Hour | Summary of Events and Information | Remarks and references to Appendices |
|---|---|---|---|---|
| LILLERS AREA | 1/4/18 | a.m. 2.0 | Coy HQ & pett Supplies moved by road to MORBECQUE | AFG |
| " | " | | Captain F.C. Smith admitted to Hospital | AFG |
| MORBECQUE | " | a.m. 7.0 | In Billets and quarters | AFG |
| " | 2/4/18 | a.m. 7.30 | Coy H.Q. moved to ST JAN-TER-BIEZEN area | AFG |
| | | | LIEUT. P.R.R. DIBBEN reported for duty as S.O. Vice Capt. Smith sick — | AFG |
| ST-JAN-TER BIEZEN | " | a.m. 4.0 | In Camp | AFG |
| | 3/4/18 | | Belgian labourers attd. for duty | AFG |
| | 4/4/18 | a.m. 2.0 | Coy H.Q. & pett Supplies moved by road to 2912 Camp YPRES (West) | AFG |
| YPRES (WEST) | " | a.m. 5.0 | In Camp | AFG |
| | " | | 1 driver evacuated sick by 64th C.C.S. | AFG |

Andrew Capt —
OC 515 Coy A.S.C. 39 Divn.

(A8004) Wt. W1771/M2 31 730,000 5/17 Sch. 52 Forms/C2118/14
D. D., & L., London, E.C.

Army Form C. 2118.

# WAR DIARY
## or
## INTELLIGENCE SUMMARY.
*(Erase heading not required.)*

Instructions regarding War Diaries and Intelligence Summaries are contained in F. S. Regs., Part II. and the Staff Manual respectively. Title pages will be prepared in manuscript.

| Place | Date | Hour | Summary of Events and Information | Remarks and references to Appendices |
|---|---|---|---|---|
| YPRES WEST | 5/4/18 | | 515 Coy A.S.C. 39th Div Train } April 1918 Return on ration strength | |
| | | | 39th Div: M.G.C. | |
| | | | 2/1st Field Amb. 467 Coy R.E. | |
| | | | 2/2nd " " 469 " R.E. | |
| | | | 2/3rd " " 470 " R.E. | |
| | | | 1/1 1st Royal Fus. Train } | |
| " | 7/4/18 | | LIEUT. J.C. FAIRFAX ROSS proceeded to VIII Corps (pro rehet) | |
| | | | M.V.S. DADOS A+E GRENADE DUMP. AREA Comdt (YPRES) BRANDICK } Came on ration strength | |
| | | | T.H.Q. S.A.A. Seetn 16th Welsh Regt | |
| | | | D.H.Q. MMP.+ type 20. Royal Fus. 2/3 of advance by | |
| | | | C.R.E. 306 Coy R.E. 9/2 Shr Signals 746 Empt Coy | |
| | | | 81st SAN. SECTION | |
| " | 8/4/18 | | 1 R.C.O. with 20 men of Royal Fus to push reported for wood cutting | |
| " | 9/4/18 | | 16 Welsh Regt } struck off ration strength | |
| | | | 20 Royal Fus } | |
| | | | | H.A. Brown Capt. o/c 515 Coy A.S.C. 39 Div Tn |

Army Form C. 2118.

# WAR DIARY
## or
## INTELLIGENCE SUMMARY.
(Erase heading not required.)

Instructions regarding War Diaries and Intelligence Summaries are contained in F. S. Regs., Part II. and the Staff Manual respectively. Title pages will be prepared in manuscript.

575 Coy ASC 39th DW — April 1918

| Place | Date | Hour | Summary of Events and Information | Remarks and references to Appendices |
|---|---|---|---|---|
| YPRES WEST | 9/4/18 | | Supplies drawn by H.T. from VLAMERTINGHE Rail Head | |
| " | 10/4/18 | | Camp heavily shelled by Enemy artillery | |
| " | 11/4/18 | | 1 H.D. evacuated to 2/1st M.V.S. | |
| " | 12/4/18 | | LIEUT. A.J. LIDDIARD proceeded on 3 months employment leave | |
| " | | | 1 Surplus HD evacuated to 2/1st M.V.S. | |
| " | | 6.0 | Coy HQ with Supplies moved by road to BRISTOL CAMP | |
| BRISTOL CAMP | | 7.0 | In Camp | |
| " | 13/4/18 | 2.0 | Coy HQ moved by road to the WATOU Area | |
| WATOU AREA | " | 6.0 | LIEUT. J.G. FAIRFAX ROSS reported on line of march from VIII Corps Gas School | |
| | | | In Camp and Billets | |

A. Green Capt. —
OC 575 Coy, ASC 39 Divl.

D. D. & I., London, E.C.
(A5004) Wt. W17711/M2 31 750,000 5/17 Sch. 52 Forms/C2118/14

# WAR DIARY

## INTELLIGENCE SUMMARY

Army Form C. 2118.

575 Coy A.S.C. 39th Div.  April 1918

| Place | Date | Hour | Summary of Events and Information | Remarks and references to Appendices |
|---|---|---|---|---|
| WATOU AREA | 14/4/18 | 4 p.m. 1.0 | Coy. H.Q. 6th with supplies moved by road to HOOGRAF area — | KEL |
| HOOGRAF AREA | " | a.m. 6.0 | In camp and billets — | AG |
| " | 15/4/18 | | 306. R.C.C. 746th Empt. Coy. 81st Gen. Sec. Area Comdt YPRES and BRANDIOK } struck off ration strength | EL |
| | | | 2 drivers wounded one of whom since discharged. Corpl. PEACOCK died 15th | CC |
| " | | | 7th Lieut. F.A.A WHITFIELD reported for duty from 9th Sup Train | AG |
| " | 16/4/18 | | 59th A.A. Salvage } 7th Field Amb } struck off ration strength 467 th Coy R.E.   470.E.) R.E.S | YE |
| " | 17/4/18 | a.m. 10.0 | attempted delivery of supplies to Bde group held up by shell fire these were afterwards successfully delivered afterwards by another | KEL |
| " | 18/4/18 | | 1 Roader of 7/4th Lincolns wounded on duty | AG |

Authors Entries - O 575 - Coy. A.S.C

Army Form C. 2118.

# WAR DIARY
## INTELLIGENCE SUMMARY
(Erase heading not required.)

575 Coy A.S.C. 59th Div. April 1918

| Place | Date | Hour | Summary of Events and Information | Remarks and references to Appendices |
|---|---|---|---|---|
| HOOGRAF AREA | 20/4/18 | 5.0 a.m. | Coy. HQ.rs moved by road to No. 6 Camp PESELHOEK. | A.G. |
| PESELHOEK | " | 7.30 a.m. | In Camp | A.G. |
| " | 21/4/18 | 7 a.m. | 2⅓ Field Ambs struck off ration strength | A.G. |
| " | " | 11.0 a.m. | Coy HQrs with Supplies moved by road to HOUTKERQUE (area) | A.G. |
| HOUTKERQUE AREA | " | 4.0 p.m. | In camp and Billets | A.G. |
| " | " | | @ HQ T.M.O. C.R.E. DADOS MVS 59th Divn Coys } struck off ration strength | A.G. |
| " | 23/4 | | 8 H.D. Horses transd to No. 514 Coy A.S.C. | A.G. |
| " | " | | 1 Driver (Reinforcement) received from Base | A.G. |
| " | 26/4/18 | 4 p.m. 7.45 | Coy HQrs with Supply lines moved by road to Schools Camp, ST JANTJE (RIJZEN) (area) | A.G. |

A.Green Capt— OC 575 Coy A.S.C 59th Div

Army Form C. 2118.

# WAR DIARY
## or
## INTELLIGENCE SUMMARY.
(Erase heading not required.)

515 B. A.S.C. 59th Div. Summary of Events and Information April 1918.

| Place | Date | Hour | Summary of Events and Information | Remarks and references to Appendices |
|---|---|---|---|---|
| SCHOOLS CAMP | 26/4/18 | 12.0 (mid night) | In Camp | A.C. |
| " | 27/18 | 4 a.m / 5.0 | Coy HQ & motor supplies moved by road to FARM. E.30.d.4.0. sheet 27 | A.C. |
| FARM E.30.d.4.0 sheet 27 | " | a.m. 6.0 | In Camp and Billets | A.C. |
| " | 29/4/18 | 4 a.m / 6.0 | Coy HQ & motor supplies moved by road to HOUTKERQUE area. | A.C. |
| HOUTKERQUE area | " | a.m 9.0 | In Camp | A.C. |
| " | 30/18 | | M.M.P. & Supplies of Nitrate beds 2nd & J. struck off ration strength. 469 Coy R.E. 59th M.G.C. 2/5 Field Amb came on ration strength | A.C. |
| " | | | General health of the company during the month has been good. Four H.D. Horses were slightly wounded by shell fire and on the whole the general condition of horses fairly good. [signature] Capt. O.C. 515 Coy 59th Div. | A.C. |

War Diary. O.I. 516 Coy A.S.C. (N°4)
59th Div. Train

for April 1918

Army Form C. 2118.

# WAR DIARY
## *or*
## INTELLIGENCE SUMMARY

*(Erase heading not required.)*

Instructions regarding War Diaries and Intelligence Summaries are contained in F. S. Regs., Part II. and the Staff Manual respectively. Title Pages will be prepared in manuscript.

| Place | Date | Hour | Summary of Events and Information | Remarks and references to Appendices |
|---|---|---|---|---|
| | | | | |

2449 Wt. W14957/M90 750,000 1/16 J.B.C. & A. Forms/C.2118/12.

Army Form C. 2118.

# WAR DIARY
or
## INTELLIGENCE SUMMARY

(Erase heading not required.)

516 Coy. A.S.C.
59th Div. Train

Instructions regarding War Diaries and Intelligence Summaries are contained in F.S. Regs., Part II. and the Staff Manual respectively. Title Pages will be prepared in manuscript.

| Place | Date | Hour | Summary of Events and Information | Remarks and references to Appendices |
|---|---|---|---|---|
| ECQUEDECQUES | April 1st 1918 | | Coy moves by route march 9AM — Arrives MORBECQUE 8.30 PM — Horses on road — Men in drums. | M.T. |
| MORBECQUE | 2nd | | Reveille 5.30 AM — Coy moves at 8.30 AM and arrives at Road Camp St. JANSTER BIEZEN at 4 PM | M.T. |
| ST JANSTER 3rd BIEZEN | 3rd | | Coy in huts — Horses in stables — S.R.P. at X Cross 1½ mile from WATOU on POPERINGHE ROAD | M.T. |
| " | 4" | | One O.R. reports from leave. | M.T. |
| " | 5" | | Two O.R's report from leave. — | P.T. |
| " | 6" | | Advance party sent to take over Camp from No 4 Coy 33rd Div Train at VLAMTINGHE — CASSELL ROAD | |
| " | 7" | | Coy moves by route march at 12 noon to Camp on STEENVOORDE — CASSELL ROAD — Men in huts — horses in lines — Advance party recalled from VLAMTINGHE | M.T. |
| STEENVOORDE | 8" | | ORs transferred to Surplus Transport Depôt and struck off strength together with 6 HD/Horses and 3 G.S. wagons. S.R.P. near Coy from main STEENVOORDE | M.T. |
| | 9 | | Coy moves by route march at 1 P.M. to CARBINE CAMP YPRES WEST taking over from No 2 Coy 41st Div Train. — S.R.P. in Coy Lines. — Camp is shelled during the night | M.T. |
| | 10" | | Supplies drawn by 1st Line transport — Train Coy ordered to draw supplies for Bdy Group by H.T. from VLAMTINGHE — Railhead — but order is cancelled without being carried out. b. GRUBHAM | M.T. |
| YPRES | 11" | | Coy moved by route march at 10 AM. for DRANOUTRE but owing to hostile shelling was ordered to stay in LOCRE — Accommodated in Y.M.C.A | M.T. |
| | 12" | | | I.D.T. |

2449 Wt. W14957/M90 750,000 1/16 J.B.C. & A. Forms/C.2118/12.

Army Form C. 2118.

# WAR DIARY
or
## INTELLIGENCE SUMMARY

*(Erase heading not required.)*

Instructions regarding War Diaries and Intelligence Summaries are contained in F. S. Regs., Part II. and the Staff Manual respectively. Title Pages will be prepared in manuscript.

| Place | Date | Hour | Summary of Events and Information | Remarks and references to Appendices |
|---|---|---|---|---|
| LOCRE | 13th | | COY moves by route march at 8AM and proceed to CANADA CORNER and remains there till 4PM and then moves just NORTH of WESTOUTRE. — STP in COY lines — Supplies kept on. Supply wagons out all night. | M.O. |
| WESTOUTRE | 14th | | Supplies delivered to units and wagons again refilled remaining on COY lines for the night. | M.O. |
| | 15th | | T.HQ parties out & is accommodated with the COY. | M.O. |
| | 17th | | The Area is heavily shelled and preparations are made for a move. — Hostile shelling causes in afternoon and COY area not being of camp. | M.O. |
| | ADV | | COY moves by route march to PESEL HOEK. — Supplies delivered to B.H.Q in BRANDHOEK AREA. — Hostile aircraft over Camp at night and dropped a bomb near PESEL HOEK drop fuel in the vicinity. — STP obtained at CAMP & PESEL HOEK | M.O. |
| PESELHOEK | 21st | | COY moves by route march to SHRUBYE CAMP HOUTKERQUE at 11.30 AM and are accommodated in tents. — Supplies delivered in TY/BO AREA — STP in road west 1/2 mile N.W of HOUTKERQUE | M.O. |
| HOUTERQUE | 22nd | | COY moves by route march to a farm on the HOUTERQUE — HERZEELE ROAD at 2PM | M.O. |
| | 24th | | LIEUT F. PIGGIN and 30 ORs proceed to CALAIS to draw remounts | M.O. |
| | 25th | | W/H L/CPL reverted to permanent grade (DVR 4th class) for inefficiency. | M.O. |
| | 27th | | COY moves by route march to ST JANSTER BIEZEN for 24 hrs and is accommodated in farm SW of Village. — STP at VILLAGE CHURCH | M.O. |

Army Form C. 2118.

# WAR DIARY
## or
## INTELLIGENCE SUMMARY
*(Erase heading not required.)*

| Place | Date | Hour | Summary of Events and Information | Remarks and references to Appendices |
|---|---|---|---|---|
| ST. JANSTER BIEZEN | 48" | | Billetting in afternoon and troops remain packed over night in Coy lines | |
| | 29" | | Coy moves by route march at 8 am to HOUTKER QUE and to HERZEELE ROAD — SRP on second place as from on HOUTKER QUE — HERZEELE ROAD. That time Coy was in the area. | |
| HOUT KERQUE | | | The following units have been referred by S.O. 178.14. Billy for the following units of Issues inclusive during April 1918. | |
| | | | HQ 178/M Bdg. 1.4.18 — 30.4.18 | |
| | | | 2/5 Sherwood Foresters 1.4.18 — 30.4.18 | |
| | | | 3/5 " | |
| | | | 4/5 " | |
| | | | 4 Coy 59 Div Train | |
| | | | 2/2 N.M. Field Ambulance 1.4.18 — 4.4.18 | |
| | | | 470 Fld Coy R.E. 1.4.18 — 4.4.15 — 14.4.18 — 30.4.18 | |
| | | | 6/7 Royal Scots Fusiliers 1.4.18 — 4.4.18 | |
| | | | 59 Batt. M.G.C. 1 — 4 — 18 — 6 — 4 — 18 | |
| | | | 178 T.M.B. 5.4.18 — 30.4.18 | |
| | | | A Coy 59 Bath M.G.C. 11.4.18 — 23.4.18 | |
| | | | 2/3 N.M. Field Ambulance 22.4.18 — 30.4.18 | |
| | | | B Coy 59 Bath M.G.C. 29.4.18 — 30.4.18 | M Wstam Johnston 516 Coy ASC 59 Div Train |

No 16

Confidential

War Diary

Headquarters 59th Divisional Train

From 1/5/18 to 31/5/18.

Volume XVI

Army Form C. 2118.

# WAR DIARY
## or
## INTELLIGENCE SUMMARY
(Erase heading not required.)

Vol XVI

HEADQUARTERS 50TH DIVISIONAL TRAIN

Instructions regarding War Diaries and Intelligence Summaries are contained in F.S. Regs., Part II. and the Staff Manual respectively. Title pages will be prepared in manuscript.

| Place | Date MAY | Hour | Summary of Events and Information | Remarks and references to Appendices |
|---|---|---|---|---|
| BAMBECQUE | 1st | | R.H. ROUSBRUGGE. R.P. North right Church. ST JANSTER-BIEZEN. 177 & 44 - 173 y y4 - 174 ½<br>Et. ½ 6, 4 (SL ½ 27) No! 3&4 Coys LE HOUTKERQUE | |
| | 3rd | | R.H. EBBLINGHEM. R.P. La Barre | ½ |
| | 5th | | R.H. EBBLINGHEM. No 4 Coy move to ROBROECK near Rubly. No nos wheel pontoon | ½ |
| | | | to ST OMER. No 3 R.P. at La Remarde ST OMER | ½ |
| ST OMER | 6th | | R.H. EBBINGHEM. T.H.Q. move to ST OMER. No 4 Coy move to La Remarde ST OMER. | ½ |
| | | | Nos 2 & 3 Coys move to KINDERBECK. R.P. 170 & 171 (Ru Groule) La KINDERBECK | ½ |
| | 9th | | R.H. EBBLINGHEM. No 3 Coy 2 R.P. 29. 177 - 178 B.A.G. & Lunc, MAMETZ. | ½ |
| | | | No 4 Coy move to BLESSY. R.P. 9 175 R.P. move to La Remarde ST OMER | ½ |
| HESTRUS | 10th | | R.H. DIEVAL. THQ moves HESTRUS. No 2 Coy move to METZ. R.P. Ru L | ½ |
| | | | No 3 Coy 2 R.P. 177 B.A.G. move to SACHIN. No 4 Coy + R.P. Ru Un move to ROURS | ½ |
| | 11th | | R.H. DIEVAL. No 2 Coy + R.P. 176 R.U. move to FIEFS. Sieur + R.P. move at | ½ |
| | | | GAUCHIN - LEGAL. Ip the Galusiar Guards work | ½ |
| | 12th | | No 3 Coy move to HERIPRE. R.P. 27 Rueport La GAUCHIN - LEGAL | ½ |
| | | | No 4 Coy move to SAUCHIN. R.P. 73 B.s.G y met at SAUCHIN | ½ |
| | 14th | | No 2 Coy move to ROCOURT. R.P. 76 Rue Le AVESNES LE COMTE | ½ |
| | 16th | | No 2 Coy move to AVESNES Le COMTE. Arlew Rep Supply Dept between | ½ |
| | | | Johnny I place blended at PERIEZ Artless MJA Artless to FieFS | ½ |

Army Form C. 2118.

# WAR DIARY
## or
## INTELLIGENCE SUMMARY.
(Erase heading not required.)

HEADQUARTERS 59TH DIVISIONAL TRAIN    VOL XVI

| Place | Date | Hour | Summary of Events and Information | Remarks and references to Appendices |
|---|---|---|---|---|
| HESTRUS | MAY 1st | — | 24 Wagons Iron Shoes to but Ammunition Park [?] | R |
| | 10th | — | R.H. DIEVAL to RATION dump N° 2 ESQ for [?] | R |
| | | | in the [?] through Humank LEBIEZ | R |
| | 21st | — | N° 2 Coy to TIEFS, R.P. de B. les FIEFS | R |
| | 23rd | — | R.H. DIEVAL N° 1 Coy R.P. du [?] THÉROUANNE R.H. | R |
| | | | [?] de AIRE | R |
| | 31st | — | R.H. DIEVAL to [?] HESTRUS N° 1 Coy ELERDRÉE R.H. TIÉRÉIN | R |
| | | | le GAUCHIN-LEGAL N° 3 [?] to INSTALL at GACHIN | R |
| | | | N° 2 Coy — R.P. [?] as at THÉROUANNE R.H. [?] AIRE | R |
| | | | N° 1 Coy [?] with N° 2 Supply Column FEBvIN | |
| | | | [?] R.P. le HÉNO. CH. DE SAULTY | |

[signature]
COMMANDING
59TH DIVISIONAL TRAIN

*Confidential*

WAR DIARY

— of —

O.C. 513 Coy A.S.C. 59th Divn.

from 1st to 31st May 1918.

Vol. 15.

VOL XVI

# WAR DIARY

## INTELLIGENCE SUMMARY.

(Erase heading not required.)

Army Form C. 2118.

Instructions regarding War Diaries and Intelligence Summaries are contained in F. S. Regs., Part II. and the Staff Manual respectively. Title pages will be prepared in manuscript.

| Place | Date | Hour | Summary of Events and Information | Remarks and references to Appendices |
|---|---|---|---|---|
| Field | 15/4/16 to 31/5/16 | | 513 Coy A.S.C. 59 Division. Employed in Beets and Jumps at HENU. Horses in lines to be in Stables. Supplies drawn by M.T. Columns from SAULTY. Rations drawn at HENU. | |

NO. 1 COMPANY
59th DIVL. TRAIN
(No. 513 Coy. A.S.C.)

Confidential

War Diary

No 2 Coy 5th Sqn Bde Res
5th G. H.S.(C.)

From 1/5/18 to 31/5/18

Volume XVI

Army Form C. 2118.

# WAR DIARY
## or
## INTELLIGENCE SUMMARY

(Erase heading not required.)

Vol. XVI

O.C. N° 2 Coy. 59th Divisional Train.

PAGE 1.

Ref. Maps. Lens 11. Hazebrouck 5A.
Belgium sheet 27.

| Place | Date | Hour | Summary of Events and Information | Remarks and references to Appendices |
|---|---|---|---|---|
| ST JAN TER BIEZEN | 1.5.18 | | Commenced work with Coy. HQrs and supply section situate at ST JAN TER BIEZEN (Belgium Sheet 27 — L.2.a.53). Baggage wagons being dealt with units. Brigade Groups (176") for Ration purposes consisting of HQ + 3 Batres. 176 I.J. Bde. N°2 Sec. 59 Div. Train. 2/1 N.M Fld Amb, 59 Machine Gun Battn., C.R.E. 59 Div., 467 468 + 470 Field Coys R.E., 6/7 Battn. Royal Scots Fusiliers, 5.a.a. sec. 59 Tn Cy. HQ. 59 D.T.W. 59 Div Sig. Coy., M.M.P. and Supplies. Refills at ST JAN TER BIEZEN. HQ Allowance for an addition 21 offrs. Rations supplied for 3 1/2 Div Supply Sec. wagons | TWIT |
| " | 6.5.18 | | Delivered rations 15 17/8 Bde HQ + 3 Battns in TRIPPOTE FARM AREA at 5 AM, & 3 Brd Cav Corp. in ST JAN TER BIEZEN AREA, and moved Coy HQ and Supply Sec. via WATOU, HOUTKERQUE, WORMHOUDT, in POPERINGHE WEST AREA. ES M 5th Battn. in ST JAN TER BIEZEN ZEGGARS CHAPEL to KINDERBELEK (2/5 miles E.N.E. of ST MOMELIN) delivering supplies on route to 6/7 Royal Scots Fusiliers at HOUTKERQUE + 2/1 N M Fld Amb. at RUBROUCK. | TWIT |
| KINDERBELEK | 7.5.18 | | Refills at KINDERBELEK and delivered to "Bulk HQ" at ST MOMELIN. 3 1/2 wagons 176 T.M.B. + M of KINDERBELEK, also 2 other wagons 2/1 N M Fld 21/NM 310 Amb. 3 Brigade Ration Supply trade E. of ERNESSBRIDGE (3m N. of RUBROUCK) allowance for transport personnel of the train with water & others to ST OMER. | TWIT |
| " | 8.5.18 | | Refill at KINDERBELEK and delivered in KINDERBELEK, ST MORELIN and LEDERZEELE AREA. 467, 468 + 470 Field Coys. R.E. c.R.E. — 2/1 N M Mer Vet Sec. taken in ration 1/178 Bde. Group. | TWIT |
| " | 10.5.18 | | Refills at ST OMER. Moved Company wagons and Supply Section from KINDERBELEK via ST MOMELIN — ST OMER — BLARINGQUES — ECQUES — REBECQ to MAMETZ and delivered supplies at ECQUES, REBECQ and MAMETZ. | TWIT |
| MAMETZ | 11.5.18 | | Refills at MAMETZ and moved Coy HQrs. Supply Section via ENTREE BLANCHE — AUCHY-AU-BOIS — WESTREHEM to FIEFS and delivered supplies at FIEFS and NEDONCHELLE. | TWIT |
| FIEFS | 12.5.18 | | Refills at FIEFS. 467 Fld Co R.E. added to Brigade Ration Group for one day only and rations for 175 + 176 Inf Bde. Group | TWIT |
| " | 13.5.18 | | Refills at 9 A.M. and delivered in Work in FIEFS and NEDONCHELLE. Refills arrive at 6 p.m. and despatched to unit ordering. Supply Wagons of 2/1 N.M. Fld Amb. S.a.a. Sec. 59 D.A.C., 79 H Gun Battn and one Sup: Section Supply Wagon 2/6 N Staffs, 2/6 North Staffs (including transport personal of same) to report to O.C. N°4 Coy. 59 Div Train at SHOWN LE Stationery; Supply wagons 176 7 Roy. Scot Fusiliers to report to O.C. N°3 Cy. 59 Div Train at SMOUTH LEGAL after delivering rations Coy lines. 1 Supply wagon each HQ 176 Inf. Bde., 2/6 S. Staffs, 2/6 N Staffs, 5 North Staff with rations for training cables. | TWIT |
| " | 14.5.18 | | Moved Coy HQrs + Supply Section via SAINS LES PERNES — TANGRY — VALHUON — MONCHY LE BRETON to ROCOURT + delivered supplies at MAGNICOURT EN COMTE. | TWIT |
| ROCOURT | 15.5.18 | | Moved Coy HQrs + Supply Section via CHELERS — TINQUES — PENIN to AVESNES LE COMTE. Refills received and delivered to HQ 176 Bde. at AVESNES, 2/5 South Staff at SOMBRIN, 2/6 N staff at HABARCQ + 2/5 N staff at HAUTEVILLE. | TWIT |
| AVESNES LE COMTE | 16.5.18 | | Taken on ration strength III Corps School, 4/2 Bad. Roy. Welch Fusiliers, and 1st, 2nd + 3rd + 75th Prov. Garrison Guard Battns. 24 G.S. Wagon, 48 H.D. horses 2 Riders 1 officer + 37 O.Rs. joined of 66th Division (sic) Horse of 65th Div Train is very distinctive staff. | TWIT |
| " | 19.5.18 | | Despatched 2/Lieut E.H.ALBRICH (66 Train) 1/c Supply wagons of 2/6 N.Staffs.T.C. 4 Rank, 9, 9, B, 4 + 5 Gram. Br. R. W. F. to proceed with these units to THEROUANNE AREA Staging at MAGNICOURT EN COMTE — FIEFS AND MAMETZ 1/1 London, Mot. Vet. Sec. 2 H.D. horses of 66 Div. Train. Refills removes in command of Group at AVESNES and delivered. Recruit + mule stores from S.A.A. Sec. 59 D.A.C. is distributed as required. Despatched all Baggage wagons to units | TWIT |

2149 Wt. W14957/M90 750,000 1/16 J.B.C. & A. Forms/C.2118/12.

# WAR DIARY
## INTELLIGENCE SUMMARY

Army Form C. 2118.

No 2 Coy. 59th Divisional Train. Vol. XVI. (Continued)
Page 2.

*(Erase heading not required.)*

Instructions regarding War Diaries and Intelligence Summaries are contained in F.S. Regs., Part II. and the Staff Manual respectively. Title Pages will be prepared in manuscript.

| Place | Date | Hour | Summary of Events and Information | Remarks and references to Appendices |
|---|---|---|---|---|
| AVESNES-LE-COMTE. | 20.5.18. | | Despatched 2/Lieut A.M. BANISTER i/c Supply Convoy of 5th N. Staff T.C. and 5th Prov. C.G. Battn to proceed to MAISNIL-COURT EN COMTÉ - FIEFS & MANIETZ, refilling and delivering supplies en route. Refilled remainder of 176 Fd. Coy. group at AVESNES LE COMTE and distributed. | Pmk. |
|  | 21.5.18. | | Proceeded with HdQrs of Coy. Supply Wagon M.T. 176 Bde., Supply Wagons of 2/5 S. Staff T.C., 2nd & 3rd Prov. C.G. Battns via TINQUES to MAGNICOURT-EN-COMTÉ. There delivered for consumption 2nd unit & 3 lieutenants unit and handed over their Supply Wagons to G.T. No 3 Coy, 59 Div Train on change of Units to ration strength of 177th Bde. group. | Pmk. |
| FIEFS. | 22.5.18. | | Thence proceeded with HdQrs of Coy. via VALHUON to FIEFS and there joined 2/Lt A.M. BANISTER's Convoy, refilled & stood by until [word], 4 Bde Fd. Coy. R.E. taken over & then refilling B group for consumption 23 inst. Despatched Supply Wagon 4 Bq. Sig. Coy. R.E. after refilling to CLARQUES - Bq. supplies Coy. at THÉROUANNE on 23 inst. Despatched Supply Wagon H.Q. 176 Bde with transport of Bde H.Q. via FLÉCHIN to THÉROUANNE. Delivered supplies to FIEFS and BAILLEUL LES PERNES to 5 N. Staff T.C., 1st & 5th Prov. C.G. Battns wagons from S.A.A. Sec. 59 D.A.C. Stores further transport units. | Pmk. |
| FIEFS. | 23.5.18. | | Moved HdQrs of Coy. with Supply Wagons of 5 N. Staff T.C., 1st & 5th Prov. C.G. B. to NIELLES (1000 yds S.W. of THÉROUANNE) Refilled at Railway Station THÉROUANNE & delivered. 431 & 432 Field Coys R.E. taken on ration strength of Brigade group. | Pmk. Pmk. |
| THÉROUANNE. | 24.5.18. | | Refilled at THÉROUANNE. | Pmk. |
|  | 28.5.18. | | Took over Supply rations strengths for consumption 27th May. C.R.E. 59 Div. and 6/7 Batn. Royal Scots Fusiliers. Also 135 & 538 A.T. Cos. R.E. | Pmk. |
|  | 29.5.18. 31.5.18. | | Transferred to 66th Div. Train 2 G.S. Wagons, 2 G.S. Wagons, 4 horses (RD) 2 turnouts accompanying Training Cadres of 2/6 N. Staff & 2/5 S. Staff respectively on 28 & 29 May to Etaples and made the 16.5.18 handed over to 2nd Coy. 59 Div. Train as from 48 H.D. Lorum, 24 Bureus of 66 Div. Train as approved by minute date 16.5.18 Authority G.H.Q. 6196 (QRB.). 5 HD horses & carts having been deposited been deposited until recently possibility. | Pmk. |

M.H. Taylor, Capt.
O.C. No 2 Coy, 59 Div. Train.

Confidential

War Diary

of

515 Company. A.S.C. sqt Division

From 1.5.18 to 31.5.18

( Volume I )

Army Form C. 2118.

Vol XVI

# WAR DIARY
# INTELLIGENCE SUMMARY.

(Erase heading not required.)

515 Coy. A.S.C. Sgt Bearson    May 1918.

| Place | Date | Hour | Summary of Events and Information | Remarks and references to Appendices |
|---|---|---|---|---|
| HOUTKERQUE (area) | 1/5/18 | | In camp | |
| " | 5/5/18 | 8.0 a.m. | 1 Driver Reinforcement received from the Base | |
| " | 6/5/18 | 6.0 a.m. | Coy. H.Q. with supplies for Bde Group moved by road to ST MOMELIN area | |
| ST MOMELIN (area) | 6/5/18 | | In Camp | |
| " | 6/5/18 | | T.M.O. 2/1st M.V.S. } Came on ration strength fr 6/5/18 only<br>DADOS. 59th Div Laundry } | |
| " | 8/5/18 | | Captain F.J.G. Smith reported for duty as S.O. from hospital | |
| " | 9/5/18 | | Coy. H.Q. moved by road to MAMETZ area | |
| MAMETZ | 9/5/18 | 5.0 p.m. | In Billets and quarters | |
| " | 10/5/18 | 11.0 a.m. | Coy H.Q. moved by road to SACHIN | |
| SACHIN | 10/5/18 | 3.0 p.m. | In Billets and quarters. | |

A Green Capt.
O/c No. 515 Coy. A.S.C.
50th Division.

Army Form C. 2118.

# WAR DIARY
## or
## INTELLIGENCE SUMMARY.
*(Erase heading not required.)*

Summary of Events and Information  May 1918.  VOL XVI

515 Coy. A.S.C. 59th Division

| Place | Date | Hour | Summary of Events and Information | Remarks and references to Appendices |
|---|---|---|---|---|
| SACHIN | 11/5/18 | | 59th D.H.Q.  Div. Salvage Coy  <br> M.M.P. + Traps  DADOS <br> 59th Div. Signals  Div. Laundry <br> 250 Empty | |
| " | 12/5/18 | 9.30 a.m | Coy H.Q. moved by road to HERIPRE | |
| HERIPRE | 12/5/18 | 3.0 p.m | In Billets and quarters | |
| " | 12/5/18 | | C.R.E.  34th M.U.S. } came on ration strength <br> 469 Coy. R.E.  %  DL 1 <br> 15th ESSEX.  23rd LIVERPOOLS <br> 11th S.L.I. | |
| " | 13/5/18 | | 469 Coy R.E. %  36th DL1  } came on ration strength | |
| " | 14/5/18 | | 1 Wheeler driver transferred from 516 Coy A.S.C. 59th Divn | |
| " | 14/5/18 | | 470 Coy. R.E. came on ration strength | |

K. Green Capt.
o/c No. 515 Coy. A.
59th Division.

Army Form C. 2118.

# WAR DIARY
## or
## INTELLIGENCE SUMMARY.
(Erase heading not required.)

Vol XVI

| Place | Date | Hour | Summary of Events and Information | Remarks and references to Appendices |
|---|---|---|---|---|
| HERIPPE | 15/5/18 | | 515 Coy. A.S.C. 59th Division May 1918. | |
| " | 15/5/18 | | 11 G.S. Wagon. 22 H.D. Horses 11 Drivers Transferred from 61st Div¹ Train | AG |
| " | 16/5/18 | | 2/Corpl H. Simons (Supply detail surplus) sent to the base. | AG |
| " | 16/5/18 | | 1 G.S. Wagon. 2 H.D. Horses. 1 Driver Transferred from 61st Div¹ Train | AG |
| " | 17/5/18 | | X Corps Horse adviser inspected all G.S. Horses etc. | AG |
| " | 21/5/18 | | 4 G.S. Wagons. 8 H.D. Horses. 4 Drivers Transferred from 66th Div¹ Train | AG |
| " | 23/5/18 | | 2/6th South Staffs 2nd Field Cos. R.E. 23rd K.R.R. 13th West Riding Reg¹ } Came on ration strength | AG |
| " | 23/5/18 | | 2/Lieut. F.A.A. WHITFIELD Transferred to 576 Coy, A.S.C. 59th Div¹ | AG |
| " | 24/5/18 | | Lieut. M.C. JOHNSTON Transferred from 576 Coy A.S.C. 59th Div¹ | AG |

A.H. Green Capt.
O/c No. 515 C.T. A.S.C.
59th Division.

Army Form C. 2118.

Vol XVI

# WAR DIARY
or
# INTELLIGENCE SUMMARY.
(Erase heading not required.)

515 Coy. A.S.C. 59th Division.    Summary of Events and Information    May 1918.

| Place | Date | Hour | Summary of Events and Information | Remarks and references to Appendices |
|---|---|---|---|---|
| HERIPRE | 25/5/18 | 9.0 a.m. | Coy HQ62 moved by road to HERMIN but returned to original Billets and quarters at HERIPRE at 2.0 p.m. | |
| " | 28/5/18 | | 1 G.S. Wagon. 2 H.D. Horses 1 Driver transferred to 30th Div. Train | |
| " | 28/5/18 | | 1 H.D. Horse of 66th Div. Train transferred to the Coy. Evacuated to 32 M.V.S. | |
| " | 29/5/18 | | 3 H.D. Horses. 1 Driver transferred to 573 Coy A.S.C. 59th Div. | |
| " | | | 1 H.D. Horse transferred to 516 Coy A.S.C. 59th Div. | |
| " | 30/5/18 | | 6 H.D. Horses transferred to 574 Coy A.S.C. 59th Div. | |
| " | 31/5/18 | | 2/5th Lincolns O/R South Staffs struck off ration strength | |
| " | 31/5/18 | | 2 Drivers transferred to 72nd Field Amb., 1 Driver transferred to H.Q. 2/7 77th Bde. General health of the Company during the month was only fair. Horses in good condition. | |

A. Green Capt.
o/c No. 515 Coy. A.S.C.
59th Division.

Confidential

War Diary.

of

O.C. No. 4 Coy A.S.C
59th Div. Train

From :- 1-5-18   To 31-5-18

Volume 16.

Sheet No. I

Vol XVI

Army Form C. 2118.

# WAR DIARY
## or
## INTELLIGENCE SUMMARY.

51st (No. 4) Coy: A S C
59th Div: TRAIN.

(Erase heading not required.)

| Place | Hour, Date | Summary of Events and Information | Remarks and references to Appendices |
|---|---|---|---|
| HOUTKERQUE | MAY 1st 1918. | Coy still at same Camp as was occupied on April 29th. S.R.P. the same. Refilling 9.0 am. | W |
| HOUTKERQUE | 3rd | Refilling 9.0 am. Lieut. M.C. Johnson & 2 O.R. proceed to ST OMER for remounts. | M |
| HOUTKERQUE | 4th | Refilling 9.0 am. Coy expecting orders to move. | M |
| HOUTKERQUE | 5th | Refilling 8.30 am. Coy nucleus moved at 1.0 pm — arrived RUBROUCK at 9.0 pm. Supply wagons of D.C.I. (coast) with all its respective B.H.Q. Units. Horses on lines, men in barns. | M |
| RUBROUCK | 6th | Coy moves by route march at 10.0 am (advance party sent up to take over new S.R.P.) arrives ST OMER at 2.30 pm. Men in BARRACKS, horses on lines S.R.P. is situated within Barracks. Refilling 4.30 pm. | M |
| ST OMER | 7th | Lieut M.C. Johnson & 2 O.R. return with Remounts. | M |
| ST OMER | 8th | Orders received for move on the morrow. Refilling 6.0 pm. 1 O.R. detailed for Base & to step on strength. | M |
| ST OMER | 9th | Coy moves by route march at 8.0 am (advance party sent on) arrives at BLESSY at 3.0 pm. Men in barns & increases horses on lines. S.R.P. is situated at a spot by main road about 2 miles N of village. Refilling 4 pm. | M |
| BLESSY | 10th | Coy moves by route march at 8.0 am (advance party sent on) arrived at GRICOURT le BOURG at 3.0 pm. Men in Huts, horses in a line similarly. New S.R.P. on BOURS - DIEVAL road. Refilling 4.0 pm. | M |

Army Form C. 2118.

Vol LXVI

SHEET No. 2

# WAR DIARY
or
# INTELLIGENCE SUMMARY.

(Erase heading not required.)

Instructions regarding War Diaries and Intelligence Summaries are contained in F.S. Regs., Part II and the Staff Manual respectively. Title pages will be prepared in manuscript.

| Hour, Date, Place | Summary of Events and Information | Remarks and references to Appendices |
|---|---|---|
| GRICOURT (BOURS) 11.10 | S.R.P. moved to opposite Church at BOURS Refilling 9.0am Two O.R's Inlisted from Base and are laken on strength. | W |
| GRICOURT (BOURS) 12.10 | Refilling at 9.0am Advance party sent on. Coy moves by route march at 11.0am — arrives SACHIN at 12.30 p.m. Take over billets plus vacated by No. 3 Coy of Troop. New S.R.P. on ch road connecting village itself with main PERNES- TANGRY road. 11 O.R's & Pairs attached from No. 3 Coy. | |
| SACHIN 13.10 | Preparations made for a long stay. Bains taking over as Coy Officers Cpl. Stores Ordnance Shops etc. | W |
| SACHIN 14.10 | 3 O.R's are posted to 2/13 N.M. Field Ambulance 1 Who Dvr transferred to No 3 Coy & struck off strength. Waggons of 177" Inf. Bde return to No 3 Coy 11 Dvrs & Pairs attached from No 2 Coy of Draws. 1 Dvr & pair attached from 59" Batt M.G.C. | W |
| SACHIN 15.10 | Refilling 9.0am Small field taken over as alternate horse lines. | W |
| SACHIN 17.10 | 1 Cpl transferred from No 2 Coy & taken on strength | W |
| SACHIN 18.10 | S.R.P. moved into village opposite the Church 1 supply O.R. transferred to Base, surplus to establishment & struck off strength. Additional watering parade for animals during summer months, commenced. Various attached wagons returned to original units. | W |
| SACHIN 19.10 | Refilling 9.0am Church Parade Service at 6.30 p.m. | W |
| SACHIN 20.10 | 6 O.R's of A.R.F. from Base enlisted on strength 1 O.R. attached from No. 1 Coy | W |
| SACHIN 21.10 | One O.R. transferred to No 2 Coy & struck off strength. | W |

(73989) W4141—463. 400,000. 9/14. H.&J.Ltd. Forms/C. 2118/10.

SHEET No 3

Army Form C. 2118.

# WAR DIARY
## or
## INTELLIGENCE SUMMARY.
(Erase heading not required.)

Instructions regarding War Diaries and Intelligence Summaries are contained in F.S. Regs., Part II and the Staff Manual respectively. Title pages will be prepared in manuscript.

Vol XII

| Hour, Date, Place | Summary of Events and Information | Remarks and references to Appendices |
|---|---|---|
| SACHIN 22nd May | O.C. inspected all horses | W |
| SACHIN 23rd | 2nd Lt. F. WHITFIELD & 1 O.R. transferred from No 3 Coy & taken ON strength | W |
| SACHIN 24th | 2nd Lieut M.C. JOHNSON & 1 O.R. transferred to No 3 Coy & are struck OFF the strength | W |
| SACHIN 25th | 1 O.R. evacuated from O.C. 3 to Base & struck off the strength. | W |
|  | O.C. visited the Coy wagons detailed for duty with the Balloon Commands. | W |
|  | X Corps LIETTRES | W |
| SACHIN 26th | Machine Gun Course opened. Instructors 1 O.R. from the M.S. of the M.G.C. | W |
|  | 1 NCO & 3 men attached from 9th Battn. by local W.O. to construct his course & mount | W |
|  | night attacks from No 3 Coy for a similar purpose. | W |
|  | Enemy shells PERNES railhead during night. | W |
| SACHIN 27th | Refitting 9 a.m. Hostile aircraft very active after dusk, & many bombs | W |
|  | dropped in the vicinity. | W |
| SACHIN 28th | 1 O.R. transferred to No 3 Coy & struck off the strength | W |
|  | 1 O.R. transferred from No 3 Coy & taken ON the strength | W |
|  | O.C visited B.L. Transport Groups & interviewed G.m.s | W |
|  | Intermittent shelling during day in vicinity by enemy long range guns. | W |
| SACHIN 29th | Full Company Parade at 6.30 p.m. when AA's W3go were distributed | W |
|  | 1 WAR CPL reported for duty & taken ON strength. | W |
|  | 2 O.Rs reported for duty on gradn. from 364 (?) Bn N Fus. | W |
|  | Hostile aircraft very active after dusk. Enemy bombs dropped in locality | W |
| SACHIN 30th | Two men from each of 2nd (?) (3) Bn. Cheshires & 11 (3) Bn RSF who had gone | W |
| SACHIN 31st | Two O.Rs proceed on leave. Hostile aircraft very active. PA guns bring one plane | W |
|  | down close by PERNES | W |

Army Form C. 2118.

Vol. XVI

SHEET No. 4.

# WAR DIARY
*or*
# INTELLIGENCE SUMMARY.
(*Erase heading not required.*)

Instructions regarding War Diaries and Intelligence Summaries are contained in F.S. Regs., Part II and the Staff Manual respectively. Title pages will be prepared in manuscript.

| Hour, Date, Place | Summary of Events and Information | Remarks and references to Appendices |
|---|---|---|
| | The following Units have been relieved by the S.O. 178 Inf Bde for the following states of recent influenza during MAY 1918. | |
| (1) | H.Q. 178th Inf Bde | 1-5-18 — 31-5-18 |
| (2) | 2/5 Sherwood F. | 1-5-18 — 31-5-18 |
| (3) | 2/6 Sherwood F. | 1-5-18 — 31-5-18 |
| (4) | No 4 Coy, 59th Div Train | 1-5-18 — 31-5-18 |
| (5) | 2/3 N.M. Fd Amb | 1-5-18 — 31-5-18 |
| (6) | 7th Sherwood F. | 1-5-18 — 29-5-18 |
| (7) | 178 T.M Batty. | 1-5-18 — 7-5-18 |
| (8) | 2/1 ND M.V.S. A.V.C. | 1-5-18 — 5-5-18 } 9-5-18 — 11-5-18 } 13-5-18 — 31-5-18 |
| (9) | D.A.D.O.S. 59th Dn | 1-5-18 — 5-5-18 } 7-5-18 — 10-5-18 } 13-5-18 — 31-5-18 |
| (10) | 59th Div Laundry | 1-5-18 — 5-5-18 } 7-5-18 — 10-5-18 } 13-5-18 — 31-5-18 |
| (11) | H.Q. 59th Div Train | 1-5-18 — 5-5-18 } 7-5-18 — 10-5-18 } 13-5-18 — 31-5-18 |
| (12) | H.Q. 59th Dunelog | 7-6-18 — 10-5-18 |
| (13) | 59th Dn (Signal) Coy R.E. | 7-5-18 — 10-5-18 |
| (14) | M.M Pa Traffic | 7-6-18 — 10-5-18 |
| (15) | 467 (Field) Coy R.E. | 9-5-18 — 11-5-18 |
| (16) | 468 " " | 9-5-18 — 12-5-18 |
| (17) | 470 " " | 9-5-18 — 13-5-18 |
| (18) | H.Q. 59th Div. R.E. | 9-5-18 — 13-5-18 |
| (19) | 59th Divl Salvage Coy | 9-5-18 — 13-5-18 { 3-5-18 — 17-5-18. |
| (20) | 16th Essex Regt. | 9-5-18 — 13-5-18 { 12-5-18 — 14-5-18. |
| (21) | 25th (Kings) 2nd Jacob Regt. | 12-5-18 { one day only |
| (22) | 4 Punebes | 13-5-18 — 14-5-18 |
| (23) | 2/5 Borders | 13-5-18 — 14-5-18 |
| (24) | 2/1 Leicesters | 13-5-18 — 14-5-18 |
| (25) | 2/1 N.M. F Amb. | 13-5-18 — 14-5-18 { 12-5-18 — 17-5-18. |
| (26) | 11th R Scots Fus. | 13-5-18 — 31-5-18 |
| (27) | 36th N Fus. | 13-5-18 — 31-5-18 |
| (28) | 4 Siege Bay R.M. R.E. | 14-5-18 — 15-5-18 |
| (29) | SAR (F) Coy R.E. | 15-5-18 — 31-5-18 |
| (30) | 158th (F.Y) Coy R.E. | 15-5-18 — 25-5-18 |

SHEET No 5.

Army Form C. 2118.

# WAR DIARY
## or
## INTELLIGENCE SUMMARY.
*(Erase heading not required.)*

Instructions regarding War Diaries and Intelligence Summaries are contained in F.S. Regs., Part II. and the Staff Manual respectively. Title pages will be prepared in manuscript.

Vol XVI

| Hour, Date, Place | Summary of Events and Information | Remarks and references to Appendices |
|---|---|---|
| | Reliving of Units cont'd | |
| (31) | 59th Bde M.G.C. T | 15-5-18 |
| (32) | 2/6th S. Staffords T | 15-5-18 — One day only — two waves. |
| (33) | " N " T | 15-5-18 — 1st issue Training Course |
| (34) | 2/5th N " T | 15-5-18 — 2nd issue, gas-post only |
| (35) | 2/1st N.M. Field amb | 16-5-18 — 16-5-18 |
| (36) | 4th Kinsahos T | 17-5-18 |
| (37) | 2/5 Hantshire T | 17-5-18 — One day only |
| (38) | 2/4 Rs Scots Fus T | 17-5-18 |
| (39) | 6/7 R Scots Fus T | 17-5-18 |
| (40) | No 3 (Fareways) Coy R.E. | 17-5-18 — 31-5-18. |
| (41) | 23rd Bde Machine Rgt. | 26-5-18 — 31-5-18 |
| (42) | 59th Bde School (H.Q only) | 25-5-18 — one day only |

Stoke Field 1/6/18

Vol 17

Confidential

War Diary

of

Headquarters 59th Divisional Train.

1st/6/18 to 30th/6/18.

Volume XVII.

# WAR DIARY

## or INTELLIGENCE SUMMARY.

Army Form C. 2118.

Vol XVII

Headquarters 59th Bn L Group

| Place | Date | Hour | Summary of Events and Information | Remarks and references to Appendices |
|---|---|---|---|---|
| HESTRUS | June 1 | | Marched DIEVAL to 177 & 178 Bde Groups. R.H. to 176 Bde. AIRE R.Ps. 176 Bde. THEROUANNE 177 Bde. BOUCHIN-LEGAL 178 Bde SACHIN | M3 |
| " | 10 | | R.H. & R.Ps. No change. No 2 Coy. sent 12 G.S. wagons C.T.O. to 16 Division at SAMER. No 3 Coy sent 112 G.S. wagons C.T.O. to 4 Guards Bde at CRENAS | M3 |
| " | 17 | | R.H. & R.Ps. No change. T.H.Q. moved to GREUPPE. No 2 Coy Moved from THEROUANNE to BEAUMETZ.-G.-AIRES No 3 Coy Moved from HERIPRIE to SACHIN No 4 Coy Moved from SACHIN to LISBOURG | M3 |
| GREUPPE | 18 | | R.H. No change R.Ps. 176 Bde Beaumetz-les-Aires 177 Bde Sachin 178 Bde. LISBOURG. New G.O.C. Division held Conference of all O.C. Formations. 11 a.m. | M3 |
| " | 19 | | R.H. 177 & 178 Bdes PERNES R.Ps. 176 Bde AIRE No 2 Coy moved to RUPIGNY. | M3 |
| " | 20 | | R.H. No change R.Ps. No 177 & 178 Bdes same R.P. 176 Bde RUPIGNY | M3 |
| " | 23 | | R.H. No change R.Ps. 176 Bde GREUPPE 177 Bde SACHIN 178 Bde LISBOURG No 3 Coy moved from SACHIN to COYECQUE | M3 |

# WAR DIARY
## or
## INTELLIGENCE SUMMARY.
(Erase heading not required.)

Army Form C. 2118.

Vol XVII

Headquarters 59th Div. Train

| Place | Date June | Hour | Summary of Events and Information | Remarks and references to Appendices |
|---|---|---|---|---|
| GREUPPE | 24 | | A.H. PEARES. B's. 176 + 178 / i/c Charge 177 Bde & COYECQUE Sn. B.H. & R.P's i/c Charge F.C. Train with B.A.D.V.S. inspected horses &c. of new Bn. 121 Line Transport several times during the month & considerable improvement was noticed at the end of the month. Transport Officers of 1st Line Transport have all been allotted to Horses Coys | |
| " | 30 | | for a weeks course of instruction. No 1 Coy who are detached with 59th Div' Artillery have been inspected 3 times during the month, the horses are in good condition. The health of the men generally is good, but we had about 30 cases of the new Influenza, the horse Transport is in good condition. | |

Ch. Brown
Capt & RASC
for OC 59th Div' Train

Confidential.

War Diary.

513 Coy. of A.S.C. 59th Division
(No 1 Coy. 59th Divl Train)

From 1-6-18 to 30-6-18.

Volume XVIII

# WAR DIARY or INTELLIGENCE SUMMARY

Army Form C. 2118.

**513 Coy. A.S.C.**

| Place | Date | Hour | Summary of Events and Information | Remarks and references to Appendices |
|---|---|---|---|---|
| Hesdin | 1/6/18 to 21/6/18 | | Coys in billets & quarters at HENU & HERIN and in Shelters. Supplies drawn by R.T. Column from Saulty 1/6/18 to 15/6/18. "  "  "  "  " Authieule 16/6/18 to 21/6/18. Refilling point at Herrin. | |
| | 22/6/18 | | Coy moved by route march to WANQUETIN. Supplies drawn by R.T. Column from Authieule. Refilling point at Humbercourt. | |
| | 23/6/18 | | Coy moved by route march to Foist Couche. Coy quartered in Billets, Huttments and Tents. Horses in Shelters. | |
| | 24/6/18 | | Supplies drawn by R.T. Column from SAVY. Refilling point at Foist Couche. | |
| | 25/6/18 | | Supplies drawn by (Horse) transport from Savy. Refilling point at Foist Couche. | |
| | 26/6/18 | | Coy moved to EPS. Coy route march. Coy quartered in billets & tents. Horses in lines. | |
| | | | Supplies drawn by R.T. Column from SAVY. Refilling point at TANGRY. | |
| | 30/6/18 | | Coy moved by route march to ESTREE BLANCHE. Coy quartered in billets & tents. Horses in lines. Supplies drawn by R.T. Column from SAVY. Refilling point at ESTREE BLANCHE | |

Major
Commanding

NO. 1 COMPANY
59th DIVL. TRAIN

(No. 513 Coy. A.S.C.)

Confidential

War Diary
of
514 Company A.S.C. 59th Division
(No 2 Coy. 59th Divl Train)

From 1.6.18 to 30.6.18

Volume XVIII

Army Form C. 2118.

# WAR DIARY

## INTELLIGENCE SUMMARY

*(Erase heading not required.)*

VOL. XVII

O.C. N° 2 Coy. 59 Div. Train.

Instructions regarding War Diaries and Intelligence Summaries are contained in F.S. Regs., Part II. and the Staff Manual respectively. Title Pages will be prepared in manuscript.

| Place | Date | Hour | Summary of Events and Information | Remarks and references to Appendices |
|---|---|---|---|---|
| NIELLES. | 1.6.18. | | HQrs of Company located at L.34.a.8.6 (Sheet 36D/40,000), Supply Refilling Point 176 Inf. Bde Group located at L.28.d.7.2. (Sheet 36D) following units on rations strength of 176 Inf. Bde. Group: HQ 176 Inf. Bde, 4th G.B. Reg. Sussex R., 17th G.B. Reg. Welch Fus., 23rd G.B. Lancs. Fus., N° 2 Coy. 59 Div. Train, C.R.E. 59 Div., 469 Field Co. R.E., 431 & 432 Divl Emp. Co. R.E., 6/7 Roy. Scots Smar T.C., 136 A.T. Coy. R.E., 158 A.T. Coy. R.E., 568 A.T. Coy. R.E., 2/5 N° Staff T.C. | MMH |
| | 2.6.18 | | RAILHEAD-AIRE. Bulk drawn by lorries, details delivered by Train Supply Wagons. 1 G.S. Wagon complete element transferred to 16th Divl. Train on 2/5 N° Staff T.C. proceeding to join 16th Div. 2/5 N° Staff T.C. struck off ration strength of 176 Inf. Bde. Group, effect 3.6.18. G.H.Q. horses taken on strength from N° 3 Coy. 59 Div. Train, 1 H.D. horse transferred to 431 Divl Coy. R.E. | MMH |
| " | 5.6.18 | | 2/1 N.M. 3td Amb. Andrew on ration strength of 176 Inf. Bde Group. | MMH |
| " | 10.6.18 | | 2/Lieut. W. Todd proceeded via COYECQUE & BLEQUIN to SAMER to hand over to 16th Division Andrew G.S. Wagon turnouts which were struck off Coy. Strength on from 12.6.18 on transfer to 16th Div. Train. | MMH |
| " | 12.6.18 | | 2/Lieut C.H. ALDRICH and 7 other ranks of 46th Div. proceeded to WOINCOURT to rejoin 46th Div. Train. 2 Ride horses of 66th Div. Train taken on Coy. Strength. 1 Ride horse evacuated to 11th Corps V.S.S (strained wound), 1 H.D. horse transferred to 432 Divl Coy R.E. to replace H.D. horse evacuated to 11 Corps V.S.S on 12.6.18. | MMH |
| " | 14.6.18 | | 432 Divl. Coy. R.E., 135, 158 and 568 Army Troops Coy. R.E. drawn from S.O. 176 Inf. Bde. for last time for consumption 17th June. 6/7 Reg. Scots Smar T.C. above for last time for consumption 18th June. 1 turnout of G.S. Wagon handed over to Train. 17th G.B. Sussex Reg., 4th G.B. Welch Fusr., 2/1 N.M. 3rd Amb. delivered in LAIRES area. | MMH |
| " | 17.6.18. | | Supplies of HQ 176 Inf. Bde, 469 Divl. Coy. R.E., 431 Divl. Coy. R.E. + 431 Divl. Coy. R.E. drawn from S.O. 176 Inf. Bde. for last time for consumption 18th June. HQrs of Coy. and Supply Refilling Point move to BEAUMETZ Les AIRE (X26.a.1.9. Sheet 36D). | MMH |
| BEAUMETZ LEZ AIRE. | 18.6.18 | | Despatched Supply Wagons to 17th G.B. Worcestershire Regt. and 23rd G.B. Lancs Fusrs at St MARTIN AU LAERT also Supplies for consumption 19th June which had struck off Unit strength of Brigade Ration strength on transfer to 40th Div. — 2 Supplies + Baggage Wagons handed over to each Battalion. | MMH MMH |
| RUPIGNY. | | | Moved HQrs of Coy. to RUPIGNY (X.2.c. - Sheet 36D). | |
| | 19.6.18 | | 25 Guns Bath Liverpool Regt. Andrew on rations strength of 176 Inf. Bde Group for consumption 19th June. | MMH |
| " | 20.6.18. | | 23rd G.B. Cheshire Regt. Supplies delivered at St MARTIN AU LAERT for consumption 20th June. Unit taken on ration strength on 1 day only. | MMH |
| " | 24.6.18. | | 25. G.B. Kings Royal Rifle Corps Andrew on Brigade ration strength. | MMH |
| " | 26.6.18. | | HQ 59 Div, 59 Divl. Sig. Coy., M.I.P. 57 Bd., 2/1 N.M. Mtd. V.J. Sec. HQ 59 Div Train, 59 Div Lumbury, 59 Div Baker Coy taken on ration strength of Brigade Group. C.R.S. 59 Div. taken on Group ration strength. | MMH |
| " | 30.6.18. | | Health of Coy. during month excellent until 24th on and after which Lt. 19 other ranks were admitted to Hospital suffering from P.U.O. | MMH |

M.M. Hagen[?]  
CAPT.  
O.C. N° 2 COY. 59. DIV. TRAIN.

Confidential

War Diary
of
515 Company. A.S.C. 59th Division

From 1-6-18 to 30-6-18

(Volume XVII)

Army Form C. 2118.

# WAR DIARY
## INTELLIGENCE SUMMARY
*(Erase heading not required.)*

| Place | Date | Hour | Summary of Events and Information June 1918. | Remarks and references to Appendices |
|---|---|---|---|---|
| HERIPRE | 1/6/18 | | In Billets and quarters | GE |
| " | 2/6/18 | | 1 G.S. Wagon Complete Turnout (Baggage) transferred to 39th Leicesters and jars rations 16th Div. Train | GE |
| " | 4/6/18 | | 1 Sergt and 1 Driver Reinforcements received from Base | GE |
| " | 4/6/18 | | 1 H.D. Horse of 66th Div. Train attached | GE |
| " | 9/6/18 | | 1 Sergt. Surplus to establishment transferred to 573 Coy A.S.C. 59 Div. | GE |
| " | 10/6/18 | | 12 G.S. Wagon Complete Turnouts transferred to 4th Guards Bde. | GE |
| " | 10/6/18 | | LIEUT. M.C. JOHNSTON proceeds on 14 days leave to England | GE |
| " | 11/6/18 | | 1 Driver reinforcement received | GE |
| " | 15/6/18 | | All Baggage Wagons of 176th Group sent to units for move | GE |

A. Green Capt.
o/c No. 515 Coy. A.S.C.
59th Division.

# WAR DIARY

**Army Form C. 2118.**

*Instructions regarding War Diaries and Intelligence Summaries are contained in F. S. Regs., Part II. and the Staff Manual respectively. Title pages will be prepared in manuscript.*

## INTELLIGENCE SUMMARY
*(Erase heading not required.)*

515 Coy. A.S.C. 59th Division — June 1918.

| Place | Date | Hour | Summary of Events and Information | Remarks and references to Appendices |
|---|---|---|---|---|
| HERIPRE | 16/6/18 | | 1 H.Q. Horse of 373 Coy A.S.C. evacuated to 32nd M.V.S. | AG |
| " | 17/6/18 | 10.0 a.m. | Coy H.Q.'s with supplies of Bde Group move by road to SACHIN | AG |
| SACHIN | 17/6/18 | 6.0 p.m. | In Billets and quarters | AG |
| " | 18/6/18 | | 470 Field Coy R.E. 2nd Field Squadron R.E. 25th Kings 13th W.R.R. } struck off ration strength | AG |
| " | 19/6/18 | | 7th Leicesters and 23rd K.R.R. struck off ration strength | AG |
| " | 23/6/18 | 9.0 a.m. | Coy H.Q.'s move by road to PONCHE. | AG |
| PONCHE | 23/6/18 | 3.30 p.m. | In Billets and quarters | AG |
| " | 27/6/18 to 30/6/18 | | LIEUT. N.C. JOHNSTON reports back from leave. General health of the Coy during the month was only fair, all horses now in very good condition. A/Grace Capt. o/c No. 515 Coy. A.S.C. 59th Division. | AG |

Confidential

War Diary

of

O.C. No 4 Coy A.S.C. 59th Div Train

From 1-6-18
To   30-6-18

Volume 17.

Army Form C. 2118.

# WAR DIARY
## or
## INTELLIGENCE SUMMARY
(Erase heading not required.)

SHEET No I

516th (No 4) Coy A.S.C
59th Divn Train

Instructions regarding War Diaries and Intelligence Summaries are contained in F. S. Regs., Part II. and the Staff Manual respectively. Title Pages will be prepared in manuscript.

| Place | Date | Hour | Summary of Events and Information | Remarks and references to Appendices |
|---|---|---|---|---|
| SACHIN | 1st JUNE | | Coy still at same camp as were occupied on MAY 31st. S.E.P the same. Refilling 9.0 am | M. |
| SACHIN | 2nd | | Various attached pairs & wagons attached from Nos 2 & 3 Coys returned to respective Units. 3 O.R. posted to 2/1st N Mid F.A. & struck off strength. | M. |
| SACHIN | 3rd | | C.O visited Rwia & Billets | M. |
| SACHIN | 4th | | 2 O.R reported from BASE & taken on strength. M.Gun course completed. Coy secure two "firsts" & a "second" | M. |
| SACHIN | 6th | | Capt E EAMES 1 O.R. proceeded on leave to U.K | M. |
| SACHIN | 8th | | 1 O.R evacuated to CCS & struck off strength. 2 O.R proceeded on leave to U.K. | M. |
| SACHIN | 9th | | 1 attached pair & wagon of 2nd Div MG Batt taken on strength. 1 F.S.S kicked & admitted to C.C.S | M. |
| SACHIN | 10th | | 1 H.D evacuated to M.V.S. | M. |
| SACHIN | 11th | | 1 F.S.S & 1 O.R returned from C.C.S & retaken on strength. | M. |
| SACHIN | 12th | | O.C accompanied C.O on tour of Inspections around new G Battns' Transport. | M. |
| SACHIN | 13th | | 1 Shoeing Smith attached from No 1 Coy on account of Coy largely undertaking Bde shoeing. A second Shoeing Smith attached from No 2 Coy. 1 O.R returned from detachment. 1 pony hospital. | M. |
| SACHIN | 14th | | 1 O.R admitted to Hospital. Jack Spurs withdrawn in accordance with G.R.O. | M. |
| SACHIN | 15th | | Influenza rife in Coy. 3 O.R admitted to Hospital. | M. |
| SACHIN | 16th | | Sudden orders to send out Baggage Wagons received by Coy at 7.30 pm Wagons despatched by 8.15 pm. Refilling 9 am as usual. Coy expecting orders to move. Wagons & escort & Pickets etc cleaned up. Supply Convoy 1.30 pm. 2 O.R proceeded on leave to U.K. 2 O.R discharged to Coy from Hospital. 5 O.R admitted to Hospital. Definite orders to move by the morrow received by O.C | M. |

# WAR DIARY or INTELLIGENCE SUMMARY

Army Form C. 2118.

SHEET No. II

*(Erase heading not required.)*

Instructions regarding War Diaries and Intelligence Summaries are contained in F.S. Regs., Part II. and the Staff Manual respectively. Title Pages will be prepared in manuscript.

| Place | Date | Hour | Summary of Events and Information | Remarks and references to Appendices |
|---|---|---|---|---|
| SACHIN | 17th | JUNE | Reveille 5 am. Refilling at same. SRP at 7.0 am. OC, 1·SSM & 1·Sgt. Left in advance at 7.0 am. for new quarters at LISBOURG to arrange billets etc. Company men to move by route march at 11.0 am. On arr: LISBOURG at 3.30 pm Men accommodated in barns, horses and lines wagons parked on road side. Wagons are off-loaded whilst rations are made for a long stay. 1 OR discharged from Hospital & admitted. 1 OR promoted on 10 days leave in France. 467 CF Coy RE Supply Wagon detached. Two pairs of wagons attached from 13th W. Riding Regt. SRP situated on LISBOURG — LAIRES road. | M. |
| LISBOURG | 18th | " | Refilling. 9.0 am. Two coudars attached from new batters of Bde vs 13th W. Ridings. Influenza very prevalent. Full Coy parade waited by MO 11th RSF. who visited disinfectant fluid. | M. |
| LISBOURG | 20th | " | 3 OR admitted to Hospital and discharged. 1 OR reposted from FA v taken on strength. | M. |
| LISBOURG | 21st | " | Full meeting of Senior NCO's when OC explained competition arrangements of Units = Div. 4 OR posted to FA & 2 OR reposted back to Coy from FA. 1 OR transferred from 31st DN. TRAIN v taken on strength. | M. |
| LISBOURG | 22nd | " | SRP removed to a site just outside village on LISBOURG – HEUCHIN road. CO. inspected SRP Billets. Lines etc during morning. 1 OR discharged from Hospital. OC reorganised driven horses wagons to suit requirements of new Units of Bde. | M. |
| LISBOURG | 23rd | " | 4 OR discharged from Hospital. Daily Diet Sheet form M9 & M11 start for animals commenced. | M. |
| LISBOURG | 24th | " | Capt EPPES & 1 OR reposted back from leave. 1 OR reposted from Base & taken on strength. | M. |
| LISBOURG | 25th | " | 2 OR reposted back from leave. 1 OR proceeded on leave to UK. | M. |
| LISBOURG | 26th | " | 2/Lt WHITFIELD detached to Company cluty as SO Divisional Troops. | M. |
| LISBOURG | 29th | " | 1 OR returned off 10 days leave to France. | M. |
| LISBOURG | 30th | " | 1 showing smith attached from Mot. Coy returned to Unit. 1 OR returned from APM upon completion of sentence. 1 Officer from Bde Battn attached for course of draught duty. | M. |

Army Form C. 2118.

# WAR DIARY
## or
## INTELLIGENCE SUMMARY

(Erase heading not required.)

Sheet No. III

Instructions regarding War Diaries and Intelligence Summaries are contained in F. S. Regs., Part II. and the Staff Manual respectively. Title Pages will be prepared in manuscript.

| Place | Date | Hour | Summary of Events and Information | Remarks and references to Appendices |
|---|---|---|---|---|
| | | | The following Units have been relieved by the S.O 178th Inf Bde for the following dates of arrival influenza during JUNE 1918. | |
| | | | (1) H.Q 178th Inf Bde — 1-6-18 — 30-6-18 | |
| | | | (2) 2/5th Shou For: — 1-6-18 — 2-6-18 | |
| | | | (3) 2/6th Shou For: — 1-6-18 — 30-6-18 | |
| | | | (4) Coy 59th D Train — 1-6-18 — 30-6-18 | |
| | | | (5) 467(F) Coy RE — 1-6-18 — 18-6-18 | M. |
| | | | (6) 2/3 NMID FA — 1-6-18 — 30-6-18 | |
| | | | (7) S.AA Section 59th DAC — 1-6-18 — 30-6-18 | |
| | | | (8) HQ 59th Div — 1-6-18 — 22-6-18 | |
| | | | (9) 59th Div Sig Coy RE — 1-6-18 — 22-6-18 | |
| | | | (10) 59th Div MMP Traff BC — 1-6-18 — 22-6-18 | |
| | | | (11) 2/1st NMID MVS AVC — 1-6-18 — 22-6-18 | |
| | | | (12) HQ 59th Div Train — 1-6-18 — 22-6-18 | |
| | | | (13) DADOS — 1-6-18 — 30-6-18 | |
| | | | (14) 11th RS Fus — 1-6-18 — 30-6-18 | |
| | | | (15) 36th (S) N Fus — 1-6-18 — 30-6-18 | |
| | | | (16) 25th (S) Cheshires — 1-6-18 — 13-6-18 | |
| | | | (17) 3rd Forway Coy RE — 1-6-18 — 16-6-18 | |
| | | | (18) 13th (DofW) West-Ridings — 13-6-18 — 30-6-18 | |
| | | | (19) 59th Lannay — 19-6-18 — 22-6-18 | |
| | | | (20) 59th 19 vet School — 19-6-18 — 30-6-18 | |
| | | | (21) 178th LTMB — 24-6-18 — 30-6-18 | |

OC 4Coy SO Sw Ploon

Confidential

War Diary

of

Headquarters, 59th Divisional Train

From 1st.7.18 to 31st.7.18.

Volume XVIII

Army Form C. 2118.

# WAR DIARY
## or
## INTELLIGENCE SUMMARY.
(Erase heading not required.)

Vol XVIII

Headquarters 59 Divn E [Train]

Ref. for Map sheet LENS. 11.

| Place | Date | Hour | Summary of Events and Information | Remarks and references to Appendices |
|---|---|---|---|---|
| GREUPPE | July 1 | | Railhead PERNES. R.P. 176 Bde. GREUPPE. 177 Bde GOYECQUE | A/2 |
| " | 9 | | 178/Bde. LISBOURG | A/3 |
| | | | R.H. and R.P.'s same as last week. No 2 Coy. moved from RUPIGNY to | A/3 |
| | | | HERBEVAL | A/3 |
| " | 10 | | R.H. hd change R.P. 176 Bde HESTRUS 177 Bde GOYECQUE 178Bde LISBOURG | A/3 |
| | | | No 3 Coy. moved from GOYECQUE to TENURE | A/3 |
| " | 11 | | R.H. hd change R.P. 177 Bde TENURE 176×178 no change | A/3 |
| | | | J.H.Q. moved from GREUPPE to CREPY | A/3 |
| CREPY | 15 | | R.H. WAVRANS R.P.s no change | A/4 |
| " | 22. | | R.H. & R.P. no change. No.2 & 4 Coys moved to GOUY-en-ARTOIS | A/3 |
| " | 24 | | R.H. TINCQUES R.P. 176×178 GOUY-en-ARTOIS 177 Bde TENURE | A/3 |
| " | 25 | | R.H. GOUY. R.P.s all at GOUY. THQ & No3 Coy move to GOUY | A/3 |
| " | 28 | | R.H. & H.Q. same. Lt. TOLLER reported for duty | A/5 |
| " | 29 | | " " Capt SMITH [O.I.] 177Bdd died n.19 C.C.S | A/6 |
| " | 30 | | No 1 Coy delated from Division with Dirt. Artilly at BOSEGHEM | A/7 |
| | | | Transport in good condition. Health of men excellent except for the eruption of 30 cases of the new Influenza during the month. | |

Capt. & Adjt.
59th Divisional Train

Confidential.

> NO. 1 COMPANY
> 59th DIVL. TRAIN
> O1/99.
> (No. 513 Coy. A.S.C.)

# WAR DIARY

(21·1) — of —
OC 513 Coy ASC 59th Division.
from 1st to 31st July 1918.

(Vol. 17.)

Army Form C. 2118.

# WAR DIARY
## or
## INTELLIGENCE SUMMARY.

(Erase heading not required.)

513 Coy ASC 59th DIVISION. Summary of Events and Information

| Place | Date | Hour | Summary of Events and Information | Remarks and references to Appendices |
|---|---|---|---|---|
| Auch. | 1/7/18 | | Company in Bivouac and billets at ESTREE – BLANCHE. Refilling point at ESTREE – BLANCHE. | |
| | 14/7/18 | 11 a.m | Company moved by March Route to LES OSSEHX. Company in Camp & Bivouac in Lines. Supplies drawn by M.T. Col. from AIRE. Refilling point at BOESEGHEM. | |
| | 14/7/18 to 31/7/18 | | Company moved by March Route to BOESEGHEM. Quartered in Camp and billets. Stores in Lines. Supplies drawn by M.T. Columns from AIRE. Refilling point at BOESGHEM. | |

Major
Commdg.

NO. 1 COMPANY
59th DIV¹. TRAIN
(No. 513 Coy. A.S.C.)

Confidential

War Diary
of
(N°2) 514 Company A.S.C — (No 2 Coy. 59th Divl Train)

1/7/18 to 31/7/18.

Volume XVIII.

Army Form C. 2118.

# WAR DIARY
## INTELLIGENCE SUMMARY
*(Erase heading not required.)*

VOL. XVIII

O.C. No 3 Coy. 59th Div. TRAIN.

Ref Map. Sheets 36b II.

Instructions regarding War Diaries and Intelligence Summaries are contained in F. S. Regs., Part II. and the Staff Manual respectively. Title Pages will be prepared in manuscript.

| Place | Date | Hour | Summary of Events and Information | Remarks and references to Appendices |
|---|---|---|---|---|
| RUPIGNY | 1.7.18. | | Commenced month with following Units on ration strength of 176 Inf. Bde Group — Hdqrs, 176 Inf. Bde. 2/5th G.B. Liverpool Regt, 4th G.B. Royal Welsh Fust, 17th G.B. Royal Sussex Regt, 2/5th G.B. K.R.R.C. No 2 Coy. 59 Div Train. 2/1. N.M. Fld. Amb. HQ 59th Div. CRE. 59th Div. 59th Div. Signal Coy. R.E. M.M.P. + Traffic Control. 2/1 N.M. Mob. Vet. Sec. HQ 59th Div. Train. 59th Div. Salvage Co. 59th Div. Laundry. | Prest. |
| " | 3.7.18 | | 59th Div Signal School taken on and 25/4/18. K.R.R.C. struck off ration strength of Bridge Group. In-complete Q.S. 15 men movements taken on Coy. Strength from Base and 2 Hill horses from Camp Commandant. 59th Div. Towards completion of Establishment. | Prest. |
| " | 8.7.18 | | S.O.A. See S.1 D.A.G letters re new ration strength of 176 Inf Bde Group. 59 Div Sig School struck off ration strength of Bde Group after consumption. | Prest. Prest. |
| " | 9.7.18 | | Bdys & wagons despatched to pick up H.Q. and details. Moved Coy H.Q. and remaining Sections via Bovy LEZ AIRE — LINARES — FIEFS — TAMGRY — HESTRUS to HERBEVAL and delivered supplies to Units in TAMGRY area. | Prest. |
| HERBEVAL | 10.7.18 | | S.A.A. Sec. 59 Div. D.A.C. attached to 176. Supply Refilling Point 176 Inf. Bde Group moved to M.4.d.57. (Sheet 44B). | Prest. |
| " | 11.7.18 | | Mt Bde. Supply to consumption 12.00 mdt. | |
| " | 12.7.18 | | 59 Div. Laundry struck off ration strength of 176 Bde. Group. | |
| " | 13." 18 | | HQ 57 Div. Train struck off ration strength of Group and 176 F brand Mobile Baths taken. | Prest. Prest. |
| " | 21.7.18 22.7.18 | | 13th Shucs Rly Coy completing unit on receipt of Mobile Bathing trailer. HQ.59 Div. CRE. 59 Div. 59 Div. Sig. Coy. M.M.P. + TRAFFIC, 2/1 N.M. Mob Vet Sec. 59 Div. Salvage Coy. struck off ration strength of Bde. Group after consumption. | Prest. Prest. |
| " | 23.7.18 | | 24:- Rejoined with 176 Bde Group in last times running of 222? HQ. of Coy. Supply etc. moved via HESTRUS, VALHUON, TINQUES, AVESNES LE COMTE to GOUY EN ARTOIS and supplies were delivered at BRETENCOURT, BELLACOURT, FERMONT and WAILLY. | Prest. |
| GOUY EN ARTOIS | 24.7.18 | | 4/67, 5/469 Bill Camp R.E. refills at 7 p.m. for consumption 25th inst. | Prest. |
| " | 28.7.18 | | Sent nothing Running for all Units of Bde. Group. Ration supplies received on fields for night. | Prest. |
| " | 29.7.18 | | 4/70 Bde Coy R.S. 1 2/5 Batt M.G. taken on ration strength of Bde. Group. | Prest. |
| " | 31.7.18 | | 4/9 Div. 2/4 R.S. 470 Fd. Amb. R.S. Shuck off strength of Bde Group. 59 Div. Reception Camp taken on ration strength. Health of company during month excellent | Prest. |

T M Taylor Capt.
O.C. No 2 Coy. 59th Div. Train

Confidential

War Diary
of
(1"-3) 515 Coy. A.S.C. 59th Division
From 1-7-18 to 31-7-18

Volume XVII

# WAR DIARY

## INTELLIGENCE SUMMARY.
*(Erase heading not required.)*

Army Form C. 2118.

515 Coy. A.S.C. 59th Division.    July 1918

| Place | Date | Hour | Summary of Events and Information | Remarks and references to Appendices |
|---|---|---|---|---|
| PONCHE | 1/7/18 | | In Billets and quarters | WG |
| " | 1/7/18 | | Battn Transport Officers of the 177th Bde Group attd for 7 days course | WG |
| " | 3/7/18 | | Wheeler Staff Sergt Evacuated Sick | WG |
| " | 3/7/18 | | 2 Complete G.S. Wagon turnouts Transferred from 514 Coy A.S.C. to complete | WG |
| " | 3/7/18 | | 23rd Batt. K.R.R.C. taken on ration strength till the 11th inst. | WG |
| " | 9/7/18 | | Baggage Wagons of the Bde Group report to units for move | WG |
| " | 10/7/18 8.0 a.m | | Coy. H.Q. with Supplies of the Bde Group move by road to TENEUR | WG |
| TENEUR | 10/7/18 2.0 a.m | | In Billets and quarters | WG |
| " | 10/7/18 | | 1 H.D. Horse evacuated to M.V.S. | WG |

W Green Capt
o/c No. 515 Coy. A.S.C.
59th Division.

# WAR DIARY
## INTELLIGENCE SUMMARY.
(Erase heading not required.)

Army Form C. 2118.

515 Coy A.S.C. 59th Division    July 1918

| Place | Date | Hour | Summary of Events and Information | Remarks and references to Appendices |
|---|---|---|---|---|
| TENEUR | 12/7/18 | | S.A.A. Section 59th Divn. taken on ration strength | KG |
| " | 13/7/18 | | Lieut. M.C. Johnston reports to T.H.Q. as A/ADT | KG |
| " | 13/7/18 | | T.H.Q. and 59th Divl Laundry taken on ration strength | KG |
| " | 15/7/18 7.0 a.10.0 | | F.G.C.M. at CANLERS on No 380682 Pte A. Marshall. | KG |
| " | 17/7/18 2.15 | | Promulgation of F.G.C.M. | KG |
| " | 21/7/18 | | Lieut. J.G. Fairfax Ross transferred to Special Bde R.E. | KG |
| " | 22/7/18 | | Lieut. P.R.R. Dibben reports for temporary duty | KG |
| " | 24/7/18 | | D.A.D.O.S. 59th Divn Signal, M.V.S. <br> D.H.Q. 23rd K.R.R.C. commandant <br> C.R.E. M.M.P. + Traffic Platoon H.A.C. } taken on ration strength | KG |

K Green Capt -
o/c No. 515 Coy. A.S.C.
59th Division.

# WAR DIARY
## or
## INTELLIGENCE SUMMARY.
(Erase heading not required).

Army Form C. 2118.

Summary of Events and Information  July 1918.

| Place | Date | Hour | Summary of Events and Information | Remarks and references to Appendices |
|---|---|---|---|---|
| TENEUR | 25/7/18 | A.M. 7.30 | 515 Coy A.S.C. 59th Division Coy. H.Qts. move by road to GOUY en ARTOIS. | AEG |
| GOUY en ARTOIS | 25/7/18 | P.M. 6.30 | In Camp | AEG |
| " | 26/7/18 | | CAPTAIN F.J.G. SMITH admitted to 19th C.C.S. | AEG |
| " | 28/7/18 | | LIEUT. W.G. TOLLER reported for duty | AEG |
| " | 28/7/18 | | One Staff Sergt Wheeler reports for duty | AEG |
| " | 29/7/18 | | CAPTAIN. F.J.G. SMITH dies of NEPHRITIS at the 19th C.C.S. | AEG |
| " | 29/7/18 | | 469. Coy. R.E. taken on ration strength | AEG |
| " | 31/7/18 | A.M. 3.0 | Inspection of Coy by the D.D. of S+T. 3rd ARMY | AEG |
| " | 31/7/18 | | LIEUT. M.C. JOHNSTON reports back for duty | AEG |

A.E. Green Capt
o/c No. 515 Coy. A.S.C.
59th Division.

Army Form C. 2118.

# WAR DIARY
## ~~INTELLIGENCE SUMMARY~~
(Erase heading not required.)

Instructions regarding War Diaries and-Intelligence Summaries are contained in F. S. Regs., Part II. and the Staff Manual respectively. Title pages will be prepared in manuscript.

515 Coy A.S.C 59th Divsn.            July 1918

| Place | Date | Hour | Summary of Events and Information | Remarks and references to Appendices |
|---|---|---|---|---|
| GOUY. EN. ARTOIS | 7 3/18 | | 1 H.D Horse with Broken leg was destroyed by the V.O — General health of the Company during the month was much below the normal. 60% being sick for 4 or 5 days with P.U.O. — Horses all in good condition | Ag ——— Vog Ag |

Green Capt
o/c No. 515 Coy. A.S.C.
59th Division.

o/c No. 515 Coy. A.S.C.
59th Division.

Confidential

War Diary

of

O.C., N: H. Coy. 59th Divisional Train

From:- 1-7-16.    To:- 31-7-18.

Volume 18.

Army Form C. 2118.

# WAR DIARY
## or
## INTELLIGENCE SUMMARY

516 (No 4) Coy. A.S.C.
59 Divisional Train.

(Erase heading not required.)

Instructions regarding War Diaries and Intelligence Summaries are contained in F. S. Regs., Part II. and the Staff Manual respectively. Title Pages will be prepared in manuscript.

| Place | Date | Hour | Summary of Events and Information | Remarks and references to Appendices |
|---|---|---|---|---|
| LISBOURG | 2.7.18 | | 1 O.R. discharged from Hospital | W |
| " | 3.7.18 | | 3 O.R. Proceeded on leave to U.K. | W |
| " | 5.7.18 | | 2 O.R. Proceeded on leave to U.K. – 2 O.R. posted to Field Ambulance – 2 O.R. returned to Coy from Field Ambulance. | W |
| " | 6.7.18 | | 178 Bde Transport Officer completed Course & returned to their unit. | W |
| " | 7.7.18 | | 4 O.R. Proceeded on leave to U.K. | W |
| " | 8.7.18 | | 1 O.R. Proceeded on leave to U.K. – 1 H.D. evacuated to M.V.S. | W |
| " | 10.7.18 | | 2 O.R. Proceeded on 14 days leave. | W |
| " | 11.7.18 | | 2/Lt J.H. DENTON, reported back to duty. | W |
| " | 12.7.18 | | Horse Lines moved to a drier position. | W |
| " | 13.7.18 | | 4 O.R. Proceed on leave to U.K. | W |
| " | 14.7.18 | | 3 O.R. Proceed on leave to U.K. | W |
| " | 15.7.18 | | 1 O.R. Proceeded on leave to U.K. | W |
| " | 17.7.18 | | 3 O.R. Proceeded on leave to U.K. | W |
| " | 18.7.18 | | C.O. Train inspected lines etc. | W |
| " | 19.7.18 | | 3 O.R Proceed on leave to U.K – 1 O.R admitted to hospital | W |
| " | 22.7.18 | | 3 O.R. Proceed on leave to U.K – Baggage wagon sent to unit – 1 H.D. evacuated – 1 O.R. discharged from Hospital | W |
| " | 23.7.18 | | Coy now to rail march to GOUY-EN-ARTOIS – 1 H.D evacuated. | W |

Army Form C. 2118.

# WAR DIARY
## or
## INTELLIGENCE SUMMARY

(Erase heading not required.)

Instructions regarding War Diaries and Intelligence Summaries are contained in F. S. Regs., Part II. and the Staff Manual respectively. Title Pages will be prepared in manuscript.

| Place | Date | Hour | Summary of Events and Information | Remarks and references to Appendices |
|---|---|---|---|---|
| GOUY-EN-ARTOIS | 25.7.18 | | 2 O.R. proceed on leave to UK. - 3 trays spare report hours for Labour Commandant IX Corps | 1-1 |
| " | 26.7.18 | | Coy moves Camp to rest field. | " |
| " | 27.7.18 | | 2 O.R. proceed on leave. - 1 Ride Horse evacuated. - Baggage wagons return to Coy. | " |
| " | 28.7.18 | | Supplies wagon 7 days R.E. refills to Coy. | " |
| " | 29.7.18 | | 1 wagon spare report hours for Labour Commandant X Corps. | " |
| " | 30.7.18 | | 1 O.R. proceed on leave to UK. - A.D.S.T. 3rd Army inspects horses. | " |

[signature]

O.C. 4 Coy 59 Div. Train.

Army Form C. 2118.

# WAR DIARY
## or
## INTELLIGENCE SUMMARY
(Erase heading not required.)

Summary of Events and Information

The following units have been fed & S.O 178 Inf Brigade during the month of July:—

| Unit | Date | |
|---|---|---|
| Hq 178 Inf Brigade | 1.7.18 | to 31.7.18 |
| 2/6 Sherwood Foresters | 1.7.18 | to 31.7.18 |
| 178. T.M.B | 1.7.18 | to 31.7.18 |
| No 4 Coy Div. Train | 1.7.18 | to 31.7.18 |
| 2/3 Field Ambulance | 1.7.18 | to 31.7.18 |
| D.A.D.O.S 59 Divison | 1.7.18 | to 23.7.18 |
| 59 Div School | 1.7.18 | to 23.7.18 |
| 36 Northumberland Fusiliers | 1.7.18 | to 31.7.18 |
| 13 West Riding | 1.7.18 | to 31.7.18 |
| A Royal Scot Fusiliers | 1.7.18 | to 31.7.18 |
| (R.A.P. details) 59 D.A.C. | 1.7.18 | to 6.7.18 |
| 25. K.R.R.C. | 11.7.18 | to 23.7.18 |
| 490 Field Coy R.E. | 29.7.18 | to 31.7.18 |

W. Denton
O.C. 4 Coy. 59 Div Train

WAR DIARY

OF

HEADQUARTERS 59th DIVISIONAL TRAIN

1st Aug 1918 to 31st Aug 1918

VOLUME XIX

Army Form C. 2118.

# WAR DIARY
## or
## INTELLIGENCE SUMMARY.
*(Erase heading not required.)*

Headquarters 59th Divisional Train

VOLUME XIX

Instructions regarding War Diaries and Intelligence Summaries are contained in F. S. Regs., Part II. and the Staff Manual respectively. Title pages will be prepared in manuscript.

Map Ref: Lens 11. Sheet 36A.

| Place | Date | Hour | Summary of Events and Information | Remarks and references to Appendices |
|---|---|---|---|---|
| | August 1918 | | | |
| Gouy-En-Artois | 1st | | Railhead Gouy-En-Artois. R.P.'s 176th Bde, 177th Bde & 178th Bde at Gouy-En-Artois. | |
| Gouy-En-Artois | 4th | | T.2/Lieut C Kraul reported for duty and posted to No 3 Coy of Train. | |
| Gouy-En-Artois | 22nd | | Lieut F Piggin transferred from No 4 Coy to No 1 Coy of Train. | |
| Gouy-En-Artois | 23rd | | THQ and Four Companies move by route march to Rebreuvette. | |
| Rebreuvette | 24th | | THQ moved to Conchy-La-Canche. No 2 Coy to Nunc q wy to Monchy Cateau, No 3 Coy to Wail, on to Anvin, No 4 Coy to Buire-Au-Bois and on to Wavrans. | |
| | | | THQ moved again later on day to Anvin. R.H. Frevent | |
| Anvin | 25th | | THQ moved to La Goulee (Fontes) No 2 Coy to Bouriecq. No 3 Coy to Lambres & No 4 Coy to Mollinghen. R.H. Frevent R.P's. 176th, 177th & 178th Bdes at Norrens Fontes. | |
| La Goulee | 26th | | No 2 Coy moved to Guarbecque. No 3 Coy to Busnes & No 4 Coy to Guarbecque. R.H.-Aire. R.P's as from 25/8/18. | |
| La Goulee | 27th | | THQ moved to Busnes. No 1 Coy rejoined Train R.H. Aire R.P's - Div' Troops. 176th Bde, 177th Bde at Busnes, and 178th Bde at Guarbecque. | |
| | | | Transport in good condition, Health of Men good on whole. | |

M. Brown
Capt. & Adjt.
59th Divisional Train

Confidential

# WAR DIARY

of

No. 1
OC 513 ASC 59 Division

from 1st to 31st Aug. 1918.

Vol. 18.

NO. 1 COMPANY
59th DIVL TRAIN
81/99/208
(No. 513 Coy. A.S.C.)

Army Form C. 2118.

# WAR DIARY
## or
## INTELLIGENCE SUMMARY.
(Erase heading not required.)

Instructions regarding War Diaries and Intelligence Summaries are contained in F. S. Regs., Part II. and the Staff Manual respectively. Title pages will be prepared in manuscript.

| Place | Date | Hour | Summary of Events and Information | Remarks and references to Appendices |
|---|---|---|---|---|
| Field | | | 513 Coy. A.S.C. 59 Division. | |
| | 11/8/18 | | Company in Camp & Quarters at BOESEGHEM. Horses in lines. Supplies drawn by M.T. Column from AIRE. | |
| | 27/8/18 | 12 noon | Company moved by March Route from BOESEGHEM to BUSNES. | |
| | 28/8/18 to 31/8/18 | | Company in Camp & Quarters at BUSNES. Horses in lines. Refilling point at BUSNES. Supplies drawn by M.T. Column from AIRE. | |

[signature]
MAJOR,
COMMANDING 513 Coy. A.S.C.

No 2 Company. 59. Divisional Train.

War Diary. Vol. XIX. - August.

Army Form C. 2118.

# WAR DIARY
## or
## INTELLIGENCE SUMMARY
*(Erase heading not required.)*

Vol. XIX
O.C. No 2 Coy. 59 Div. Train.

| Place | Date | Hour | Summary of Events and Information | Remarks and references to Appendices |
|---|---|---|---|---|
| GUY EN ARTOIS | 1.8.18 | — | Commenced march with Advance Guard to Relieve Strength of Brigade Group, 26th Bn Royal Welsh Fusrs, Mgy 176 and 1 Bn, 25th Bn R.E., Liverpool Regt, 17th Bn Sussex Regt, 26th Bn Royal Welsh Fusrs, No 2 Coy 59 Div Train, 467 Fld Co R.E. | W.Y. |
| " | 6.8.18 | — | 2/1 N.M. 3rd Ambl. 25th Bn M. Gun Corps. 59th Div School. 59th Div Veterinary Section. Reinforcements 1 Rd., 2 N.D. horses from Remount Depot, Abbeville. | W.Y. WY WY WY |
| " | 9.8.18 | — | 2 N.D. and 1 Thoroughbred to 2/1 N.M. Mobile Veterinary Section. Reinforcements 1 Ride, 2 N.D. horses from Remount Depot, Abbeville. | |
| " | 16.8.18 | — | Capt T.M. Hazlerigg proceeded on leave to United Kingdom. 2/Lieut. W. Todd assumes command of Company. | |
| " | 16.8.18 | — | 23rd Bn E. Batt goes off ration strength. 59th Bn Amm. Coln D.A.A. Goes on | |
| " | 20.8.18 | — | ration strength. 98.5%. | |
| " | 23.8.18 | — | refilled at 8.0 A.M. As ordered and delivered supplies. Baggage wagon despatched to Unit at 3.0 P.M. Orders from T.H.Q. 2nd refilling at 4.0 P.M. for consumption 23rd Gd. received time H.D. horse from remounts. Drawn from lorries of No. 3 Coy. Left GOUY-EN-ARTOIS 8.30 P.M. under orders from T.H.Q. and arrived at REBREUVIETTE noad. BARLY, AVESNES-LE-COMTE, ETREE-WAMIN where we stayed for night 23-24. | W.Y. |
| REBREUVIETTE | 24.8.18 | — | 6.30 A.M. left REBREUVIETTE for NUNCQ via FREVENT and arrived 8.30 A.M. near ardnes. 2.30 P.M. orders from Divisor supplies by further orders from T.H.Q. Coy moved to MONCHY CAYEUX arriving there at 11.0 P.M. under orders. Here the Coy stayed for night 24-25. Up till this time nothing had been seen in heap. of the Brigade Transport. No orders from O.C. Train supplies remained on road. Weather wet horse and Gear. Gone doubt existing as to whether supplies had left for consumption. | W.Y. |
| MONCHY-CAYEUX | 25.8.18 | — | At 3.30 A.M. found that transport of 23rd Bn Loyal North Lancashire, 2/1 N.M F.A., 176 Lays, 806 H.Q Royal Lancashire had some failed feelings clearing the night. We therefore received Forage and Ration to these Units and sent Coy left MONCHY-CAYEUX at 6.30 A.M. under orders from O.C. Train and ant for BOURECQ. Supplies for D.A.A. Below were handed over at coal to 59 Div D.A.C. 46 Field Coy. R.E. being formed Coffs Coy marched Left Coffs for 17 Hussar Reg were handed over to 1st HILAIRE Y detrained at R.M. this | W.Y. |
| BOURECQ | 26.8.18 | — | Arrived as MORRENT-FONT at 10.0 A.M | |
| GUARBECQUE | 27.8.18 | — | All supps wagons travelled with Unit to whom over and Coy H.Q. moved to GUARBECQUE. Uptilling at BUSNES. Coy H.Q moved to BUSNES | WY WY |
| BUSNES | 28.8.18 | — | Although the horses wet, no horse east ration/ whist flesh, wee, for shoeing. Baggage wagons recalled. | WY |
| " | 29.8.18 | — | Gram fresh ration for prisoners Ret. 10th H.D. to the other the health of the Coy is Good. William Todd 2/Lt | WY |

Confidential

War Diary
of
No 3
515 Company, A.S.C. 59th Division

From 1.8.18 to 31.8.18

(Volume VIII)

Army Form C. 2118.

# WAR DIARY
## or
## INTELLIGENCE SUMMARY.
(Erase heading not required.)

Instructions regarding War Diaries and Intelligence
Summaries are contained in F. S. Regs., Part II.
and the Staff Manual respectively. Title pages
will be prepared in manuscript.

Summary of Events and Information  August 1916

| Place | Date | Hour | Summary of Events and Information | Remarks and references to Appendices |
|---|---|---|---|---|
| GOUY EN ARTOIS | 1/8/18 | | 515 Coy A.S.C. 59th Division In camp | — |
| " | 1/8/18 | | LIEUT. W. G. TOLLER. Proceeded on 14 days leave to England | — |
| " | 1/8/18 | | 2. H.D. Encounts received | — |
| " | 1/8/18 | | C.R.E. H.Q. 59th Div. } Came on ration strength 1/8/16 to 17/8/16 DADOS. H.Q. 59th TRAIN. 2/Lieut M.M.S. M.M.P and TRAFFIC. S.A.A. 59th Divl Signals. 59th Divl Laundry 59th Divl Salvage | — |
| " | 10/8/16 | | 1. H.D. Remount received | — |
| " | 10/8/16 | | 1. H.D. Evacuated to 14.V.S. | — |
| " | 14/8/18 | | LIEUT R.R.R.DIBBEN. Posted as Supply Officer | — |
| " | 14/8/18 | | 2/LIEUT C. KAUL. appointed R.O. and attd to Coy | — |

W. Green Capt
o/c No. 515 Coy. A.S.C.
59th Division.

**Army Form C. 2118.**

# WAR DIARY
## or
## INTELLIGENCE SUMMARY.
*(Erase heading not required.)*

Instructions regarding War Diaries and Intelligence Summaries are contained in F. S. Regs., Part II. and the Staff Manual respectively. Title pages will be prepared in manuscript.

515 Coy A.S.C. 59th Division.   Summary of Events and Information   August 1918

| Place | Date | Hour | Summary of Events and Information | Remarks and references to Appendices |
|---|---|---|---|---|
| GOUY EN ARTOIS | 17/8 | p.m. | LIEUT. W.G. TOLLER reports back from leave. | AG |
| " | 18/8 | | Inspection of all horses by the D.A.D.V.S | AG |
| " | 23/8 | | 2 H.D Remounts received | AG |
| " | 23/8 | p.m. 8.30 | Coy H.Q. with supplies of Bde Group move by road to new area | AG |
| " | 24/8 | a.m. 2.0 | Stayed for 4 hours at REBREUVIETTE. | AG |
| REBREUVIETTE | 24/8 | a.m. 6.30 | moved on to WAIL. | AG |
| WAIL | 24/8 | a.m. 12.10 | Stayed for 3 hours | AG |
| " | 24/8 | p.m. 3.0 | moved on to ANVIN. | AG |
| ANVIN | 24/8 | p.m. 8.30 | In Camp and Billets | AG |
| " | 25/8 | a.m. 6.20 | moved on to LAMBRES | AG |
| LAMBRES | 25/8 | p.m. 5.0 | In Camp and Billets | AG |

A Green Capt.
c/o No. 515 Coy. A.S.C.
59th Division.

Army Form C. 2118.

# WAR DIARY
## or
## INTELLIGENCE SUMMARY.

(Erase heading not required.)

Instructions regarding War Diaries and Intelligence Summaries are contained in F. S. Regs., Part II. and the Staff Manual respectively. Title pages will be prepared in manuscript.

Summary of Events and Information August 1918

| Place | Date | Hour | Summary of Events and Information | Remarks and references to Appendices |
|---|---|---|---|---|
| LAMBRES | 25th | | 515 Coy. A.S.C. 59th Division | |
| | | | 1. H.Q. Horse Evacuated | AG |
| " | 26th | a.m 3.0 | Coy. H.Q.rs move by road to BUSNES | AG |
| BUSNES | 26th | a.m 6.0 | In Camp and Billets | AG |
| " | 27th | | 1 Driver Evacuated to C.C.S. | AG |
| " | 28th | | 1 Driver Evacuated to C.C.S. | AG |
| " | 30th | | Lieut. C. Kave, reports to T.H.Q. | AG |
| " | 30th | | Sub. Area Comdt. at BUSNES. 59th Mt. Reception Camp } Came on ration strength | AG |
| " | 31st | | 36th Fab. Coy came on ration strength. General health of the Company during the month was only fair. Horses all in good condition | AG |

A Green Capt
o/c No. 515 Coy. A.S.C.
59th Division.

Confidential

"War Diary"
of
Headquarters 59th Divisional Train

From:- 1-8-18    To:- 31-8-18.

Volume 19.

Army Form C. 2118.

576 Coy. (N₂ L₁ Cᵢ) A.S.C.
39 Divisional Train

# WAR DIARY or INTELLIGENCE SUMMARY

*(Erase heading not required.)*

Instructions regarding War Diaries and Intelligence Summaries are contained in F. S. Regs., Part II. and the Staff Manual respectively. Title Pages will be prepared in manuscript.

| Place | Date | Hour | Summary of Events and Information | Remarks and references to Appendices |
|---|---|---|---|---|
| GOUY-EN-ARTOIS | 1.8.18 | | 2 H.D. taken on Strength. | M |
| | 3.8.18 | | O.C. Coy & 1 O.R. proceed on leave. | M |
| | 4.8.18 | | 3 O.R. proceed on leave — 2 attached M.G.C. waggons sent to 196th L.T.M.B. restored. | M |
| | 5.8.18 | | 2 O.R. proceed on leave — 4 O.R. return from leave. | M |
| | 6.8.18 | | C.O. inspect Lewis & Coy. | M |
| | 7.8.18 | | | M |
| | 9.8.18 | | 1 O.R. admitted to Hospital — 3 O.R. return from leave — Divisional Commander inspects horses | M |
| | | | 3 O.R. return from leave. | |
| | 10.8.18 | | | M |
| | 11.8.18 | | 1 O.R. admitted to Hospital — 1 O.R. discharged from Hospital. | M |
| | 12.8.18 | | 1 O.R. admitted to Hospital. | M |
| | 13.8.18 | | 1 O.R. return from leave. | M |
| | 14.8.18 | | D.A.D.O.S. inspects Company stores. | M |
| | 15.8.18 | | 3 O.R. return from leave. | M |
| | 17.8.18 | | 1 S.S.M. reports to Train H.Qrs. for duty — 1 S.S.M. return from 2/3 Field Ambulance to duty. | M |
| | 18.8.18 | | A.D.M.S. inspects horses — 3 O.R. proceed on leave. | M |
| | 19.8.18 | | O.C. Coy return from leave. | M |
| | 20.8.18 | | 1 O.R. return from leave — 10 O.R. proceed on leave. | M |
| | 21.8.18 | | | M |
| | 22.8.18 | | 1 O.R. returned from leave — Baggage wagons refit & await — 1 O.R. discharged from Hospital | M |
| | | | 2 O.R. returned from leave — Major M.I. Coy 52 Divisional Train seconded to duty with 1st Portuguese | |
| | 23.8.18 | | Signal M¹ shingle on trucks. E. Nº1, Coy 59 Div. Train | M |
| REBREUVETTE | 24.8.18 | | 4 H.D. taken on Strength — 1 H.D. evacuated to M.V.S. — Coy move to REBREUVETTE. | M |
| HAVRANS | 25.8.18 | | Coy move to BURE-AU-BOIS and later in day to WAVRANS. | M |
| MOLLINGHEM | 27.8.18 | | Coy move to MOLLINGHEM — w/Van from NORRENT-FONTES. | M |
| | | | 1 Captain & 20 N.R. detailed C 195 Lewis Section CoY R.E. — 1 O.R. proceeds on leave — 1 O.R. drill bill Coy. | M |
| GUARBECQUE | 28.8.18 | | Coy move to GUARBECQUE. | M |
| | 29.8.18 | | 2 H.D. transferred to Nº 1 Coy 59 Div. Train. | M |
| | 30.8.18 | | 2 O.R. proceed on leave. | M |
| | 31.8.18 | | 1 O.R. admitted to Hospital — 1 O.R. returned from leave. | M |

Army Form C. 2118.

# WAR DIARY
## or
## INTELLIGENCE SUMMARY.
(Erase heading not required.)

Sib^10 (No.4) Coy A.S.C
59th Divisional TRAIN

Instructions regarding War Diaries and Intelligence Summaries are contained in F.S. Regs., Part II and the Staff Manual respectively. Title pages will be prepared in manuscript.

| Hour, Date, Place | Summary of Events and Information | Remarks and references to Appendices |
|---|---|---|
| | The following units were on the strength of the 176 Inf Brigade group for rations during dates shown:— | |
| | Hq 176 Infantry Brigade | 1.8.18 to 31.8.18 | No 3 Field Survey Batt | 28.8.18 to 31.8.18 |
| | 2/6 Stewart Howitzers | 1.8.18 to 2.8.18 | 89 Motor Air Line Sectn | 28.8.18 to 31.8.18 |
| | 36 Batt Northumberland Fusiliers | 1.8.18 to 31.8.18 | 221 Transport Workers | RE 28.8.18 to 31.8.18 |
| | 11 Royal Scots Fusiliers | 1.8.18 to 31.8.18 | S.P.O. GUARBEC QUE | 28.8.18 to 31.8.18 |
| | 13 West Riding Regiment | 1.8.18 to 31.8.18 | S.A.E. BUSNES | 28.8.18 only |
| | 178 T.M.B | 1.8.18 to 31.8.18 | Det 7th B.N.I. Regt | 28.8.18 |
| | 4/10 Field Coy RE | 1.8.18 to 31.8.18 | Conv. Officers & 9 men | 29.8.18 to 31.8.16 |
| | No 4 Coy A.S.C 59 Div Train | 1.8.18 to 31.8.18 | 21 N.M Mobile Vet Sectn | 30.8.18 to 31.8.18 |
| | 2/3 N.M Field Ambulance | 1.8.18 to 31.8.18 | | |
| | 432 Field Coy R.E | 28.8.18 to 31.8.18 | | |
| | No 3 Sectn 12 Aux H.E Coy | 28.8.18 | | |
| | 56 Labour Coy | 28.8.18 | | |
| | 64 Labour Coy | 28.8.18 | | |
| | 135 A.T Coy RE | 28.8.18 to 31.8.18 | | |
| | 284 A.T Coy RE | 28.8.18 to 31.8.18 | | |
| | R.H 2/1 Pontoon Park RE | 28.8.18 to 31.8.18 | | |
| | "D" Coy Oxf & Bucks L.I | 28.8.18 to 31.8.18 | | |
| | 11 G.B Ox Bucks 2/5" | 28.8.18 | | |
| | No 1 R.O Coy RE | 28.8.18 to 31.8.18 | | |
| | 79 Area Employment Coy | 28.8.18 to 31.8.18 | | |
| | 47 Ballon Sec 11 Coy | 28.8.18 to 31.8.18 | | |

O.C. No 4 Coy 59 Div Train

Confidential

WAR DIARY

OF

HEADQUARTERS

59 DIV TRAIN

For month of

Sept 1918 (1st to 30th)

VOLUMME XX

**Army Form C. 2118.**

# WAR DIARY
## or
## INTELLIGENCE SUMMARY.
(Erase heading not required.)

**HEADQUARTERS 59th DIVL TRAIN**

VOLUME XX

Instructions regarding War Diaries and Intelligence Summaries are contained in F. S. Regs., Part II. and the Staff Manual respectively. Title pages will be prepared in manuscript.

| Place | Date | Hour | Summary of Events and Information | Remarks and references to Appendices |
|---|---|---|---|---|
| | Sept 1918 | | Map Reference Sheet 36A | |
| Busnes | 1st | | Railhead Berguette. SRP's Div RA, 176 & 177 Bdes, Busnes. 178 Bde at Guarbecque. No 1 Coy moved to Carvin (P.24 b.3.4 Sheet 36A), No 2 Coy moved to St Floris, No 3 Coy Carvin (P.24 d.b.4. Sheet 36A) No 4 Coy to St Floris | |
| Busnes | 2nd | | SRP's Div RA. Carvin, No 176 Bde St Floris, 177 Bde Carvin. 178 Bde St Floris | |
| Busnes | 4th | | Railhead St Venant. | |
| Busnes | 7th | | THQ moved to Carvin. No 1 Coy to Calonne (Q5.a), No 2 Coy Goods Yards R.H. Calonne. | |
| | | | SRP's Div RA. 176, 177 & 178 Bdes moved to Merville | |
| Carvin | 9th | | No 1 Coy moved to L.32.d.8.6. Sheet 36A, Nos 2 & 3 Coys to Calonne - Merville road (Q.5.a central Sheet 36a) No 4 Coy to Beaupre. 2/Lt Whitfield detached from No 4 to No 1 Coy as S.O. 2/Lt Kaul detached from THQ to No 4 Coy for Transport duty. 3 H.D. Horses of No 3 Coy detached with 177 BHQ Killed by enemy shell fire. | |
| Carvin | 14th | | Div RA. SRP moved to L.32.d.8.6. Sheet 36A. | |
| Carvin | 15th | | 176 Bde SRP moved to Q.5.d.b.8 Sheet 36A or Calonne - Merville road. Major V.B.R Conran O.B.E A.S.C. SSO 59th Division posted to R.A.F. Capt R.W Harvey S.O 176 Bde assumed duties of S.S.O 59 Div. 2/Lt Kaul detached from No 4 to No 2 Coy and assumed duties of S.O. 176 Bde. Captain H.H Collins ASC reported for duty. | |

Army Form C. 2118.

# WAR DIARY
## or
## INTELLIGENCE SUMMARY.
(Erase heading not required.)

VOLUME XX

HEADQUARTERS 59 DIV TRAIN

Instructions regarding War Diaries and Intelligence Summaries are contained in F. S. Regs., Part II. and the Staff Manual respectively. Title pages will be prepared in manuscript.

| Place | Date | Hour | Summary of Events and Information | Remarks and references to Appendices |
|---|---|---|---|---|
| | Sept 1918 | | | |
| CARVIN | 15th | | SAPs of 177 Bde moved to MERVILLE — PARADIS road a 178 Bde to BEAUPRÉ. R.H. MERVILLE. | |
| CARVIN | 16th | | THQ moved to PARADIS (Q.18.A.2.7. Sheet 36A). | |
| PARADIS | 17th | | Capt EARNES detached from No 4 to Non. Hq. and assumed duties of SO Div RA 2/Lt WHITFIELD returned to No 4 Coy a assumed duties of SO 176 BDE. | |
| PARADIS | 19th | | SAPs 176 Bde moved to R.3.c.8.8 Sheet 36a — LA GORGUE, 177 Bde also to LA GORGUE. | |
| PARADIS | 21st | 12.00 | CRE 59 Div inspected Camps of 4 Coys. | |
| | | 16.00 | ADVS 59 Div inspected Train animals | |
| PARADIS | 27th | | XI Corps ADVS & AQMG 59 Div inspected Train animals Major N.B. CLEGG DSO reported for duty & posted to command of No.1. Coy, vice Major M.G.H. LAMBERT (invalided). | |

Health of men good on whole. Transport in good condition

[signature]
CAPT & ADJT
59TH DIVISIONAL TRAIN

Confidential.

WAR DIARY
— OF —
OC 53 Coy A.S.C.
for Month of
SEPTEMBER 1918
(1st to 30th)

Vol. No. 19 20

# WAR DIARY or INTELLIGENCE SUMMARY

**Army Form C. 2118**

513 Coy. A.S.C.

| Place | Date | Hour | Summary of Events and Information | Remarks and references to Appendices |
|---|---|---|---|---|
| FIELD | 1/9/18 | — | Company in Camp & Quarters at BUSNES. Horses on lines. Refilling point at BUSNES. Supplies drawn by M.T. Col. from BERGUETTE. | |
| | 1/9/18 | 5pm | Coy. HdQrs. and 3 Supply wagons of 295 and 296 Bakes R.F.H. at 6 Supply wagons of Coys 1, 2, 3 and 4 of the DAC moved to Vieille Hunte from BUSNES to P24 d. 3. 4. | |
| | 2/9/18 | — | Company in Camp and Quarters at GARVIN. Supplies drawn and transport from BERGUETTE. Refilled point at GARVIN. | |
| | 7/9/18 | 7am | Coy HQrs. and Supply wagons of 295 and 296 Bdes RFH and Supply wagons of 1, 2 & 3 of the DAC moved to march rdezvs. Bigger wagons from P24 to 3.4 to Q.5.a Coy in camp [illegible] town Quarters at NEVILLE E. drawn by H.T. from CALONNE. Refilling point at [illegible] | |
| | 9/9/18 | 7am | Coy HQtrs. and Supply wagons of 295 and 296 Bdes R.F.H. and Supply wagons of 1st, 2nd & 3rd sections DAC. baggage wagons of coys 1, 2, 3 & 4 still 36a. from Q.5.a. to S.1. 32 d. 8. 6. Supplies drawn by H.T. from CALONNE. Refilling point NEVILLE. Coy in camp. Horses in stables. | |
| | 10/9/18 | | Refilling point changed from NEVILLE to L.32. d. 8. 6. | |
| | 14/9/18 | | Supplies drawn by Horse transport and M.T. Col from NEVILLE. | |
| | 27.9.18 | | Major N.B. CLEGG. D.S.O. assumed command as from 27.9.18 of 513 Coy ASC Vice Major M.L.B. H. LAMBERT (invalided) | |

Frank Clegg

COMMANDING No. 1 Coy, 59 DIVL. TRAIN.

*Confidential*

War Diary

of

514 Coy A.S.C

for

Month of

Sept 1918 (1st to 30th)

Vol XX

**WAR DIARY**
**INTELLIGENCE SUMMARY.**
*(Erase heading not required.)*

Army Form C. 2118.

VOL. XX.

O.C. No 2 Coy. 59th Div

Instructions regarding War Diaries and Intelligence Summaries are contained in F.S. Regs., Part II. and the Staff Manual respectively. Title pages will be prepared in manuscript.

| Hour, Date, Place | Summary of Events and Information | Remarks and references to Appendices |
|---|---|---|
| 1.9.18. BUSNES. | Capt. T.M. McAuliffe assumed command of [?] and following units the ration strength of 176th Inf. Bde. Group: — HQ 176 Inf Bde. 2.5 Bn Liverpool Regt, 2.6 Bn R. Welch Fus., 17 Bn R. Sussex R., 4/5 Bn Coy R.E., 2/1 N.M. Fld. Amb. B.O.Q. Sec. 59th D.A.C., C.R.E. 59th Div. 2/1 N.M. Mob V.A.T. Sec. — supplies drawn ex Pres [?] with for consumption 2 Sept and transported to station strength of 177 Inf. Bde. Group. Rations at Busnes and delivered at Robecq St Venant + St Floris. Moved HQ of Coy at 5 p.m. to ST FLORIS. (P.B. b.O.S/36A) & S.R.P. of 176 Inf Bde. Group 15. P.6.a.3.3. | mut. |
| 2.9.18. ST FLORIS. | Drew supplies in bulk from BERGETTE Railhead, 1st Line Transport drew rations from S.R.P. (4 wagons used on R.H. convoy) | mut. mut. |
| 3.9.18. ST FLORIS | Drew supplies in bulk from ST VENANT Railhead with Train transport (18 wagons used on R.H. convoy) | mut. |
| 4.9.18. " | ditto | mut. |
| 5.9.18 " | Battn ration strengths forwarded to various sections of Brigade Group. Baggage wagons permitted to move. Action strength of Brigade Group. 198 Labour Co. attd. | mut. |
| 6.9.18 " | Drew supplies in bulk from CALONNE Railhead – 16 wagons employed. S.R.P. moved to MERVILLE Goods Sta. | mut. |
| 7.9.18 " | Drew supplies in bulk from CALONNE Railhead – 14 wagons employed. No 36 Labour Group HQ taken on ration strength of Bde. Group. | mut. |
| 8.9.18 " | | mut. |
| 9.9.18 Q.S.A — SheT 36A | No 8 Railway C.O. R.G.S. taken on Ration Strength of Brigade Group. 13 G.S. wagons attached to 26th Bn. Royal Welsh Fus. Coy. helpers moved to CALONNE. R.H. 10 wagons used. | mut. |
| 10.9.18 | MERVILLE – CALONNE Road (Q.S. of ShT 36 A). Supplies drawn in bulk from CALONNE R.H. – 8 wagons employed. | mut. |
| 11.9.18 " | Baggage wagons attached to HQ, 176 VB Bde, 25th Liverpool R, & 17 R. Sussex R. | mut. |
| 12.9.18 " | Supplies drawn in bulk from CALONNE R.H. by Train wagons – 2 wagons employed. | mut. |
| 13.9.18 " | ditto | mut. |
| 14.9.18 " | ditto | mut. |
| 15.9.18 " | ditto | mut. |
| 19.9.18 " | Horse supplies in bulk by H.T. from MERVILLE Railhead. Ration Return of 176 Inf Bde. Group appended to Q.S. dt 6.8. Supply Refilling Point moved to R.3.c.8.2 (LAGORGUE – Sheet 36 A) | mut. |
| 23.9.18 " | Capt. R.W. HARTLEY transferred from Coy, Sp. Div. Train. 2/LT C. MAIR assumed duties as S.O. 176 Inf. Bde. | mut. |
| 25.9.18 " | 119 Labour Coy taken on ration strength of Brigade Group. | mut. |
| 26.9.18 " | Y.M.C.A., CALONNE taken on ration strength of Brigade Group. | mut. |
| 30.9.18 " | Supply wagon of M. Gun Coy lent to 176 L.T.N.B. 2nd Adv. [?] of Coy. Health of men others during month continued excellent in spite of adverse conditions and accommodation. | mut. |

M McAuliffe Capt
O.C. No 2 Coy. 59 Div Train

Confidential

War Diary

of

515 Company, A.S.C. 59th Division

From 1.9.18 to 30.9.18

Volume XX.

Army Form C. 2118.

# WAR DIARY
## or
## INTELLIGENCE SUMMARY.
(Erase heading not required.)

VOL XX

Instructions regarding War Diaries and Intelligence Summaries are contained in F. S. Regs., Part II. and the Staff Manual respectively. Title pages will be prepared in manuscript.

515 Coy. A.S.C. 59th Divn.

Summary of Events and Information September 1918.

| Place | Date | Hour | Summary of Events and Information | Remarks and references to Appendices |
|---|---|---|---|---|
| BUSNES | 1/9/18 | | In Camp and Billets | |
| " | 1/9/18 | | 5 Surplus Ride Horses transferred to 469 Cy R.E. | |
| " | 1/9/18 | A.m 3.30 | Coy H.Q. moved by Road to POMPADOUR FARM. P.24.A.6.4. pdometer 36¼ | |
| POMPADOUR FARM | 1/9/18 | A.m 4.30 | In Camp and quarters | |
| " | 2/9/18 | | Supplies of Bde Group drawn from Railhead by Train Transport | |
| " | 6/9/18 | | CAPT. F. J. GREEN proceeds on leave to ENGLAND. — LIEUT M.C. JOHNSTON acting O.C. | PCI |
| " | 9/9/18 | 8.AM | Coy HQ moves by route march to MERVILLE AREA. (Q.5.a.6.2 Sheet 36A) In Camp. horses on open lines men in bivouacs — Baggage wagons detached to line with units. — 3 H.D. horses detached 177 B.H.R. | PCI |
| | | | Killed by enemy shell fire. | |
| | 13/9/18 | | 2 L.D. and 2 H.D. remounts received | |
| MERVILLE | 15/9/18 | | 1 H.D. horse of No 1. Coy attached temporarily to 2/1 M.V.S. by V.O. | |

M. Johnston O/C No. 515 Coy. A.S.C.
59th Division

# WAR DIARY or INTELLIGENCE SUMMARY

Army Form C. 2118.

VOL. XX

515 Coy. A.S.C. 59th Div. September 1918

| Place | Date | Hour | Summary of Events and Information | Remarks and references to Appendices |
|---|---|---|---|---|
| MERVILLE | 18/9/18 | | WHL S. SERGT reposted from (H.T. & S. Base Depot HAYNE). Surplus to establishment — 10R EVACUATED | MET |
| | 19/9/18 | | Surplus WHL DVR transported to 47". DIV TRAIN OFF Strength 4 | MET |
| | 20/9/18 | | Baggage wagon sent to 25 M.G.C. 177 Brig SRP moved to R 3 c 88 Sht. 36.A. — Supply wagons of 2/1 NM Field Ambulance and 4 bg Field Coy R.E sent to live with units — E, M, & 9 Special Coy's R.E: No 5 Observation group; 59 Div. Reception Camp: 291 Transportation Coy R.E: AREA COMMANDANT BUSMES: 56" Labour group OFF Brig Ration Strength. | MET |
| | 21/9/18 | 12 noon | C.O. and CRE 59" DIV inspect Camp with view to winter quarters. Camp condemned. | MET |
| | | 4.50 | C.O. – DADYS – V.O. ½ Train inspect all horses. — Condition satisfactory. | |
| | 22/9/18 | | CAPTAIN R. J. GREEN, returns from leave and assumes command | KG |
| | 23/9/18 | | 1 driver reinforcement — received | KG |
| | 25/9/18 | | 6 privates from Battⁿ of Bde Group report for wheelwrights Course | KG |

R. J. Green Capt.
o/c No. 515 Coy. A.S.C.
59th Division.

# WAR DIARY
## or
## INTELLIGENCE SUMMARY.

(Erase heading not required.)

Army Form C. 2118.

VOL XX

515 Coy. A.S.C. 59th Div. Summary of Events and Information September 1918.

| Place | Date | Hour | Summary of Events and Information | Remarks and references to Appendices |
|---|---|---|---|---|
| MERVILLE | 2/9/18 | | Surplus R.H.S. & Sgts sent to Base H.T. Depot HAVRE | nil |
| " | 27/9/18 | 2 to 4.0 | XI Corps A.D.V.S. and C.O. inspected all Horses and Coy lines | nil |
| " | 30/9/18 | | General health of the Coy during the month was only fair. All horses in good condition | nil |

A. Green Capt.
o/c No. 515 Coy. A.S.C.
59th Division.

Confidential

War Diary
of
46th (N.H.) 9th Divisional Train.

From :- 1-9-16    To :- 30-9-16.

Volume 20.

# WAR DIARY
## or
## INTELLIGENCE SUMMARY.

*(Erase heading not required.)*

816 Coy (No 4 Coy) ASC   Army Form C. 2118.
59 Divisional Train

Instructions regarding War Diaries and Intelligence Summaries are contained in F.S. Regs., Part II and the Staff Manual respectively. Title pages will be prepared in manuscript.

| Hour, Date, Place | | Summary of Events and Information | Remarks and references to Appendices |
|---|---|---|---|
| QUARBECQUE | 1.9.18 | Coy moves to ST. FLORIS | N. |
| ST. FLORIS | 4.9.18 | 1 Baggage wagon der Balk. killed — 1 O.R. wounded by kick — 1 O.R. from leave | N. |
|  | 5.9.18 | 1 N.O. on leave. | N. |
|  | 6.9.18 | 1 O.R. on leave — 1 O.R. To Hospital | N. |
|  | 7.9.18 | 1 O.R. on leave — Supply Dump moves to MERVILLE. | N. |
|  | 8.9.18 | 2 O.R. from leave — 1 O.R. from Hospital. 2/Lt KAUL reports for duty. | N. |
| BEAUPRÉ | 9.9.18 | 2/Lt WHITFIELD detached to No 1 Coy — Coy moves to BEAUPRÉ | N. |
|  | 10.9.18 | 1 N.O. & 1 O.R. on leave — remaining Baggage wagons report to unit | N. |
|  | 11.9.18 | 1 O.R. from Hospital | N. |
|  | 12.9.18 |  | N. |
|  | 13.9.18 | 2/Lt KAUL proceeds to No 2 Coy. | N. |
|  | 14.9.18 | 1 O.R. from leave | N. |
|  | 17.9.18 | Supply Dump moves from MERVILLE to BEAUPRÉ. Capt E.J.N EADIES attached to No 1 Coy — 2/Lt F WHITFIELD returns from No 1 Coy | N. |
|  | 18.9.18 | — 1 O.R. on leave | N. |
|  | 19.9.18 | 2 O.R. from leave. | N. |
|  | 20.9.18 | 1 O.R. on leave — 1 O.R. on sickness (rheumatism). | N. |
|  | 21.9.18 | 1 Cpl attached to Camp Commandant for duty. | N. |
|  | 22.9.18 | C.R.E with C.O visits Coy to advise on stable building — Co inspects lines — | N. |
|  | 23.9.18 | 1 O.R. To Hospital | N. |
|  |  | 1 N.O. From leave — Building huts & stables commenced — | N. |
|  | 24.9.18 | 1 O.R. From leave. | N. |

Army Form C. 2118.

# WAR DIARY
or
## INTELLIGENCE SUMMARY.
(Erase heading not required.)

Instructions regarding War Diaries and Intelligence Summaries are contained in F.S. Regs., Part II. and the Staff Manual respectively. Title pages will be prepared in manuscript.

| Hour, Date, Place | Summary of Events and Information | Remarks and references to Appendices |
|---|---|---|
| BEAUPRE. | | |
| 25.9.18. | 1 O.R. from Hospital | M. |
| 26.9.18. | 1 Sgt proceeds to 2nd Army Rest Camp — 1 attached Supply killed sent there | M |
| | 1 O/N.C.O — 1 Baggage know wounded by shell | |
| 27.9.18 | 1 O.R. on leave — ADVS XI Corps, AQMG 59 Div & C.O inspected horses — | M |
| | 1 O.R From leave. | |
| 28.9.18 | 5 Horses received from Brigade to condemning | M |
| 29.9.18 | 1 O.R. on Special leave — | M. |
| 30.9.18 | 1 R.S.M.A conducted few met returned convoy from 196 Tunnel Drainage Cy R.E. | M. |

O.C. No. 4 Cy 59 Divisional Train

# WAR DIARY or INTELLIGENCE SUMMARY

Army Form C. 2118.

516 (No 4 Coy) A.S.C.
59 Divisional Train

| Hour, Date, Place | Summary of Events and Information | Remarks and references to Appendices |
|---|---|---|
| | List of units fed by Supply Officer 178 Infantry Brigade during Month of September:— | |
| | Headquarters 178 2nd Bde. 1.9.18 to 30.9.18 | 794 Area Employment Coy 19.18 to 7.9.18 |
| | 56 Northumberland Fusiliers ditto | 221 Transport (World's Coy) 19.18 to 3.9.18 & 22.9.18 to 30.9.18 |
| | 11 Royal Scots Fusiliers ditto | 89 Motor Amb. Line 1.9.18 only |
| | 13 West Riding Regiment ditto | SAC GUARDECAUE 17.9.18 to 7.9.18 |
| | 178 Trench Mortar Battery ditto | Agricultural Officers (Militia) 1.9.18 to 12.9.18 |
| | 470 Field Coy RE ditto | (continued) |
| | No 4 Coy 59 Divisional Train ditto | 19.18 to 29.18 |
| | 64 Labour Coy ditto | 57 Labour Coy 19.9.18 to 30.9.18 |
| | 294 A.T. Coy R.E. ditto | No 3 Wasservern Crusts 22.9.18 to 30.9.18 |
| | R14 2/Porter Park R.E. ditto | 308 RCE RE detachment 27.9.18 to 30.9.18 |
| | 47 Balloon Section 11 Corps ditto | Y Coy Agricultural Labour 3.9.18 to 22.9.18 |
| | No 2 Field Survey Bn ditto | 70 Sec B A.A. Battery 4.9.18 to 7.9.18 |
| | 41 Mobile Veterinary Section 1.9.18 to 6.9.18 | 33 Sec B A.A. Battery 9.9.18 to 29.9.18 |
| | 432 Field Coy R.E. 1.9.18 to 4.9.18 | 56 Labour Coy 30.9.18 to 30.9.18 |
| | No 3 Sec 15 Aux Horse T Coy 1.9.18 to 4.9.18 | M. Special Coy R.E. 22.9.18 to 30.9.18 |
| | 135 Q.T. Coy R.E. 1.9.18 to 11.9.18 | 225 Labour Coy 24.9.18 to 30.9.18 |
| | D Coy by Bucks L.I. 1.9.18 to 3.9.18 | 130 Labour Coy 3.9.18 to 30.9.18 |
| | 11 Field Bn Bucks Regt 1.9.18 to 9.9.18 | 107 Sec B AA Battery 22.9.18 to 30.9.18 |
| | No 2 LR Coy RE 1.9.18 to 3.9.18 | |

M. Chartres
OC 4 Coy 59 Divl Train

Vol 21

Confidential

War Diary

of

H.Q. 59th Divisional Train

From 1-10-18
To 31-10-18

Volume XXI

Army Form C. 2118.

# WAR DIARY
## or
## INTELLIGENCE SUMMARY.
(Erase heading not required.)

Headquarters 59th (N.M.) Divisional Train

Volume XXI

Instructions regarding War Diaries and Intelligence Summaries are contained in F. S. Regs., Part II. and the Staff Manual respectively. Title pages will be prepared in manuscript.

| Place | Date | Hour | Summary of Events and Information | Remarks and references to Appendices |
|---|---|---|---|---|
| OCTOBER 1918 | | | Map References Sheets 36a, 36 & 37 | |
| PARADIS | 1st | - | SRP3. Div R.A. L32.d 8.6/36a. 176 Bde R3 c 8.8/36a. 177 Bde R3 c 8.8/36a (La Gorgue) 178 Bde - Beaupre/36a. R.H. Merville. | |
| PARADIS | 2nd | - | S.R.P. 178 Bde to Estaires. | |
| PARADIS | 3rd | - | SRP3. Div R.A. 176, 177, 178 Bdes moved to Sailly-Sur-La-Lys/36 | |
| PARADIS | 4th | - | T.H.Q. moved to Chayulle Deville (L.27.c/36). No 1 Coy to L27. c 7.4/36a. No 2 Coy to K.24.d 3 6/36a. (Neuf Berquin), No 3 Coy to Estaires & No 4 Coy to Neuf Berquin. | |
| Chayulle Deville | 6th | - | No 1 Coy to G27.6.6/36. No 2 Coy to G27 6.2.2/36. R.H. La Gorgue. Captn H.S. Cowins took over duties of S.O. 176 Bde vice 2/Lt C Kaul | |
| Chayulle Deville | 17th | - | T.H.Q moved to Bac St Maur. No 3 Coy to Sailly-Sur-La-Lys. No 4 Coy to Sailly-Sur-La-Lys. 176 Bde S.R.P. to Wez-Macquart. | |
| Bac St Maur | 18 | - | T.H.Q moved to St Andrée, No 1 Coy to Lambersart. No 2 Coy to Lambersart, No 3 Coy to Lambersart. No 4 Coy to Lambersart. 4 SRP3 also at Lambersart R.H. Laventie. | |
| St Andrée | 19 | - | T.H.Q. moved to Flers, 1.2.3 & 4 Coys to St Andrée. 4 SRP3 also to St Andrée | |
| FLERS | 20 | - | T.H.Q moved to Petit Lannoy (Hem). No 1 Coy L.29 & 4 6/36 (Hemponpont), No 2 Coy to Hemponpont, No 3 Coy to Flers Berg, No 4 Coy to Hem. 4 SRP3 or Flers - Hemponpont road. | |
| FLERS | 24 | - | R.H. at Perenchies 26/10/18 R H St Andrée | |

Army Form C. 2118.

# WAR DIARY
### or
# INTELLIGENCE SUMMARY.
(Erase heading not required.)

Volume XXI

Headquarters 59' (N.M) Divisional Train

| Place | Date | Hour | Summary of Events and Information | Remarks and references to Appendices |
|---|---|---|---|---|
| October 21st 1918 | | | Map References Sheet 36a 36 & 37 | |
| HEM | 21st | | T.H.Q moved to Saint Léz. Lannoy. Health of troops during month good save for influenza. Transport in good condition. | |

CAPT. & ADJT.
FOR DIVISIONAL TRAIN

WAR DIARY

of

O.C. 53 Coy A.S.C. 59th Divn

Nov 1st to 31st October 1915

(Vol. 20.)

Army Form C. 2118.

# WAR DIARY
## or
## INTELLIGENCE SUMMARY.

(Erase heading not required.)

Instructions regarding War Diaries and Intelligence Summaries are contained in F. S. Regs., Part II and the Staff Manual respectively. Title pages will be prepared in manuscript.

513 Coy A.S.C. 50th DIVISION

| Place | Date | Hour | Summary of Events and Information | Remarks and references to Appendices |
|---|---|---|---|---|
| Field | 1/10/15 | — | Company in billets at L.32 d 9 6. Refilling point at L.32 d 9 6. Sheet 36 N. Supplies drawn from MERVILLE. | |
| | 3.10.15 | | Refilling point moved to SAILLY-SUR-LYS. Supplies drawn by M.T. and M.T. from MERVILLE. | |
| | 4.10.15 | | Supplies drawn by M.T. from MERVILLE. | |
| | 4.10.15 | 10 am | Coy HQrs with Suppy wagons at L.29. d.6. 1/6 Bgde R.F.A. and HQrs No 1 & 2 Sections D.A.C. and wagons at HQrs No 1 & No 2 Sects D.A.C moved to L.27 c 7, Sheet 36. Horse & Limber shelters. Veterinary detail Camp and Officers' Horses in huts & open shelters. | |
| | 6.10.15 | 9 am | Coy HQrs moved to Horse Route from L.27 d. 7.4. to G 27. h. 6.6 Sheet 36. | |
| | 7.10.18 | 8 am | Refilling point moved to H.21.d. Sheet 36. | |
| | 15.10.18 | 8.30 am | Coy HQrs moved to Horse Route from G 27. h. 6.6. to J.30. b. 5. 9. Quartered in Billets at AMBARSART known as Refilling point and LAMBERSART. Supplies drawn by M.T. from LAVENTIE. | |
| | 19.10.18 | 11.30 am | Coy HQrs moved to Horse Route from J.30. d. 5. 9. to St ANDRÉ. Refilling point at St ANDRÉ. Supplies drawn by M.T. from LAVENTIE. | |
| | 20.10.15 | 1 pm | Coy HQrs and Suppy wagons 1/5 Bgde R.F.A. moved to Horse Route from St ANDRÉ to L.29 F. 4. 6. Refilling point at L.29 F.h. 4. 6. Supplies drawn by M.T. from LAVENTIE. | |
| | 24.10.15 | | Supplies drawn by M.T. from St ANDRÉ. | |
| | 30.10.18 | | Coy in Billets at L.29. h. 4. 6. Horses in Stables & open sheds. | |

COMMANDING 513 Coy. A.S.C.
[signature] MAJOR,

Confidential

War Diary

of

O.C No 2 Coy 59' (NM) Divisional Train

From 1-10-18
To 31-10-18

Volume XXI

Army Form C. 2118.

VOL. XXI

# WAR DIARY
## INTELLIGENCE SUMMARY
*(Erase heading not required.)*

O.C. N° 2 Coy. Sq II~w~. TRAIN.

Instructions regarding War Diaries and Intelligence Summaries are contained in F.S. Regs., Part II. and the Staff Manual respectively. Title pages will be prepared in manuscript.

| Hour, Date, Place | Summary of Events and Information | Remarks and references to Appendices |
|---|---|---|
| 1st Oct 1918. Q.S.a./Sh.J 36.A. 1000 yds. S.W. of MERVILLE. | Commenced march with HQrs. party at Q.S.a./31.a. and S.R.P. 176 Inf. Bde. Group at R.3.c.8.8/36.A. following Mule lorry on ration strength of Brigade Group HQ. 176 Inf. Bde., 7-3 Battns of fds, 176 L.T.M.B. N°2 Coy, 59 Div. Train, 447-312 Co. R.E., 2/1 N.M. Fd. Amb. 118 and 199 Lab. Corps, 7 M.G.C. Colonels. Adv. & 73 BattMen 175 Inf. Bde drawing supplies by 1st Line Transport from this Train Supply wagons. Supplies being drawn in bulk from MERVILLE Railhead K5 S.R.P. by Train Supply wagons (8 daily) | Truck |
| 3rd Oct 1918. | HQ. 36 Lab. Group drawn for last time for consumption 3rd Oct. also 26th Regt. Welsh drawn to 447 Fd. Co. R.E. Undermentioned Units taken on ration strength of Bde. Group for consumption 4th Oct: | Mist, Truck |
| 4th Oct 1918. N.24.d.3.b. Sh.J 36.A | St Germain Group, 20th Balloon Sec., XI Corps Cyclists, 196th Lnd Draw. Coy. 164th Anti Aircraft Sec. 70th A Auxy. Bn. 351 2nd M. Coy. 11th Reg Sigs. Bde 3rd 470 Sld Co.R.S. Following units drew for last consumption 4th Oct. 198th Labour Coy. | Mist, Truck |
| 6th Oct 1912. | Royal Artillery 176 Fd. Bttn. moved to K.24.d.3.b & moved from MERVILLE to NEUF BERQUIN. 5th Australian Light Ry. Drawing Coy drew for last time for consumption 6th Oct. (SAILLY SUR LA LYS.) who XI Corps Cyclists. | Mist, Brit |
| G.27.b.6.6./Sh J 36. | Moved 8 27.b.6.6 on main Road from ESTAIRES to SAILLY SUR LA LYS. Horse day Horse Transport from LA GORGUE Railhead. | Mist. |
| 13th Oct 1918. | Capt. H.S. Collins taken on strength of Company and assumed duties of Supply officer. 176 Inf. Bde via 2/1 Z. Kent. | Mist |
| 14th Oct 1918. | 70th Anti Aircraft Sec. reduced for this day & shewn off strength of Brigade Group. | Mist |
| | 142nd Anti Aircraft Sec. shewn on ration strength of Brigade group. XI Corps Cyclists restored to this day and shewn off strength of Brigade Group. | Mist |
| 15th Oct 1918. LAMBERSART. | S.R.P. 176 Inf. Bde. moved to I.16.D/Sh J 36 W. of WEZ MACQUART. Headquarters of Coy & Supply Section moved via FLEURBAIX - CHAPELLE D'ARMENTIERES - WEZ MACQUART and LOMME to LAMBERSART. | Mist |
| 19th Oct 1918. LAMBERSART. ST ANDRE | S.R.P. 176 Inf. Bde. to 19th - LAMBERSART. Supplies delivered by Train Transport to Units in FLERS & BROEUCQ areas. | Mist |
| 20th Oct 1918. ST ANDRE HEMPONPONT. | Headquarters of Coy. moved to ST ANDRE. S.R.P. 176 Inf. Bde. to 20th - ST ANDRE. Headquarters of Coy. moved via LA MADELEING - TEMPLEUVE - SAILLY LES LANNOY - | Mist |
| 21st Oct 1918 HEMPONPONT. | FYVES - FLERS AT HEMPONPONT. Supplies delivered Kit Kdwnds there & N Corps Cyclists rations for last time by Train Supply wagons. CHAS and HEM by Train Supply wagons. S.R.P. 176 Inf. Bde. to 21st - HEMPONPONT. Supplies delivered by Train Transport. | Mist |
| 22 Oct 1918 HEMPONPONT. | at SAILLY LES LANNOY and TEMPLEUVE. | Mist |
| 31 Oct 1918. | S.R.P. HEMPONPONT. 25th Township Coy. R.C. taken on ration strength of 59th Div. Group. Ration at HEMPONPONT to end of month. Relieved supplies daily to SAILLY LES LANNOY - TOUFFERS and TEMPLEUVE. Made Company transliteration of pieces of work & throughout month. | Mist |

T.W.M.A??? Capt.
O.C. N°2 Coy. S.9 IV. TRAIN.

Confidential
War Diary
of
515 Company, A.S.C. 59th Division
from 1·10·18 to 31·10·18.
(Volume XXI)

Army Form C. 2118.

Volume XXI

# WAR DIARY
## or
## INTELLIGENCE SUMMARY.
(Erase heading not required.)

Instructions regarding War Diaries and Intelligence Summaries are contained in F. S. Regs., Part II. and the Staff Manual respectively. Title pages will be prepared in manuscript.

515 Coy. A.S.C. 59th Divn.    Summary of Events and Information October 1918.

| Place | Date | Hour | Summary of Events and Information | Remarks and references to Appendices |
|---|---|---|---|---|
| MERVILLE | 1/10 | | In camp | AG |
| " | | | One NCO proceeds to England on transfer to R.A.F. | AG |
| " | | | NCO goes from 516 Coy A.S.C. to complete establishment | AG |
| " | | | D.H.Q. M.V.S. MMP & Traffic | |
| " | | | I.H.Q. DADOS 59th Div. Signals } Came on ration strength 1/10/18 to 4/10/18 | AG |
| " | | | C.R.E. S.A.A. Sec. 59th Salvage Coy } | |
| " | 3/10 | | 2 Drivers reinforcements reported from Base | AG |
| " | | | 177 Bde, R.F.P. moved up to SAILLY SUR LA LYS. | AG |
| " | 4/10 | 10am | Coy HQ moved by road to ESTAIRES | AG |
| ESTAIRES | 4/10 | 12.0 | In camp and quarters | AG |
| " | 5/10 | | 23rd Battn M.G.C. struck off ration strength on leaving Division | AG |
| " | 6/10 | | One NCO sent on course to XI Corps Gas school | AG |
| " | 7/10 | | Squadron of K.E.H. came on ration strength | H.G. Gr— Capt o/c No. 515 Coy. A.S.C. 59th Division. |

Army Form C. 2118.

# WAR DIARY
## or
## INTELLIGENCE SUMMARY.
(Erase heading not required.)

Volume XXI

Instructions regarding War Diaries and Intelligence Summaries are contained in F. S. Regs., Part II. and the Staff Manual respectively. Title pages will be prepared in manuscript.

| Place | Date | Hour | Summary of Events and Information | Remarks and references to Appendices |
|---|---|---|---|---|
| ESTAIRES | 10/18 | | 515 Coy. A.S.C. 59th Divn. October 1918 | |
| | 10/10 | | One Driver sent to 2nd Army Rest Camp | W.G. |
| " | 10/18 | | 59th DAC Canteen came on ration strength | W.G. |
| " | 13/10 | | XI Corps Cyclist Corps came on ration strength | W.G. |
| " | 17/10 14.15 | | Coy H.Q. moved by road to SAILLY SUR LA LYS | W.G. |
| SAILLY SUR LA LYS | 17/10 11.0 | | In Camp | W.G. |
| " | 18/10 6.15 | | Coy H.Q. moved by road to LAMBERSART | W.G. |
| LAMBERSART | 18/10 3.0 | | In Camp & Billets | W.G. |
| " | 19/10 2.30 | | Coy H.Q. moved by road to ST ANDRE | W.G. |
| ST ANDRE | 19/10 3.30 | | In Billets | W.G. |
| " | 19/10 | | 1. H.D. Horse Transport to 2/1st M.V.S. | W.G. |
| " | 20/10 9.30 | | Coy H.Q. moved by road to FLERS-BERG | W.G. |
| FLERS-BERG | 20/10 3.0 | | In quarters and Billets | W.G. |

H Green Capt
o/c No. 515 Coy. A.S.C.
59th Division

Army Form C. 2118.

Volume XXI

# WAR DIARY
or
# INTELLIGENCE SUMMARY.
*(Erase heading not required.)*

515 Coy. A.S.C. 59. Divn.   Summary of Events and Information   October 1918

| Place | Date | Hour | Summary of Events and Information | Remarks and references to Appendices |
|---|---|---|---|---|
| FLERS-BERG | 24/10 | | One Supply N.C.O. evacuated to C.C.S. | A/L |
| " | 31/10 | | Co. Camp and Billets. General health of the Coy. during the month has been good. All horses in good condition. | NL |

W. Green Capt
o/c No. 515 Coy. A.S.C.
59th Division.

Confidential

War Diary

of

96. N.H. Inf. 59ᵗʰ Divnl. Train

From 1-10-18   To: 31-10-18

Volume 21

Army Form C. 2118.

516 Coy (No 4 Coy) ASC

# WAR DIARY
## or
## INTELLIGENCE SUMMARY. 59 Divisional Train

(Erase heading not required.)

Instructions regarding War Diaries and Intelligence Summaries are contained in F.S. Regs., Part II. and the Staff Manual respectively. Title pages will be prepared in manuscript.

| Hour, Date, Place | | Summary of Events and Information | Remarks and references to Appendices |
|---|---|---|---|
| 1.10.18 | BEAUPRE | 2 OR FROM leave | M |
| 2.10.18 | | 1 WO (Lieut T) TO Hospital — Supply Dump TO ESTAIRES | M |
| 3.10.18 | | 1 OR FROM Hospital — 2 OR reinforcements ON strength — Supply dump | |
| 4.10.18 | ASHILLY-SUR-LACYS | Coy move to Premesques n NEUF-BERQUIN | M |
| 6.10.18 | NEUF-BERQUIN | 1 OR ON leave | M |
| 7.10.18 | | | M |
| 8.10.18 | | 2/Lt DENTON J proceeds on a gas course | M |
| 9.10.18 | | 2 OR ON leave — 1 OR FROM Base — | M |
| 11.10.18 | | 1 OR TO hospital | M |
| 14.10.18 | | 1 OR Wounded + struck off — | M |
| 17.10.18 | | 1 OR ON leave — 1 OR FROM Hospital | M |
| 18.10.18 | SAILLY-SUR-LYS | Coy move to SAILLY-SUR-LYS — Supply Dump TO WEZ-MACQUART + | M |
| 19.10.18 | LAMBERSART | Coy moves FLAMBERSART — Dump moves to same place as Coy | M |
| 20.10.18 | ST ANDRE | 1 OR ON leave | M |
| 22.10.18 | | Coy + Dump move to ST ANDRE | M |
| 27.10.18 | HEM | Coy + dump move to HEM | M |
| 28.10.18 | | 1 OR transferred to No 1 Coy | M |
| 29.10.18 | | 1 OR FROM leave — Capt E.J. KEARNES return to Coy | M |
| 30.10.18 | | 2 OR FROM leave — hospital — 1 OR On leave | M |

Army Form C. 2118.

516 Coy (No. 4 Coy) ASC
59 [?] Divisional Train

# WAR DIARY
or
## INTELLIGENCE SUMMARY.
(Erase heading not required.)

Instructions regarding War Diaries and Intelligence Summaries are contained in F.S. Regs., Part II. and the Staff Manual respectively. Title pages will be prepared in manuscript.

| Hour, Date, Place | Summary of Events and Information | Remarks and references to Appendices |
|---|---|---|
| | List of units rationed by 178 Infantry Bde from during month of October :— | |
| H.Q. 178 Inf Brigade | 1.10.18 — 31.10.18 | 1.10.18 — 2.10.18 |
| 36. Northumberland Fusiliers | | 2.10.18 — 31.10.18 |
| 11 Royal Scots Fusiliers | 2.10.18 | 3.10.18 — 9.10.18 |
| 13 West Riding Regiment | 1.10.18 | 3.10.18 — 31.10.18 |
| 178. T.M. Battery | | |
| 470 Coy R.E. | | 5.10.18 — 31.10.18 |
| 4 Coy 5/9 Inf Train | 1.10.18 | |
| 64 Labour Coy | 1.10.18 | |
| 284 A.T. Coy R.E. | | |
| R.H. 7 Pontoon Park R.E. | | |
| 47 Balloon Section " Coy | | |
| 2 Field Survey 1 Sect | | |
| 101 Sig B A A Battery | | |
| 59 Labour Coy | | |
| 56 Labour Coy | 2.10.18 | |
| 5 Observation Group | | |
| M Special Coy R.E. | 10.10.18 | |
| 221 Transport Supply Coy | | |
| 308 R.C.C. R.E. | | |

(73989) W4141—463. 400,000. 9/14. H.&J.Ltd. Forms/C. 2118/10.

CONFIDENTIAL.

WAR. DIARY.

59th (N.M.) DIVISIONAL TRAIN.

From 1-11-18 to 30-11-18

# WAR DIARY
## or
## INTELLIGENCE SUMMARY.

Army Form C. 2118.

(Erase heading not required.)

VOLUME XXII

59th (N.M.) DIVISIONAL TRAIN. H.Qs.

Instructions regarding War Diaries and Intelligence Summaries are contained in F.S. Regs., Part II. and the Staff Manual respectively. Title pages will be prepared in manuscript.

| Place | Date | Hour | Summary of Events and Information | Remarks and references to Appendices |
|---|---|---|---|---|
| NOVEMBER | | | | |
| SAILLY-LES-LANNOY. | 1st | | T.H.Q. SAILLY-LES-LANNOY. No.1 Coy. L 29. b. 6. (Sheet 36) No.2 Coy HEMPONPONT. No.3 Coy FLETSBURG. No.4 Coy HEM. All four SRP's on FLERS – HEMPONPONT road. Railhead at ST. ANDRÉE. Supplies drawn by M.T. | M.T. |
| | 2nd | | No.3 Coy moved to PETIT LANNOY. (Nov.6th) | M.T. |
| | 3rd | | Railhead moved to FIVES. Supplies drawn by M.T. Lieut. Col. T. HAZELRIGG. D.S.O. Proceeded on leave to UNITED KINGDOM. Major H.B. CLEGG. D.S.O. in command. | M.T. |
| | 7th | | No.4 Coy moved to FOREST. | M.T. |
| | 9th | | SRP's Div Arty. H.14 d. (Sheet 37). 176. Brig. NECHIN. 177. Brig and 178. Brig. NECHIN. | M.T. |
| | 10th | | T.H.Q moved to BAILLEUL. No.1 Coy to H. 26. d. (Sheet 37). No.2 Coy. NECHIN. No.3 Coy. CATNOIS. Farm. H. 26. a. (Sheet 37). No.4 Coy to NECHIN. | M.T. |
| BAILLEUL. | 11th | | All SRP's at ESQUELMES on banks of river SCHELT. L 13. d (Sheet 37). Supplies drawn by M.T. from ST. ANDRÉE | M.T. |
| | 15th | | No.2 Coy moved to TEMPLEUVE. 176 SRP L 13. b.9.o. (Sheet 37). No.3 Coy moved to LE MARIE QUIET. SRP. L. 13. d. (Sheet 37). 178 SRP moved to NECHIN. | M.T. |
| | 16th | | T.H.Q moved to WATTIGNIES. No.1 Coy to WATTIGNIES. No.2 Coy. L'ABRISSEAU. No.3 Coy to SECLIN. No.4 Coy to WILLEMS. SRP's DIV. Troops. 176 +177. at WATTIGNIES. 178. NECHIN. | M.T. |
| WATTIGNIES | 17th | | Supplies drawn by M.T. from ST. ANDRÉE. 176 SRP moved to Q 26. A 7. 1. (Sheet 36) | M.T. |

# WAR DIARY
## or
## INTELLIGENCE SUMMARY.
(Erase heading not required.)

Army Form C. 2118.

VOLUME XVII

59 (N.M.) DIVISIONAL TRAIN HQs

| Place | Date | Hour | Summary of Events and Information | Remarks and references to Appendices |
|---|---|---|---|---|
| NOVEMBER | | | | |
| WATTIGNIES | 19 | | 177 S.R.P. moved to CRAND. PLACE SECLIN. No 4 Coy moves to PETIT RONCHIN. | M.J. |
| | 22 | | 176 S.R.P. to PETIT RONCHIN. | M.J. |
| | | | CAPT. J.K. BROWN Adj 59 Div. Train to Hospital sick. LIEUT. M.C. JOHNSTON as A/Adjutant. | M.J. |
| | 25 | | LIEUT. COL. T. HAZLIE TIGG. D.S.O. returns from leave and resumes command. VICE MAJOR N.B. CLEGG. D.S.O. | M.J. |
| | 30 | | Health of troops good save for influenza of which there were many case. Horses in excellent condition in spite of heavy work occasioned by frequent moves and rapid advance of troops. Supply sections of No 1. 2. & 4. Coys doing as much as 30 a day at one period. | M.J. |

M Chanton Johnston Lt Col
59 Div. Train

Confidential

WAR DIARY

:of:-

O.C. 513 Coy A.S.C. 59 Division

from 1st to 30th November 1918

Vol. 21.

Army Form C. 2118.

# WAR DIARY
## or
## INTELLIGENCE SUMMARY.
(Erase heading not required.)

Instructions regarding War Diaries and Intelligence Summaries are contained in F.S. Regs., Part II. and the Staff Manual respectively. Title pages will be prepared in manuscript.

| Place | Date | Hour | Summary of Events and Information | Remarks and references to Appendices |
|---|---|---|---|---|
| Field | 1.11.18 | — | 513 Coy ASC 59 Division | |
| | | | Coy in Billets at L29 b, 4, 6. Horses in Stables and open sheds. | |
| | | | Refilling point at L29 b, 4, 6. Supplies drawn by M.T. from ST ANDRE. | |
| | 3.11.18 | — | Supplies drawn by M.T. from FIVES. | |
| | 9.11.18 | — | Refilling point moved to H.14 D. Sheet 37. | |
| | 10.11.18 | 0930 | Coy HdQrs moved by Manda. Route to H.16 d. Central Sheet 37. Quartered in Billets therein. Stables. Supplies drawn by M.T. from FIVES. | |
| | 14.11.18 | — | Supplies drawn by M.T. from ST ANDRE. | |
| | 16.11.18 | 0700 | Coy HdQrs and Supply wagons 295 Bde RFA moved by March route from H.16 d. Sheet 37 to WATTIGNIES. Quartered in Billets. Horses in open sheds. Refilling point at WATTIGNIES. Supplies drawn by M.T. from ST ANDRE. | |
| | 17.11.18 to 30.11.18 | | No CHANGE. | |

30th November, 1918.

[signature]
MAJOR,
COMMANDING 513 Coy. A.S.C.

Army Form C. 2118.

# WAR DIARY
## INTELLIGENCE SUMMARY.
(Erase heading not required.)

VOL XXII.
O.C. N° 2 Coy. 59th Div. TRAIN.

Instructions regarding War Diaries and Intelligence Summaries are contained in F.S. Regs., Part II and the Staff Manual respectively. Title pages will be prepared in manuscript.

| Hour, Date, Place | Summary of Events and Information | Remarks and references to Appendices |
|---|---|---|
| 1st November 1918. HEMPEMPONT. L.29.b.8.6 /Sht. 36 | Commenced month with Baggage Wagons detached with units, Coy. Hdqrs. & Supply Sec. quartered at and S.R.P. at HEMPEMPONT. Supplies drawn by M.T. to S.R.P. and thence by Train Transport to Armn Sects. at SAILLY LES LANNOY, TOUFFLERS and TEMPLEUVE. Supplies delivered to Bde. HQ. & 2/8th Bn. R.W. Regt. & GOURNIERE. T.18 sheet 37. | mut. |
| 7." " " | | mut. |
| 10. " NECHIN. H.19.II.7.8 /Sheet 37. | S.R.P. 176 Bde. party moved to NECHIN and supplies delivered by train. Supply wagons at VELAINES & DEL PRE distance covered by Supply Convoy being from 30 to 32 miles. Coy. Hdqrs. moved to NECHIN. H.14.II.7.8 | mut. |
| 11. " " | S.R.P. 176 Bde. moved to T.13. b.9.0. | mut. |
| 12. " " | "DEL PRE" distance covered by Supply convoy 25–27 miles. Supplies delivered to units at HEL PLANQUE, QUATRE VENTS, GOURDINIERE & FRAN D ROGER. | mut. |
| 15. " TEMPLEUVE. H.33.A.9.7 /Sheet 37. | Refilled at I.13.b.9.0. Moved Hdqrs. of Coy. and Supply Sec. to TEMPLEUVE and delivered to units in TEMPLEUVE and WILLEMS. | mut. |
| 16. " L'ARBRISSEAU. Q.26.C.7.2 /Sheet 36. | Moved Coy. Hdqrs. & Supply Sec. via WILLEMS - SIN - ASCQ - RONCHIN - THURYESNIL to L'ARBRISSEAU, Supply Sec. proceeded to WATTIGNIES, refilled there and delivered to units in THURMSNIL Area. | mut. |
| 17. " " | 467 M.T. Co. R.P. taken on ration strength of Brigade Group. | mut. |
| 26. " " | 2/2 N.M. Fd. Amb. taken on ration strength of Brigade Group. S.R.P. moved to Q.26.a.7.1/36. | mut. |

MHughes Capt
O.C. N° 2 Coy. 59th Div. Train.

Confidential

War Diary

of

515 Company A.S.C. 59th Division

From 1/4/18 to 30/4/18

(Volume XXII)

Adjutant
59th Bn C.E.F.

Strength war Diary for
the month of November 1918

R. Green Capt
O.C. No 3 Company
59 Bn C.E.F.

1/12/18

# WAR DIARY
## or
## INTELLIGENCE SUMMARY.
*(Erase heading not required.)*

Army Form C. 2118.

Volume XXII

November 1918.

| Place | Date | Hour | Summary of Events and Information | Remarks and references to Appendices |
|---|---|---|---|---|
| FLERS-BERG | 1/11 | | 515 Coy. A.S.C. 59th Div. In quarters and Billets | |
| " | 2/11 | 9.30 a.m. | Coy HQ moved by road to PETIT LANNOY | |
| PETIT LANNOY | 2/11 | 1.0 p.m. | In quarters and Billets | |
| " | 3/11 | | LIEUT. P.R.R. DIBBEN proceeded on Special leave to ENGLAND | |
| " | 4/11 | | 2/LIEUT. F.A.A. WHITFIELD takes over duties as S.O. vice LIEUT. P.R.R. DIBBEN | |
| " | 10/11 | 9.30 a.m. | Coy HQ move by road to CARVOG FARM. H.26.a sheet 37 | |
| CARVOG FARM | 10/11 | 12.30 p.m. | In quarters and Billets | |
| " | 11/11 | 11.0 a.m. | ARMISTICE reported signed | |
| " | 11/11 | | One N.C.O. seconded to C.C.'s strength off strength | |
| " | 12/11 | | 467 Field Coy R.E. 3rd G.B. Pte A5 <br> Bdy of Amm't. 3rd C.S.M Forts Pd 45 } one on ration strength to this date only | |
| " | 14/11 | | One Corpls Turner transferred to 513 Coy A.S.C. 59th Div. <br> V. Sec. Field Survey Coy | |
| " | 15/11 | 9.0 a.m. | Coy HQ move by road to LE MARQUIET | |
| LE MARQUIET | 15/11 | 1.0 p.m. | In quarters and Billets | |
| " | 16/11 | 9.30 | Coy HQ in ch't of Supplies of Bde Group now by road to SEC LIN | |

K. Green Capt.
o/c No. 615 Coy. A.S.C.
59th Division

# WAR DIARY
## or
## INTELLIGENCE SUMMARY.
*(Erase heading not required.)*

Army Form C. 2118.

Volume XXII

November 1918

| Place | Date | Hour | Summary of Events and Information | Remarks and references to Appendices |
|---|---|---|---|---|
| SECLIN | 16/18 | | 515 Coy. A.S.C. 59th Divn. | |
| | | | In quarters and Billets — | KG |
| | | | 59th D.H.Q. 59th ZA TRAF712 Coy | |
| | | | 59th T.H.Q. 2/1 M.V.S. 59th Signal } struck off station strength | Coy |
| | | | M.M.P. D.A.D.O.S. 59th 2 Salvage | |
| | | | C.R.E. S.A.A. Sec. 59th Div. Canteen | |
| | 16/18 | | 470 Field Coy R.E. 2 Ports M/G Batt } taken on ration strength | KG |
| | | | 2/1 N.F.A. 6th Corps Field Amb. | |
| | | | 2/3rd Field Amb. | |
| | | | Baggage Wagons withdrawn for all units | KG |
| | 18/18 | | 2/1 M.V.S. struck off ration strength | KG |
| | | | 4 Drivers Reinforcements received from Base | KG |
| | 21/18 | | LIEUT. M.C. JOHNSTON posted to No.3 Coy A.S.C. as R.O. | KG |
| | 22/18 | | One Driver evacuated to C.C.S | KG |
| | 23/18 | | One Surplus Cycle Orderly transferred to 513 Coy. A.S.C. | KG |
| | 30/18 | | One Driver evacuated to C.C.S | KG |

General Health of the Coy satisfactory — also good all ranks in good condition

W.Green Capt.
o/c No. 515 Coy. A.S.C.
59th Division.

Confidential

"War Diary"
of
O.C., 11th Bn. 59th Inval. Train.

From:- 1-11-18   To:- 30-11-18

Volume:- 22.

Army Form C. 2118.

# WAR DIARY
## or
## INTELLIGENCE SUMMARY
*(Erase heading not required.)*

Instructions regarding War Diaries and Intelligence Summaries are contained in F. S. Regs., Part II. and the Staff Manual respectively. Title Pages will be prepared in manuscript.

| Place | Date | Hour | Summary of Events and Information | Remarks and references to Appendices |
|---|---|---|---|---|
| Hem | 1/11/18 | | 1 O.R. discharged from Hospital. | W |
| " | 3/11/18 | | 1 O.R. Admitted to Hospital. – 1 O.R. returns off leave. | W |
| " | 5/11/18 | | 1 O.R. Admitted to Hospital – 1 O.R. discharged from Hospital. | W |
| Hem | 7/11/18 | | Coy. moves to a farm on the Forest-Hem Road. | W |
| " | 9/11/18 | | Supply Dump moves to Nechin. – 2 O.R. admitted to Hospital. | W |
| Hem | 10/11/18 | | Coy. moves to Nechin – 1 O.R. proceeds on leave. | W |
| Nechin | 11/11/18 | | Supply Dump moves to Esquelmes – 1 O.R. proceeds on leave. | W |
| " | 12/11/18 | | 1 – O.R. proceeds on leave. | W |
| " | 13/11/18 | | 8 – O.R. admitted to Hospital. | W |
| " | 14/11/18 | | 1 – O.R. returns off Leave. | W |
| " | 16/11/18 | | Supply Dump moves to Nechin. – 2 O.R. discharged from Hospital. – 1 O.R. transferred to H.Q. Coy. 57 Divl. S. | W |
| Nechin | 16/11/18 | | Coy. moves to Willems – 1 O.R. proceeds on leave. | W |
| Willems | 17/11/18 | | Coy. moves to Petit Ronchin – 2 O.R. discharged from Hospital. | W |
| Petit Ronchin | 19/11/18 | | 1 – O.R. returns off Leave – 4 O.R. discharged from Hospital – 1 O.R. proceeds on leave. | W |
| " | 21/11/18 | | 3 O.R. report from 800 an M.G.C. w loaders – 6 O.R. report for duty (Reinforcements) | W |
| " | 22/11/18 | | H O.R. posted to 21/15 N.M. Fol. Ambce. – 1 Yr/Srr. returns to H/ 1 Coy. | W |
| " | 28/11/18 | | 1 – O.R. returns off Leave – 1 O.R. admitted to Hospital – 1 O.R. proceeds on leave | W |
| " | 29/11/18 | | 2 – O.R. returns off Leave – 1 – O.R. admitted to Hospital. | W |

106 H Coy. Sig. divnl. S—

2449  Wt. W14957/Mgo 750,000  1/16  J.B.C. & A.  Forms/C.2118/12.

Instructions regarding War Diaries and Intelligence Summaries are contained in F. S. Regs., Part II. and the Staff Manual respectively. Title Pages will be prepared in manuscript.

# WAR DIARY
*or*
## ~~INTELLIGENCE SUMMARY~~
*(Erase heading not required.)*

Army Form C. 2118.

| Place | Date | Hour | Summary of Events and Information | Remarks and references to Appendices |
|---|---|---|---|---|
| | | | List of Units fed. | |
| H.Q. 178th Inf Bde | | | 1-11-18 - 30-11-18. | |
| 36th Bn N.Fs. | | | 1 11/18 - 15 11/18 & 22 11/18 - 30 11/18. | |
| 11th R.S.F | | | 1-11-18 - 30-11-18 | |
| 13th West Ridings | | | 1-11-18 - 30-11-18. | |
| 178th L.T.M.B. | | | 1-11-18 - 30-11-18. | |
| 467 Fd Cy. R.E. | | | 1-11-18 - 15-11-18. | |
| No 4 Cy. 59th Divl Train | | | 1-11-18 - 30-11-18. | |
| 2/3 N.M. Fd Ambce | | | 1 11/18 - 12 11/18 & 12 11/18 - 15 11/18. | |
| 200 Bn M.G.C. | | | 1-11-18 - 30-11-18. | |
| U Section Field Survey | | | 1 11/18 - 11 11/18 & 13 11/18 - 16 11/18. | |
| 78 Road Section 69 Anse Stem Cy. | | | 1 11/18 - 11 11/18. | |
| 59th Div Recept. Camp | | | 1-11-18 - 11-11-18. | |
| No 3 G.B.A. Portugese | | | 1 11/18 - 2 11/18 | |
| 14th Inf Portugese | | | 1 11/18 - 2 11/18 | |
| No 3 C.S.M. 13 Fd Cy Portugese | | | 1 11/18 - 11 11/18 & 13 11/18. | |
| HQ 295 Bde R.F.A.<br>A Bty 295 R.F.A.<br>B<br>C<br>D<br>H.Q. 296 Bde R.F.A.<br>A<br>B<br>C<br>D | | | } 12-11-18. | |
| | | | 22nd Portugese Inf. Bn. 14-11-18 - 15-11-18. | |
| | | | 21st do do 14-11-18 - 15-11-18. | |
| | | | 34th do do 14-11-18 - 15-11-18. | |
| | | | 6th Fd. Ambce Portugese 14-11-18 - 15-11-18. | |
| | | | 284 A.T. Cy. R.E. 16-11-18 - 16-11-18. | |
| | | | 42nd Squad. R.A.F. 16-11-18 - 16-11-18. | |
| | | | 164 Anti Aircraft Sec. 16-11-18 - 19-11-18. | |
| | | | 142 do do do 16-11-18 - 19-11-18. | |
| | | | A. Sqdn. King Edwards H. 16-11-18 - 19-11-18. | |
| | | | 257 Tunnel Cy. 16-11-18 - 19-11-18. | |
| | | | No 4 Sec. do 16-11-18 - 18-11-18. | |
| | | | 721 Labour Cy. R.E. 16-11-18 - 19-11-18. | |
| | | | 14 Anti Aircraft Sec. 16-11-18 - 16-11-18. | |
| | | | 44 do do. 16-11-18 - 16-11-18. | |
| | | | XI Corps Cyclists 16-11-18 - 16-11-18. | |
| | | | 59th Div Laundry 16-11-18 - 23-11-18. | |
| | | | 2/2nd Fd. Ambce 17-11-18 - 30-11-18. | |
| | | | 470 Fd Cy. R.E. 22-11-18 - 30-11-18. | |

[illegible signature] Capt.
OC 4 Cy. 59th Divl Train

2449 Wt. W14957/M90 750,000 1/16 J.B.C. & A. Forms/C.2118/12.

WA 23

Confidential

War Diary
of
Headquarters 59th Divl Train

1-12-18 to 31-12-18

Volume XXIII

# WAR DIARY
## or
## INTELLIGENCE SUMMARY.
(Erase heading not required.)

Army Form C. 2118.

VOLUME XXIII

59" DIVISIONAL TRAIN HEADQUARTERS

| Place | Date | Hour | Summary of Events and Information | Remarks and references to Appendices |
|---|---|---|---|---|
| DECEMBER | 1918. | | | |
| WATTIGNIES. | 1st | | THQ at WATTIGNIES. No1 Coy WATTIGNIES. No2 Coy L'ABRISSEAU. No3 Coy SECLIN. No4 Coy PETIT RONCHIN. SRP's with respective companies. All in billets, horses in stables. Supplies drawn from ST. ANDREE by M.T. Orders received that 178 Inf. Bde. would proceed to DUNKIRK on 3rd inst. No4 Coy TRAIN going with them. | M.O. |
| " | 3rd | | No4 Coy started with transport of 178 Inf. Bde. to DUNKIRK. Orders for move cancelled and transport turned off on the road to FOURNES-EN-WEPPES to billet for the night. Orders received for No1 Coy to proceed to FOURNES-EN-WEPPES on 4th inst. to HOUCHIN. | M17. |
| " | 4th | | No1 Coy moved to HOUCHIN with supply wagons under local Dir. Arty. S.R.P. moved to HOUCHIN for 5" issue. No4 Coy moved to RUITZ. Supplies of 178 Inf. Bde. dumped at RUITZ for 5" issue. 176 S.R.P. moved after issue to BARLIN to receive supplies for 6" consumption. 177 S.R.P. moved to BRACQUEMONT after double supplying to receive supplies for 6" consumption. Orders for move of No2 & No3 Coys on 5th inst. issued. | M17. |
| " | 5th | | No3 Coy moved to BRACQUEMONT. S.R.P 177 Inf Bde. also moved to BRAQUEMONT. THQ moved to VERQUIN. No2 Coy to BARLIN (billeted night 5/6 Dec at FOURNES). No4 Coy to RUITZ. R.H. at NOUEX-les-MINES.; S.R.Ps. - Div. Troops, HOUCHIN; 176 Inf. Bde., BARLIN, 177 INF BDE. BRACQUEMONT ; 178 INF BDE at RUITZ. | M17. |
| " | 6th | | | M17. |

Army Form C. 2118.

# WAR DIARY
## or
## ~~INTELLIGENCE SUMMARY~~
*(Erase heading not required.)*

Vol: XXIII

HEADQUARTERS :- 59TH DIVISIONAL TRAIN

MAP REF: Sheet 36, 44 B.

| Place | Date | Hour | Summary of Events and Information | Remarks and references to Appendices |
|---|---|---|---|---|
| VERQUIN | DECEMBER 1918 7th | - | Supplies drawn from R.H. by Horse Transport and continued during the month. | MT |
| " | 10th | - | No 4 Coy a S.R.P. a 178 INF Bde left Divl Divl AREA & proceeded by Train to DUNKIRK. | MT |
| " | 11th | - | 277th Bde AFA taken on ration strength of Division & allotted to 176 INF Bde S.R.P. | MT |
| " | 18th | - | Billets & Lines of No 3 Coy inspected by A.D.M.S. 59 Div. | MT |
| " | 21st | - | T/Lt F.A.A. WHITFIELD posted to No 2 Coy from No 4 Coy. | MT |
| " | 27th | - | F.G.C.M. on T/Cpl GERNON & Cpl DOWRY (att: from 250 Divl Emp Coy L.C.). | MT |
| " | 29th | - | No 2 Coy dispatch Baggage & Supply wagons of 176 INF Bde Units to Units in view of impending move of Bde | MT |

M. Chiston Johnston
Lieuty Adjt
59 Divl Train

Confidential

# WAR DIARY

NO. 1 COMPANY
59th DIVL. TRAIN
(No. 513 Coy. A.S.C.)

of

O.C. 513 Coy ASC. 59th Divn

from Dec 1st to 3rd 1918

Vol. 22.

# WAR DIARY
## INTELLIGENCE SUMMARY

Army Form C. 2118.

| Place | Date | Hour | Summary of Events and Information | Remarks and references to Appendices |
|---|---|---|---|---|
| Field | 1/5/18 | | 513 Coy A.S.C. 5a Divisional Train. Refilling Point at WATTIGNIES. Supplies loaded at WATTIGNIES. | |
| | 2/5/18 | | Company moved by M.T. from WATTIGNIES to HOUCHIN. Another in-Café forms for Open Letter. Supplies drawn by M.T. from ST ANDRE. Refilling Point at HOUCHIN. | |
| | 3/5/18 to 31/5/18 | | Supplies drawn by M.T. from NOEUX-LES-MINES. No change. | |

(Sgd.) ...............
MAJOR,
COMMANDING 513 Coy. A.S.C.

Confidential

War Diary

of

514 Coy R.A.S.C. 59 Division

From 1-12-18 To 31-12-18

Volume XXIII

**Army Form C. 2118.**

# WAR DIARY
## or
## INTELLIGENCE SUMMARY.
*(Erase heading not required.)*

Instructions regarding War Diaries and Intelligence Summaries are contained in F.S. Regs., Part II. and the Staff Manual respectively. Title pages will be prepared in manuscript.

| Hour, Date, Place | Summary of Events and Information | Remarks and references to Appendices |
|---|---|---|
| 1st December 1918. L'ARBRISSEAU. Q26.c.7.2. Sht 36. | Commenced month knowing on strength of 1/176 Inf. Bde. Group HQ + 3 Sections 176 Inf Bde, 2/1 and 2/2 N.M.Fd.Amb. 4+7 3rd Co. R.E. ttt 2 Coy. 59 Div. Train | Tw/st. |
| 2nd " " | 2/C A.M. BANISTER commenced duties as S.O. 176 Inf. Bde in 2/Lt C. KAVIL proceeding to U.K. on leave. | Tw/st. |
| 3rd " " | 470. 3rd Co. R.E. taken on ration strength of 176 Bde. Group. | |
| 4th " " | 13 wagons despatched to units in readiness for move. Stands refilled (for consumption by) divisional ordins for two personnel to units there for road party. 2/2 N.M. Fd. Amb. and 470 3rd. Co. R.E. struck off ration strength of 3 Bde. Group. Moved | Tw/st. |
| 5th " " | Hdqrs of Coy & Supply Sec. to FOURNES | Tw/st. |
| 6th " FOURNES. BARLIN. | Moved Headquarters of Coy. via LA BASSEE + NOEUX LES MINES to BARLIN, refilled at K.27.a.1.3 Sht 44 B. and billeted to Coy. three in BARLIN area. | Tw/st. |
| 7th " " | Recd Baggage wagons from wild 2/1 N.M. Mob. Vet. Sec. and 74" San. Sec. taken on ration strength of Group. | Tw/st. |
| 10th " " | Commenced drawing supplies in bulk from NOEUX LES MINES Railhead by Horse transport and continued delivering by horse transport to Units | Tw/st. |
| 11th " " | 10 G.S. wagons lent to 176 Bde than 5 Baggage wagons. 277 Army GT Coy Rly came to consumption strength for commutation this day. | Tw/st. |
| 21st " " | Ceased to deliver supplies to Units by Train transport | Tw/st. |
| 22nd " " | on receipt of 22 wagons in div. 2/Lieut. F.A.A. WHITFIELD posted to Company. 25th Battn K.R.R.C taken on ration strength of Brigade Group. Lieut. F.A.A WHITFIELD Leave to U.K. assumed duty as S.O. 176 Inf Bde on 2/Lieut A.H. BANISTER proceeding on leave to U.K. | Tw/st. |
| 29th " " | Started refilling P.T.O. 176 Bde. 26th Bn. Middlesex + 467 Field Co R.E. to HONDEGHEM Area and baffage | Tw/st. |
| 30th " " | supply wagons continued to move with these Units. Started transport of 25th Battn K.R.R.C. and ex. of 277 Army Old Arty Bde in preparation for the Div. Train. | Tw/st. |

Mullagleno Capt.
OC. 2 Coy. 59 Div. Train.

Confidential

War Diary

of

515 Company R.A.S.C. 59th Division

From 1-12-18 to 31-12-18

Volume XXIII

Army Form C. 2118.

# WAR DIARY
## or
## INTELLIGENCE SUMMARY.
(Erase heading not required.)

Instructions regarding War Diaries and Intelligence Summaries are contained in F. S. Regs., Part II. and the Staff Manual respectively. Title pages will be prepared in manuscript.

515 Coy R.A.S.C. 59th Divn.   December 19.

| Place | Date | Hour | Summary of Events and Information | Remarks and references to Appendices |
|---|---|---|---|---|
| SECLIN | 1/12/18 | | In quarters and Billets | A.G. |
| " | 1/12 | | LIEUT. P.R.R DIBBEN reports sick from Influenza | A.G. |
| " | 2/12 | | LIEUT. F.A.A WHITFIELD Returns to 515 Coy R.A.S.C | A.G. |
| " | 2/12 | 11.30 | C.O. and V.O. inspect all horses of Coy | A.G. |
| " | 3/12 | | G.O.C. 59th Divn. inspects the Coy in GRAND PLACE | A.G. |
| " | 5/12 | | R.Q.M.S. with supplies of Bde Group moved road to BRAQUEMONT | A.G. |
| BRAQUEMONT | 5/12 | 2.0 | In Billets and Quarters | A.G. |
| " | 5/12 | | One Supply Issuer transferred to 516 Coy R.A.S.C | A.G. |
| " | 7/12 | | One Supply Issuer evacuated to C.C.S | A.G. |
| " | 7/12 | | 200 Baths M.C.C. taken on Ration strength | A.G. |
| " | 7/12 | | One Supply Issuer reports from Base | A.G. |
| " | 10/12 | | On N.C.O. one Driver evacuated to C.C.S | A.G. |
| " | 10/12 | | Area Commdt. NOEUX LES MINES Special C.R.E. came on Ration strength | A.G. |
| " | 13/12 | | 1st Pack by Coy on Ration strength | A.G. |

A. Green Capt.
c/o No. 515 Coy R.A.S.C.
59th Division.

# WAR DIARY
## INTELLIGENCE SUMMARY
*(Erase heading not required.)*

Army Form C. 2118.

515 Coy R.A.S.C. 59th Divn.  December 1918

| Place | Date | Hour | Summary of Events and Information | Remarks and references to Appendices |
|---|---|---|---|---|
| BRAQUEMONT | 15/12/18 | | 59th T.H.Q. arrive on return strength. Vernon went to XI Corps troops taken on Ration Strength 19 units in add—return strength of advanced HQ. Men 2700 Horses 75 | A.C. |
| " | 16/12/18 | | 2 lorries sent to Hardres to deliver Ordnance to Corps heads to Saarbourg hereafter to England relinquishing as reserve | |
| " | 17/12/18 | | | |
| " | 18/12/18 | | Inspection of Coy at Braquemont by A.D.M.S. 59 Division | |
| " | 19/12/18 | | Two reinforcements reported from Base 1 Turner 1 Sullivan date 2 horses cast Rubbell Ct 2 Turner Frost | |
| " | 20/12/18 | | | |
| " | 24/12/18 | | One Sub Bus Driver to Bucquoy to 515 Company A.S.C. | |
| " | 27/11/18 | | Lieut Tollen proceeds 14 days Ordinary leave to U.K. | |
| " | 28/12/18 | | One M.T. cart 15 M.V.S. to Gosnay | |
| " | 27/12/18 | | H.Q. C.M. on 7 Cal. Gunners | |
| " | 29/12/18 | | C/ERJ Ingram proceed to U.K. on 14 days Ordinary leave. Commence this absence Lieut PLPD Stay | |
| " | 30/12/18 | | Lieut. RS Tinkler proceeds to England duty on demobilization of 59th Division on to Sergt Simcoe T. Relieved 15 Humsby | |
| " | 31/12/18 | | Cmg Billets Herald of Company turn all horses cast to Coult | |

O/C No. 515 Coy R.A.S.C.
59th Division.

## 515 Coy RASC 59th Division

The 515 Coy RASC, originally known as the 2/1 (NM) Divl. T&S Column, equipped thro the LRK & gwn Manchester, was recruited in September & October 1914 & after several weeks training proceeded to Luton on Jany 21st/15 to join the 2/1 (NM) Division, afterwards known as the 59th Division, which was then being concentrated in that area (the Dvn. consisting of the 176, 177 & 178 Bde Groups).

The Company moved to St Albans by road on the 5/8/15 – At this time it was known as No.2 Coy 59th Divl. Train & was affiliated to 177th Inf Bde of the 59th Division (which was comprised of the 2/4 & 2/5 Lines & 2/4 & 2/5 Leycs)

While at this station, the Coy Supply Wagons of the Bde Group drew rations from the Divl. S.A.P. Rubber Works, St Albans delivering in detail daily in detail to units of the Bde Group –

On 16/5/16 orders were received to proceed to Watford the Company then being temporarily attached to the 178 Inf. Bde in place of No.4 Coy of the Train.

While here rations were drawn from the Bde S.A.P & delivered to the 178 Inf Bde Group.

Easter Monday night

On 25/4/16 the Company received orders to proceed at a few hours notice with the 178 Inf Bde to Ireland to assist in the suppression of the Sinn Fein Rebellion which had broken out in Dublin

The Coy disembarked at Kingstown on 26/4/16. & proceeded to Kilmainham Hospital on the 27th.

During the trek from Kingstown to Kilmainham, considerable resistance was encountered the convoy being attacked by rebels & held up on the Sth Circular Road for 5 hours, most of the NCO's & men coming into action - ultimately the ~~company~~ convoy passed through the 7th & 8th Sherwood Foresters into the grounds of Kilmainham Hospital, where they remained in quarters for a fortnight -

During this period, supplies were drawn under great difficulties from Kingsbridge Station for the garrison & in addition the Company did valuable work in supplying the Brigade with grenades & ammunition -

Later, the Company moved to Balls Bridge, Dublin & rejoined the 177th Inf Bde -

On leaving the 178 Bde, it received from Bde Genl (?) Maconchy, ~~commdg~~ through the Division, a letter of recognition for valuable services rendered, a copy of which is attached.

On the 28/5/16, with the Bde, the Coy, moved to the Old Barracks Fermoy, in the south of Ireland, & remained there until the end of 1916.

The Supplies for the Bde groups were delivered by Coy transport at such places as Tralee, Killarney, Old & New Barracks, Fermoy & Kilworth & Moore Park in the vicinity

In Aug & Sept 1916, the Coy was inspected by Genl Maxwell, GOC, Irish Command, & Fld Marshal Sir John French, obtaining excellent observations on its state of efficiency —

In Jany 1917 the Coy proceeded to Fovant, Salisbury Plain, for final training before going to France — While at this station, it was inspected by H.M. the King.

Before proceeding overseas, the nomenclature of the Coy was altered, it now being known as 575 Coy RASC or No. 3 Coy. 59 Divl. Train.

It embarked at Southampton, on Jany 17th 1917 on H.M. Troopship Huntscraft, & on its sea journey, went on the rocks 14 miles N.W. of Havre, at Cape Antifor at midnight 20/2/17 — After standing to, all night, the Company was transferred to torpedo boats & tugs & landed in Havre harbour later in the day —

Eventually the troopship came into harbour & all transport was disembarked —

The following day the Coy entrained for Amiens joining the III Corps, the division relieving the 50th Divn in the line near Foureaucourt on the 5th March —

On the 17th March the Germans commenced their retirement on the Somme, the Division following them up, & the Company crossed the Somme during the night 25/6 March —

as supplies were being drawn + delivered at a
19 miles depth - /-

During to the exceptional bad weather & the complete lack of accommodation, the Company suffered considerably from exposure during their advance & there were several casualties amongst the horses.

During this period considerable difficulties had to be overcome to maintain contact with units of the Bde Group & get the Supplies delivered.

The Coy. moved to Roisel 7/5/17, the Divn at this time occupying a sector of the line forward of this town—

On the 21 May the Divn was relieved by the 4th Cav Divn. & were withdrawn into Camps in the neighbourhood of Bouzincourt, subsequently taking another sector of the line near Havrincourt Wood, the Coy. being in camp near Ytres.

On the 10th July the Divn was withdrawn from the line & proceeded to the Barastre rest area, the Coy being encamped at Rocquigny, from which Railhead supplies were drawn & delivered in detail to the 177 Inf Bde Group—

After about a month in this area the Divn proceeded north to take part in the battle for Passchendale, which was then raging near Ypres. & on 20 Sept marched into the Ypres sector to relieve the 55 Divn in the St Julian-Wieltje area— the Coy being situated at Slamertinghe—

While in this area, the Coy. ration convoys were working under great difficulties owing to the continuous shelling of roads from hostile artillery.

Several casualties were sustained at this time thro' the activities of the enemy's bombing raids, the Company losing some of its best men.

Owing to the severe casualties the Divn. was withdrawn into rest on the 28th Sept, subsequently relieving the 4 Canadian Divn. in front of Lens, the Coy. being situated at Carency, delivering supplies to the Bde under fairly easy conditions.

After a month in this area, the Coy moved with the Divn, which was withdrawn to take part in the Cambrai battle. It subsequently relieved the Guards Divn. in Bourlon Wood after the successful advance on Cambrai.

The Divn took part in the retirement from Bourlon Wood + also in repulsing the sudden German attack on Gouzeaucourt.

When the Germans penetrated the line in this area, the Coy. + SRP. was left on the ridge outside Metz en Couture, orders to retire having failed to reach them. The Camp, Horselines + SRP was subjected to a severe shelling + orders were eventually received to retire to the outskirts of Havrincourt Wood. During this occasion Major DR Conlan, RASC, SSO 59 Divn, who happened to be on the spot, fetched ammunition in his car, taking it up into the line + remaining there assisting them. For this he was awarded the D.S.O.

The Divn remained in this Sector until the end of Decr when they were withdrawn into rest, the Coy moving to Ambrines on the 24/25 Decr 1917 ~~Christmas Day 1917~~ During this trek severe climatic conditions had to be contended with —

After 6 weeks rest the Divn went into the line again under the tr Corps in the Bullecourt Area the Coy being stationed at Gomiecourt.

They were in this sector when the great German offensive of the 21st March 1918 commenced — At 4.45 am on this day the Coy came under shellfire eventually being forced to abandon the camp & retire to Ayette. The following day it was again compelled to fall back, this time on Hannes camps — ※

During this critical period there was desperate fighting round Bullecourt & Ecoust, the Germans only succeeding in driving the 176 & 178 Bdes back a few miles & entirely failing to cross the Arras Bapaume Road, which was one of their objectives. In this defence these 2 Bdes were partly wiped out but gallantly held on until relieved on the morning of the 22nd by the 177 Inf Bde who remained in the line doing splendid work under the 40 Divn, while the remainder of the Divn was withdrawn to be refitted.

-X-

During the general confusion in the retirement the Coy S Sty with a convoy of Supply Wagons, was cut off from the Coy & was unable to rejoin ~~the Coy~~ for a period of 7 or 8 days.

After further fighting, the 177 Bde ~~with~~ the Coy was withdrawn from the line, eventually rejoining the Division in the Houdain Area, greatly to the relief of the C.O. train, as it had ~~been~~ persistently reported that the Officers & half the Company had been captured by the enemy.

During a short rest here, H.M. the King visited the 177th Inf. Bde, & personally thanking Officers & men for their valuable services —

Shortly afterwards the Div again proceeded to the Ypres Salient, relieving the 33 Div in the line. ~~While~~ holding this sector, the 2nd German offensive commenced necessitating the withdrawal from Passchendale. — During this period the Coy was encamped in the vicinity of Ypres — where they came under heavy hostile shellfire from 10 p.m. to 4 a.m. on the a/n April 18.

fighting the Div was withdrawn & hurriedly put into the heavy fighting round Kemmel, sustaining casualties amounting to nearly 2500.

Great difficulty was experienced in delivering supplies in this area, the Coy being situated behind Locre.

On several days the convoys had to turn back &

While in this area the Coy sustained a severe loss by the death of Capt J.G. Smith the S.O. 77th Inf Bde, which occurred on July 29th. This officer had been with the Coy since its formation, reporting for duty Sept. 25th 1914

at the Magazine

the Bde being part of the Fifth Army, it went into rest in the back areas, the Second + Fifth Armies only being chosen to go forward into Germany

times owing to the intense hostile artillery fire on the roads.

Several casualties were sustained to men & horses but by proceeding in open order, the rations were eventually delivered.

Here again the Camp came under shellfire. The Division was ultimately withdrawn from the line & on 16/5/18 proceeded to St. Omer where orders were received for the Division to be reduced to a Training Cadre Establishment.

On June 14th it was again made up with Category B men & the following units now comprising the 177 Inf Bde Group — 15th Bn Essex Regt 2/6 D L I & 11th S L I.

Since then the Coy has accompanied the new 177 Inf Bde when in the line in the Mercatel Sector in July & August & again in the Merville Sector during September.

About this time the Germans commenced their great retirement in this area, the Division closely following them up, crossing the rivers; Lawe, Deule, Marq & L'Escaut — The Company encountered considerable difficulties in negotiating the roads & bridges which the Germans had destroyed during his retreat. These difficulties however were successfully overcome, contact with the Bde Group being maintained throughout the whole advance Lestrem to the River Scheldt.

At this point the Division was squeezed out owing to the sudden shortening of the front, & on the

While in this area, great attention has been directed to Education, Sports & Social events.

16/11/18 The Division was withdrawn & put in quarters in the Wattignies Area the Coy being stationed at Seclin —

A letter of recognition was received from the GOC XI Corps, expressing his appreciation of the very fine achievements accomplished during the above advance.

On Dec 2/1918, the Coy was inspected by the GOC 59 Divn in the Square Seclin & was complimented by the Divl Genl & Brig Genl on the high state of efficiency it had maintained. Actual copy of parade State is attached, originals having been retained by the Generals inspecting the parade —

The Coy is now in rest at Braquemont, NOEUX les MINES having finished its duties, & is expected to return to Eng as a skeleton Cadre.

The Company, as a Unit of 177th Inf Bde has taken its part in most of the big battles fought on the British Front since Feby 1917 & has gained for itself Distinction by the efficient manner in which it always carried out its duties.

With the exception of the period 29/1/15 to 15/3/15 when appointed as Adjutant of the Train, & for 2 short periods OC Headquarter Coy I have always held the honour of OC 515 Coy RASC

## 515 Coy. A.S.C. 59th Division

Parade State, December 3rd 1918, SECLIN, B.E.F FRANCE
at Inspection by Major Genl N.M Smyth. V.C. C.B.

|  | Personnel | Rides | L.D | H.D | Vehicles Wagons G.S. | Wagons Limbd | Water Cart |
|---|---|---|---|---|---|---|---|
| Officers | 3 | 3 |  |  |  |  |  |
| W.O Class I | 1 | 1 |  |  |  |  |  |
| A/C.S.M. | 1 | 1 |  |  |  |  |  |
| Sr. Sgt Artificers | 2 | 2 |  |  |  |  |  |
| Section Corporals | 2 | 2 |  |  |  |  |  |
| Drivers | 27 |  | 6 | 48 | 24 | 2 | 1 |
| Loaders | 8 |  |  |  |  |  |  |
| Water duty man | 1 |  |  |  |  |  |  |
| Bugler attached | 1 |  |  |  |  |  |  |
| Supply Details | 4 |  |  |  |  |  |  |

No. of original men who came out to France with the Company in Feby. 1917 and still on the strength — 58%.

Casualties to Personnel

| Officers died | 1 |
| NCOs killed | 1 |
| NCOs wounded | 1 |
| Drivers killed | 2 |
| Drivers wounded | 6 |
| Loaders died of wounds | 1 |
| Loaders wounded | 2 |

No. of original men of Company evacuated sick & struck off the strength — 11%.

Casualties to Horses

| H.D. killed | 7 |
| H.D. wounded | 5 |
| Rides wounded | 2 |

N.C.O.s & men who have received Commissions — 6.

H/A Shaw Capt.

o/c No. 515 Coy. A.S.C.
59th Division.

59

Headquarters
59 Division

War Diary

of flow Coy of this formation
(now on detachment) herewith

M Chortons / ? ? ?
Lieut & adjt
for Lieut Colonel
Cmdg 59 Divl Train

6/1/19

Confidential

War Diary
of
A.E. 516 Coy. R.A.S.C.

From: 1/12/18   To: 31/12/18

Volume 23

# WAR DIARY
or
## INTELLIGENCE SUMMARY

*(Erase heading not required.)*

Army Form C. 2118.

516 Coy (M+ Coy) R.A.S.C.

by [signature]

Instructions regarding War Diaries and Intelligence Summaries are contained in F. S. Regs., Part II. and the Staff Manual respectively. Title Pages will be prepared in manuscript.

| Place | Date | Hour | Summary of Events and Information | Remarks and references to Appendices |
|---|---|---|---|---|
| PETIT RONCHIN | 2.12.18 | | 1 O.R. on leave — 2 O.R. M. & Capt Griffith Hogan were admd to No.2 Coy — 470 Coy R.E. Supply main work to No.2 Coy. — | |
| | 3.12.18 | | Coy moved to FOURNES. Lt. moved work. | |
| | 4.12.18 | | Coy moved to RUITZ. Lt. moved work. | |
| FOURNES | | | | |
| RUITZ | 6.12.18 | | 2 O.R. on leave — 2 O.R. from leave | |
| | 9.12.18 | | Brigade & Supply units are detailed to units. Separation to move — 1 O.R. to Hospital | |
| | 10.12.18 | | All personnel of 350 Employment Coy returned to their units. — 1 O.R. transferred to No.1 Coy. — 1 O.R. taken on strength No.3 Coy. — 1 O.R. taken on from No.1 Coy. — Coy under orders to move to | |
| CALONNE - RICOUART | 11.12.18 | | CALONNE - RICOUART between Béthune & Auboinville. Coy moved by rail to DUNKIRK. | |
| DUNKIRK | 12.12.18 | | 2/Lt. DENTON on leave. — 1 O.R. on leave — 1 O.R. to Hospital | |
| | 13.12.18 | | All vehicles of Brigade group are sorted to Brigade & Building of Demobilization Camps | |
| | 14.12.18 | | 1 O.R. on leave | |
| | 15.12.18 | | 1 O.R. on leave | |
| | 16.12.18 | | 1 O.R. to Hospital — 1 O.R. admitted as Civilian | |
| | 17.12.18 | | 1 O.R. discharged as Civilian — 1 O.R. on leave — F.Q.S.M. on Thompson R.T. — | |
| | 21.12.18 | | 1 O.R. on leave — 1 O.R. to Hospital | |
| | 23.12.18 | | 1 S.S.M. + 1 O.R. returned to duty. — | |
| | 27.12.18 | | 1 O.R. from Hospital | |
| | 28.12.18 | | 2 O.R. on leave | |
| | 29.12.18 | | 1 O.R. from leave | |
| | 30.12.18 | | 2 O.R. from leave | |

2449 Wt. W14957/M90 750,000 1/16 J.B.C. & A. Forms/C.2118/12.

516 Co. (N24 Co.) R.A.S.C. Army Form C. 2118.
59 Divisional Train.

# WAR DIARY
## or
## INTELLIGENCE SUMMARY.
(Erase heading not required.)

Instructions regarding War Diaries and Intelligence Summaries are contained in F. S. Regs., Part II. and the Staff Manual respectively. Title pages will be prepared in manuscript.

| Hour, Date, Place | Summary of Events and Information | Remarks and references to Appendices |
|---|---|---|
| | Units fed during month of December 1918 by Supply Officer 178 Inf Bde :—  Headquarters 178 Inf Bde   1.12.18 to 31.12.18  36 Northumberland Fusiliers            Ditto  11 Royal Scots Fusiliers                 Ditto  13 Duke of Wellingtons Regt           Ditto  178 T.M.B.                                     Ditto  No 4 Coy 59 Divisional Train  470 Field Coy R.E.                         1.12.18 to 2.12.18 and 5.12.18 to 9.12.18  Bn. R.S.C. M.G.C.                          1.12.18 to 2.12.18  2/2 N.M. Field Ambulance             5.12.18 to 31.12.18  201 2nth Coy R.E.                           31.12.18 only  202 2nth Coy R.E.                           31.12.18 only  | |

[signature]
O.C. N⁰ 4 Coy 59 Divisional Train

War Diary
of
Headquarters, 50th Divisional Train.

From 1st Jan. 1919 to 31st Jan. 1919

Volume XXIV

# WAR DIARY
## or
## INTELLIGENCE SUMMARY.
(Erase heading not required.)

Army Form C. 2118.

VOLUME XXIV
59. (N.M.) DIVISIONAL TRAIN.

| Place | Date | Hour | Summary of Events and Information | Remarks and references to Appendices |
|---|---|---|---|---|
| VERQUIN | Jan/Feb. 1st | | THQ. VERQUIN. No 1 Coy and Div Troops S.R.P. at HOUCHIN. No 2 Coy and 176 S.R.P. at BARLIN. No 3 Coy and 177 S.R.P. at BRACQUEMONT. No 4 Coy and 178 S.R.P. at DUNKIRK. Supplies for Div Troops 176 and 177 Brigs. drawn from NOEUX-LES-MINES. RAILHEAD by H.T. Numerous units of CORPS TROOPS on the Div. Ration strength. Ration Strength (8000 men, 4000 horses) Horses in open stables. | MT |
| | 7th | | No 2 Coy moved to ST. VENANT. | MT |
| | 8th | | No 1 Coy moved to BARLIN. (K 27 d 2 2 Sheet 44 B). No 2 Coy to LES CINQ RUES nr HAZEBROUCK. Div Troops S.R.P. BARLIN. 176 Brig. ST. SYLVESTRE CAPPEL. | MT |
| | 9th | | No 2 Coy moved to WALLON CAPPEL. 176 S.R.P. HONDEGHEM. | MT |
| | 11th | | No 2 Coy moved to HONDEGHEM. Railhead for 176 Brig BAVINCHOVE by H.T. Div Troops and 177 Brig NOEUX-LES-MINES. LIEUT. COL. T. HAZLERIGG D.S.O. O.C. 59 Div Train proceeded for duty to ENGLAND (with WAR OFFICE instructions. CAPT. T.W. BARTLEY S.S.O. 59 Div assumed temporary command of the Train pending return from leave of MAJOR N.B. CLEGG D.S.O. 14 Cat Y. horses sent by No 3 Coy to XIX CORPS COLLECTING CAMP AFFIQUES for repatriation to ENGLAND | MT |
| | 13 | | No 1 Coy moved to K 26 d. 8. 6. Sheet 44 B. (BARLIN) Supplies for Div Troops and 177 Brig drawn from BARLIN R.H. Orders for move of No 3 Coy with 177 Brig to DIEPPE received. | MT |
| | 15 | | 177 Brig moved to DIEPPE taking Supply and Baggage wagons of No 3 Coy with them. H.Q.s of No 3 Coy did not move under orders of | MT |
| | 17 | | XI CORPS. 177 BRIG. S.R.P. closed down. MAJOR N.B. CLEGG D.S.O. returns from leave and assumes command | MT |

Army Form C. 2118.

# WAR DIARY
## or
## INTELLIGENCE SUMMARY.
*(Erase heading not required.)*

Instructions regarding War Diaries and Intelligence Summaries are contained in F. S. Regs., Part II. and the Staff Manual respectively. Title pages will be prepared in manuscript.

VOLUME XXIV

| Place | Date | Hour | Summary of Events and Information | Remarks and references to Appendices |
|---|---|---|---|---|
| VERQUIN | 26.1.19 | | CAPT. J.K. BROWN ADJT. 59. Div. TRAIN despatched for demobilization. LIEUT M.C. JOHNSTON. appointed ADJUTANT | M.J |
| | 28.1.19 | | MAJOR - GENERAL N.M. SMYTH V.C. CB. GOC 59 Div inspects No 1 and 3 Coys. of the TRAIN | M.J |
| | 30.1.19 | | 176 Brig. moved to DUNKIRK leaving No 2 Coy under orders of XIX CORPS. No 3 Coy moved to VERQUIN | M.J |
| | 31.1.19 | | The health of both men and horses throughout the month has been good. Demobilization has been carried on at the rate of 6 per week. This is very slow compared with the numbers despatched by units of other arms of the service. Considerable difficulty has been experienced throughout the month in finding sufficient fatigue parties to handle rations, and to keep vehicles in clean condition owing to the large withdrawals of men for demobilization by the 250 (Div) Employment Coy. Boots and clothing have been difficult to obtain owing to the very short supply from Base. This has entailed considerable hardship in some cases as the weather has been bad at periods and the mens' boots were far from satisfactory and the very ragged clothing they have been forced to wear has a depressing effect, and causes men to cease to take a pride in their personal appearance. Div Ration strength 8000 men 3100 horses | M.J |

M Chatham Johnston Capt Adjt
59 Div. Train

Confidential.

# WAR - DIARY
## - of -
### Of 513 Coy. RASC 59th Division.
from 1st to 31st Jany. 1918

(Vol. 23).

Army Form C. 2118.

# WAR DIARY
## or
## INTELLIGENCE SUMMARY

(Erase heading not required.)

Instructions regarding War Diaries and Intelligence Summaries are contained in F. S. Regs., Part II. and the Staff Manual respectively. Title Pages will be prepared in manuscript.

| Place | Date | Hour | Summary of Events and Information | Remarks and references to Appendices |
|---|---|---|---|---|
| Field. | | | 513 Coy. R.A.S.C. 59 Division. | |
| | 1/1/19 | | Company in Camp at HOUCHIN. Horses in open sheds. Refilling point at HOUCHIN. Supplies drawn by H.T. from NOEUX-les-MINES. | |
| | 8/1/19 | | Company moved to BARLIN. K27.d.2.2 Sheet 44.S. Quartered in Camp. Horses in open sheds. Refilling point at BARLIN. Supplies drawn by H.T. from NOEUX-les-MINES. | |
| | 13/1/19 | | Company moved to K26.d.8.6. Sheet 44.S. Quartered in Camp. Horses in open sheds. Refilling point at BARLIN. Supplies drawn by H.T. from BARLIN. Mileage to S.R.P. | |
| | 14th-31st | | No change. | |

31st Jany 1919.

[signature]
Major
COMMANDING 513 Coy. A.S.C.

War Diary
of
No 2 Coy. 5 T.Gph. Dvl. Train.

From 1/1/19 to 31/1/19.

Volume 24

Army Form C. 2118.

# WAR DIARY
# INTELLIGENCE SUMMARY.
(Erase heading not required.)

VOL. XXIV

O.C. No 2 Coy. 59 Div. Train.

Instructions regarding War Diaries and Intelligence Summaries are contained in F.S. Regs., Part II and the Staff Manual respectively. Title pages will be prepared in manuscript.

| Hour, Date, Place | | Summary of Events and Information | Remarks and references to Appendices |
|---|---|---|---|
| BARLIN. | 1. January 1919. | Communed month with Company Lines and S.R.P. at BARLIN. HQ. 176 Inf. Bde. 467 Fld. Co. Rt. + 26" R. Welsh Fus. having proceeded to HONDEGHEM area and being no longer on ration strength of Brigade Group. | Nil. |
| " | 5. " | Despatched Baggage and supply wagons to 1/7" Battn Royal Sussex Regt in readiness for move to HONDEGHEM AREA on 4 inst. | Nil. |
| " | 6. " | Despatched supply wagons 15 2/1 N.M. Fld. Amb. to move with same to EBLINGHEM. Orders for move of 25" Battn. Kings Liverpool Regt having been cancelled Baggage and supply remained in the unit. | Nil. |
| ST VENANT. | 7. " | Moved HQrs of Company to ST VENANT + refills line. | Nil. |
| LES CINQ RUES. | 8. " | Moved HQrs of Coy. to LES CINQ RUES — 2 miles WEST of HAZEBROUCK and drew supplies for consumption 10th inst from XIX Corps Dump at ST SYLVESTRE CAPPEL. | Nil. |
| WALLON CAPPEL. | 9. " | Moved Headquarters 1/Company to WALLON CAPPEL. Rejd Mid at HONDEGHEM. | Nil. |
| HONDEGHEM. | 11. " | Despatched bus mares Co 1/23rd Veterinary Hospital for repatriation | Nil. |
| " | 12. " | Commenced drawing supplies in bulk from BAVINCHOVE Railhead by Horse Transport and to reduce distance travelled moved HeadQuarters of Coy. to HONDEGHEM | Nil. |
| " | 13. " | Despatched 1 Ride. 2 Draught, 11 HD (Heavy) to XIX Corps Collecting Camp ARCQUES. 10 wagons used for Railhead Convoy. | Nil. |
| " | 16. " | Capt. T.M. Warburg proceeded to United Kingdom on 28 days leave. 2/Lieut A.M. Bampton assumed command of Coy. | Act. 2 |
| " | 17. " | 3 reinforcements arrived — C.S.M. J. Belderley 1 Driver. 25" B. Kings Liverpool Regt came for Brigade Group. Drawing rations for remainder of Jany. | Act. 2 |
| " | 19. " | Lieut. W.G. Toller under order of HQ 59 Div. Train assumed command of Coy. during absence of Capt. T.M. Warburg on leave. | Act. 2 |
| " | 29. " | Despatched Baggage + Supply Wagons to 3 Battn + Brigade HQ. with rations for consumption 30/1. 31.2.19. | Act. 2 |
| " | 30. " | 1/6 B.N.F. & 3 Lothians moved to DUNKIRK area + struck off ration strength 2/Lieut A.M. Bampton accompanied Hqs. 176 Inf Bde to DUNKIRK for the purpose of conducting Baggage + Supply Wagons back to Company. Despatched 1 Riding Horse (Class B) to XIX Corps Descriting Camp. 2/L Battn Welsh Foot (W.Co) Came on ration strength + drew for consumption 31st. | Act. 2 |

K.G. Toller
Lieut

Confidential

War Diary
of
515 Coy R.A.S.C. 59th Division

From 1-1-19 to 31-1-19

Volume XXIV

# WAR DIARY
## or
## INTELLIGENCE SUMMARY.

*(Erase heading not required.)*

Army Form C. 2118.

**515 Coy. R.A.S.C. 59th Division** Volume XXIV  January 1919

| Place | Date | Hour | Summary of Events and Information | Remarks and references to Appendices |
|---|---|---|---|---|
| BEAULIEU MT. | 1/1/19 | | In quarters at B.Mt. | |
| " | 1/1/19 | | Supply lorry once transferred to 513 Coy RASC | |
| " | 4/1/19 | | One Leyland lorry (Spare Vehicle) transferred to the 59 S.M.T.Coy | |
| " | 7/1/19 | | One Supply lorry (Spare Vehicle) from the 59 SMT Coy | |
| " | 7/1/19 | | Lieut. W. G. TOLLEY Proceeded on Furlough & Leave to U.K. | |
| " | 9/1/19 | | Lieut F.C. TURTON Returned to 515 Coy RASC | |
| " | 12/1/19 | | NCO returned from the Base to Enable establishment | |
| " | 13/1/19 | | Supplies transferred to 513 Coy RASC | |
| " | 13/1/19 | | 2 Ca. B/M.G.C. 2nd rgtl cont of 1st Bttn Kings R. | |
| " | 13/1/19 | | 00 Battery Majors MCR Brigade 1 Bde Group | |
| " | 13/1/19 | | 011 Bty DMC Wagons Taken over and upkeep by the unit | |
| " | 14/1/19 | | 013 Rations & 1/2 to 513 Coy RASC | |
| " | 15/1/19 | | CAPTAIN R.T. GREEN reported to supplies officer U.K. | |
| " | 16/1/19 | | LIEUT. P.R.R. DIBBEN w/o 3 app1 detail Brigade Office | |
| " | | | BARLIN S.R.R and taken over as MT Troops S.O. | |
| " | 16/1/19 | | 177 S.R.P. Above Lieut | |

R. G. Green Capt. o/c No. 515 Coy. A.S.O. 59th Division.

# WAR DIARY
## or
## INTELLIGENCE SUMMARY.
*(Erase heading not required.)*

Army Form C. 2118.

Volume XXV

515 Coy R.A.S.C. 59th Divsn    January 1919

| Place | Date | Hour | Summary of Events and Information | Remarks and references to Appendices |
|---|---|---|---|---|
| BRAQUEMONT | 18/19 | | LIEUT W.G. TOLLER goes to take over 514 Cy R.A.S.C. 59th Divn | Nil |
| | 19/19 | | Sergt S.C. RODWELL proceeds to TH.Q on special Course | Nil |
| | 20/19 | | One N.C.O evacuated to C.C.S and struck off strength | Nil |
| | 21/19 | | Classification of Horses by the 59th Div Vet. | Nil |
| | 28/19 | | Inspection of Camp and transport by the G.O.C 59th Div. | Nil |
| | " | | The S.C.M reports to 573 Cy R.A.S.C for duty | Nil |
| | 29/19 | | 7 men Drivers Brown transferred to the 33rd Div trans | Nil |
| | " | | Coy H.Q move by road to VERQUIN | Nil |
| | 30/19 | 11.30 a.m | | Nil |
| VERQUIN | 30/19 | 12.30 p.m | H.Q Camp and transport Arrive | Nil |
| | 31/19 | | A Cook and Painter the 4th Bn R.W.F sent on return Type 1 strength of Coy H.Q 66 in Each Section | Nil |

W.P. Green Capt.
o/c No. 515 Coy. A.S.C
59th Division.

Army Form C. 2118.

516 Coy (No 4 Coy)
59. Divisional Train
R.A.S.C

# WAR DIARY
or
## INTELLIGENCE SUMMARY.
(Erase heading not required.)

Instructions regarding War Diaries and Intelligence Summaries are contained in F.S. Regs., Part II and the Staff Manual respectively. Title pages will be prepared in manuscript.

| Hour, Date, Place | Summary of Events and Information | Remarks and references to Appendices |
|---|---|---|
| DUNKIRK. 2.1.19 | 1 OR ON leave | M. |
| 3.1.19 | 1 OR. dispatched to Dunkirk | W. |
| 4.1.19 | 1 OR. FROM leave | M. |
| 5.1.19 | 1 OR FROM Hospital | W. |
| 6.1.19 | 1 OR TO Hospital. 1 OR FROM leave | W. |
| 7.1.19 | 1 OR TO Hospital 1 OR ON leave | W. |
| 9.1.19 | 1 OR. TO Hospital | W. |
| 14.1.19 | 1 OR FROM Hospital 1 OR ON leave + 1 OR ON Strength | W. |
| 16.1.19 | 5 OR taken ON strength reinforcement | W. |
| 18.1.19 | 1 OR ON leave | W. |
| 19.1.19 | 1 OR. sent to Dunkirk | W. |
| 20.1.19 | 1 OR TO Hospital. 1 OR FROM Hospital | W. |
| 21.1.19 | 1 OR FROM leave | W. |
| 22.1.19 | 1 OR FROM Hospital 1 OR ON leave | W. |
| 27.1.19 | 1 OR ON leave | W. |
| 28.1.19 | 2 OR sent to Dunkirk | W. |
| 30.1.19 | 1 OR ON leave | W. |

(73989) W4141—463. 400,000. 9/14. H.&J.Ltd. Forms/C. 2118/10.

56 Coy (No 4 Coy) Army Form C. 2118.
5th Divisional Train
R.A.S.C.

# WAR DIARY
## or
## INTELLIGENCE SUMMARY.
(Erase heading not required.)

| Hour, Date, Place | Summary of Events and Information | Remarks and references to Appendices |
|---|---|---|
| January 1919 | The undermentioned units have been released by Supply Officer 178 Ord Brigade :—<br><br>Headquarters 178 Inf Bde  1.1.19 to 31.1.19<br>36 Multinational Drainer  1.1.19 to 31.1.19<br>11 Royal Scots Fusiliers  1.1.19 to 31.1.19<br>13 Duke of Wellington  1.1.19 to 31.1.19<br>178 Trench Mortar Battery  1.1.19 to 31.1.19<br>576 Coy R.A.S.C  1.1.19 to 31.1.19<br>2/2 N.M. Field Ambulance  1.1.19 to 31.1.19<br>469 Field Coy R.E  1.1.19 to 31.1.19<br>97 Field Ambulance  9.1.19 to 31.1.19<br>1/6 Chaplin  3.1.19 to 7.1.19<br>2/15 London Regiment  15.1.19 to 31.1.19<br>176 Brigade Headquarters  31.1.19<br>25 Kings Liverpool Regt  31.1.19<br>26 Royal Scots L R. F  31.1.19<br>17 Royal Sussex Regt  31.1.19 | [signature]<br>56 Coy ROSC |

31
59th Div Series

Jul 25

WAR DIARY

VOL XXV

# WAR DIARY
## or
## INTELLIGENCE SUMMARY.

Army Form C. 2118.

VOL XXV

HQ 59. Div Train

| Place | Date | Hour | Summary of Events and Information | Remarks and references to Appendices |
|---|---|---|---|---|
| VERQUIN | Feb 1st 1919 | | Train HQ VERQUIN No 1 Coy and Div Troops SRP BARLIN No 2 Coy and 176 Brig SRP units XIX Corps HONDEGHEM. No 3 Coy without an SRP at VERQUIN No 4 Coy and 178 SRP DUNKIRK. Horses in open stables men in Camp and Billets. Supplies often Div Troops and attachments drawn by H.T. from BARLIN Railhead 178 Brig drawing at DUNKIRK | MT |
| | 11" | | No 2 Coy moved to DUNKIRK | MT |
| | 14" | | Capt R W HARTLEY SSO 59 Div proceeded for demobilization and struck off strength temporary duty in United Kingdom and returned from temporary duty in United Kingdom and | MT |
| | 17" | | Major T/Lieut Col T HAZLERIGG DSO appointed SSO 59 Div vice Major N/S CLEGG DSO resumes command of M Train vice Major N/S CLEGG DSO appointed for demobilization and struck off strength LIEUT W G TOLLER No 3 Coy proceeded for demobilization and struck off strength Col Y horses despatched to BASE 46 HD received from XI Corps Heavy Artillery Capt A N PEACH evacuated to England | MT |
| | 21 | | 10 HD received from XI Corps Heavy Artillery and struck off strength | MT |
| | 24. | | All horses in good condition and health 7 men good during month. Demobilization allotment 5 HT and 1 Supply per week. A few reinforcements received, but very difficult to carry on satisfactorily owing to shortage of NCO's men and loaders Under authority R. of T. all officers NCO's and men of 59 Div Train allowed to draw BONUS under Army Order XIV of 1919 | MT |

M Choton
Johnston Cuthsy
59 Div Train

# WAR DIARY

of

O.C. 513 Coy R.A.S.C. 59 Division

from 1st. to 28th February 1919

(Vol. 24.)

Army Form C. 2118.

# WAR DIARY
## or
## INTELLIGENCE SUMMARY.
(Erase heading not required)

Instructions regarding War Diaries and Intelligence Summaries are contained in F. S. Regs., Part II. and the Staff Manual respectively. Title pages will be prepared in manuscript.

513 Coy R.A.S.C. 59 Division.

| Place | Date | Hour | Summary of Events and Information | Remarks and references to Appendices |
|---|---|---|---|---|
| BARLIN. | 1-2-19 | | Company in Camp at BARLIN. Horses in open sheds. Refilling Point at BARLIN. Supplies drawn by M.T. from BARLIN RAILHEAD to S.R.P. | |
| | 2-2-19 to 28-2-19 | | NO CHANGE | |
| | 28-2-19 | | | |

[signature]
MAJOR,
COMMANDING No. 1 Coy, 59 DIVL. TRAIN.

1577 Wt.W10791/1773 500,000 1/15 D. D. & L. A.D.S.S./Forms/C. 2118.

# WAR DIARY or INTELLIGENCE SUMMARY

Vol 25. (FEBRUARY)
O.C. No 2 Coy 59 Div TRAIN

Army Form C. 2118.

| Place | Date | Hour | Summary of Events and Information | Remarks and references to Appendices |
|---|---|---|---|---|
| HONDEGHEM | 1.2.19 | | Commenced month with 2/11M 4th Class & 2 Coy 59 Div Train on feeding strength. Drawing supplies from BRAWNSTRUVE (railhead by H.T.) | App. 1 |
| " | 4.2.19 | | Drew supplies from XIV Corps Dump (Sylvestre Cappel) Supply Officer & details gone under instructions of XIV Corps | App. 2 |
| " | 5.2.19 | | Drew supplies from XIV Corps Dump HONDEGHEM | App. 2c |
| " | 11.2.19 | 10 am | Despatched supply wagons of 2/4 N.M. F.A. to West Hoek | App. 2c |
| " | " | 12 noon | Headquarters of Company entrained at HONDEGHEM en route for DUNKIRK under instructions XIV Corps & arrived | App. 2c |
| DUNKIRK | 12.2.19 | | at DUNKIRK 14.00 hours 12.2.19. | App. 3 |
| " | 12.2.19 | | Drew supplies for consumption 13.2.19 from S.C.P. 178 Bde. | App. 3c |
| " | 14.2.19 | | Capt T.M. HAZLERIGG resumed command of Company on return from leave. Transport pool arranged comprising transport of 175th, 178th Inf. Bde. and 514 + 516 Coys R.A.S.C. with two field ambulances, from which pool transport for the two Brigades and Demobilization Camps detailed. Average strength (mounted) being 5 I.H. Coy for purposes of work being 10 G.S. wagons daily. | |
| | | | four G.S. wagons detailed under B.T.O. 176 Inf. Bde. | |
| | | | Running records on our supply establ. and also Bruno & bars drawn Demobilising | |
| | | | Details of same rendition of ratios permanents app 3 | |

TMHazlerigg Capt
O.C. No 2 Coy 59 Div Train

Confidential

War Diary
of
515 Company. R.A.S.C. 59th Division

From 1-2-19 to 28.2.19.

Volume XXV

Army Form C. 2118.

# WAR DIARY
## INTELLIGENCE SUMMARY.

*(Erase heading not required.)*

Volume XXV

Instructions regarding War Diaries and Intelligence Summaries are contained in F. S. Regs., Part II. and the Staff Manual respectively. Title pages will be prepared in manuscript.

| Place | Date | Hour | Summary of Events and Information February 1919 | Remarks and references to Appendices |
|---|---|---|---|---|
| VERQUIN | 1/2/19 | | 515 Coy. R.A.S.C. 59th Division In camp and quarters | AFG |
| Do | 2/2/19 | | 1 H.S. horse evacuated to M.V.S. | AFG |
| Do | 9/2/19 | | 1 Driver demobilised | AFG |
| Do | 14/2/19 | | 1 Officer (Lt W.G. TOLLET) demobilised | AFG |
| Do | 15/2/19 | | 1 N.C.O evacuated to C.C.S. | AFG |
| Do | 17/2/19 | | 1 N.C.O reinforcement - reports from base | AFG |
| Do | 21/2/19 | | 8. H.S. horses received from XI Corps Heavy Arty. | AFG |
| Do | 22/2/19 | | 2 Riders and 8 H.S. Group Y horses transferred to No.5 Base R.F. Depot | AFG |
| Do | 28/2/19 | | 1 Driver transferred from 514 Coy R.A.S.C. towards completing estt. Health of Company during the month was good. Horses in good condition | AFG |

A. Green Capt
o/c No. 515 Coy R.A.S.C.
59th Division.

Confidential

War Diary
of
O/C. 516 Coy. R.A.S.C.

From:- 1-2-19  To 28-2-19

Volume 25.

# WAR DIARY
## or
## INTELLIGENCE SUMMARY.

*(Erase heading not required.)*

Army Form C. 2118.

516oby (No. 4 Coy)
57 Divisional Train R.A.S.C.

| Hour, Date, Place | Summary of Events and Information | Remarks and references to Appendices |
|---|---|---|
| ST. POL SUR MER Feb. 1. 1919 | 1 O.R. admitted to Hospital | W/D |
| " 3. 1919 | 2 O.Rs admitted to Hospital | W/D |
| " 4. | 1 O.R. proceeded to Dispersal Station for Demobilisation | W/D |
| " 7. | 1 S.R. proceeded on leave | W/D |
| " 8. | 1 O.R. admitted to Hospital | W/D |
| " 9. | 1 Officer proceeded on leave. 1 O.R. struck off strength. 1 O.R. proceeded to Dispersal Station for Demobilisation | W/D |
| " 10. | 1 O.R. reported for duty. 3 O.Rs reported to Hospital. 2 O.Rs returned from leave | W/D |
| " 13. | 1 O.R. proceeded to Dispersal Station for Demobilisation | W/D |
| " 14. | 1 O.R. proceeded on leave. 1 Officer + 1 O.R. reported for duty | W/D |
| " 15. | 1 O.R. discharged from Hospital. 2 O.Rs admitted to Hospital. 1 O.R. returned from leave. 1 O.R. struck off strength. | W/D |
| " 15. | 1 O.R. proceeded to Dispersal Camp for Demobilisation | W/D |
| " 16. | 1 O.R. discharged from Hospital. 3 O.Rs struck off | W/D |
| " 17. | 1 O.R. discharged from Hospital, strong it | W/D |

Army Form C. 2118.

516/(No 4) Century
57th Divisional Train R.A.S.C.

# WAR DIARY
or
# INTELLIGENCE SUMMARY.
(Erase heading not required.)

Instructions regarding War Diaries and Intelligence Summaries are contained in F.S. Regs., Part II. and the Staff Manual respectively. Title pages will be prepared in manuscript.

| Hour, Date, Place | Summary of Events and Information | Remarks and references to Appendices |
|---|---|---|
| ST POL sur MER Feb 18 | 1 O.R. admitted to Hospital. 1 O.R. proceeded on Leave | 8/19 |
| " 20 | 1 O.R. proceeded on Leave | 8/19 |
| " 21. | 1 O.R. admitted to Hospital | 8/19 |
| " 22 | 1 Officer returned from Leave | 8/19 |
| " 23 | 1 Officer admitted to Hospital | 8/19 |
| " 24 | 1 O.R. proceeded on Leave | 8/19 |
| " 27 | 1 O.R. discharged from Hospital | 8/19 |
| List of Units fed Feb 1st - 28th 1919 | HQ 178 Infantry Bde.    Feb 1st - 28th       HQ 176 Infantry Bde  Feb 26th-28th | |
| | 32. Northumberland Fus.      "           25 K. Liverpool Regt.     "    | |
| | 11. R. Scots Fus.            "           26 Royal Welsh Fus.       "    | |
| | 13. W. Riding Regt.          "           17 Royal Sussex Regt.     "    | |
| | 178 M.T.M.B.                 "           574 Coy. R.I.P.E.      Feb 12-28 | |
| | 516 Coy. R.A.S.C.            Feb 1st - 26th   2/1 Field Ambulance " | }  M/19 |
| | 2/2 Field Ambulance          Feb 1st - 28th   2/15 London Regt. Feb 1-6th | |
| | 2/6. Field Amb. Regt.        "           | |
| | 97th Field Ambulance         "           | |

JJ Warren Capt.
O.C. 516 Coy. R.A.S.C.

WAR DIARY

59th (N.M.) DIVISIONAL TRAIN.

VOL XXVI

from 1.3.19 to 31.3.19

# WAR DIARY or INTELLIGENCE SUMMARY

Army Form C. 2118.

(Erase heading not required.) HQ 59th (N.M.) DIV TRAIN

VOL XXVI

| Place | Date | Hour | Summary of Events and Information | Remarks and references to Appendices |
|---|---|---|---|---|
| VERQUIN | 1st March | | THQ VERQUIN. No1 Coy BARLIN. Div Troops, SRP BARLIN. RAILHEAD for DIV TROOPS, BARLIN. Supplies drawn by HT. No2 Coy ST POL SUR MER DUNKIRK. 176 SRP not functioning, being amalgamated with 178 BRIG. No3 Coy. HQ's at VERQUIN. Bn Baggage and Supply wagons of No3 Coy in CALAIS area with 177 Inf Brig. No4 Coy and 178 BRIG SRP. at ST POL SUR MER. DUNKIRK. | MVI |
| | 6th | | All Baggage and Supply Wagons of 59 Div Arty (full turnout less drivers) despatched to respective units. (74 H.D. 2 LD horses 37 GS wagons 1 limbd. GS wagon) | MVI |
| | 7th | | No3 Coy and THQ TRANSPORT started by ROUTE MARCH to CALAIS AREA staying at AIRE BARRACKS. | MVI |
| | 8th | | THQ personnel moved by lorry to BALINGHEM via CALAIS. Route march of No3Coy and THQ Transport continued staying night at SERQUES. | MVI |
| BALINGHEM | 9th | | THQ in Camp. No3Coy and Transport arrived in the course of the day. | MVI |
| | 11th | | 25 H.D. remounts from XI Corps H.A. distributed to No.2 and 4 Coys. | |
| LE BEAU MARAIS | 14th | | THQ proceeds to LE BEAU MARIS and is accommodated in Camp with Div HQ Horses in Stables. | MVI |
| | 15th | | CAPT MC JOHNSTON proceeds on leave. LIEUT PRR DIBBIN assumes duties of ADJUTANT. | MVI |
| | 17th | | No3 Coy moved from BALINGHEM to No19 Vet Hospital FRETHUN and collect in all wagons of Coys from 177 BRIG. Whole of 177 Brig TRANSPORT pooled under O.C. No3 Coy. 28 Cat.X horses despatched | MVI |
| | 20. | | T/MAJOR NB CLEGG DSO SSO 59 Div proceeded for duty with RIGHT DIV TRAIN | MVI |
| | 22nd | | T/ LIEUT F.G. TURTON No1Coy 59 Div Train proceeded for duty with 34 Div Train. | MVI |
| | 27th | | T/MAJOR NM NEWELL TF. All surplus personel despatched to the Brig Coys. All wagons of RE No1Coy reduced to cadre strength and all surplus personel despatched to the Brig Coys. Brig Pioneer B.M. still attached as their white self Coys HQ Group THQ Field Ambulances. M/E B.M. Pioneer B.M. reported for duty from 18th Div Train Ln hd strength as ISSO 59 Div. | MVI |
| | | | posted as SO 177 Inf BRIG VICE LIEUT PRR DIBBIN posted R.O. T/CAPT PH LOUPTE reported for duty and posted as ADJUTANT. CAPT MC JOHNSTON resumes duty as ADJUTANT. | MVI |
| | 30. | | Demobilization carried on slowly throughout the month, but with the exception of No1 Coy Train is being retained at hand. "CLEARING UP ARMY". All HORES in good condition and health of men good. Departmental orders now issued from T.D.T. NORTHERN for the Train. 178 Brig have a large number of attached units to feeding at DUNKIRK. | MVI |

M Christie Johnston Capt Adjt
59 Div Train

CONFIDENTIAL.

# WAR DIARY

OF

## O.C. 513 COMPANY RASC 59 DIVISION

### FROM 1-3-19 TO 31-3-19

VOLUME 25

Army Form C. 2118

# WAR DIARY
## or
## INTELLIGENCE SUMMARY

(Erase heading not required.)

Instructions regarding War Diaries and Intelligence Summaries are contained in F. S. Regs., Part II. and the Staff Manual respectively. Title Pages will be prepared in manuscript.

| Place | Date | Hour | Summary of Events and Information | Remarks and references to Appendices |
|---|---|---|---|---|
| BARLIN. | 1/3/19 | | 513 COMPANY RASC 59 DIVN. Company in camp at Barlin. Horses in open sheds. Refilling Point at BARLIN. Supplies drawn by A.T. from BARLIN Railhead to S.R.P. | |
| | 6/3/19 | | All baggage and supply wagons of 59 Divl Artillery (full turn-out less drivers) despatched to respective units. (74 A.B. and 2 D. Stores, 37 R.S. & 1 Limber & Wagon, in all) | |
| | 9/3/19 | | S.R.P. ceases to be functionary. | |
| | 10/3/19 | | Supplies for Company drawn from R.S.O. BARLIN Railhead. | |
| | 18/3/19 | | 2 6 Horses & 2 Ride Horses of "X" Category despatched to Base. 4 Ride Horses to St. Pol for sale. ("Z" Category) | |
| | 23/3/19 | | | |
| | 27/3/19 | | Company reduced to cadre strength and all surplus personnel despatched to H.Q. 59 Divl Train CALAIS, for reporting, in accordance with instructions from H.Q. 59 Divl Train by wire. | |
| | 28/3/19 to 31/3/19 | | No CHANGE. | |

3/3/19

J.S.Moore
2/Lieut
COMMANDING No. 1 Coy, 59 DIVL. TRAIN.

Army Form C. 2118.

# WAR DIARY
# INTELLIGENCE SUMMARY.
*(Erase heading not required.)*

Vol. XXVI

O.C. N° 2 Coy. 59th Div. Train.

| Place | Date | Hour | Summary of Events and Information | Remarks and references to Appendices |
|---|---|---|---|---|
| DUNKERQUE | 1.3.19 | | Company stationed at ST POL SUR MER. Transport was in general pool for service in respect of Demobilization Camps | |
| | 8.3.19 | | Thirteen other ranks reinforcements taken on strength | |
| | 11.3.19 | | Twenty H.D. Reserves taken on strength from HQ 59 Div Train | |
| | 12.3.19 | | Six H.D. Reserves returned to N° 4 Coy, 59 Div Train | |
| | 21.3.19 | | Five other ranks sent for dispersal | |
| | 23.3.19 | | Five other ranks reinforcements taken on strength | |
| | 28.3.19 | | Further twelve other ranks reinforcements received from O.C. 59 Div Train and taken on strength | |

M. Taylroft Capt.
O.C. N° 2 Coy. 59 Div. TRAIN.

## Confidential

## War Diary.
## 515 Coy R.A.S.C.
## Volume xxvi
from 1/3/19 to 31/3/19.

# WAR DIARY

## INTELLIGENCE SUMMARY

(Erase heading not required.)

Army Form C. 2118.

Volume XXVI

515 Coy R.A.S.C. 59th Divn   March 1919

| Place | Date | Hour | Summary of Events and Information | Remarks and references to Appendices |
|---|---|---|---|---|
| VERQUIN | 1/3/19 | | In camp and quarters | |
| Do | 1/3/19 | 23.00 | Summer time comes into force | |
| Do | 2/3/19 | | 2. Lt. 19 Horses (Remounts) | |
| Do | 3/3/19 | | 1. N.C.O. Reports back from leave to U.K. | |
| Do | 7/3/19 | | 1 N.C.O. and 1 Driver demolished. 1 Jam Point and 4 Drivers transferred from 573 Coy R.A.S.C. | |
| Do | 7/3/19 | 0.900 | Coy H.Q.'s move by road to new station. Staged at AIRE BARRACKS night - 7/8th | |
| AIRE BARRACKS | 8/3/19 | 0.900 | Continued march to new station : staged at SERQUES night - 8/9th | |
| SERQUES | 9/3/19 | 0.900 | Continued march to new station at BALINGHEM | |
| BALINGHEM | 9/3/19 | 16.00 | In camp and quarters | |

A Green Capt
O/C 515 Coy
R.A.S.C.
59th Divn

Army Form C. 2118.

# WAR DIARY
## or
## INTELLIGENCE SUMMARY. Volume XXVI

(Erase heading not required.)

515 Coy R.A.S.C. 59th Div. March 19

| Place | Date | Hour | Summary of Events and Information | Remarks and references to Appendices |
|---|---|---|---|---|
| BALINGHEM | 14/3/19 | | 2 Drivers demobilized | AG |
| Do | 14/3/19 | | 1 Driver reports back from leave to U.K. | AG |
| Do | 15/3/19 | | W.O. Class II demobilized | AG |
| Do | 16/3/19 | | 1 Sergt reports back from leave to U.K. | AG |
| Do | 17/3/19 | 10-9.00 | Coy H.Q. 59 moved by road to 8914 Veterinary Hospital at FRETHUN | AG |
| | 17/3/19 | 12.15 | In Camp and quarters at 82/19 Veterinary Hospital | AG |
| FRETHUN | 17/3/19 | | 1 Saddler Driver proceeds on leave to U.K. | AG |
| Do | 17/3/19 | | 1 Driver proceeds on leave to U.K. | AG |
| Do | 19/3/19 | | 1 Sergt. and 1 Driver demobilized | AG |
| Do | 21/3/19 | | 1 H.D. Horse transferred to 514 Coy R.A.S.C. | AG |
| Do | 21/3/19 | | 1 Sergt and 3 Private Supply details transferred from 573 Coy R.A.S.C. | AG |
| Do | 24/3/19 | | | AG |

D. Green Capt
o/c No. 515 Coy, A.S.C.
59th Division.

Army Form C. 2118.

# WAR DIARY
## or
## INTELLIGENCE SUMMARY.   Volume XXVI

(Erase heading not required.)

515 Coy. R.A.S.C. 59 Div².   March 1919

| Place | Date | Hour | Summary of Events and Information | Remarks and references to Appendices |
|---|---|---|---|---|
| FRETHUN | 25/3/19 | | Iron rations drawn | AG |
| D⁰ | 28/3/19 | | QMS Boote transferred from 513 Coy. RASC and posted to 513 N.M.F.A. | AG |
| D⁰ | 28/3/19 | | 1 S.Q.M.S. and 5 N.C.O. with 11 drivers transferred from 513 Coy. RASC | AG |
| D⁰ | 28/3/19 | | 1 Wheeler Corpl. transferred from 516 Coy. RASC | AG |
| D⁰ | 30/3/19 | | 1 Driver proceeds on leave to U.K. | AG |
| D⁰ | 30/3/19 | | T/Capt. H.P.P. LOUFFTE. R.A.S.C. reports for duty as S.O. 197 to Bde vice, T/Lieut. P.R.R. DIBBEN. posted as R.O. | AG |
| D⁰ | 31/3/19 | | 1 N.C.O. demobilized | AG |
| D⁰ | 31/3/19 | | All Train Baggage Wagons withdrawn from Bde Group including the 25th 1st R.R.C. and 200. M.G.B.  Health of the Company during the month has very good. Horses in good condition. | AG |

H Green Capt.
o/c No: 515 Coy. A.S.C.
59th Division.

Confidential

War Diary

06.516 Coy R.A.S.C.

From:- 1/3/19 To 31/3/19

Volume 28.

# WAR DIARY
## or
## INTELLIGENCE SUMMARY.
(Erase heading not required.)

Army Form C. 2118.

516 Coy. R.A.S.C.

| Hour, Date, Place | Summary of Events and Information | Remarks and references to Appendices |
|---|---|---|
| St. Pol sur Mer 2/3/19 | 6 - O.R. report for duty - 3 O.R. proceed to Verquin for Remounts 1 O.R. returns off leave. | |
| do 6/3/19 | 1 - O.R. proceeds to Dispersal Station for Demobilisation - 1 - O.R. admitted to Hospital | |
| 7/3/19 | 1 - O.R. proceeds on leave. | |
| 8/3/19 | 10 - O.R. report for duty | |
| 9/3/19 | 1 - O.R. proceeds to Dispersal Station for Demobilisation | |
| 10/3/19 | 1 - O.R. reports for duty. | |
| 12/3/19 | 1 - O.R. returns off leave - 26 - O.R. report for duty - 5 - M.D. Horses Taken on strength. | |
| 13/3/19 | 1 - O.R. admitted to Hospital. | |
| 14/3/19 | 1 - O.R. proceeds on leave - 1 - O.R. admitted to Hospital | |
| 16/3/19 | 2 - O.R. proceed to Dispersal Station for Demobilisation | |
| 17/3/19 | 1 - O.R. returns off leave - 1 - O.R. proceeds on leave. | |
| 20/3/19 | 1 - O.R. admitted to Hospital | |
| 21/3/19 | 1 - O.R. admitted to Hospital | |
| 22/3/19 | 1 - O.R. admitted to Hospital - 2 - O.R. proceed to Dispersal Station for Demobilisation | |
| 23/3/19 | 1 - O.R. admitted to Hospital | |
| 24/3/19 | 1 Off. proceeds on leave. - 1 - O.R. returns off leave. | |
| 25/3/19 | 1 - O.R. discharged from Hospital reports for duty. | |
| 27/3/19 | 2 - O.R. discharged from Hospital. | |
| 28/3/19 | 2 - O.R. proceed on leave - 1 O.R. discharged from Hospital. | |
| 29/3/19 | 13 - O.R. report for duty. | |
| 30/3/19 | 3 - O.R. proceed on leave - 1 O.R. returns off leave. | |
| | 2 - O.R. proceed on leave - 1 - O.R. discharged from Hospital | |

O.C. 516 Coy. R.A.S.C.

**Army Form C. 2118.**

516 Coy. R.A.S.C.

# WAR DIARY
## or
## INTELLIGENCE SUMMARY
*(Erase heading not required.)*

Instructions regarding War Diaries and Intelligence Summaries are contained in F.S. Regs., Part II. and the Staff Manual respectively. Title Pages will be prepared in manuscript.

| Place | Date | Hour | Summary of Events and Information | Remarks and references to Appendices |
|---|---|---|---|---|
| | | | Units fed during month of March 1919 by Supply Officer 178th Inf. Bde. | |
| | | | H.Q. 178th Inf. Bde. 1/3/19 to 31/3/19 | |
| | | | 36th Northumberland Fus. 13/3/19 to 31/3/19 | |
| | | | 11th Royal Scots Fus. do. | |
| | | | 13th West Ridings do. | |
| | | | 516 Coy. R.A.S.C. do. | |
| | | | 2/1st N.M. Fd. Amblce. do. | |
| | | | 2/2 N.M. Fd. Amblce. do. | |
| | | | 469 Fd. Coy. R.E. do. | |
| | | | 94th Fd. Amblce. do. | |
| | | | H.Q. 176th Inf. Bde. do. | |
| | | | 25th Kings Liverpools 1/3/19 to 26/3/19 | |
| | | | 26th Royal Welsh Fus. 1/3/19 to 21/3/19 | |
| | | | 14th Royal Sussex 1/3/19 to 31/3/19 | |
| | | | 514 Coy. R.A.S.C. do. | |
| | | | 6th South Wales Borderers 12/3/19 to 22/3/19 | |
| | | | 201 Fd. Coy. R.E. do. | |
| | | | 225 Fd. Coy. R.E. 12/3/19 to 31/3/19 | |
| | | | 467 Fd. Coy. R.E. 12/3/19 to 31/3/19 | |
| | | | 554 A.T. Coy. R.E. 12/3/19 to 31/3/19 | |
| | | | 241 } A.W. Coys. R.E. do. | |
| | | | 575 } do. | |
| | | | 1 Lorry Detachment R.A.F. do. | |
| | | | 59th Div. M.T. detachment do. | |
| | | | 6th Works Coy. R.E. 14/3/19 to 31/3/19 | |
| | | | 10th Park Detachment R.A.F. 29/3/19 to 31/3/19 | |

178th Inf. Bde.

[signature] Capt.
O.C. 516 Coy. R.A.S.C.

# WAR DIARY or INTELLIGENCE SUMMARY

Army Form C. 2118.

VOLUME XXVII

H.Q. 59 (N.M.) DIV TRAIN

| Place | Date | Hour | Summary of Events and Information | Remarks and references to Appendices |
|---|---|---|---|---|
| LE BEAUMARIS | APRIL 1st | | 59 Div Train HQ with Div HQ at LE BEAUMARIS near CALAIS. No.1 Coy at BARLIN. Horses in open sheds. Supplies for the DIV. ART/ drawn from RSO BARLIN. No.2 Coy with 176 Brig at ST POL DUNKIRK. 176 Brig STP permanently with 178 Brig STP. No.3 Coy at No. 19 VET HOSPITAL FRÉTHUN near CALAIS. Supplies to 177 Brig drawn from Détail Issue Store CALAIS. No.4 Coy at ST POL DUNKIRK. 178 STP (railway units of 178, 179 Brigs, and a minimum of attached troops. No.4 Coy horses in open, personnel in huts. No.3 Coy horses in open sheds, personnel in huts. No.4 Coy by horses in open stables, personnel in huts. | nil |
| | 2nd | | 1/Lieut F.A.A. WHITFIELD No.3 Coy proceeded to demobilization. | nil |
| | 4th | | T/Major A.G. EDEN RASC detailed for duty and temporary posted to No.3 Coy. | nil |
| | 12th | | T/Capt H.P. LOUETTE No.3 Coy. 50 179 Inf Brig proceeded for demobilization. T/Lieut F.R.R. DUBBIN posted to SO. 177 Brig. T/2 Lieut C. KAUL transferred to CENTRAL INVESTIGATION DEPT. | nil |
| | 13th | | Horses wagons and personnel of No.1 Coy which are required for units of the Division which are being kept up to strength transferred to Brig Coys, as authorised additions on authority of DA/QMG GHQ consequent on the reduction of No.1 Coy to CADRE. | nil |
| | 15th | | No.3 Coy together with 177 Inf Brig Transport group, including 25 Bn KRRC and 200 Bn MGC moved to AUSTRALIAN VET HOSPITAL whilst OC No.3 Coy assumed command of the whole comp. Major/Lieut Col T HAZELRIGG DSO OC 59 Div Train proceeded to ENGLAND for duty at DADS.T ALDERSHOT. Major L.M. NEWALL RASC TF SSO 59 Div Div assumes command of the TRAIN. | nil |
| | 20th | | Course in WHEELWRIGHTS WORK and HARNESS MAKING commenced at No 3 and 4 Coys for infantry personnel. | nil |
| | 21st | | Lieut A/Capt E.S.H. EAMES SO 178 Inf Brig deputed to demobilization. Lieut A/Capt S. PIGGIN assumed duties of SO 178 Inf Brig. CADRE of 3/1 (N.M.) MVS attached to the Div Train and taken on by 110.4 Coy. | nil |
| | 28th | | Major A/Lieut Col A.H. MAUDE GMG DSO RASC TF deputed for duty from 47 Div Train and assumed command. | nil |
| | 29th | | Course for Farriers of Infantry Bns started at A/V Corps. | nil |
| | 30th | | Supplies to 59 Div Artillery drawn in bulk by MT from RSO BARLIN RAILHEAD and distributed by respective units from STP. The condition of the horses throughout the month has been excellent and a number of good sub chargers have been purchased and all OR over 7 establishment. Health of personnel good. A large number of labour allotments have been received with but dissatisfaction and very small only 26 having been received to date. Demobilization of ranks without leave absconded. The smallness of demobilization allotments caused much dissatisfaction among the men, as there are still left over 300 releasable men of whom 160 are 1914 men. 155 (1915 men) and 135 are over 41 years of age and enlisted after 1.1.16. Many efforts have been made by OC Train to obtain a larger allotment from DIV destinate but without result |  |

M Newall Major RASC
59 Div Train

CONFIDENTIAL

WAR DIARY

of

O.C. 513 Coy R.A.S.C. 59 DIVN.

From 1/4/19 To 30/4/19

VOLUME 26

**Army Form C. 2118**

# WAR DIARY
## or
## INTELLIGENCE SUMMARY
*(Erase heading not required.)*

Instructions regarding War Diaries and Intelligence Summaries are contained in F. S. Regs., Part II. and the Staff Manual respectively. Title Pages will be prepared in manuscript.

| Place | Date | Hour | Summary of Events and Information | Remarks and references to Appendices |
|---|---|---|---|---|
| BARLIN. | 1/4/19 | | 513 Company R.A.S.C. 59 DIVN. Company in camp at Barlin. Horses in open sheds. Supplies for company drawn from R.S.O. Barlin Railhead. | |
| BARLIN. | 30/4/19 | | Supplies for 59 Divl. Artillery drawn in bulk by M.T. from R.S.O. Barlin Railhead and distributed to respective units from S.D.S. | |
| | 30/4/19 | | | |

J. Brown
2/Lieut

COMMANDING No. 1 Coy, 59 DIVL. TRAIN.

1875 Wt. W593/826 1,000,000 4/15 J.B.C. & A. A.D.S.S./Forms/C. 2118.

Army Form C. 2118.

# WAR DIARY
## INTELLIGENCE SUMMARY
*(Erase heading not required.)*

Vol. XXVII
O.C. Nº 2 Coy, 59 Div. TRAIN

| Place | Date | Hour | Summary of Events and Information | Remarks and references to Appendices |
|---|---|---|---|---|
| DUNKERQUE | 1.4.19 | | Commenced month with Company stationed at S¹ Pol Sur Mer DUNKERQUE, Baggage & Supply wagons & | |
| | | | 25th Battⁿ Kings Liverpool Regt being attached with Batt'n at CALAIS | |
| | | | Capt. J. F. PIGGIN Anken on Strength of Coy and assumed duties as S.O. 176 July 13 & 2/Lieut C. KAVI posted to | ℳ |
| | | | Nº 4 Coy, 59 Div Train. | ℳ |
| " | 16.4.19 | | 2 HD horses taken on strength from Nº 1 Coy, 59 Div Train (viz 2/2 N.M. Fld Amb) | ℳ |
| " | 17.4.19 | | 2 HD horses taken over from Nº 1 Coy 59 Div Train (viz 2/1 N.M. Fld Amb) | ℳ |
| " | 23.4.19 | | 10 Men surplus to Cadre taken on strength from 2/1 N.M Fld Amb. 1 HD vacated to Veterinary Detachment M.T.O | ℳ |
| " | 27.4.19 | | 1 Rde taken on strength from 2/1 N.M.Mtd. Vet Sec. | ℳ |
| " | 28.4.19 | | Capt F. PIGGIN posted to Nº 4 Coy 59 Div Train. | ℳ |

M. Hayden J. Capt
O.C. Nº 2 Coy, 59 Div. Train.

Secret.
War Diary.
515 Coy R.A.S.C.
April/19
Volume XXVII

Army Form C. 2118.

# WAR DIARY
## or
## INTELLIGENCE SUMMARY
(Erase heading not required.)

Volume XXVII

Instructions regarding War Diaries and Intelligence Summaries are contained in F. S. Regs., Part II. and the Staff Manual respectively. Title pages will be prepared in manuscript.

515 Coy. R.A.S.C. 59 Divn.       April /19

| Place | Date | Hour | Summary of Events and Information | Remarks and references to Appendices |
|---|---|---|---|---|
| FRETHUN | 1/4/19 | | In camp and quarters | MG |
| " | 1/4/19 | | 1 Driver reports back from leave to U.K. | MG |
| " | 2/4/19 | | 1 R.C.O. transferred from 516 Coy R.A.S.C | MG |
| " | 2/4/19 | | 1 Driver reports back from leave to U.K. | MG |
| " | 3/4/19 | | 5 Drivers proceed on leave to U.K | MG |
| " | 4/4/19 | | 3 R.C.O. proceed on leave to U.K. | MG |
| " | 5/4/19 | | 1 R.C.O, 2 Drivers proceed on leave to U.K. | MG |
| " | 6/4/19 | | 1 R.C.O. 1 Driver proceed on leave to U.K. | MG |
| " | 7/4/19 | | 1 R.C.O. 1 Driver proceed on leave to U.K | MG |
| " | 8/4/19 | | 2 Drivers proceed on leave to U.K. | MG |
| " | 9/4/19 | | 1 Driver proceeds on leave to U.K. | MG |

M. Green Capt. o/c No. 515 Coy. A.S.C.
59th Division.

Army Form C. 2118.

# WAR DIARY
or
INTELLIGENCE SUMMARY.

(Erase heading not required.)

Volume XXVII

Instructions regarding War Diaries and Intelligence Summaries are contained in F. S. Regs., Part II. and the Staff Manual respectively. Title pages will be prepared in manuscript.

| Place | Date | Hour | Summary of Events and Information | Remarks and references to Appendices |
|---|---|---|---|---|
| | | | 515 Coy. R.A.S.C. 50th Divn. April/19 | |
| FRETHUN | 10/4/19 | | 2 Drivers 1 Private Proceed on leave to U.K. | |
| " | 12/4/19 | | 3 Drivers 1 Private Proceed on leave to U.K. | |
| " | 12/4/19 | | 1 R.C.O. 14 Drivers posted to Coy from the 2/3rd Field Amb. | |
| " | 12/4/19 | | Capt. H.P.R. LOUETTE Proceed to Dispersal Camp for Demobilization | |
| " | 12/4/19 | | 1 R.C.O. 1 Driver (serving soldier) despatched to U.K. | |
| " | 13/4/19 | | 3 R.C.O. 28 Drivers 5 Privates 93 H.D. Horses 5 L.D. 3 R.D.'s transferred from 573 Coy R.A.S.C. and held on add^l authorised establishment for HQ 50th Divn. and 59th Bde Troops in CALAIS area | |
| " | 13/4/19 | | 2 Drivers Proceed on leave to U.K. | |
| " | 14/4/19 | | 1 Driver transferred from 573 Coy R.A.S.C. | |
| " | 14/4/19 | | CAPTAIN. R.J. GREEN and 2 Drivers Proceed on leave to U.K. | |
| " | 14/4/19 | | 1 Driver Reports back from leave to U.K. | |

H.J. Green Capt. o/c No. 515 Coy. A.S.P.
50th Division.

Army Form C. 2118.

# WAR DIARY
## or
## INTELLIGENCE SUMMARY.
(Erase heading not required.)

Volume XXVII

Instructions regarding War Diaries and Intelligence Summaries are contained in F. S. Regs., Part II. and the Staff Manual respectively. Title pages will be prepared in manuscript.

515 Coy. R.A.S.C. 59th Divn.    April/19

| Place | Date | Hour | Summary of Events and Information | Remarks and references to Appendices |
|---|---|---|---|---|
| FIRETUN | 14/4/19 | 14.00 | MAJOR. A.G. EDEN. R.A.S.C. reports and takes over command | AGE |
| " | 15/4/19 | | Coy. proceed by road to Australian Vety Hospital. COQUELLES | AGE |
| COQUELLES Vety. Hospital | 16/4/19 | | 1 Private transferred from D.A.D.V.S. 59th Divn | AGE |
| " | 17/4/19 | | 1 2.C.O. 1 Driver despatched for demobilization | AGE |
| " | 17/4/19 | | 1 Driver proceeds on leave to U.K. also 1 Driver reports back | AGE |
| " | 18/4/19 | | 3 2.C.O. 2 Drivers 1 Private report back from leave to U.K. | AGE |
| " | 19/4/19 | | LIEUT. P.R.R.DIBBEN posted to S.O. 177th Bde | AGE |
| " | 19/4/19 | | 2 Drivers proceed on leave to U.K. | AGE |
| " | 20/4/19 | | 2 2.C.O. 3 Drivers report back from leave to U.K. | AGE |
| " | 21/4/19 | | 1 2.C.O. 1 Driver proceed on leave to U.K. | AGE |
| " | 21/4/19 | | 2 2.C.O. despatched for demobilization | AGE |
| " | 22/4/19 | | 2 Drivers report back from leave to U.K. | AGE |

A.G. Green Capt.
o/c No. 515 Coy. A.S.C.
59th Division.

Army Form C. 2118.

# WAR DIARY
## or
## INTELLIGENCE SUMMARY.
(Erase heading not required.)

Volume XXVII  

515 Coy. R.A.S.C. 59 Div.  April/19

| Place | Date | Hour | Summary of Events and Information | Remarks and references to Appendices |
|---|---|---|---|---|
| COQUELLES VET HOSPITAL | 22/4/19 | | 2 Drivers Proceed on leave to U.K. | ACG |
| " | 23/4/19 | | 2 Drivers deputated for demobilization | ACG |
| " | 23/4/19 | | 3 Driver transferred from 573 Coy. R.A.S.C. | ACG |
| " | 24/4/19 | | 1 W.O Proceeds on leave to U.K. | ACG |
| " | 24/4/19 | | 5 Drivers 1 Private Whart-han from leave to U.K. | ACG |
| " | 24/4/19 | | 1 Driver Proceeds on leave to U.K. | ACG |
| " | 26/4/19 | | 1 Mule Horse transferred from No 513 Coy R.A.S.C. | ACG |
| " | 26/4/19 | | 1 R.C.D. 4 Drivers 1 Private report back from leave to U.K. | ACG |
| " | 26/4/19 | | 3 Driver transferred to 514 Coy R.A.S.C. | ACG |
| " | 26/4/19 | | 3 Drivers Proceed on leave to U.K. | ACG |
| " | 26/4/19 | | 2 Ride Horses transferred from 2/1st M.V.S. | ACG |
| " | 27/4/19 | | 2 Drivers transferred from 514 Coy R.A.S.C. | ACG |
| " | 27/4/19 | | 1 Driver Proceed on leave to U.K. | ACG |

A Green Capt — o/c No. 515 Coy. A.S.C.
59th Division.

# WAR DIARY
## or
## INTELLIGENCE SUMMARY.
*(Erase heading not required.)*

Army Form C. 2118.

Volume XXVII

| Place | Date | Hour | Summary of Events and Information | Remarks and references to Appendices |
|---|---|---|---|---|
| CORQUELLES VET HOSPITAL | 27/4/19 | | 515 Coy. RASC. 59 Divn — April/19. 1 Driver reports back from leave to U.K. | AS |
| " | 28/4/19 | | 2 Drivers despatched for demobilization | AS |
| " | 28/4/19 | | 1 A.C.O. 1 Driver proceed on leave to U.K. | AS |
| " | 29/4/19 | | 1 Driver reports back from leave to U.K. | AS |
| " | 29/4/19 | | 1 Senior 1 Private proceed on leave to U.K. | AS |
| " | 29/4/19 | | CAPTAIN R. J. GREEN reports back from leave to U.K. | AS |
| " | 30/4/19 | | 1 Driver reports back from leave to U.K. | AS |
| " | 30/4/19 | | 3 Drivers transferred to 515 Coy. RASC. | AS |
| " | 30/4/19 | | 2 H.D. Horses transferred to 516 Coy. RASC. | AS |
| " | 30/4/19 | | 3 H.D. Horses transferred to 104 VET. HOSPITAL | AS |
| " | 30/4/19 | | 3 H.D. Horses received from 92 S. Remount Depot — | AS |
| " | 30/4/19 | | CAPTAIN R. J. GREEN, RASC, assumes command of 515 Co. RASC and assumes command of 1/77 & 1/75 Bde Transports the vice MAJOR A. G. EDEN, RASC, who proceeds to take over 21st Divn H.T. Co. RASC. Health of the Coy & horses in good condition during the month — | AS |

Kobler Capt
o/c No. 515 Coy. A.S.C.
59th Division.

Confidential

War Diary

of

O.C. 516 Coy. R.A.S.C.

From:- 1/4/19 - To 30/4/19

Volume - 24.

# WAR DIARY
## or
## INTELLIGENCE SUMMARY

Army Form C. 2118.

(Erase heading not required.)

516 Coy. R.A.S.C.

Instructions regarding War Diaries and Intelligence Summaries are contained in F. S. Regs., Part II. and the Staff Manual respectively. Title Pages will be prepared in manuscript.

| Place | Date | Hour | Summary of Events and Information | Remarks and references to Appendices |
|---|---|---|---|---|
| St. Pol-sur-Mer | 3/4/19 | | 3- O.R. proceed on leave. | W |
| | 4/4/19 | | 2- O.R. proceed to Dispersal Station for Demobilisation. – 3- O.R. proceed on leave. | W |
| | 5/4/19 | | 1- O.R. proceed on leave. – 2- O.R. admitted to Hospital. – 1- O.R. returns off leave. | W |
| | 6/4/19 | | 1- O.R. proceed on leave. – 1- O.R. admitted to Hospital. | W |
| | 7/4/19 | | 4- O.R. proceed on leave. – 1- O.R. reports for duty. | W |
| | 8/4/19 | | 6- O.R. proceed on leave. | W |
| | 9/4/19 | | 4- O.R. proceed on leave. | W |
| | 10/4/19 | | 4- O.R. Transferred from 2/1st N.M. Sub Ambce. – 2- O.R. proceed on leave. – 1- O.R. returns off leave. | W |
| | 11/4/19 | | 1- O.R. admitted to Hospital. | W |
| | 12/4/19 | | 2/Lt. Stone transferred to Central Investigation Staff. – 1- O.R. proceeds to Dispersal Station for Demobilisation. | W |
| | 13/4/19 | | Capt. C.J.N. Games returns off leave. – 3- O.R. reports for duty. | W |
| | 14/4/19 | | 3- O.R. proceeds on leave. | W |
| | 15/4/19 | | 2- O.R. admitted to Hospital – 2- O.R. proceed on leave – 2- O.R. returns off leave. | M |
| | 16/4/19 | | 1- O.R. admitted to Hospital. – 1- O.R. proceeds on leave. | M |
| | 17/4/19 | | 1- O.R. attached T.H.Q. | M |
| | 18/4/19 | | 2- O.R. proceeds on leave. – 1- O.R. returns off leave. | M |
| | 19/4/19 | | 2- O.R. admitted to Hospital. – 1- O.R. returns off leave. | W |
| | 20/4/19 | | 5- O.R. returns off leave. | W |
| | 21/4/19 | | 1- O.R. returns off leave. – 1- O.R. discharged from Hospital. | W |
| | 22/4/19 | | 2- O.R. proceed on leave. | W |
| | 23/4/19 | | 4- O.R. proceed to Dispersal Station for Demobilisation. – 3- O.R. proceed on leave. | M |

Army Form C. 2118.

# WAR DIARY
## or
## INTELLIGENCE SUMMARY

(Erase heading not required.)

516 by J. RAB C

| Place | Date | Hour | Summary of Events and Information | Remarks and references to Appendices |
|---|---|---|---|---|
| St. Polsure. mes | 24/4/19 | | 1 - O.R. return off leave — 4 - O.R. proceed on leave. | (1) |
| | 25/4/19 | | 2 - O.R. return off leave. | (1) |
| | 26/4/19 | | 2 - O.R. return off leave — 1 - S.S.M. reports for duty | (1) |
| | 27/4/19 | | 2 - O.R. return off leave — 2 - O.R. return to dispersal — 1939 E.J.N. Kerr proceeds. | (1) |
| | 28/4/19 | | 3 - O.R. proceed to dispersal station for Demobilisation — 2 O.R. K.R.R. report | (1) |
| | | | for shoeing course 1 - O.R. K.R.R. report for shoeing course — | (1) |
| | 29/4/19 | | 1 - O.R. proceeds on leave — 3 - O.R. taken on strength — | (1) |
| | 30/4/19 | | 3 - O.R. return off leave. | (1) |

Instructions regarding War Diaries and Intelligence Summaries are contained in F. S. Regs., Part II. and the Staff Manual respectively. Title Pages will be prepared in manuscript.

Army Form C. 2118.

# WAR DIARY
## or
## INTELLIGENCE SUMMARY

516 Coy RASC

(Erase heading not required.)

Instructions regarding War Diaries and Intelligence Summaries are contained in F. S. Regs., Part II. and the Staff Manual respectively. Title Pages will be prepared in manuscript.

| Place | Date | Hour | Summary of Events and Information | Remarks and references to Appendices |
|---|---|---|---|---|
| | April 1919 | | The undermentioned Units have been rationed by Supply Officer. | |
| | | | 118th Inf. Bde. | |
| | | | H.Q. 178th Inf. Bde. 1/4/19 to 30/4/19 | 1/4/19 to 30/4/19 |
| | | | 36th N. Fs. do. | do. |
| | | | 11th Bn. R.S.F. do. | do. |
| | | | 13th W.R.R. do. | do. |
| | | | 516 Coy R.A.S.C. do. | do. |
| | | | 211st H.M. Fd. Ambce do. | |
| | | | 210th N.M. Fd. Ambce do. | |
| | | | 469 Fd. Coy R.E. do. | |
| | | | 94th Fd. Ambce do. | |
| | | | H.Q. 176th Inf. Bde do. | |
| | | | 26 Royal Welsh Fus do. | |
| | | | 17 Royal Sussex do. | |
| | | | 514 Coy R.M.S.C. do. | |
| | | | 467 Fd. Coy R.E. do. | |
| | | | 470 Fd. Coy R.E. do. | |
| | | | 225 Fd. Coy R.E. | 1/4/19 to 30/4/19 |
| | | | 595 A.M. Coy R.E. | do. |
| | | | 554 A.S. Ind R.E. | do. |
| | | | W⁺ Tent Det RAF | do. |
| | | | W⁺ 10 Tent Det RAF | do. |
| | | | 59th Div. M.T. Det | do. |
| | | | 241 A.W. Coy R.E. | 1/4/19 to 15/4/19 |
| | | | 6 Works Coy R.E | 1/4/19 to 22/4/19 |

[signature] Capt
OC 516 Coy RASC

War Diary.

H.Qs. 59th Divisional Train

from 1/5/17 to 31/5/17.

Volume 28.

No 28

Confidential

Army Form C. 2118.

# WAR DIARY
## or
## INTELLIGENCE SUMMARY

(Erase heading not required.)

VOL XXVIII
H.Q. 59 DIV TRAIN

Instructions regarding War Diaries and Intelligence Summaries are contained in F.S. Regs., Part II. and the Staff Manual respectively. Title Pages will be prepared in manuscript.

| Place | Date | Hour | Summary of Events and Information | Remarks and references to Appendices |
|---|---|---|---|---|
| BEAUMARIS NEAR CALAIS | MAY 1st 1919 | | 59 TH Q with Div HQ LE BEAUMARIS NEAR CALAIS. No 1 Coy BARLIN. Horses & own skins. Supplies for 59 Div ARTY drawn in bulk by MT from T50 BARLIN RAILHEAD and distributed to units from S.R.P. No 2 Coy ST POL SUR MER near DUNKIRK 176 and 178 INF BRIG. SRPs amalgamated. No 3 Coy at AUSTRALIAN VET HOSPITAL CALAIS with transport of 177 Bay group 200 M/U and 25 Bn KRRC. Supplies for 177 Inf Bay group drawn from DETAIL ISSUE STORE CALAIS. No 4 Coy ST POL SUR MER DUNKIRK. Supplies for 176 and 178 Inf Brigs drawn in bulk from DIS DUNKIRK and distributed to units by 60. 178 Inf Brig. Horses & in open skins | [M.D.] |
| | 2nd | | T/Major A G EDEN RASC proceeded to take command of 21st ARMY AUXILIARY HORSE COY (ARMY QP/AS/ 22716/2) | [M.D.] |
| | 11th | | MAJOR A/LIEUT COL A H MAUDE GMG DSO RASC TF O.C. 59 DIV TRAIN proceeded in leave to UNITED KINGDOM. MAJOR L.M. NEWELL OBE TD assumed command of 59 DIV TRAIN | [M.D.] |
| | 13th | | T/LIEUT P.R.R. DISBEN No 3 Coy proceeded to join CADRE 7 63 DIV TRAIN (ARMY QP/AS/ 23019/5-5-19) | [M.D.] |
| | 17th | | T/2 LIEUT W.J. JEMMETT-BROWNE No 1 Coy 59 Div TRAIN promoted T/LIEUT with seniority 26.2.'19 | [M.D.] |
| | 21st | | LIEUT F. REYNOLDS 200 BNH M/C reported for duty as ADS to OC No 3 Coy. Comm'dt Aktant 59 Div TRANSPORT CAMP. | [M.D.] |
| | 25th | | LIEUT COL A.H. MAUDE GMG DSO returned from leave and resumed command 59 Div TRAIN | [M.D.] |
| | 26th | | MAJOR L.M. NEWELL OBE TD RASC TF 550 59 Div proceeded as OC RASC PERSONNE SUB- AREA No 3 Coy (AARG (T) QP/AS/ 22949 dated 7.5.'19) | [M.D.] |
| | 29th | | Warning order issued for No 1 Coy to move from BARLIN to MARDICK nr DUNKIRK | [M.D.] |
| | 31st | | CAPT H.W. DAWES. RAVC T.F. yd attached 59 Div TRAIN proceeded to ENGLAND for demobilisation. CAPT H WHITEHEAD RAVC reported as V.O. | |

During the month steady progress was made with demobilisation and some reinforcements received. Weather was excellent and health of men good. All horses in excellent condition. Difficulty had been experienced in obtaining artificers especially farriers and wheelers. Various courses in farriery, wheeling's work and horse making, for the hoof, in Division carried out during the month.

M Plowton Johnson Captain
59 Div Train

Army Form C. 2118.

Vol. XXVIII

O.C. N°2 Coy 59th Div. TRAIN

# WAR DIARY
## INTELLIGENCE SUMMARY.
(Erase heading not required.)

Instructions regarding War Diaries and Intelligence Summaries are contained in F. S. Regs., Part II. and the Staff Manual respectively. Title pages will be prepared in manuscript.

| Place | Date | Hour | Summary of Events and Information | Remarks and references to Appendices |
|---|---|---|---|---|
| DUNKIRK. | 1.5.19 | | Commenced month with Coy Hdqrs and Baggage & Supply Sections stationed at S<sup>t</sup> Pol sur Mer, DUNKIRK. Baggage and Supply Wagons of 2/5<sup>th</sup> Batt<sup>n</sup> Kings Liverpool Reg<sup>t</sup> being detached with that Battalion at CALAIS. Detached to 26<sup>th</sup> Batt<sup>n</sup> Royal Welsh Fusiliers stationed at MALO les BAINS three G.S. wagons, Unit having disposed of all transport | |
| " | 12.5.19 | | Downgraded four other ranks. | Nil. |
| " | 19.5.19 | | Downgraded nineteen other ranks. | Nil. |
| " | 22.5.19 | | Detachment returned from CALAIS on departure of 2/5<sup>th</sup> Kings Liverpool Reg<sup>t</sup> to Egypt. | Nil. |
| " | 23.5.19 | | One W.O. Horse died. | Nil. |
| " | 28.5.19 | | Received from O.C. 2/1 N.M. Fld Amb. six Drivers surplus to reduced Cadre. | Nil. |
| " | 30.5.19 | | Received 3 O.R. reinforcements from Base Depot. | Nil. |

CAPT.
O. C. N°. 2 COY. 59. DIV. TRAIN.

CONFIDENTIAL

WAR DIARY

OF

O.C. 513 Coy. R.A.S.C. 59TH DIVN.

FROM 1/5/19 TO 31/5/19

VOLUME 27.

Army Form C. 2118.

# WAR DIARY

(Erase heading not required.)

Instructions regarding War Diaries and Intelligence Summaries are contained in F.S. Regs., Part II. and the Staff Manual respectively. Title pages will be prepared in manuscript.

513 Coy. R.A.S.C. 59th DIVN.

| Place | Date | Hour | Summary of Events and Information | Remarks and references to Appendices |
|---|---|---|---|---|
| BARLIN. | 1/5/19 | | Company in camp at BARLIN. Stores in open sheds. Supplies for 59 Divn. Artillery drawn in bulk by M.T. from R.S.O. BARLIN Railhead and distributed to units from S.R.O. | |
| BARLIN. | 29/5/19 | | Warning order received from H.Q. 59 Divl. Artillery to be prepared to entrain at NOEUX-LES-MINES for ENGLAND on JUNE 3rd 1919. | |
| BARLIN. | 31/5/19 | | Warning order for entrainment confirmed. | |

31/5/19.

[signature]
Lieut.
COMMANDING No. 1 Coy, 59 DIVL. TRAIN.

# WAR DIARY.

## 515 Company. R.A.S.C.

### 59th. Division.

### May 1919.

### Vol. XXVIII.

Army Form C. 2118.

# WAR DIARY
## or
## INTELLIGENCE SUMMARY
(Erase heading not required.)

Instructions regarding War Diaries and Intelligence Summaries are contained in F. S. Regs., Part II. and the Staff Manual respectively. Title pages will be prepared in manuscript.

515 Coy R.A.S.C. 59 Division  VOL XXV/11   May 1919

| Place | Date | Hour | Summary of Events and Information | Remarks and references to Appendices |
|---|---|---|---|---|
| COQUELLES VET HOSPITAL | 1/5/19 | | In camp and quarters | |
| " | 1/5/19 | | 1 N.C.O. Proceeds on leave to U.K. | |
| " | 1/5/19 | | 1 Driver reports back from leave to U.K. | |
| " | 2/5/19 | | 1 Driver Proceeds on leave to U.K. | |
| " | 2/5/19 | | 2 Drivers report back from leave to U.K. | |
| " | 3/5/19 | | 2 Drivers demobilized | |
| " | 5/5/19 | | 2 Drivers transferred to 516 Coy R.A.S.C. | |
| " | 5/5/19 | | 1 Driver reports back from leave | |
| " | 5/5/19 | | 5 Drivers transferred from 514 Coy. M.T. + S.C. | |
| " | 6/5/19 | | 3 Drivers proceed on leave to U.K. | |
| " | | | 1 N.C.O. reports back from leave to U.K. | |
| " | | | 1 H.D. Horse died | |

H. Green Capt o/c No. 515 Coy. A.S.C.
59th Division.

Army Form C. 2118.

# WAR DIARY
## INTELLIGENCE SUMMARY.
(Erase heading not required.)

VOL. XXVIII.

| Place | Date | Hour | Summary of Events and Information | Remarks and references to Appendices |
|---|---|---|---|---|
| COQUELLES VET HOSPITAL | 5/7/19 | | 51st Coy. R.A.S.C. 59th Division. May 1919. 1 Driver proceed on leave to U.K. | AG |
| " | 5/8/14 | | 3 Drivers proceed on leave to U.K. | AG |
| " | 5/12/19 | | 1 A/C Horse died at Dunkerque of Attack. | AG |
| " | 5/14/19 | | Shewing board held at Camp under DRO 33343 | AG |
| " | 5/17/19 | | Detachment of Lieut Burns, MC & proceed to Baringham & move the Cadre of 3/3rd NM Field Amb. to Dunkerque | AG |
| " | 5/19/19 | | 12 R. & O. and men proceed to U.K. for demobilization ( 2 H. & O. Horses transferred to 76th DL 1 178 = Bde A. 9 ) | AG |
| " | 5/19/19 | | 2 H. & O. " | AG |
| " | 5/20/19 | | Detachment proceed to H.Q. 25th Bden Kings Own &c & move unit to Fortinettes Rail Head | AG |

A.F. Green Capt.
o/c No. 515 Coy. A.S.C.
59th Division

Army Form C. 2118.

# WAR DIARY
## or
## INTELLIGENCE SUMMARY.

(Erase heading not required.)

VOL XXVIII

Instructions regarding War Diaries and Intelligence Summaries are contained in F. S. Regs., Part II. and the Staff Manual respectively. Title pages will be prepared in manuscript.

| Place | Date | Hour | Summary of Events and Information | Remarks and references to Appendices |
|---|---|---|---|---|
| COQUELLES VET HOSPITAL | 21/5 | | 515 Coy. R.A.S.C. 59th Divn. May 1919 | |
| | 21/5 | | 1 Capt. 3 O.Rnks transferred from 513 Coy. R.A.S.C. | |
| | | | LIEUT. F. REYNOLDS M.G.C. reports for duty | |
| | 22/5 | | detachments returns from duty to DUNKERQUE as day — | |
| | 22/5 | | 2 Privates Report for Course in Wheelwrights shops | |
| | 23/5 | | 1 O.Rnk proceed on leave to U.K. | |
| | 24/5 | | 2 O.Rnks Report from Leave from U.K. | |
| | 25/5 | | 1 O.Rnk proceeds on leave to U.K. | |
| | 28/5 | | Sheep heard collected camp under D.R.O. 2362 | |
| | 28/5 | | 3 N.C.O. 1 O.Rnk proceed to U.K. for demobilisation | |
| | 29/5 | | 3 H.D. Horses (Remounts) received | |
| | 30/5 | | 12 O.Rnks (Reinforcements) report from 5P E Dist. Depot | |
| | | | Barber Capt. o/c No. 515 Coy. A.S.C. 59th Division. | |

Army Form C. 2118.

# WAR DIARY
## or
## INTELLIGENCE SUMMARY.  VOL. XXVIII.

(Erase heading not required.)

515 Coy. R.A.S.C. 59th Division    Summary of Events and Information    Aug 1919

| Place | Date | Hour | | Remarks and references to Appendices |
|---|---|---|---|---|
| COQUELLES VET HOSPITAL | 31 | | In Camp and quarters.<br>There has been certain amount of unrest in the Unit during the month about demobilisation this was properly explained to the N.C.O.s on their retrospection at a so% of up 1914 men being released. Health of the Coy during the month been excellent. All Horses in very good condition. | GG<br><br>GG |

K Green Capt<br>o/c No. 515 Coy A.S.C<br>59th Division

Instructions regarding War Diaries and Intelligence Summaries are contained in F. S. Regs., Part II. and the Staff Manual respectively. Title pages will be prepared in manuscript.

Confidential

War Diary
of
H.Q. 516 Coy. R.A.S.C.

From:- 1/5/19   To:- 31/5/19.

Volume - 28

Army Form C. 2118.

# WAR DIARY
## or
## INTELLIGENCE SUMMARY

*(Erase heading not required.)*

Instructions regarding War Diaries and Intelligence Summaries are contained in F. S. Regs., Part II. and the Staff Manual respectively. Title Pages will be prepared in manuscript.

| Place | Date | Hour | Summary of Events and Information | Remarks and references to Appendices |
|---|---|---|---|---|
| St. Pol-sur-mer | 1/5/19 | | 1-O.R. struck off strength - 2-O.R. return off leave - 1-O.R. admitted to Hospital. | M |
| | 2/5/19 | | 2-O.R. return off leave. | M |
| | 3/5/19 | | 1-O.R. admitted to Hospital. | M |
| | 4/5/19 | | 1-O.R. admitted to Hospital - 2-O.R. proceed on leave - 2-O.R. return off leave | M |
| | 5/5/19 | | 1-O.R. demobilised - 1-O.R. admitted to Hospital - 1-O.R. discharged from Hospital - 3-O.R. report for duty | M |
| | 6/5/19 | | 3-O.R. proceed on leave. | M |
| | 7/5/19 | | 1-O.R. admitted to Hospital | M |
| | 8/5/19 | | 4-O.R. proceed on leave - 3-O.R. return off leave. | M |
| | 9/5/19 | | 2-O.R. return off leave - 2-O.R. discharged from Hospital | M |
| | 10/5/19 | | 2-O.R. proceed on leave - 3-O.R. return off leave - 1-O.R. discharged from Hospital. | M |
| | 11/5/19 | | 1-O.R. return off leave. | M |
| | 12/5/19 | | 1-O.R. demobilised - 2-O.R. struck off strength - 2-O.R. proceed on leave. | M |
| | 14/5/19 | | 1-O.R. proceeds on leave. | M |
| | 15/5/19 | | 3-O.R. proceed on leave - 3-O.R. report from 2/2/9 N.M. Fd. Amblce. | M |
| | 17/5/19 | | 1-O.R. admitted to Hospital. | M |
| | 18/5/19 | | 1-O.R. returns off leave. | M |
| | 19/5/19 | | 1-O.R. return off leave - 1-O.R. proceeds on leave - 8-O.R. demobilised. | M |
| | 20/5/19 | | 1-O.R. returns off leave - 2-O.R. proceeds on leave - 8-O.R. report for Artillery Course - 1-O.R. | M |
| | 21/5/19 | | admitted to Hospital | M |
| | 22/5/19 | | 1 Officer + 1 D.R. proceed on leave - 4-O.R. return off leave. | M |
| | 23/5/19 | | 3-O.R. return off leave - 1-O.R. proceeds on leave. | M |
| | 24/5/19 | | 2-O.R. return off leave. | M |
| | 25/5/19 | | 2-O.R. proceed on leave - 3-O.R. proceed on leave. | M |
| | 26/5/19 | | 1-O.R. return off leave - 3-O.R. proceed on leave. | M |
| | 28/5/19 | | 5-O.R. report for duty from 3/2ⁿᵈ N.M. Fd. Amblce. - 1-O.R. demobilised | M |
| | 29/5/19 | | report for duty from 3/3ʳᵈ N.M. Fd. Amblce. - 2-O.R. report for instruction in Signalling | M |
| | 30/5/19 | | 2-O.R. return off leave - 1-O.R. discharged from Hospital - 1-O.R. proceeds on leave | M |
| | 31/5/19 | | 1-O.R. returns off leave. | M |

Army Form C. 2118.

# WAR DIARY
## or
## INTELLIGENCE SUMMARY

(Erase heading not required.)

| Place | Date | Hour | Summary of Events and Information | Remarks and references to Appendices |
|---|---|---|---|---|
| | May 1919 | | The undermentioned Units have been rationed by Supply Officer 178ᵗʰ Inf. Bde. | |
| | | | H.Q. 178ᵗʰ Inf Bde  15/5/19 to 31/5/19. | 1/5/19 to 31/5/19 |
| | | | 36ᵗʰ Bn. N. Fs.   do. | do. |
| | | | 11ᵗʰ R. S. F.   do. | do. |
| | | | 13ᵗʰ Y. R.   do. | |
| | | | 516 Coy. R.A.S.C.   do. | |
| | | | 2/1ˢᵗ W. M. Sct Amblee   do. | 20/5/19 to 31/5/19 |
| | | | 2/3ʳᵈ   "   "   do. | 1/5/19 to 31/5/19 |
| | | | H.Q. 176ᵗʰ Inf. Bde.   do. | do. |
| | | | 26ᵗʰ Royal Welsh Fus:   do. | |
| | | | 19ᵗʰ Roy. W. Surrase   do. | |
| | | | 511ᵗʰ Coy. R.A.S.C.   do. | |
| | | | 464 Fd. Coy. R.E.   do. | |
| | | | 286   do.   do.   R.E.   do. | |
| | | | 596 Fd. Coy. R.E   do. | |
| | | | 564 D.W. I R.E.   do. | |
| | | | No. 1 Lowland etach. M.P.P.   do. | |

[signature]

R.E. Westbass, Capt.
Supt.

**Army Form C. 2118.**

# WAR DIARY
## or
## INTELLIGENCE SUMMARY
*(Erase heading not required.)*

VOL. "XXIX"

HQ. 59. DIV. TRAIN

Instructions regarding War Diaries and Intelligence Summaries are contained in F.S. Regs., Part II. and the Staff Manual respectively. Title Pages will be prepared in manuscript.

| Place | Date | Hour | Summary of Events and Information | Remarks and references to Appendices |
|---|---|---|---|---|
| BEAUMARIS. | JUNE 1st 1919 | | HQ 59 Div TRAIN at WINDSOR CAMP LE BEAUMARIS CALAIS with HQ 59 DIV. No1Coy 59 Div TRAIN at DUNKIRK (HARDICK CAMP) No2 Coy ST POL-SUR-MER DUNKIRK in CAMP Horses on open lines. No3 Coy at 59 DIV TRANSPORT CAMP. COCQUELLES CALAIS OC 3Coy acting as OC Camp. No4 Coy at ST POL-SUR-MER DUNKIRK Horses in open stables. Personnel in CAMP All Coys employed in LOCAL TRANSPORT WORK. No SRPS functioning All units drawing direct from Detail Issue Stores CALAIS and DUNKIRK. Three officer reinforcements received (Lt Hq WARD Lt CR MIDDLECOAT 2/Lt JRD DAVIDSON) | PM17 |
| | 2nd | | CADRE of No 1 Coy left DUNKIRK to England 2/Lt AJ PETTIT reported for duty | M17 |
| | 10th | | LIEUT CR MIDDLECOAT posted to TRAINING Lt AJ WICKS reported for duty | M17 |
| | 13th | | CAPT TD HAZLERIGG MC OC 2Coy proceeds on leave to UK. CAPT F.TRIBBY assumes command of 2 Coy 59 Div TRAIN LIEUT JM JEMMETT BROWNE posted to 30th DIV TRAIN | M17 |
| | 15th | | Demobilization of all 1914 enlisted ORs completed except for those who voluntarily wish to stay with Colours | M17 |
| | 16th | | 1st Line Transport of 176 Inf. Brigade HQ attached to 2Coy 59 Div TRAIN pending orders of dispersal Lt AJ WICKS proceeds to join Rifle Army Depot DUNKIRK to take over 19th Inf Brig which No2 Coy 59 Div TRAIN move from DUNKIRK to FORT NIEULAY CALAIS to take over same Camp and | M17 |
| | 19th | | 1st Line Transport of 197 Inf Brig. 656 line Transport of 19 Inf Brig in same camp has joined DIVISION in place. OC 2Coy appointed OC Camp. | |
| | 27. | | CAPT FM HAZAR RIGG MC struck off strength of unit pending posting to RUSSIA. CAPT F TRIBBIN posted as OC No 2 Coy 59 Div TRAIN | |
| | 29. | | Secret Orders received that No 2 3 4 Coys. 59 Div TRAIN shall be reduced to CADRE strength Many horses, less harness, hand back over to units. Supply and Baggage wagon's complete. Less horses. During the month over 100 reinforcements have been received and about the same number of men demobilised. All ORs taken or enlisted for 3½ months or till return at wish. 5½ months Officers 3½ months. Counters have carried out to Transaine infantry personnel for Supplies, Wheelers Farriers hand Supply Details. | |
| | 30. | | Lewin has been going very well 1st 2nd and 3rd Brigs also won by 59 Div TRAIN at CALAIS RACE HORSE shoe. Horses in excellent condition. A large amount of local transport work being done. Health of men has been good. | |

M Christian Johnston Capt & Adj
59 Div Train

# WAR DIARY
## INTELLIGENCE SUMMARY
*(Erase heading not required.)*

Army Form C. 2118.

Vol XXI
O.C. No 2 Coy. S of Div. Train

Instructions regarding War Diaries and Intelligence Summaries are contained in F. S. Regs., Part II. and the Staff Manual respectively. Title pages will be prepared in manuscript.

| Place | Date | Hour | Summary of Events and Information | Remarks and references to Appendices |
|---|---|---|---|---|
| DUNKIRK | 1.6.19 | | Commenced work with troops of 5 Coy & Baggage & Supply Sections boarded at 87 Poste sur Mer | T.W.T. |
| | 3.6.19 | | Blood draws 176, 177, 178 B.T. Supply Refilling Points and all units of the 29th Brigade Supplies drawn Supply Depot from Depot | T.W.T. |
| | 4.6.19 | | Received 7 Drivers reinforcements from 1st Cavalry Reserve Park | T.W.T. |
| | 6.6.19 | | Sent for Embarkation four Drivers to the Supply Depot | T.W.T. |
| | 7.6.19 | | Six Drivers reinforcements received from 7th Div. Train | T.W.T. |
| | 10.6.19 | | These 1910 men sent for demobilization | T.W.T. |
| | 11.6.19 | | Seven 1914 men sent for demobilization completing similar to all personnel other than those volunteering for duration | T.W.T. |
| | | | period of service. | |
| | 13.6.19 | | Capt F. Piggin assumed command during absence on leave of Capt T.M. Hinzie Rigg, M.C. | T.W.T. |
| | 16.6.19 | | 2 G.S. wagons (6 mules) 10 D Horses & (attached) from Bde HQ of 17th Inf. Bde (whose | 11 |
| | | | transport) | 11 |
| FORT NIEULAY | 19.6.19 | | HQ of Sup. & Baggage Supply Sections with 17 Inf. Bde left here transferred & marched to | |
| CALAIS | | | Refugees Permanent Camp at NIEULAY, CALAIS. Two sick horses left with 51st Coy RAG | |
| | | | at Fort SURVILLE. Four G.R. sent for demobilization attached 19th Infantry Advance Party | |
| | 20.6.19 | | Received 8 Drivers reinforcement from 501 Coy RASC. Five men released (3 from 15 KRRC | 11 |
| | | | 2 from N & Y MGC) for permit issue in rolled stretcher, 1st Line Transport 19th Inf Bde joined Coy | |
| | | | at FORT NIEULAY | |

**Army Form C. 2118.**

# WAR DIARY
## or
## INTELLIGENCE SUMMARY.
*(Erase heading not required.)*

Instructions regarding War Diaries and Intelligence Summaries are contained in F.S. Regs., Part II. and the Staff Manual respectively. Title pages will be prepared in manuscript.

| Place | Date | Hour | Summary of Events and Information | Remarks and references to Appendices |
|---|---|---|---|---|
| Base Depot CALAIS | 23.6.19 | | Two O.R. demobilised | |
| " | 24.6.19 | | Three O.R. demobilised | |
| " | | | Lt A/Capt. F. PIGGIN posted as O.C. No 2 Coy. 59th Divisional Train vice Capt TM HAZLERIGG MC (returned to England pending posting to RUSSIA) | |
| " | 29.6.19 | | Began handing out transport of 514 Coy RASC & 19 T Rde under detail from LTO CALAIS | |
| " | 30.6.19 | | Two O.R. sent to demobilisation | |

F. N. Pr...
CAPT.
O.C. No. 1 COY. 59, DIV TRAIN.

# War Diary.

No. 515 Coy. A.S.O.
59th Division.

June 1919.

Sir,

Herewith my return for
the month of June

[signature]
o/c No. 515 Coy. A.S.C.
59th Division.

CROQUIER
4/7/19

Army Form C. 2118.

# WAR DIARY
## or
## INTELLIGENCE SUMMARY.   VOL XXIX

(Erase heading not required.)

515 Coy. R.A.S.C. 59th Division       JUNE 1919

| Place | Date | Hour | Summary of Events and Information | Remarks and references to Appendices |
|---|---|---|---|---|
| CURVELLES | 1/6/19 | | To camp and quarters | |
| " | 1/6/19 | | LIEUT. H.G. WARD } Posted for transportation AATD ABBEVILLE | |
| " | | | LIEUT. J.D. DUDSON } | |
| " | 2/6/19 | | 1 Driver 1 Pack Horse Demobbed home to U.K. | |
| " | 3/6/19 | | 2 Drivers released from the Army to U.K. | |
| " | 3/6/19 | | 2 Drivers Released Class Z to U.K. | |
| " | 5/6/19 | | 12 Reinforcements reported for duty | |
| " | 4/6/19 | | 3 N.C.O.s and 10 Drivers released to U.K. for demob'n — | |
| " | 1/6/19 | | 1 N.C.O. transferred to 115 Coy to duty | |
| " | 4/6/19 | | 1 Pte O.R.M. 1 Driver Released from Army home to U.K. | |
| " | 4/6/19 | | 1 Driver Released Class Z Demob to U.K. | |

K.L. Green Capt.
NO 115 Coy.
63rd Division

# WAR DIARY
## or
## INTELLIGENCE SUMMARY.

*(Erase heading not required.)*

Army Form C. 2118.

VOL XXIX        JUNE 1919.

| Place | Date | Hour | Summary of Events and Information | Remarks and references to Appendices |
|---|---|---|---|---|
| | | | 515 Coy. R.A.S.C. 59th Division | |
| COQUELLES | 5/19 | | 1 other rank to UK from leave | AC |
| " | 6/19 | | 3 O/Rs on ments reported from UK to Coy | AC |
| " | 6/19 | | 2 O/Rs dispatched tho. Base to UK | AC |
| " | 6/19 | | 1 O/R from Coy to UK | AC |
| " | 6/19 | | 9 reinforcements reported from UK to Coy | AC |
| " | 7/19 | | 1 Coy. strength to 353 R&F on completion of change | AC |
| " | 8/19 | | 1 Ends. reported from Coy to UK | AC |
| " | | | 1 O/R from Coy to UK on leave | AC |
| " | 9/19 | | 1 O/R on leave from Coy to UK | AC |
| " | 9/19 | | 6 O/Rs Officer to UK | AC |
| " | 10/19 | | 3 O/Rs and one Runner dispatched UK | AC |
| " | 10/19 | | 3 O/Rs dispatched on leave to UK | AC |

Army Form C. 2118.

# WAR DIARY
## or
## INTELLIGENCE SUMMARY
*(Erase heading not required.)*

Army Form C. 2118.

**515 Coy. R.A.S.C. 59th Division**     Vol XXIX     JUNE 1919

Instructions regarding War Diaries and Intelligence Summaries are contained in F. S. Regs., Part II. and the Staff Manual respectively. Title pages will be prepared in manuscript.

| Place | Date | Hour | Summary of Events and Information | Remarks and references to Appendices |
|---|---|---|---|---|
| Courrieres | 10/6/19 | | 1 Jans Corp E sent to Givet proceed to U.K. for demobilisation | |
| " | 11/6/19 | | 2 Sin Moore on leave to U.K. | |
| " | 11/6/19 | | 1 Reinforcement received | |
| " | 12/6/19 | | 1 Air Mechanic joined from Leave to U.K. | |
| " | 14/6/19 | | 2 N.C.O. and 5 drivers proceeded Reserve | |
| " | 14/6/19 | | 1 N.C.O. and 2 drivers proceeded to U.K. for demobilisation | |
| " | 14/6/19 | | 2 drivers joined with 14 horses on leave from U.K. | |
| " | 16/6/19 | | 1 N.C.O. and 2 drivers proceeded on leave to U.K. | |
| " | 16/6/19 | | 1 N.C.O. and 2 drivers proceeded — ret. for demobilisation | |
| " | 17/6/19 | | 2 Men rejoined Coy on leave from U.K. | |
| " | 17/6/19 | | 1 driver rejoined Coy on leave from U.K. | |
| " | 18/6/19 | | 2 drivers joined on U.K. leave demobilisation | |
| | | | A. Green, Capt. O/C 515 Coy | |

D. D. & L., London, E.C.
(A501) Wt. W1771/M2031 750,000 5/17 Sch. 52 Forms/C2118/14

# WAR DIARY
## or
## INTELLIGENCE SUMMARY.

*(Erase heading not required.)*

Army Form C. 2118.

515 Coy R.A.S.C. 59th Division                VOL XXIX       JUNE 1919

| Place | Date | Hour | Summary of Events and Information | Remarks and references to Appendices |
|---|---|---|---|---|
| CONVELLES | 20/6 | | | |
| | 21/6 | | | |
| | 22/6 | | | |
| | 23/6 | | | |
| | 24/6 | | | |
| | 25/6 | | | |
| | 26/6 | | | |

o/c No. 515 Coy. A.S.C.
59th Division

Army Form C. 2118.

# WAR DIARY
## INTELLIGENCE SUMMARY.
*(Erase heading not required.)*

Instructions regarding War Diaries and Intelligence Summaries are contained in F. S. Regs., Part II. and the Staff Manual respectively. Title pages will be prepared in manuscript.

| Place | Date | Hour | Summary of Events and Information | Remarks and references to Appendices |
|---|---|---|---|---|
| CAMBRAI | 26/9 | | | |
| " | 30/9 | | | |

516

Confidential

War Diary

by

O.C. 516 Coy. R.A.S.C.

From 1/6/19 To 30/6/19

Volume 39

Army Form C. 2118.

# WAR DIARY
## or
## INTELLIGENCE SUMMARY.
*(Erase heading not required.)*

Instructions regarding War Diaries and Intelligence Summaries are contained in F. S. Regs., Part II. and the Staff Manual respectively. Title pages will be prepared in manuscript.

| Hour, Date, Place | Summary of Events and Information | Remarks and references to Appendices |
|---|---|---|
| St. Pol-sur-mer | | |
| 1/6/19. | 1-O.R. return off leave — 1 Off + 1 O.R. report for duty | |
| 2/6/19. | 2-O.R. return off leave | |
| 3/6/19. | 1 Off. + 1 O.R. report for duty — 1-O.R. discharged from Hospital. 3 O.R. demobilised. | |
| 4/6/19. | 9-O.R. report for duty — 13 O.R. demobilised. | |
| 5/6/19. | 1-O.R. returns off leave. | |
| 6/6/19. | 9-O.R. report for duty — 1 O.R. proceeds on leave. | |
| 7/6/19. | 2-O.R. report for duty — 2-O.R. return off leave. | |
| 8/6/19. | 1-O.R. returns off leave. | |
| 9/6/19. | 3-O.R. demobilised — 3-O.R. proceed on leave. | |
| 10/6/19. | 3-O.R. return off leave — 3-O.R. demobilised — | |
| 11/6/19. | 1-Off. + 1 O.R. transferred to Rhine Army. 3-O.R. proceed on leave. — 4-O.R. demobilised. | |
| 12/6/19. | 5-O.R. demobilised — 1-O.R. evacuated to stock off strength | |
| 13/6/19. | 3-O.R. demobilised — 3-O.R. proceed on leave. | |
| 14/6/19 | 3-O.R. return off leave. — 1-O.R. admitted to Hospital. | |
| 15/6/19 | 1-O.R. returns off leave — 1-O.R. demobilised | |
| 16/6/19 | 1-O.R. returns off leave — 3-O.R. proceed on leave. | |
| 17/6/19. | 4-O.R. report for duty — 1-O.R. returns off leave. | |
| 18/6/19. | 2-O.R. report for duty — 1-Off. + 1-O.R. transferred to 50th Bty. | |
| | 2-O.R. proceed on leave — 5-O.R. demobilised | |
| 19/6/19. | 1-O.R. discharged from Hospital — 2-O.R. return to work from leave | |

Army Form C. 2118.

# WAR DIARY
## or
## INTELLIGENCE SUMMARY.
(Erase heading not required.)

Instructions regarding War Diaries and Intelligence Summaries are contained in F.S. Regs., Part II. and the Staff Manual respectively. Title pages will be prepared in manuscript.

| Hour, Date, Place | Summary of Events and Information | Remarks and references to Appendices |
|---|---|---|
| Sr. Pol – sur – mer 20/6/19. | 10 – O.R. report for France – 1 – O.R. discharged from Hospital | |
| 21/6/19. | 2 – O.R. demobilised | |
| 22/6/19. | 3 – O.R. returned to Unit as unfit for France | |
| 23/6/19. | 1 – O.R. returns off leave. – 2 – O.R. demobilised | |
| 24/6/19 | 4 – O.R. demobilised – 1 – O.R. returns off leave. | |
| 25/6/19 | 2 – O.R. return off leave – 2 – O.R. report for France | |
| | 2 – O.R. proceed on leave – 1 – O.R. admitted to Hospital | |
| 26/6/19. | 1 – O.R. discharged from Hospital – 1 – O.R. returns off leave – | |
| | 1 – O.R. report for France – 2 – O.R. proceed on leave | |
| 27/6/19. | 3 – O.R. report for France – 1 – O.R. report for duty & no Estgs. on strength – 2 – O.R. returns off leave – 1 – O.R. returns to Unit from Calais – 2 – O.R. Amdld on leave. | |
| 28/6/19 | 1 – O.R. proceeds on leave | |
| 29/6/19 | 3 – O.R. returns off leave | |
| 30/6/19 | 2 – O.R. demobilised | |

W656 Coy/R.A.S.C.
Capt.

59D Train
G.H. 30

War Diary

Vol XXX

From 1-7-19 – 31-7-19

HQ 59 Div

**Army Form C. 2118.**

# WAR DIARY
## or
## INTELLIGENCE SUMMARY

HQ 59th (NM) Divisional TRAIN
VOL XXX

(Erase heading not required.)

| Place | Date | Hour | Summary of Events and Information | Remarks and references to Appendices |
|---|---|---|---|---|
| BEAUMARIS | July 1st 1919 | | T.H.Q. WINDSOR CAMP. LE BEAUMARIS with Div HQs. Horses in Div HQ Stables. No 2 Coy at FORT NIEULAY. CALAIS O.C. 2 Coy acting as Camp Commandant to 19th Inf Brig Transport Camp. Horses in great stables. No 3 Coy at COQUELLES CALAIS O.C. 3 Coy acting as Camp Commandant to 177 Inf. Brig Transport. Camp. No 4 Coy at ST POL-SUR-MER DUNKIRK. with 178 Inf Brig. No SRP's working all Supplies being drawn from D.I.S. CALAIS and DUNKIRK. Transport & Coys working under orders of LOCAL TRANSPORT OFFICE CALAIS and DUNKIRK. Horsed in excellent condition. Coys up to strength in men. Acting on instructions received on June 29th arrangements are made to reduce No 2, 3, 4 Coys to CADRE strength. Surplus men and horses less drivers are to be handed down to Units to which they are affiliated in War Establishments and Transport of Coy HQs are either absorbed within other units of the Division or handed in to REMOUNTS. CALAIS. By end of month all horse a/c closed and Coys down at CADRE A. Serial numbers allotted No 2 Coy Z.F 200 No 3 Coy Z.F 201. No 4 Coy Z.F 202. distribution of all Coys. AYTREE. All returnable men surplus to CADRE demobilized under authority of D.D.T. (N) Returnable personnel. H.T. and Volunteers for Army of Occupation despatched to ABBEVILLE H.T. Depot for reposting except a few to 501 Coy RASC under orders of D.A.D.O.B. 59 Div. Stores on excellent condition and very few deficiencies. Completed for all Coys by D.A.D.O.B. 59 Div. TRAIN deposited to KENSINGTON BARRACKS on 30th inst. LIEUT COL A H MADE C.M.G. D.S.O. O.C. 59 Div. TRAIN a/c of Coys closed down, and arrangements made to move TRAIN all to DUNKIRK for shipping to United Kingdom. Leave for all ranks has been granted. Satisfactory other ranks most been at about 4 months Officers about 3½ months. Camp at FORT NIEULAY and COQUELLES handed over to Commandants appointed by 19th and 177th Inf. Brigs respectively Orders received on 31st inst for Coys to be reduced to Equipment Overlay & CADRES. General Service ribbon has been issued to all ranks at end of month. |  |

M. Photous Johnston Cuthill
59 Div Train

2449 Wt. W14957/M90 750,000 1/16 J.B.C. & A. Forms/C.2118/12.

War Diary.

Vol. XXX

From 1.7.19 — 31.7.19

No 2 Coy 59 Div Train

Army Form C. 2118.

Vol XIX

OC No 2 Coy 59 Div Train

# WAR DIARY
## or
## INTELLIGENCE SUMMARY.
(Erase heading not required.)

Instructions regarding War Diaries and Intelligence Summaries are contained in F. S. Regs, Part II. and the Staff Manual respectively. Title pages will be prepared in manuscript.

| Place | Date | Hour | Summary of Events and Information | Remarks and references to Appendices |
|---|---|---|---|---|
| FORT NIEULAY nr CALAIS | 1.7.19 | | Commenced work with HQ Baggage Supply Section at FORT NIEULAY CALAIS with 1st line Transport of 19th Infantry Bde attached | A.1 |
| | 4.7.19 | | Supply & Baggage wagons (14 G.S. wagons, 1 Cooker) handed in to Demobilisation Depot BEAUMARIS with 15 sets of harness, wagon equipment accompanying. | A.2 |
| | 5.7.19 | | 15 pairs of horse passed to 19th Infantry Bde. (without equipment) for supply & Baggage maintenance at points in their possession. (28 HD 2 Draught, 10 R Draw bleed) | A.2 |
| | 6.7.19 | | 3 Draught 3 HD horses handed over to 6th Batt Queens (RWS) Reg. | A.2 |
| | 9.7.19 | | Nine OR sent to demobilisation | A.2 |
| | 12.7.19 | | 5 Riding 11 HD horses handed in to Base Remount Depot CALAIS | A.2 |
| | 15.7.19 | | 10 Draught horses handed over (8 to 6th Batt Queens, 2 to 19th I Bde HQ) | A.2 |
| | 19.7.19 | | Nine OR sent for demobilisation | A.2 |
| | 25.7.19 | | Lance Corpl DR (Intercomm) reported to A.H.T.D Depot Abbeville | A.2 |
| | 30.7.19 | | 2 HD horses handed over to 19th Brigade HQ 1 Riding Dn Sta & 1 Riding to HQ RA winter Coy | A.2 |
| | 31.7.10 | | SSm Robinson Noceska to AHTD Depot Abbeville | A.2 |

Confidential.

WAR DIARY.

VOL xxx

From 1·7·19 — 31—7—19

No 3 Coy 59 Div Train

Army Form C. 2118.

# WAR DIARY
## or
## INTELLIGENCE SUMMARY.   VOL. XXX.

(Erase heading not required.)

515 Coy R.A.S.C. 59th Division    July 1919

| Place | Date | Hour | Summary of Events and Information | Remarks and references to Appendices |
|---|---|---|---|---|
| COQUELLES | 1/7/19 | | In camp and quarters | AG |
| " | 1/7/19 | | 5 Complete turnouts transferred to 200th M.G.B. in reduction of reduction CADRE. Strength 4 | AG |
| " | 3/7/19 | | 4 Complete turnouts transferred to 2/6th D.L.I. | AG |
| " | 3/7/19 | | 1 H.C. and 1 Driver reported from leave to U.K. | AG |
| " | 4/7/19 | | 4 Complete turnouts transferred to 15th Essex Regt. | AG |
| " | 4/7/19 | | 1 Driver proceeds on leave to U.K. | AG |
| " | 5/7/19 | | 1 Driver arrived on leave to U.K. | AG |
| " | 5/7/19 | | 4 Complete turnouts transferred to 25th T.M.B.C. | AG |
| " | 7/7/19 | | 3 H.D. and 3. L.D. turnouts transferred to 6th Queens T.W'S | AG |

W. Green Capt.
o/c No. 515 Coy. A.S.C.
59th Division.

# WAR DIARY
## or
## INTELLIGENCE SUMMARY

Army Form C. 2118.

515 Coy. R.A.S.C. 59th Division    Vol XXX    JULY 1919.

| Place | Date | Hour | Summary of Events and Information | Remarks and references to Appendices |
|---|---|---|---|---|
| C DQUELLES | 8/7/19 | | 3 Drivers report back from leave to U.K. | |
| " | 9/7/19 | | 8 Drivers proceed to U.K. for demobilization | |
| " | 5/7/19 | | 5 Returnable Drivers posted to 177th B.H.Q. | |
| " | 2/7/19 | | 2 Reberville return from 177 Bn to Coy lines | |
| " | 9/7/19 | | 3 Completed turnover transferred to 177 B.H.Q. | |
| " | 9/7/19 | | 1 L.D. Horse died | |
| " | 9/7/19 | | 2 R. C O 2 and 14 Drivers proceed to U.K. for demobilization | |
| " | 11/7/19 | | 3 16 Returnable Drivers posted to 59 D.H.Q. | |
| " | 11/7/19 | | 1 Reberville returns from 59 D.H.Q. | |
| " | 12/7/19 | | 7 R.D. 9.H.D. and 3 L.D. transferred to No 5 Remount Depot | |
| " | 13/7/19 | | 2 A.D. transferred to No 5 Remount Depot | |

o/c No. 515 Coy. A.S.C. 59th Division.

Army Form C. 2118.

# WAR DIARY
## or
## INTELLIGENCE SUMMARY.   VOL XXX

(Erase heading not required.)

Instructions regarding War Diaries and Intelligence Summaries are contained in F. S. Regs., Part II. and the Staff Manual respectively. Title pages will be prepared in manuscript.

515 Coy R.A.S.C.   Sgt Stevens   Summary of Events and Information   JULY 1919.

| Place | Date | Hour | Summary of Events and Information | Remarks and references to Appendices |
|---|---|---|---|---|
| CAQUERLES | 14th | | This date was observed as the French Peace Celebrations | A.G. |
| | 15/7/19 | | 9 Drivers forward to the U.K. for demobilization | A.G. |
| | 16/7/19 | | 11 Drivers proceed to U.K. to accompany | A.G. |
| | 17/7/19 | | 4 Drivers proceed to U.K. for Hostilities for | A.G. |
| | 17/7/19 | | LIEUT J.D. DUDSON returns from leave to U.K. | A.G. |
| | 17/7/19 | | 1 Driver proceeds to U.K. for leave to U.K. | A.G. |
| | 18/7/19 | | 8 Army Tracel to U.K. for demobilization | A.G. |
| | 19/7/19 | | This date was observed as the English Peace Celebrations | A.G. |
| | 19/7/19 | | 1 Driver returns proceeds to U.K. on leave to U.K. | A.G. |
| | 20/7/19 | | 2 Drivers proceed to U.K. for demobilization | A.G. |
| | 21/7/19 | | | |
| | 22/7/19 | | 1 Tech. R. Sgt. proceeds to U.K. D.4.R | A.G. |

W. Allen Capt A
o/c No. 515 Coy. A.S.C.
59th Division

Army Form C. 2118.

# WAR DIARY
## or
## INTELLIGENCE SUMMARY.

VOL XXX

(Erase heading not required.)

**515 Coy R.A.S.C.** 29th Division

**JULY 1919**

| Place | Date | Hour | Summary of Events and Information | Remarks and references to Appendices |
|---|---|---|---|---|
| COQUELLES | 22/7 | | 1 other ranks proceeded on leave to U.K. | |
| " | 23/7 | | N.C.O. reported from leave ex U.K. | |
| " | 24/7 | | Cadre of the 59th Siege Coy moved by two M.T. lorries to DUNKERQUE under Lieut T.D. Dodson | |
| " | 24/7 | | 1 Sergt. S. Sgt. and 3 N.C.O.'s transferred to 501. H.T. & M.T. Coy. | |
| " | 23/7 | | 1 M.S.S. Sgt. and 2 Drivers transferred to A.H.T.D. ABBEVILLE | |
| " | 25/7 | | 1 N.C.O. proceeded on leave to U.K. | |
| " | 26/7 | | CAPTAIN R.J. GREEN proceeded on leave to U.K. | |
| " | 26/7 | | LIEUT H.C. WARD RASC (T.F.) was assumed Command of Unit during absence of Capt Higgins F.J. taken on Strength of Train. | |
| " | 28/7 | | Temp Lieut a/Capt. Higgins proceeded to C.C.K. | |
| " | 30/7 | | 1 Driver proceeded on leave to FRANCE | |
| " | 31/7 | | Lt Col A.H. MAUDE C.M.G. D.S.O. left for U.K. | H/Ward Lieut a/c Coy RASC 515 Coy |

Confidential.

War Diary

of

66,516 Coy. R.A.S.C.

From:- 1/4/19   To:- 31/4/19.

Volume 30.

Army Form C. 2118.

# WAR DIARY
## or
## INTELLIGENCE SUMMARY.
(Erase heading not required.)

Instructions regarding War Diaries and Intelligence Summaries are contained in F.S. Regs., Part II. and the Staff Manual respectively. Title pages will be prepared in manuscript.

| Hour, Date, Place | Summary of Events and Information | Remarks and references to Appendices |
|---|---|---|
| ST-POL-SUR-MER 1/4/19 | 1-O.R. to Hospital — 1 O.R. from Leave | |

**Army Form C. 2118.**

# WAR DIARY
## or
## INTELLIGENCE SUMMARY
*(Erase heading not required.)*

59th N.M. DIVISIONAL TRAIN

Vol. XXXI

| Place | Date | Hour | Summary of Events and Information | Remarks and references to Appendices |
|---|---|---|---|---|
| BEAUMARIS | Aug 1st | | TRAIN HEADQUARTERS with 59 Div HQ's BEAUMARIS. No 2 Coy FORT NIEULAY. No 3 Coy COQUELLES. No 1 Coy ST-POL-SUR-MER. DUNKIRK. All companies at CADRE strength. | |
| | " 2nd | | No 4 Coy and THR reduced to Equipment Guard. All remaining horses disposed of. | |
| | " 4th | | No 2 Coy company Cadre moved by road to ST-POL-SUR-MER DUNKIRK. Horses being provided by 14" Inf Bgde. | |
| | " 5th | | No 2 Coy Cadre reduced to Equipment Guard. Surplus personnel sent for demobilization. | |
| | " 6th | | No 3 Coy Cadre moved by road to ST-POL-SUR-MER DUNKIRK. Horses being provided by 177 Inf Bgde. | |
| | " 7th | | No 3 Coy Cadre reduced to EQUIPMENT GUARD Surplus personnel sent for demobilization. | |
| | " 14th | | All baggage, stores and vehicles of all companies loaded on to barges at DUNKIRK and shipped for RICHBOROUGH en route for AINTREE. | |
| | " 15th | | Personnel of Equipment Guards sent for demobilization from DUNKIRK. SSM KIRKDALE found three drivers who were cells in Hospital Prison on absent offences. | |
| | " 19th | | Authority detained to strike off strength W. SSM KIRKDALE found. three drivers who were cells in Hospital Prison on Absent offences. | |
| | " 22nd | | Postings of Surplus officers viz. 59 Div Train received. Authority D. of S. & T. STP. 22308 dated 15.8.19. CAPT H.R. GODDARD to Command No 6 Auc. Auc. Petrol Coy. CAPT R.J. GREEN to 59 Div MT Coy. CAPT F. PIGGIN to 61 Div MT Coy. LIEUT A.M. BANNISTER and J.D. DUDSON to 13th GHQ Res MT Coy. LIEUT A.J. PETTET to No. 9 GHQ Reserve MT Coy. Authority to release of CAPT M.C. JOHNSTON received on 31st Aug. | |
| | " 22 to 31 | | Time spent in clearing up all accounts and stores. | |
| | | | HQ's 59 Div Train closes on Aug 31st 1919 having existed since Oct 1914 and having been in France since Feb 13th 1917. On no occasion has this Train never failed to feed its Division during its whole period of active service. | |
| | | | Honours Gained Officers: O.B.E. 1. P.B.E. 1. M.C. 1. Mentions 7. D.S.O. 2. | |
| | | | Other Ranks: M.S.M. 7. D.C.M. 1. M.M. 6. Mentions 9. | |

M. Murton Lieut Colonel
59 Div Train

Army Form C. 2118.

# WAR DIARY
## or
## INTELLIGENCE SUMMARY.
(Erase heading not required.)

Instructions regarding War Diaries and Intelligence Summaries are contained in F. S. Regs., Part II. and the Staff Manual respectively. Title pages will be prepared in manuscript.

| Place | Date | Hour | Summary of Events and Information | Remarks and references to Appendices |
|---|---|---|---|---|
| Baileul | 1.9.19 | | Commences month with Coy at Baileul under Orders | |
| Lumbres | 4.9.19 | | Coy to Lumbres to St Pol for training | |
| " | 9.9.19 | | Coy H.Q. returned to Lumbres after training | |
| | 14.9.19 | | Whitehead Hodd + Gill on A.T.R.C. | |
| | 15.9.19 | | Lawrence Gill on 5 day leave to UK | |

# WAR DIARY
## or
## INTELLIGENCE SUMMARY.
(Erase heading not required.)

Army Form C. 2118.

| Place | Date | Hour | Summary of Events and Information | Remarks and references to Appendices |
|---|---|---|---|---|
| Catterick | 1.8.19 | | Commenced month with Coy. H.Q. returned to Cadre Strength stationed at Fort Musselburgh Camp | |
| Scotland | 4.8.19 | | Coy. H.Q. moved to St Roy Son then Scottish Area | |
| " | 9.8.19 | | Coy. H.Q. returned to Equipment Guard, N.C.O. sent for demobilization | |
| " | 14.8.19 | | Mobilization Stores shipped for AINTREE. | |
| " | 15.8.19 | | Equipment Guard of 5 O.R. demobilized | |

# WAR DIARY
## or
## INTELLIGENCE SUMMARY.
*(Erase heading not required.)*

Army Form C. 2118.

Vol XXXI  Aug 1919

| Place | Date | Hour | Summary of Events and Information | Remarks and references to Appendices |
|---|---|---|---|---|
| CORBELLES | 1/8/19 | | 4 H.D. Horses transferred to M.G.S. Base Remounts | |
| " | " | | 2 Relays to Camp Canvas and 59 Div | |
| " | 6/8/19 | | Cadre (of) moved to DUNKIRK by road | |
| DUNKIRK | 7/8/19 | | Cadre reduced Equipment found short. 1L 2 NCO's & drum. Lieut. (SO) | |
| " | 8/8/19 | | An N.CO reported back from leave to U.K. | |
| " | 9/8/19 | | one N.CO demobed. Cap' Green reports back from leave | |
| " | 14/8/19 | | 4 G.S. Wagon M/C. Cook 1 Cook. Lamps Lo truck scales ma [?] | |
| " | | | Received one Bracket. Locks to Cy hounds & L.R. | |
| " | | | No vehicles A/67826 received. Now on sloan & returned | |
| " | | | From S.E. Cy Captured [?] | |
| " | 15/7/19 | | Employed hands [illegible] for our holiday & [?] | |

M.M... [signature]
o/c No. 515 Coy. A.S.C.
59th Division.

Army Form C. 2118

516 Coy RASC

# WAR DIARY

## INTELLIGENCE SUMMARY

(Erase heading not required.)

Instructions regarding War Diaries and Intelligence Summaries are contained in F. S. Regs., Part II. and the Staff Manual respectively. Title Pages will be prepared in manuscript.

| Place | Date | Hour | Summary of Events and Information | Remarks and references to Appendices |
|---|---|---|---|---|
| ST POL-SUR-MER | 2/5/19 | | 1 – O.R. returns off leave | W. |
| | 5/8/19 | | 9 – O.R. demobilised. | W. |
| | 7/8/19 | | 1 – O.R. demobilised – 1- O.R. admitted to Hospital | W. |
| | 12/8/19 | | 1 – O.R. struck off strength. | W. |
| | 14/8/19 | | Equipment guard proceeds to U.K.   R.I.P. | W. |

Ashland Capt.
O.C. 516 Coy RASC

www.ingramcontent.com/pod-product-compliance
Lightning Source LLC
Chambersburg PA
CBHW080811010526
44111CB00015B/2543